Handbook of Research on Cross-culture Business and Management

Edited by
Dr. Chandan Maheshkar
East Nimar Society for Education (ENSE), Indore, India
Dr. Vinod Sharma
SCMHRD, Symbiosis International University Pune, India

Series in Business and Finance

VERNON PRESS

www.vernonpress.com

In the Americas:
Vernon Press
1000 N West Street, Suite 1200
Wilmington, Delaware, 19801
United States

In the rest of the world:
Vernon Press
C/Sancti Espiritu 17,
Malaga, 29006
Spain

Series in Business and Finance

Library of Congress Control Number: 2022950727

ISBN: 978-1-64889-887-7

Also available: 978-1-64889-601-9 [Hardback]; 978-1-64889-686-6 [PDF, E-Book]

Table of Contents

Kurt April
University of Cape Town, South Africa

Meltem Yavuz Sercekman
Brunel University, London, UK

Joana Vassilopoulou
Brunel University, London, UK

José G. Vargas-Hernández
Instituto Tecnológico José Mario Molina Pasquel y Henríquez, Unidad Zapopan, Jalisco

Ernesto Guerra García
Autonomous Indigenous University of Mexico, México

List of Figures

List of Tables

Foreword

Prof. Dr. Dileep Kumar M.

Deputy Vice Chancellor (DVC)

Nile University of Nigeria

More industries are engaging in business overseas, and the advancement of technology has sped up this development, a workforce with possible assimilation of people from diverse backgrounds, gender, culture, and values, with the right set of knowledge and skills for business growth. Internationalization invites attention from leaders, policymakers, strategists, functional managers, human resource managers, technologists, and business operations specialists to cross-cultural management. Successful managers and leaders in the organization must deal with multiple cultural differences that have become the new global business reality. Simultaneously, human behavior at work is influenced by diverse backgrounds, including gender, culture, beliefs, and values. Modern organizations must understand the reality that multiple cultures exist simultaneously, and they need proper synchronization and synthesis for robust decision-making business development.

This handbook of research on cross-cultural business and management—vol 1 is one of the books that integrates a collection of themes related to cross-cultural business and management and encompasses the perspectives of several writers from various countries. The book shares the cultural influence of various regions; ethnographic differences; utilization of cultural intelligence; cultural impact on buying behavior of customers; cross-boundary businesses; power relations in organizations; diversity and group norms; and cultural impact on business communication in the context of uncertain and complex business processes in the VUCA world. The book argues that globalization and technological advances have thinned topographical borders. Digital tools and mass media are transforming the business ecosystem through which business firms can constantly interact with their customers.

Some of the chapters in the book that have invited my special academic interest and attention are the ones about the role of theories, specifically fundamental ones like *Scientific Management Theory, System Management Theory, Theory X and Y, and Contingency Management* in handling cross-cultural issues and effective decision-making. From an academic point of view, these chapters have given a wider opportunity for teachers and research scholars to have effective deliberations in the context of changing work culture as well as cross-cultural communications. With respect to the current dynamic world, modern organizations must look at various cultural theories to explore and exploit the resources and capabilities to move with fidelity and accuracy. The books pay due attention to the fact that understanding human behavior at work requires special attention to the integrity of cross-cultural impact.

The book, at some point, discusses the role of cultural intelligence, relating to varied demographic diversity, experiential and cognitive diversity, and cultural capabilities in handling group dynamics in organisations. The authors, like James Phelan of the *US Department of Veterans Affairs, USA,* suggest that managing diversity by breaking the barriers of borders needs not only emotional intelligence but also more cultural intelligence. Cultural considerations are an exceptionally delicate subject that creates a multitude of prospects and consequences. Managers must devote time to discovering and developing cultural intelligence to create a thriving business environment. The authors have provided ample evidence to support their argument, and they back it up by informing managers and leaders in the organization about the future consequences of a lack of cultural intelligence.

Although the book is specially tailored for managers and leaders, the scope of the book is not just limited to them. The scope of the book breaks the borders of one country by integrating the perspectives of authors from several countries related to relevant topics, and I observed that this highly valuable book would help people from all continents understand the significance of cross-cultural impact. I would recommend this book to people from all continents and people going to live and work in another culture for a better understanding and practice of cross-cultural aspects in organizational management as well as day-to-day life.

Preface

Chandan Maheshkar

East Nimar Society for Education (ENSE), Indore, India

Vinod Sharma

SCMHRD, Symbiosis International University Pune, India

Culture is *a cumulative custom of beliefs, values, rituals, and sanctions practiced by a group of people, province or country.* It is a more sensitive dimension of internationalization of any business and making it perform in a culturally diverse environment. Sometimes, nations/states lose their normative significance in a cross-cultural setting (e.g., India). It is because they undermined their earlier philosophies of norms, values, and beliefs or neglected the cultural significance of other nations. At present, culture introduces significant changes in the core assumptions of business practices and skill expectations. This paradigm shift has forced business executives and managers to know how cultural differences affect inter-organizational as well as intra-organizational functioning. It has made gaining cross-cultural compatibility a serious concern for the business as well as scholarly society around the world.

A shift in business paradigms is a complex process because an educational change of any significance involves changes in organizational structures, communications, resource allocation, practices, beliefs, and attitudes. Organizations experienced that selecting any strategic option is significantly influenced by the country/region-specific cultural factors that demand competence to identify the socio-cultural diversities to develop an inclusive cross-cultural business environment. Successful sustenance in cross-cultural business settings needs individuals with strong knowledge, skills, and perspectives matching the working styles of context and will be –

- Able to foster relationships that create respect for all,
- Able to employ cultural sensitivity and diplomacy,
- Able to solve cultural problems synergistically,
- Able to balance conflicting demands of global integration and local responsiveness,

- Able to manage and/or work with people from diverse racial and ethical backgrounds,

- Able to maintain flexibility in strategy and tactics,

- Able to create and sustain business teams in a global setting and the like.

This volume of the *Handbook of Research on Cross-Cultural Business and Management* facilitates cross-culture business and management practices by developing practitioners and academicians with cross-cultural business and management competencies. The way to improve these skills is to fill the gaps between practical implication and theoretical consideration; the focus should be on learning so that they will get more chances to enhance their knowledge, skills, and attitudes relevant to achieve business objectives.

Chapter 1, by the editors of this book, introduces cross-cultural business and management and explores how culture influences an organization's operations and, ultimately, performance. This chapter explores culture-driven opportunities and challenges of business and management practices involving individual, national and international perspectives. Authors have attempted to discover the paradigm shift due to globalization that considerably encouraged cross-cultural interaction and promoted multicultural societies and organizations.

Chapter 2, by Jeremy Kwok, exposes how to manage in Chinese culture from an institutional economic perspective. As the author claimed, the main contribution of this chapter is providing a strong case with rigorous analysis. The chapter focuses on the complexity of managing in Chinese cultural settings.

Chapter 3, by Yvonne Kamegne, discusses managing cultural differences, particularly regarding Cameroon from an ethnographic perspective. The chapter provides a better understanding of the relationship between culture, business, and technology and a perspective on cross-cultural approaches in user interface design. It would help stakeholders to understand, manage, and interact with diverse cultures.

Chapter 4, by James Phelan, describes practical ideas and measures that can be used to improve the performance of business executives/expatriates in a cross-cultural work environment. This chapter equips stakeholders to practice CQ. They learn about various measures they can utilize to gauge their practice of CQ and work towards sharpening and improving their skills.

Chapter 5, by Rupa Rathee and Madhvi Lamba, concentrates on cultural intelligence. This chapter emphasizes the importance of cultural intelligence, sources and precursors of cultural intelligence, formal education and training to enhance cross-cultural adjustments and the role mindfulness can play in cultural intelligence.

Chapter 6, by Tarika Nandedkar and Amit Kumar, explains *Scientific Management Theory, System Management Theory, Theory X and Y,* and *Contingency Management theory* concerning the current business environment and discusses its relevance in the cross-cultural world. With the help of these theories, the handling of cross-cultural issues, planning resources, and decision-making have been discussed.

Chapter 7, by Rachna Bajaj, Gaurav Gupta, and Rachna Bansal, deals with online group buying behavior. It presents a comparative picture of the USA, China and Indian markets. The chapter's primary focus is on social-demographic and psychographic features of online group-buying users, as well as likenesses and variances in their shopping habits, attitudes and motivations. It reveals that Chinese consumers are more inclined to purchase from group-buying websites than their US counterparts.

Chapter 8, by Rauno Rusko, advocates cross-cultural effects of the joint global features such as the greenhouse effect and global warming. This chapter exhibits the convergence of attitudes and rhetoric in cross-cultural business ethics due to the greenhouse effect.

Chapter 9, by Deepti Sinha and Sachin Sinha, discusses cultural cosmopolitanism. This chapter is aimed at understanding the idea of culture, multiculturalism, glocalization and the concept of the cosmopolitan consumer. The authors intend to highlight the intermingling of cultures and blurring the differentiating lines of culture.

Chapter 10, by Xiaodan Zhang, discusses paternalism in Chinese business settings. The chapter addresses mainly how managers in DPEs adopted many labor-controlling strategies and methods that the state-owned enterprises used under the socialist system before the reforms. This chapter exhibits managerial isomorphism from a neo-institutionalist point of view. The chapter argues that the persistent paternalist ideology that influences the formation of power relations in DPEs is reproduced in the interactional process.

Chapter 11, by Arti Sharma and Sushant Bhargava, discusses cross-cultural diversity in global virtual teams. In this chapter, the authors have presented a brief literature review on GVTs, emphasizing the dearth of research in a cross-cultural context. They have presented the framework to describe the dimensions of diversity across different levels of implementation in GVTs.

Chapter 12, by Chandra Sekhar Patro, discusses cross-cultural communication in digital business settings. The chapter evaluates the influence of globalization on cross-cultural communication, the adoption of various communication strategies in cross-cultural business, and cross-cultural negotiation. The chapter also discusses the issues faced by global managers in cross-cultural business communication and dealing with barriers to cultural adaptation.

Chapter 13, by Rifat Kamasak, Mustafa F. Özbilgin, Kurt April, Meltem Yavuz Sercekman and Joana Vassilopoulou, is about managing diversity in multinational organizations. The chapter focuses on the problematic lack of effective regulation of diversity in global organizations. In this chapter, the authors have proposed the GVC approach to regulate global organizations, which could effectively ensure adequate and equitable global management of diversity in the organizations.

Chapter 14, by José G. Vargas-Hernández and Ernesto Guerra García, discusses entrepreneurial socio-interculturality. This chapter concludes that socio-intercultural entrepreneurship presents a methodological frame that significantly allows entrepreneurs to perceive global and local realities.

Acknowledgements

In the Name of God, Most Gracious, Most Merciful

This first volume of *Handbook of Research on Cross-Cultural Business and Management* is made with the contribution of authors and researchers from different nations and cultural backgrounds. We thank all the authors, reviewers, and academic alliances for their sincere efforts to make this book possible.

We are highly thankful to Prof. Deelip Kumar M, Deputy Vice Chancellor (DVC), Nile University of Nigeria for sparing his valuable time and writing the foreword for the book. His generous words for this book have given us inspiration to keep moving forward with such efforts.

We would like to pay our sincere gratitude to Prof. Vaishali Mahajan, Symbiosis Centre for Management & Human Resource Development (SCMHRD), Pune, India, for serving as an external reviewer to provide independent review for the book.

Special thanks to all the reviewers who gave their precious time and made sincere efforts in reviewing all the manuscripts. Their honest suggestions and advice helped us enrich the quality of all the chapters of the book.

We are grateful to all the researchers and authors who have contributed their work to the *Handbook of Research on Cross-Cultural Business and Management*. Also, we thank the people who permitted our researchers and authors to carry out research and develop it through their state-of-the-art descriptions of situations of all times to make this book a significant contribution in the field.

We are immensely thankful to our family members, friends and colleagues for encouraging us to publish this book. Their love, sacrifice and support helped us focus and continue in this direction. Their confidence in us helped us rise above the times of self-doubt and uncertainty throughout the journey.

In the end, we wish to pray to the Almighty for his kindness and eternal grace on us at all times to help us accomplish our goals.

Chapter 1

Cross-Cultural Business and Management: Opportunities and Challenges

Chandan Maheshkar

East Nimar Society for Education (ENSE), Indore, India

Vinod Sharma

SCMHRD, Symbiosis International University Pune, India

Abstract: Cross-culture business and management, as a practice, includes considering the influence of culture on an organization's operations and performance. It is all about how an organization operates and performs across the possible cultural contexts, including inter- and intra-organizational culture, in both business environments of home and host nations. Globalization and technological advancements made cross-cultural business and management practices strategic choices for organizations looking to expand in culturally diverse markets and leverage competitive advantage. Multicultural teams become a significant part of organizations to promote effectiveness in their business operations. Numerous aspects of culture influence business in myriad ways, and it is because business cannot exist without society, and society cannot exist without culture. This chapter aims to establish the relevance of culture in business and management practices and present challenges and opportunities to assist organizations in moving forward in the cross-cultural business environment.

Keywords: Cross-Culture Business, Cross-Culture Management, Cultural Studies, Managerial Competencies, Multiculturalism, Cultural Diversity

***

Introduction

Cross-culture business and management is most often considered as a subject of international business centred on cultural encounters between nations' cultures and the organizations' perceived cultural expectations. In the global scenario, because every nation holds its specifically defined culture and social norms, the deviation in the native cultures and organizations' expectations and the ways to manage cultural differences typically lead to conflict or miscommunication (Søderberg & Hoden, 2002). However, it is now out of context due to globalization and the expansion of businesses across the markets globally (Maheshkar & Sharma, 2018, 2021). Global knowledge networks, multicultural workforce, and national and/or international collaborations are the need of business organizations in the current global business environment. There is a need to rethink the intricacies of inter- and intra-organizational frameworks for managing in cross-cultural or multicultural business contexts (Maheshkar & Sharma, 2018, 2021).

Cross-culture business and management, as a practice, includes considering the influence of culture on an organization's operations and performance. As Madhavan (2012, p.15) mentioned that "the ability to manage cross-cultural interactions, multinational teams, and global alliances has become fundamental to managing in today's globalized world." There are many cases where the power of culture and diversity is overlooked, and organizations became a great failure. No matter if it is about Walt Disney, Walmart, Nick, or Starbucks. It has been noticed that managers have a tendency to neglect the diversity and cultural elements attached to it. From a managerial perspective, as Tomar (2019) stated, "individuals from different cultural backgrounds bring a different outlook, different ideas and different approaches—as well as their own strengths and weaknesses—to the table, and they can impact an organization in vastly different ways." Here, it is significant to understand how an individual's decision-making is influenced by his/her cultural background as both customer and manager. The focus of cross-cultural management is on dealing with cultural elements and making business practices compatible with these cultural elements (Jacob, 2004, Maheshkar & Sharma, 2018, 2021).

Cultural diversity has engrossed many scholars, philosophers, travelers, and traders since ancient times (Kim, 2000). They recorded their experiences and described probable reasons for their observed cultural differences. However, a large part of their explanations was biased and influenced by their religious beliefs, philosophical orientation, and personal intuitions. Relatively, systematic exploration of cross-cultural diversity is a recent phenomenon in Business and Management (Kim, 2000, Maheshkar & Sharma, 2018). Many studies exhibited that not considering cultural differences can be a cause of business failure. For example, Walt Disney, the world's leading entertainment conglomerate, performed poorly in France. The primary reason was Disney's lack of sensitivity to French and European culture. Walt Disney's 'The American way' in its theme park' Euro Disney' in Paris was a major factor contributing to this international failure. Therefore, this chapter establishes the significance of culture in the success of an organization's business and management practices and also exhibits the opportunities and challenges in cross-cultural business and management.

Relevance of Culture in Business and Management

Culture, socio-economic status, and political dynamics are critical dimensions that considerably affect how business is done. The universality of business and management theories and practices has vanished due to socio-cultural variations in interpersonal relationships between organizations and employees, organizations and suppliers, businesses and customers, and community and competition (Maheshkar & Sharma, 2018, 2021). It can be observed that the applicability of business practices is influenced by related culture to a certain extent. It shapes and suggests ways to satisfy society's physiological, psychological and sociological needs (Schiffman et al., 2016).

According to Maheshkar and Sharma (2018), "culture is an enormous and complex assemblage that utilizes a variety of ideologies and a higher order synthesis to bind humans into a society with historically prescribed customs, rituals, values, economic and political frameworks, and skill orientation." It has impacted individuals' views, expectations, wittiness, credibility, worries and fears to different extents, which can be explicated through cultural anthropology. A society's professed beliefs, customs and religion reflect how people live and behave. It helps to get a cultural understanding of a group or country to work effectively with people and diversity. Culture offers a *sense of identity*, and thus it is directly associated with organizational identity. On the humanitarian ground, every culture holds the *'common good'* as its core, i.e. quality of life, mutual cooperation, socio-economic well-being, and tolerance for others' actions (Gilmore, 2014).

Due to the mounting business expansions and migration in global job markets, many organizations are exposed to troubles caused due to cultural insensitivity to host nations' cultures and their market dynamics as well as their own intra-organizational work environment in the home country. In the present context, "a business is a hybrid social system that includes people of different backgrounds" (Maheshkar & Sharma, 2018, p.5). An organization can only succeed if its workforce believes in its organization's leadership and has shared values. Knowledge of the cultural backgrounds of the organizational workforce makes organizations capable of developing an organizational/business culture such that every member of the organization gets informed, involved and committed to the organizational success.

Cultural factors influence management functions in different ways, such as negotiation styles adopting appropriate modes of communication, and managing culturally diverse teams. These factors influence human behavior in many ways and categorize people as individualist or collectivist (Mueller & Thomas, 2000), each taking place at a different level of depth and having a thoughtful impact on business practices. Cultural understanding enables business executives to consider market diversity, consumers' adaption patterns for products/services, and when these should be customized and standardized (Maheshkar & Sharma, 2018). For example, some specific products/services accepted in one culture are outlawed in others. "Hindus do not eat beef because of their religious beliefs, but Christians and Muslims like to eat it. Muslims do not eat pork because Islam prohibits it, but Christians eat pork." McDonald's experienced failure in different countries because of culturally inspired food consumption, which forced McDonald's to customize its offerings accordingly.

Any change associated with cultural relevance can harm the business or offer new opportunities. Thus, culture should be considered a strategic component in the present business dynamics. Socio-cultural elements determine the products, services, and performance standards acceptable to society. So, organizations must be sensitive to host nations' cultures before entering into business with them. Business executives must explore host nations' cultures to learn their market trends, consumption and impacts of cultural change. They must be attentive to how their own cultures and symbolic meanings affect the beliefs and behaviors of other cultures. "Their cultural sensitivity will facilitate improved communication and control over conflicts caused by ethnocentrism or self-reference criterion (Maheshkar & Sharma, 2018)."

Case 1: Walt Disney in Paris – An Ethnocentric Failure

Walt Disney is a well-known American multinational mass media and entertainment company headquartered in Burbank, California. Its main business divisions are studios, parks and resorts, media networks, consumer products and interactive media. Disney opened its first theme park *Disneyland* in California, USA, in 1955, which was an astonishing success. Disney repeated the same success in Florida, USA, in the 1970s. In 1983, with a well-penetrate in the American market, Disney again marked *Disneyland's* success in Tokyo, Japan (Matusitz, 2010; Bryman, 2006, 2003). Now, these consecutive successes encouraged Disney to expand further (Matusitz, 2010). It decided to open its fourth *Disneyland* in Europe, and strategically, Paris was selected. In 1992, Disney opened *Euro Disney*, the biggest and most luxurious theme park in the world (Madhavan, 2012). As Matusitz (2010) reported, instead of all the efforts, enthusiasm and expectations, the first season of *Euro Disney* was unfortunate. *Euro Disney* had incurred losses of USD 900 million until 1994. Its poor performance made the Disney team believe that it might have to be closed down. In 2005, the French government-backed Disney with a subsidy (Madhavan, 2012).

French and Europeans are closely tied to their culture and believe that their culture is better than any outsider can offer (Riding, 2006). French exemplified *Euro Disney* as a wasteland as it did match their culture (Aupperle & Karimalis, 2001; Maheshkar & Sharma, 2018, p.11). For its cultural ignorance, Disney faced many protests to shut down its *Euro Disney* by French people. The root cause for the failure of *Euro Disney* was cultural ignorance. Disney had tried to emboss a self-referenced impression of American ways over French and European culture. Disney made the following operational mistakes in Paris:

- Food and wine are central to French society. French culture is also regarded as wine culture just because of its cuisine. In contrast, Disney practiced its 'no alcohol' policy in *Euro Disney*.

- Disney's forecast for its day-wise visitors got flopped. Disney thought Monday would be lighter and Friday an extremely busy day for it.

- *Euro Disney* restaurants were in trouble because of limited seating arrangements, food offerings, and timings of breakfast and lunch. Disney thought most of the visitors would like eating on the move, the same as Americans do while visiting the park.

- Disney replicated the same staffing model in *Euro Disney*, which was functioning successfully in America and Japan but failed in France.

- One of the key issues Disney faced was that Europeans stayed at *Euro Disney* for a short duration compared to what Disney expected based on the USA vacation pattern. Americans take various short vacations during the year, whereas Europeans take fewer but longer vacations (Madhavan, 2012).

Finally, a careful evaluation made Disney realize its gaffe of using an ethnocentric strategy in the European market, which failed to accommodate the needs of Europeans (Maheshkar & Sharma, 2018, 2021). Disney recognized how European culture is significant to Europeans, particularly French cultural traditions in France. Now, Disney shifted from its American way to Europeans' way of life. Disney started making a range of strategic modifications to its business philosophy, practices and products. The first change was that it renamed *Euro Disney* 'Disneyland Paris' to strengthen the park's identity and help to locate it precisely on the European map (Hill, 2000; Kaikati & Kaikati, 2003). *Disneyland Paris* earned its first profit in 2008 (Madhavan, 2012).

Case 2: Barbie in the Arab World

Barbie is the most recognizable doll, with its presence in more than 150 nations around the world. American businesswomen Ruth Handler, while watching her daughter playing with paper dolls, noticed that young girls enjoy playing adult roles and most children's toys were infants in representation. Realizing the gap in the market, an adult-bodied doll is idealized. Handler created the doll using a German doll, '*Bild Lilli*', which was exactly what was in her mind. Handler named this dream doll of young girls after her daughter Barbra's nickname *'Barbie'.* Mattel launched Barbie at the American International Toy Fair in New York on March 9, 1959. Barbie's curvaceous and unrealistic bodily appearance and materialism have been criticized. According to critics, it is a doll with "*too much of a figure*" that endorses sexuality among children. It caused Barbie to be banned in Saudi Arabia.

Barbie entered the Arab World in the mid-1990s. Due to its American appearance and cultural representation, which is entirely different from that of Arab Islamic culture, Barbie was banned twice (1995 and 2003) in Saudi Arabia. Barbie was declared a threat to morality and offensive to Islam because of its adult-bodied appearance and revealing clothes which were already banned in the country (CBS News, 2003). As said a poster on the site of *The Committee for the Propagation of Virtue and Prevention of Vice*, officially known as Saudi Arabia's religious police,

> Jewish Barbie dolls, with their revealing clothes and shameful postures, accessories and tools are a symbol of decadence to the perverted West. Let us beware of her dangers and be careful.

According to Sheik Abdulla al-Merdas (The Sydney Morning Herald, 2003), a preacher in a Riyadh mosque,

> It is no problem that little girls play with dolls. But these dolls should not have the developed body of a woman, and wear revealing clothes…These revealing clothes will be imprinted in their minds and they will refuse to wear the clothes we are used to as Muslims.

This was not the only case Mattel faced. It cannot be disregarded that culture and social norms significantly affect consumer behavior. American and European children have almost similar expectations and attitudes, as different Barbie dolls represent. However, the situation in other culturally diverse nations was not the same. The culture of the country is one of the major factors deciding the characteristic of its market and the acceptance or rejection of products/services. Thus, products/services popular in the

American market may fail in other culturally diverse nations like India, Russia, Arab, and Brazil. As an alternative and equivalent to Barbie, the Fulla doll, specifically designed to symbolize traditional Islamic values, was launched in November 2003 in Muslim-majority nations. There were different dolls launched to match the Islamic markets' needs, such as Salma (Indonesia), Saghira (Morocco), and Sara (Iran). Muslim parents prefer these dolls because they resemble Islamic culture and expect their daughters to behave and dress. Here, Mattel needed to think about and learn the customer needs in culturally diverse markets prior to extending Barbie, particularly in terms of cultural fit, religious fit and inspirational fit.

Cultural Fit: Social norms for men and women in every culture are different. Arabian culture is collectivist, while American culture is individualist, where individual autonomy and self-gratification are greatly valued (Buda & Elsayed-Elkhouly, 1998). Barbie is completely synonymous with women in American society, which is significantly different from Arabian society. Barbie in the Arabian markets was like a subject distracting young girls from their culture and values. Customers prefer products that fit into the socio-cultural fabric of their society, particularly with regard to the roles and status of women. Therefore, according to Rohm Jr. (2010), "it is important to better understand ourselves and clean our *cultural lens* in order to understand other's cultural differences and nuances."

Religion Fit: Arabians ensure Islam as their national religion. On the other hand, Americans have an individualistic perspective where people have the liberty to decide their religious orientation. The Islamic norms of religion differ to a great extent from what Barbie has experienced in American and European markets. Barbie violated the Islamic way of life. Arabian customers want dolls that completely suit the Islamic lifestyle.

Inspirational Fit: It is a general act of parents to give their children articles that inspire them toward what their parents expect from them. At the growing age, children also prefer toys that suit their inspirations. Parents in Islamic nations want a doll that inspires their daughters towards their cultural values and helps them to choose a career path respectable in Islamic society.

Mattel came up with *Muslim Barbie Doll, 'Leyla'*. However, "Islamic dolls are criticized for promoting gender stereotypes and restrictive roles." Saudi Arabia was not the only case of cross-cultural conflict which Mattel had experienced. Russia, Japan, Iran and other nations raised their objections and took restrictive actions. From a business perceptive, these regions are diverse in culture and religion, but they have potential markets. Mattel cannot be ignored the potential of such markets to earn huge profits. In response to tapping the opportunity, there were different customized Barbie dolls launched as per the culture and social norms of the nations. For example, the costume of Chinese Barbie is inspired by the Qing Dynasty, and Indian Barbie is dressed in Sari and traditional jewelry. Barbie dolls are not only customized with traditional attires, but festivals celebrated in the nations were also considered. Barbie has adopted the cultures of varied nations successfully and still maintains its charm in young girls worldwide.

Challenges to Cross-Cultural Business and Management

Organizations are crossing geographic boundaries to expand and take a competitive advantage from cross-border markets. Many organizations' capacity to manage the concomitant cultural shifts has not kept up with the pace of globalization. The emphasis has been on removing economic, technological, political, and legal barriers; nevertheless, cultural barriers are sometimes ignored or undervalued.

Lack of awareness of cultural diversity and values of host nations/regional populous can lead a poor economic performance, opportunity losses, legal issues, reputational damage, and the early termination of partnerships and contracts. Misunderstandings, conflicts, and prejudices based on cultural differences may even result in complete business failure. The major challenges to business and management facing organizations globally have been discussed in the following sections.

'One Size Fits All' Approach

Culture has a considerable influence on consumer behavior and preference. When an organization moves to a new and culturally different market, it needs to modify its business models to respond the regional preferences, social norms, and habits. Businesses and managerial practices should not be approached in a "*one-size-fits-all*" way (Maheshkar & Sharma, 2018). International, particularly cross-cultural/multicultural, business environment, a global perspective is required for phenomenal success. Failure to adapt the regional preferences, social norms and habits can lead to business failure, for example, Walt Disney Paris in its initial phase. Organizations need to remember that every nation, and even every state, has its own culture, social norms, and business practices when they are doing or planning business in a culturally diverse nation.

The host nation's culture has an influence on every aspect of business operations, including how personnel is managed, how negotiations are made, and how risks are handled. Therefore, success in cross-cultural business depends on having a thorough awareness of regional socio-economic practices. Unfortunately, organizations enter the market without becoming familiar with local business practices, and they soon find themselves in trouble (Seah, 2021). So, when entering a new market, organizations should prepare to think, communicate, and work just as competently as any native business therein (Ordorica, 2020). They have to appreciate the cross-cultural market's finer cultural attributes.

Cross-culture/Multi-Culture Communication

Cultural communications are deeper and more complex than spoken or written messages. The essence of effective cross-cultural communication has more to do with releasing the right responses than with sending the 'right' messages.

Hall and Hall (1990)

Table 1.1: Mental constructs as barriers in cross-cultural communication

Constructs	Definition	Examples
Prejudice	Preconception having no reason or actual experience.	In India, social class claiming itself elite/upper class thought that people from other social classes (scheduled casts and scheduled tribes) have lower intelligence.
Stereotypes	A rigid belief about particular people or something which is wrong.	An American thinks all Indian food is spicy without actually experiencing the enormously diverse Indian cuisine.
Biases	A tendency to favor or oppose a particular person/group or event, especially in a way considered to be unfair.	A manager from South India only prefers South Indians and avoids hiring North Indians for the job.
Parochialism (Narrow-Mindedness)	A state of mind focused on narrow aspects of an issue instead of focusing on its wider context.	When a manager ignores the culture of the region and/or people working in the organization due to organizational norms or own cultural boundaries, and thus, cannot see its impact on the organization until crisis hits.
Ethnocentrism	The belief that the people and culture of one's own race or nation are superior to others.	Expecting others to speak English, even when people are in their own country and the local language is Hindi. "Certain castes in India consider themselves superior to other castes." (Madhavan, 2012)
Self-Reference Criterion	Considering others' culture based on one's knowledge and experience of own culture.	When McDonald's entered India believing that its global menu of non-vegetarian items would be accepted, it had to customize its menu with vegetarian items.

Mental constructs such as prejudice, stereotypes, biases, parochialism, ethnocentrism, and self-reference criteria often create problems in cross-cultural communication (Madhavan, 2012). Cultural values or assumptions that are different from others can be challenging to understand and sometimes a cause for conflicts. These cultural divides are pervasive on a global scale. There are different patterns of cultural differences, where cultures vary from each other. When business executives/managers enter into a cross-cultural dialogue, they must keep these common differences in mind.

Communication becomes even more complicated due to cultural diversity. It increases the likelihood of linguistic and other communication barriers and the risk of uncertainty, value conflicts and disparities in thinking and decision-making. Perceptions and other forms of bias can also imperil relationships and obstruct the communication process.

Managing Cross-culture and Multi-Culture Teams/Workforce

A cross-cultural or multicultural team/workforce surely is competent only when it has respect for diversity and coordination among all the members of the team. It needs to reflect traits that characterize it as a social entity. In a cross-cultural business environment, learning how to manage with own culturally influenced attributes and use them selectively is an emerging and significant issue for business executives and managers (Ochieng et al., 2013). It is because when team members belong to different cultures and geography, they possibly vary in behavioral traits and perceptions of social norms. It may create differences toward preferred styles of leadership, decision-making, and dealing with conflicts. The high level of cultural distance between team members makes it difficult to maintain cohesiveness. For example, a team having all the members from south India has fewer issues than a team made up of members from India, North America, and Europe. Thus, when the workforce spreads over culturally diverse regions, the managers' responsibilities become even more complicated. In order to manage cross-cultural ambiguity and manage constraints of time, cost and work scope, managers must have higher-order cross-cultural competencies (Kappagomtula, 2017; Maheshkar & Sharma, 2018).

In the current business environment—due to globalization, technological interventions, and choices for better career prospects—a culturally diverse workforce becomes a core of organizational strategy (Salas et al., 2004; Maheshkar & Sharma, 2018, 2021). As the cross-cultural/multicultural workforce/teams continue to increase, it becomes necessary to identify the ways through which the effectiveness of the workforce/teams can be promoted.

Adaption of Management Practices

Most management theories, models, and practices—if not all—include assumptions that are particular to a certain culture. Regardless of the fact that no organizational theory or business framework is universal, the cultural presumptions that underlie management practices are frequently ignored. Without considering cultural differences, ideas are exported to other cultural contexts. But when cultural variations aren't taken into account while adaption of managerial practices, they can fail and even result in losses.

Cross-culture Diversity and Inclusion Barriers

Managing cross-cultural diversity refers to recognizing one's uniqueness in terms of religious beliefs, one's way of life and behavior, and managing his/her individual differences (Luthans, 2005; Maheshkar & Sharma, 2018, 2021). Today's organizations hold culturally diverse stakeholders. Effective management of cultural diversity is a critical component of an organization's competence. Business executives and managers must cultivate not only empathy and tolerance for cultural differences but also a sufficient level of factual knowledge of the beliefs and values of their culturally diverse stakeholders.

Knowledge of Cross-Cultural Ecology

Table 1.2: Knowledge Category and its Sources in Cross-Cultural Business

Knowledge Type	Factors	Source of Knowledge
Business Environment	**External:** Macro - Society-economic status, Politics, and global trends Micro - Customers, Suppliers, and Investors	Inductive/Deductive Reasoning; Consumer Research; Competitor Analysis, Industry Trends; Market Research; Scientific Study
	Internal: Human Resources, Vision and Mission, Value System, and Organizational Culture	Systematic Observations; Performance Assessments; Reviews; Impact Studies
Society & Culture	Cultural Mix, Values, Social Norms, Religious Practices, Recurrent Trends	Schemas as Social Knowledge; Associational Learning; Systematic Observations; Scientific Study
Behavioral Traits	Cultural Intelligence, Mindfulness, Respect for Diversity, Creativity, Learning, Dealing with Conflicts, Empathy, Intercultural Communication	
Regulatory Framework	Lawsuits, Policies, and Procedures specified by the Government	Public Policies; Current Practices; Business and Labor Laws

It could be disastrous if an organization enters into a culturally diverse market without having adequate knowledge of its business environment, society & culture, behavioral attributes, and requirements of compliance with minimum lawsuits, policies and procedures.

An adequate level of knowledge of the business environment of culturally diverse host nations improves the rate of success for organizations doing and go do business with them. When organizations are aware of potential differences and similarities, they are able to closely address the needs of their stakeholders, which ultimately enhances trust between them.

Cultural Traditionalism

Cultural influence can be classified into two types – traditional and non-traditional cultural influence. The traditional cultural influence is caused by predominant traditions, values, beliefs, rituals, and norms established in the past and transferred from generation to generation (Shiraev & Leavy, 2010). Non-traditional cultural influence is based on new ideas, principles, and practices. National or regional culture and individual community norms, in particular reference to cross-border businesses, significantly influence business and management practices in a varied manner, such as leadership and communication styles and HR practices.

Table 1.3: Traditional vs. Non-traditional Cultural Influence

Traditional Cultural Influence	Non-traditional Cultural Influence
Emphasis is on traditional wisdom and customs.	Emphasis is on individual preferences.
Associated with technology-driven developments to some extent.	Dominance of science-based knowledge and technology-driven developments.
Largely confined to regional or national boundaries.	Largely confined in metropolitans.
Intolerant to change in established beliefs, values, and norms.	Absorbing and dynamic to change in beliefs, values, and norms.
Limited to a certain set of ideas associated with a particular religious doctrine, tribe, ethnicity, or territory.	Promote autonomy and individualism.
Most social roles are prescribed to individuals.	Most social roles are decided/adopted by individuals.
Good and evil are clearly defined.	Good and evil are purposive.

Traditional cultures follow pre-approved societal structures in which most of the actions in people's lives are prescribed to them with very little autonomy for change. Traditional cultures via religious beliefs and practices control the individuals' value orientation and actions in terms of good or evil, desirable and obnoxious, or wisdom and stupidity. It becomes a serious concern to organizations operating in a cross-cultural environment if they ignore cultural traditionalism. For example, the case of Barbie in the Arab World (*see case 2 in the previous section*). Usually, it can be considered that some societies don't want to lose their cultural identity, and traditionalism is preventing it.

Negotiating across the Cultures

As a process, negotiation follows steps: building relations, collecting information, persuasion, and agreements. The purpose of this process is to make a mutual decision or come out with an agreement. Culture influences the negotiation processes. Negotiations in cross-cultural business are multifarious in nature and involve higher transaction costs than with partners in their home country. Business executives or negotiators should be culture-savvy so that they can appreciate the cultural intricacies of cross-border business and influence their counterparts more successfully than those who ignore the relevance of culture in cross-border business negotiations. They need to understand their counterparts' business philosophy, objectives, cultural inclinations, and negotiation styles.

Subordination of Cross-culture Diversity into Inclusivity

An inclusive workplace attracts and invigorates competent people from around the world. A diversified workforce can better understand and address the needs of culturally diverse clientele. Employee diversity can increase access to a variety of perspectives and resources. The successful integration of diverse perspectives fosters novelty and creativity. However, if it is not managed sensitively, workgroups can face conflicts, which results in less cooperation and trust among them. Organizations must deal with discrimination, racism, and cultural conflicts appropriately. Those that don't deal with these internal conflicts risk losing out on the benefits of a diverse staff and being subject to face legal issues.

Opportunities for Cross-Cultural Business and Management

Globalization and technological advancements have expanded the scope of cross-cultural business and management. There is a good possibility that organizations will work with people in countries from diverse cultures, regardless of the country to which they belong.

Cultural Diversity Offers Multiple Perspectives and Can Inspire Innovation

People from culturally diverse backgrounds usually have different perspectives, skills, and experiences. In this sense, cultural diversity offers a variety of perspectives, which can offer new ideas and inspirations. It exhibits that diversity of thought fosters creativity and propels innovation and expansion in business, helps to solve issues and satisfies consumer needs in novel and exciting ways (Maheshkar & Sharma, 2018; Reynolds, 2018). For example, cultural diversity in team members or employees in an organization challenge them to be more out-of-box thinker and nurture cross-cultural intelligence. As a result, cross-cultural/multicultural business environments frequently foster greater levels of innovation and creativity. This benefits companies since more innovation generates more income.

Local Market Insights Makes Business More Competitive

As the protectionist barriers are being removed or minimized in the growing markets throughout the world, new opportunities for further business expansion or new businesses have widely opened to the organizations (Dawer & Frost, 1999; Maheshkar & Sharma, 2018, 2021). An organization can prosper if it is aware of the culture, competition, and local laws. Cultural awareness, connections and native linguistic proficiency can greatly accelerate the business in a cross-cultural setting. These give an organization a considerable advantage when expanding into new markets (Reynolds, 2018). Organizations looking to enter the global markets have to be familiar with the cultural differences of their host country and how these cultural differences can affect their business endeavors.

Glocalization – The Fusion of Global and Local

Glocalization, a blend of '*Globalization*' and '*Localization*', refers to a product or service that is developed and distributed globally but modified to sustain in local markets as per the consumer needs (Hayes, 2022). It encourages the acceptance of foreign products among local consumers. The process of glocalization can be costly and resource-intensive. It mostly offers good economic benefits to the businesses that practice it.

  Glocalization should boost the level of competition, lower prices, and make products/services more accessible by making global organizations more competitive in response to domestic players (Hayes, 2022, Ritzer, 2003). However, it is usually the practice of large multinational organizations through which they hold a large share of the market.

Attract and Retain the Best Talent Pool

An organization's competence to grow depends on its ability to attract and retain excellent personnel (Maheshkar, 2016). A surefire approach to increase earnings and market credibility is to hire the best talent, which will guarantee higher and better productivity. A culturally diverse human resource allows organizations to be more compatible with cross-cultural/multicultural business environments. Cross-cultural diversity—including gender, ethnicity, and religion—improves retention and minimizes the cost of employee turnover (Reynolds, 2018; Maheshkar & Sharma, 2018, 2021). Organizations holding a cross-cultural employee pool are more competent. A welcoming environment of cross-cultural collaboration is a great way to bring together teams and coworkers across the organization.

The most considerable advantage of culturally diverse personnel is organizations benefit from professionals with a wide array of skills, experiences and perspectives. Organizations can take the competitive advantage of a wider set of skills and potentially diverse product/service portfolio. In a present uncertain business environment, agile and adaptable organizations sustain and succeed. An organization with cultural diversity may identify market gaps quickly (Reynolds, 2018). It would have market-specific insights necessary for the adaption process in culturally diverse markets.

Diversity Ensures Effective Performance for Organizations

The diversity of experience, knowledge, and working styles that a diverse workplace provides can improve problem-solving competence and increase performance. It can be noted that organizations with cultural diversity and inclusion practices are more productive. According to a McKinsey report by Hunt et al. (2018), inclusion and diversity are regarded as "a source of competitive advantage, and specifically as a key enabler of growth." However, organizations are still not sure about the best ways to leverage diversity and inclusion to accelerate their value-creation goals.

Working in uniform teams may appear simpler, but it might lead an organization to accept the status quo. Contrarily, diversity can foster healthy competition, pushing a team to perform to its highest potential. This environment of active and fair competition can encourage the improvement of business practices for increased effectiveness (Maheshkar, 2016; Reynolds, 2018; Maheshkar & Sharma, 2018, 2021).

Conclusion

Culture is a significant concern that puts pressure on businesses to modify their practices and strategies accordingly (De Mooij, 2019; Dass &Vinnakota,

2019). Organizations must have competencies to manage cross-cultural interactions and international alliances to survive in the current dynamic business environment. Understanding culture can help business executives learn the business etiquette of different countries, explore the business environment and rationale behind different managerial practices, understand the diversity of markets, and adjust more readily to work as an expatriate (Madhavan, 2012; Maheshkar & Sharma, 2018). Cross-cultural business— however it is not new and has ancient roots—has emerged swiftly during the last two decades. From a managerial perspective, cross-cultural management focuses on appraising cultural norms and aligning business endeavors accordingly (Jacob, 2004). As a business leader, it is very significant to the organization to know how to manage cross-cultural expectations effectively in intra-organizational environments and host countries in which they are operating or thinking of expanding.

Organizations failed as they failed to appreciate the cultural norms of the host nations like KFC, McDonald's, Starbucks, and others. They cannot be successful in operating in host nations if they misunderstand the notion of *cultural adaptation.* There are many cases that have set the relevance of culture in operating in cross-cultural settings. Each brings a distinctly unique set of experiences and reveals diverse challenges and opportunities. It depends on the organizations' ability to know cultural intricacies and how they utilize this knowledge to gain competitive advantage at its maximum effect in a cross-cultural environment.

References

Aupperle, K. E., & Karimalis, G.N. (2001). Using metaphors to facilitate cooperation and resolve conflict: Examining the case of Disneyland Paris. *Journal of Change Management 2*(1), 23-32. https://doi.org/10.1080/714042 489

Bryman, A. (2003). McDonald's as a Disneyized Institution: Global Implications. *American Behavioral Scientist, 47*(2), 154–167. https://doi.org/10.1177/000276 4203256181

Bryman, A. (2006). Global implications of McDonaldization and Disneyization. In G. Ritzer (Ed.), *McDonaldization: The reader* (pp. 319-325). Pine Forge Press.

Buda, R., & Elsayed-Elkhouly, S. M. (1998). Cultural Differences between Arabs and Americans: Individualism-Collectivism Revisited. *Journal of Cross-Cultural Psychology, 29*(3), 487–492. https://doi.org/10.1177/002202219829 3006

CBS News (2003, September 11). Saudis Bust Barbie's 'Dangers'. *CBS News.* https://www.cbsnews.com/news/saudis-bust-barbies-dangers/

Dass, M., & Vinnakota, S. (2019). Cross-Cultural Mistakes by Renowned Brands – Evaluating the Success and Failures of Brands in Host Nations. *International Journal of Trend in Scientific Research and Development, 3*(2), 38-42.

Dawer, N., & Frost, T. (1999). Competing with Giants: Survival Strategies for Local Companies in Emerging Markets. *Harvard Business Review.* https://hbr.org/1999/03/competing-with-giants-survival-strategies-for-local-companies-in-emerging-markets

De Mooij, M. (2019). *Consumer behavior and culture: Consequences for global marketing and advertising.* Sage.

Gilmore, A. (2014, November 12). Raising our quality of life. *Centre for Labour and Social Studies.* http://classonline.org.uk/pubs/item/raising-our-quality-of-life

Hayes, A. (2022). Glocalization: What It Means, Advantages, and Examples. *Investopedia.* https://www.investopedia.com/terms/g/glocalization.asp

Hunt, V., Yee, L., Prince, S., & Dixon-Fyle, S. (2018). Delivering through Diversity. *McKinsey & Company.* https://www.mckinsey.com/capabilities/people-and-organizational-performance/our-insights/delivering-through-diversity

Hill, C. (2000). *International Business: Competing in the Global Marketplace.* McGraw Hill.

Jacob, N. (2004). *Intercultural Management.* Kogan Page.

Kaikati, J.G., & Kaikati, A.M. (2003). A rose by any other name: Rebranding campaigns that work. *Journal of Business Strategy, 24*(6), 17-23. https://doi.org/10.1108/02756660310509451

Kappagomtula, C. L. (2017). Overcoming challenges in leadership roles – managing large projects with multi or cross culture teams. *European Business Review, 29*(5), 572-583. https://doi.org/10.1108/EBR-12-2015-0177

Kim, U. (2000). Indigenous, cultural, and cross-cultural psychology: A theoretical, conceptual, and epistemological analysis. *Asian Journal of Social Psychology, 3*(3), 265–287. https://doi.org/10.1111/1467-839X.00068

Luthans, F. (2005). *Organization Behavior.* McGraw Hill.

Maheshkar, C., & Sharma, V. (2018) (Eds.). Cross-cultural Business Education: Leading Businesses around the Cultures. In *Handbook of Research on Cross-Cultural Business Education* (pp. 1-35). IGI Global. https://doi.org/10.4018/978-1-5225-3776-2.ch001

Maheshkar, C., & Sharma, V. (2021) (Eds.). Cross-cultural Business Education: Leading Businesses around the Cultures. In *Research Anthology on Business and Technical Education in the Information Era* (pp. 677-711). Business Science Reference. https://doi.org/10.4018/978-1-7998-5345-9.ch038

Maheshkar, C. (2016). HRD Scholar-Practitioner: An Approach to Filling Research, Theory and Practice Gaps. In Hughes, C. & Gosney, M. W. (Eds.), *Bridging the Scholar-Practitioner Gap in Human Resource Development* (pp 20-46). IGI Global. https://doi.org/10.4018/978-1-4666-9998-4.ch002

Madhavan, S. (2012). *Cross-Cultural Management.* Oxford University Press.

Matusitz, J. (2010). Disneyland Paris: a case analysis demonstrating how glocalization works. *Journal of Strategic Marketing, 18*(3), 223-237. https://doi.org/10.1080/09652540903537014

Mueller, S. L., & A. S. Thomas (2000). Culture and entrepreneurial potential: a nine country study of locus of control and innovativeness. *Journal of Business Venturing, 16*(1), 51-75. https://doi.org/10.1016/S0883-9026(99)00039-7

Ochieng, E.G., Price, A.D.F., Ruan, X., Egbu, C.O., & Moore, D. (2013). The effect of cross-cultural uncertainty and complexity within multicultural construction teams. *Engineering, Construction and Architectural Management, 20*(3), 307-324. https://doi.org/10.1108/09699981311324023

Ordorica, S. (2020, November 23). Getting Lost In Translation: Three Critical Ways Businesses Fail in Global Markets. *Forbes* https://www.forbes.com/sites/forbesbusinesscouncil/2020/11/23/getting-lost-in-translation-three-critical-ways-businesses-fail-in-global-markets/?sh=48050d946c4a

Reynolds, K. (2018). 13 benefits and challenges of cultural diversity in the workplace. *HULT International Business School Blog.* https://www.hult.edu/blog/benefits-challenges-cultural-diversity-workplace/

Riding, A. (2006, December 26). American culture's French connection. *The New York Times.* https://www.nytimes.com/2006/12/26/books/26martel.html

Ritzer, G. (2003). Rethinking Globalization: Glocalization/Grobalization and Something/Nothing. *Sociological Theory, 21*(3), 193-209.

Rohm Jr., F. W. (2010). American and Arab Cultural Lenses. *Inner Resources for Leaders, 3*(2).

Salas, E., Burke, C.S., Fowlkes, J.E., & Wilson, K.A. (2004). Challenges and Approaches to Understanding Leadership Efficacy in Multi-Cultural Teams. In Kaplan, M. (Ed.), *Cultural Ergonomics (Advances in Human Performance and Cognitive Engineering Research, Vol. 4)* (pp. 341-384). Emerald Group Publishing. https://doi.org/10.1016/S1479-3601(03)04012-8

Saudi police outlaw Barbie (2003, September 10). *The Sydney Morning Herald.* https://www.smh.com.au/world/saudi-police-outlaw-barbie-20030910-gdhd5i.html

Schiffman, L., Wisenblit, J., & Kumar, S. R. (2016). *Consumer Behavior (11e).* Pearson India.

Seah, L. (2021). The importance of cultural awareness in international business. *International Business Blog.* https://www.airswift.com/blog/importance-of-cultural-awareness

Shiraev, E. B. & Leavy, D. A. (2010). *Cross-Cultural Psychology: Critical Thinking and Contemporary Applications (4e).* Allyn & Bacon.

Søderberg, A.-M., & Holden, N. (2002). Rethinking Cross Cultural Management in a Globalizing Business World. *International Journal of Cross-Cultural Management, 2*(1), 103–121. https://doi.org/10.1177/147059580221007

Tomar, B. (2019). The Importance of Cross-Cultural Management. *Forbes.* https://www.forbes.com/sites/forbeslacouncil/2019/04/23/the-importance-of-cross-cultural-management/?sh=4021b971b5c3

Chapter 2

Managing in Chinese Cultural Settings: An Institutional Economic Perspective

Jeremy Kwok

University of Exeter, England

Abstract: The theoretical underpinning of this chapter is cultural theories from economics, particularly institutional economics. Explanations offered from institutional economics, for example, are particularly well-suited to explain the rise of the Chinese economy in the late 20th century, starting from the market-led economic reforms in the 1980s. The main contribution of this chapter is providing a strong case with a rigorous analysis from an economic perspective. Relevance is shown in examining the differences arising from such economic and institutional arrangements that the outcome is the fast-growing Chinese economy that we are seeing now. The second contribution comes from introducing the complexity of managing in Chinese cultural settings. This complexity arises as soft institutions such as cultural practices in business like Guanxi constantly change and morph into different practices when the geography changes.

Keywords: Chinese Culture, Institutional Economy, Chinese Economy, Cultural Theories, Guanxi, Cultural Shifts, Chinese Business

***

Introduction

Personal network or Guanxi matters less in overseas private Chinese businesses and other regions such as Hong Kong and Singapore. Due to economic activity, growth and labour migration, various Chinese communities have substantial cultural differences. For example, Hong Kong's culture differs enormously from other Chinese communities. Although the majority of inhabitants in Hong Kong are ethnically Chinese, due to its long history of British administration and the city's status as international trade and financial hub, the management culture differs greatly from mainland China. The differences are particularly prominent in terms of governance, the influence of the central government, relationships with foreign firms and down to human resources and line management. The working language, for example, is predominantly English, although most of the population communicates in Cantonese when speaking directly with each other. This prevalent bilingualism is rare in mainland China where often the sole working language is Mandarin Chinese.

As a result of the rapid changes in the Chinese economy in recent decades, the accompanying culture has also changed dramatically compared to the pre-1970s. Since then, there has been a convergence towards Western management and culture. However, there remains a distinctive difference when comparing the two. This part discusses some of these divergences and their implications. Although China is the largest economy to have Chinese businesses, a substantial population and expatriates run businesses in distinctively different institutional settings, such as Hong Kong, Taiwan, and Singapore. In this case, the cultural settings are very different due to different laws and social norms. The focus is on the rise of China. Perhaps like the rise of the Japanese economy in the 1970s and 1980s, Japanese management was exported to other countries and succeeded.

This chapter tries to illustrate the theoretical framework of institutional economics and how it can be used to understand and manage a business in a Chinese context. A strong emphasis is on institutions. The term "institution" commonly applies to informal institutions such as customs or behaviour patterns important to society and formal institutions created by law and having a distinctive permanence in ordering social behaviours. Primary or soft institutions are institutions such as the family culture that are broad enough to encompass and permeate other institutions.

Theoretical framework

To understand the institution in this context, the use of the theoretical framework from institutional economics was considered. It focuses on understanding the role of the evolutionary process and the role of institutions in shaping economic behaviour. Institutional economics has emerged from academia as one of the leading economic schools of thought that has strongly influenced how we understand development, organisational structures, and changes in economic institutions.

An economic institution is defined as "the constraints placed by law and social norms on human behaviour" or, in North's words, "the rules of the game". The purpose of the constraints is there to help reduce transaction costs. In North's (1990) introduction to his seminal book, he defined that

> Institutions are the rules of the game in a society or, more formally, are the humanly devised constraints that shape human interaction. Consequently, they structure incentives in human exchange, whether political, social, or economic. Institutional change shapes how societies evolve through time and is the key to understanding historical change. That institutions affect the performance of economies is hardly controversial. That the differential performance of economies over time is fundamentally influenced by how institutions evolve is also not controversial. (p. 7)

There has been a strong focus from economists on institutions and transaction costs in different economies. An example is the Ease of doing business index compiled by the World Bank[1] (Djankov, 2016). Higher rankings (a low numerical value) indicate better, usually simpler, regulations for businesses and stronger protections of property rights. The implication is that the economic growth impact of improving these regulations is vital. A nation's ranking on the index is based on an average of 10 sub-indices, such as starting a business, dealing with construction permits, getting electricity, registering property, getting credit, protecting investors, paying taxes, trading across borders, enforcing contracts, and resolving insolvency. In general, the index approximates how much time and effort (in other words, transaction costs) is needed when doing business in such a country. For example, a very illustrative sample was given in North's work, in which he used the example of a sports match to explain institutions:

> Institutional constraints include both what individuals are prohibited from doing and, sometimes, under what conditions some individuals are permitted to undertake certain activities. As defined here, they, therefore, are the framework within which human interaction takes place. They are perfectly analogous to the rules of the game in a competitive team sport. That is, they consist of formal written rules as well as typically unwritten codes of conduct that underlie and supplement formal rules, such as not deliberately injuring a key player on the opposing team. And as this analogy would imply, the rules and informal codes are sometimes violated, and punishment is enacted. Therefore, an essential part of the functioning of institutions is the costliness of ascertaining violations and the severity of punishment. (p. 8)

---

[1] https://www.doingbusiness.org/en/rankings

Transaction costs, as defined above, clearly indicate their implication for the development of an economy. As overall transaction costs reduce in an economy, economic performance is expected to improve. It has been a correct prediction of China's economic rise since the 1980s. Outside of China and looking into peripheral areas such as Japan, Korea, Taiwan, Hong Kong, and Singapore, a distinctive pattern of reducing transaction cost measures taken by successive governments can be noticed. The result has been an unprecedented rise in economic performance in these economies. The rest of this chapter further explores this theoretical framework and demonstrates how these can be explained in managing in Chinese cultural settings.

Institutional Economic Theories and Changes

China's Economic Growth

China's economy is now the second largest in the World. The tremendous growth since the market reforms in the 1970s is seen as the biggest impetus which caused the phenomenal growth in the following 50 years. The gross domestic product (GDP) of China's economy is $14.72 billion[2]. The below graph shows the real yearly GDP of 7 nations (in order of magnitude: USA, China, Japan, Germany, UK, India and Russia). All seven nations have been growing in terms of GDP since the 1960s, but their growth rate is very different. The US has been growing steadily since the 1960s and only suffered two small drops in 2008 and 2020 due to the great financial crash and virus pandemic. The second place is China, which accelerated its growth in the early 1990s to 10% per year on average and again accelerated in the late 2000s and only plateaued in 2020.

On the other hand, Japan has stopped growing its economy since the late 1990s due to the financial crash. A distinctive group of Western European economies is performing similarly. For example, UK and Germany are growing, but their speed of growth has paused since the early 2000s, similar to Japan. This is also the case for France, Spain, and Italy. India has experienced something like China's growth, which accelerated in the early 2000s, although the speed has since lessened. On the other hand, Russia had its country, institutions, and culture entirely changed since the collapse of the Soviet Union in 1991. This change was so profound that it only started growing again in the early 2000s, although its path is quite different from other countries, and the growth has become negative recently.

---

[2] Full data series please visit: https://data.worldbank.org/country/china

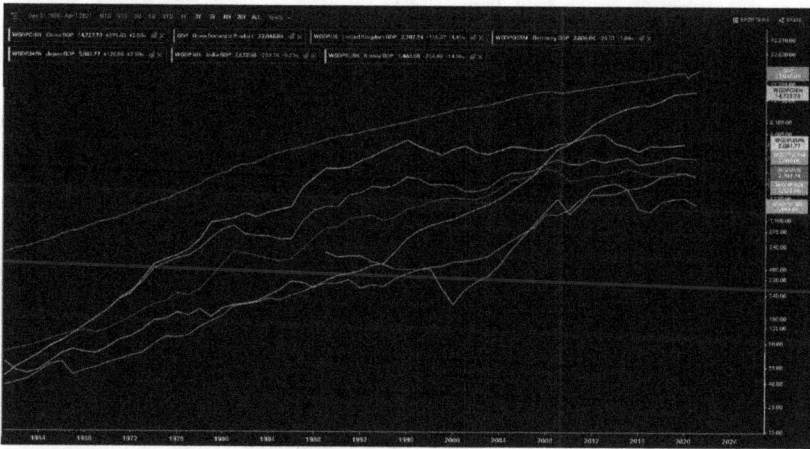

Figure 2.1: World Leading Economies Yearly GDP from 1960 to 2021, constructed from quarterly GDP data from World Bank

Institutional Economics and Development

Naturally, there is a need to explain the phenomenal growth and the different development paths taken by different economies. In this case, institutional economics is particularly relevant to demonstrate and explain the resulting growth and the divergences among countries. Considering the importance of institutions, the field of institutional economics is now one of the major contributions to the research on understanding development and growth (Bardhan, 1989; Nabli & Nugent, 1989; North, 1993; Ménard & Shirley, 2005; Tamanaha, 2015; Gray, 2016; Roland, 2016; Hodgson, 2017; Acs et al., 2018; Prasetyo & Kistanti, 2020). In effect, institutions or simply the game's rules determine how costly it is to pursue business and transactions in the economy. Such transactions can be purchasing properties, building materials, setting up private businesses and exporting to local and foreign customers. Some countries' intuitions make economic transactions much easier, while others are less productive to the entrepreneurs, thus increasing the cost of each transaction. Take China as an example. It was still running a state-led planned economy in the 1970s in which the China Communist Party (CCP) ran and decided on all economic decisions (Coase & Wang, 2012) wrote a comprehensive account of the history and institutional change of China). As experienced in numerous planned economies, this economic model was inefficient and prone to continuous market failures.

Such institutions made economic transactions difficult, if not impossible. Property rights did not exist as properties were shared; investment prediction virtually did not exist as private property was not the norm. Economic life under such an institutional arrangement naturally led to corruption and favouritism, which harmed development. The economic reforms in China in the 1970s saw a massive institutional change in which capitalist concepts and ideas were gradually introduced. The effects have been very strong on economic growth as changes in property rights, market development, the existence of private enterprises, and legal protection of investments were introduced.

Main Theories in Institutional Economics

This section discusses two aspects of intuitions – formal institutions, such as laws, and informal intuitions, such as culture.

Property Rights

Property rights are the centre of research in institutional economics. The term property is very expansive, though the legal protection for certain kinds of property varies between jurisdictions. In general, the property is owned by individuals or a group such as companies. Property rights are defined as the expected ability of an economic agent to use an asset (Barzel, 1997) freely. It represents a social institution that creates incentives to operate, maintain, and invest in assets. Property ownership rights can be extended by using patents and copyrights to protect them. Legal instruments such as property laws are part of the formal institution to protect property rights.

The enforcement of property rights is normally associated with the formal legal institution. However, as demonstrated in the literature, it is also possible to maintain rights by custom, norms and markets (see, for example, Ellickson 1991). Compared to costly legal resolutions, the custom is cheaper in addition to laws and regulations for markets to process repeated transactions.

Property rights remain one of the strongest intrinsic motivations for humans to work. The reforms of the 1970s in China saw the government allowing private ownership for the first time. This gradual introduction of property laws saw massive economic growth as the population began to reap benefits from small to medium enterprises as entrepreneurs. Under the strict governance of the CCP, private property rights did not exist until the reforms.

In this first sweeping reform, the household responsibility system (HRS) was widely adopted in rural areas, which saw the contracting and restructuring of state-owned enterprises (SOEs) in cities. Private enterprises re-emerged as self-employed and other forms, and foreign-invested companies cropped up in coastal cities such as Shanghai, Tianjin, and others. Property rights under the new reforms allowed the ownership of property again, which has since spurned the continuous growth. Since then, a new form and structure of property rights have been added to the constitution to reflect later changes to accommodate a mixed economy (Zhou, 2020).

Transaction Cost

The dictionary gave a concise and distinctive definition (Niehans, 2018): "Transaction costs arise from the transfer of ownership or, more generally, of property rights. They are a concomitant of decentralised ownership rights, private property, and exchange. They would be absent in a collectivist economy with completely centralised decision-making; administrative costs would take their place." Note that transaction costs would be absent in a completely centralised economy. However, there was never one completely centralised due to the information required to assess all components within the economy in real-time properly. As such, transaction cost was extremely high in such an economy due to the costly method of the planned economy and the absence of property rights. In its absence, rent dissipation happened rapidly, and social norms and customs were developed organically to contain the waste (see section **Rent dissipation and culture**).

Transaction cost is a concrete concept that we encounter in everyday business dealing. The employer's national insurance payment is an extra transaction cost when hiring a new employee. Value-added tax (VAT) is a transaction cost that consumers must pay when the tax authority specifies. However, other transaction costs are difficult to observe as they are implicit. For example, discounts or instant access to clubs for females are often done to attract more male customers. This is done so that more females will go into the said club at lower or no cost. As such, the club will have a higher number of females, attracting more males. There is a higher transaction cost to male customers for the entrance. This is a case of classic price discrimination in which optimised revenue can be obtained. Transaction costs also occur within the state. For example, the regulations imposed may deter businesses from creating too much carbon waste as there will be higher carbon taxes and fines. While a transaction cost increase can distort the agent's intention to conduct a business, it does not imply that it is always good or bad for its overall well-being. A keynote here is that transaction cost exists and should be examined when understanding institutions.

Different economies have different levels of transaction costs. One of the strongest arguments for the performance of a market economy over a planned economy is the much lower cost of transactions. A planned economy requires the planner to possess all information, such as the precise and changing nature of supply and demand. It has dramatically increased the cost compared to a market-based one in which this function is outsourced to the market by competition.

Rent Dissipation and Culture

An important theory of the institutional economic literature is rent dissipation. Imagine a metropolitan city centre such as London. Parking is often a severe issue, and permits can be sold very expensively for the right of permeant certainty (some are sold for upwards of £40k, and the parking lot ownership can be sold or transferred like a property deed). Now, if this parking space is free, it is easy to imagine that anyone with a car will park it until no space is left. This phenomenon is referred to as rent dissipation. This occurs when a valuable public good can be accessed with no restrictions. Under competition, its value will dissipate at the margin after being consumed by an additional person until all economic rent is wholly dispersed. By establishing a restriction to access, such as rights of a parking lot backed by a property deed, the value of the parking lot will retain and will not dissipate under this condition.

Another classic example is the case of overfishing and overfarming in public spaces. The rent of said sea or grazeland will reduce to zero as it cannot produce any fish or produce further. It would become a waste capital, referred to as the tragedy of the commons (Hardin, 1968). Similarly, rent dissipation is a major undesirable economic outcome where no private ownership is established under the communist regime. Without a formal institution established to lay the boundary of a desired publicised private good, informal institutions will be formed autonomously to reduce rent dissipation. For example, in the absence of formal rules on a shared resource such as fertile farmland, an informal system will likely be established, such as the order of access based on seniority or family prestige. Such informational institutions can then be carried over to other areas where it becomes a common culture.

Interestingly, an informal institution can sometimes be served as a reducer to rent dissipation, as noted in Feeny et al. (1990). In this case, the harsh prediction of a public resource depleting to zero may not occur, although it will still dissipate to a lesser extent. From this perspective, culture is a by-product of the complex institutions of which it is also a constraint to the action of the agents.

Hierarchy and Corruption

As seen in the above example in 'rent dissipation and culture', hierarchy naturally forms in all human and animal organisations. An interesting observation is noted that news reports of corruption and bribing during China's capitalist reforms in the 1980s. However, it was seen as a good sign by the said economist, as back in the communist era, access to resources was strictly distributed according to the ranks in the party. A higher-ranked official would have access to better-quality goods than lower-ranked officials. This restriction on resources was an explicit system created under a propertyless economy as an effort to reduce rent dissipation. When corruption and bribery were reported, it was viewed as a good sign that capitalist reforms were indeed being carried out. It was a sign of the gradual withdrawal of the rank-seniority system to a market-based system.

Market-based Economic Reform in the 1980s

On September 9, 1976, Chairman Mao Zedong, who had long been ill with Lou Gehrig's disease, died. Internal political struggles continued not until Deng Xiaoping rose to supreme power in 1978. It was perhaps the most important event in modern Chinese history as Deng represented the ideas and political friction for economic reform. Deng's economic reform goal was to raise China's standard of living from dire poverty. Although the CCP led the reform, it did not have a clear master plan on how to achieve this. It was very open to new ideas, and even capitalist ideology was gradually tolerated and accepted as part of the "socialism with Chinese characteristics" regime. The reform was so novel and drastic. It was completely different compared to the rigid adherence to the Marxist and Communist ideology of the previous leadership. As a result, many popular quotes of this era captured the experimental nature of such reform, such as "no matter if it is a white cat or a black cat; as long as it can catch mice, it is a good cat" and "across a river by groping for stones".

Due to the liberalisation and the general acceptance of the market reforms, many local initiatives in agriculture took place before gaining approval from the government. In 1979, one commune responded to a drought situation by drawing up individual contracts and basing pay on productivity. Despite some criticism from local government leaders, the effect of the private contracts worked and quickly spread to other places in the country. It quickly turned into a general nationwide abandonment of the communes and a return to the family farm, or individual household, as the basic agricultural unit. Under this new institutional arrangement, property rights were not assigned to the land, which remained collectively owned. Rights were given to the farmers who tilled the land. The output of such individual farms achieved harvests and profits. Farmers were incentivised to outperform each other and obtain the highest yield with the most efficient input. This was drastically different from the commune farm, in which farmers performed according to a set quota requested by the state and did have no profit sharing (see Coase & Wang, 2016 for a full account of the change). Soon the reform was spread into the state-run industrial sector. The most unproductive state-run factories were shut down, the responsibilities were passed onto the private market, and the state encouraged entrepreneurship. By about 1992, China had become a predominantly market economy. In 1997, the state laid off more than twenty-five million workers from state-owned enterprises within a few years. By the early twenty-first century, the former China bureau chief of the Financial Times could marvel that "China today is a great deal less socialist than any country in Europe" (Holcombe, 2017).

The wholesale institutional economic reform was not matched by its scale and depth in any economy. This is one of the reasons for China's rapid economic take-off, as it allowed the relaxation of central controls and a widespread and obsessive focus on economic growth. A relentless pursuit of economic growth and money-making was completely endowed from the top bureaus to the local office to the state. Effectively local state officials were given a profit share if they managed to bring in new investments and improved output. Under such a competitive institutional arrangement, China can be seen as a giant corporation with tens of thousands of local sales offices competing against each other and developing its businesses. On top of this competition, there was a huge, relatively well-educated and unlimited supply of comparatively low-wage labour (although this supply is dwindling as of writing, partly due to the one-child policy in the 1970s, though the upper limit is three now).

Traditional confusion ethics and culture have returned as the central values subscribed by the state and population. Again, this is a tremendous institutional change from the Marxist and Communist values of the 1940s to the 1980s, which did not provide a suitable culture for entrepreneurship. The traditional values of hardworking, respecting parents and valuing education have extensively provided soft institutions as a backbone of China.

Under Deng Xiaoping, China opened to foreign investments again compared to the previous isolated regime. One significant sign of the Chinese reform is its willingness to accept foreign investments. When comparing Japan and Korea, foreign direct investments contributed up to 30% of China's GDP when it is only a few percent in other prosperous East Asian countries. To attract outside capital and to spurn the export-led growth, four Special Economic Zones (SEZs) were initially approved in 1979 (Shenzhen, Shantou, Zhuhai, and Xiamen, all in the southeast) on the model of export processing zones elsewhere in East Asia (such as those established in Taiwan beginning in 1966), offering low taxes and other economic incentives. IN PARTICULAR, the SEZ at Shenzhen, near Hong Kong, then exploded from rural rice paddies into a bustling city that is now home to perhaps twenty million people. In addition to the SEZs, new coastal cities are also open to investments. More than 100 ports, free trade zones, and economic development zones are in China now.

To put things in perspective, 40% of the top 50 largest ports are in China, while the rest of the 30% is shared by other East Asian countries such as Taiwan, Singapore, Korea and Japan.

The Prominent Characteristic of Chinese Business – Guanxi

Chinese business broadly comprises all businesses in Greater China, including Hong Kong, Taiwan, Singapore, and other geographic areas dominated by foreign but ethnically Chinese citizens. Due to the different historical processes and institutional backgrounds, there are large differences between a state-own bank in China and a major global bank in Hong Kong or Singapore. Down to the local scales of small and medium enterprises (SMEs) that are often family businesses, there are still major differences between jurisdictions. However, it is important to note that there are still distinctive characteristics among Chinese businesses that make them *Chinese*.

The extraordinary growth rate of East Asian economies such as Japan, South Korea, Taiwan, Hong Kong and Singapore are not all Chinese but indeed share a strong common culture through historical reasons. For example, although Japan and South Korea are not Chinese, they have been heavily influenced by ancient Chinese culture for hundreds of years. The result is that despite very different language and institutional settings, all the above East Asian countries still enjoy a dominant Confucian culture, despite the major Christianity in South Korea, Shintoism in Japan and a mix of atheism, Buddhism and Taoism in China. The salient features of Confucianism explained the rise of the economies despite the damage of wars and ideology struggles in the 20th century (Kahn, 1979). Silin (1976) highlighted Confucian traits such as familism, obedience, perseverance, and thrift are the main explanation behind the economic growth in East Asia.

Of all the characteristics or features shared by East Asian countries, the concept of Guanxi (关系) is the most prevalent in organisational decision-making. It is similar to the idea of a customer relationship, but it is a lot more involved and personal. Guanxi refers to having personal trust and a strong relationship with someone and can involve moral obligations and exchanging favours. Below is an example of how Guanxi is more than just a customer relationship, taken from a Singaporean example (Tong & Yong, 2014),

> We Chinese are very flexible. We can change to suit the situation. Even though we may not have agreed on a certain dateline, if you (the supplier) cannot make it, you can ask, Can you postpone? My shipping is not ready. And it's possible. After the contract, you can still ask for amendments, to change this and that...If there is a good relationship, then we can make changes. If you make a request, we can oblige. (p. 42)

The example above shows the above-and-beyond attitude for the customer *if there is a good relationship.* In this case, a customer firm with good Guanxi will enjoy a much stronger power and advantages in business. Guanxi can also be described as a network of contacts, which an individual can call upon when something needs to be done and through which they can exert influence on behalf of another. As a result, these networks can have a direct impact when conducting with Chinese businesses. This can also be a challenge for foreigners going into the Chinese market as there is often a strong Guanxi already established with the existing networks. To better manage this obstacle, it is important to be aware that the reciprocal nature of Guanxi also dictates an informal obligation to 'return the favour'. Once the relationship has been built long and strong enough, new opportunities could be leveraged from a good Guanxi.

There also exist a few related concepts, such as Renqing (人情) and face (Mianzi, 面子). Renqing is considered to be the moral obligation to maintain a relationship. This is not only done in business but also in everyday life in which families visit each other during major holidays or festivals. These meetings are considered to be obligatory rather than causal. As a result, it is part of building Guanxi that Renqing is also considered. Face or the collective concept of social status, propriety and prestige is also very prominent in daily life and business. This concept has been so frequently understood and became part of a standard repertoire in business and everyday speech in English (e.g., saving face).

Institutional Contexts

It is important to note that Guanxi is an informal institution under the previous analysis. When compared to developed economies, China's formal institutions are much more in flux. The biggest institutional change was undoubtedly the market reforms in the 1980s. Since then, regulatory rules, government sentiment towards business and local implantation of central guidance have all changed completely in a few decades. Therefore, it is a predictable phenomenon that Guanxi has remained a major criterion for conducting business in China. Guanxi is an informal institution that secures future businesses and, crucially, the lives of many small enterprises. Frequent changes in the formal institutions, such as reforms, often bring long-term economic benefits and disruption and inefficiency in the short term. It acts as an informal institution that softens the transaction costs (such as information gathering for upcoming changes, compliance with regulations, new business organisations and guidance etc.). As a result, Guanxi has remained an important organic governance structure, particularly in China and, to a lesser extent, in Hong Kong, Taiwan, and Singapore.

The bases of Guanxi

Continuing the previous institutional analysis that Guanxi serves as an autonomous mechanism to lower transaction costs in a changing business environment, we now examine what constitutes Guanxi and the form it occurs. In a comprehensive survey by Tong and Yong (2014, p.41), the author interviewed business executives and owners of Chinese businesses on what constitutes the basis of Guanxi. Locality, Kinship, Workplace, and Friendship are noted that are included by Guanxi.

Locality / Dialect / Associations / Club

In the earlier stages of Chinese capitalism, such as the 1960s in Singapore / Hong Kong, Guanxi was particularly important for new immigrants from China to their new hosts. The new arrivals often depend on members from the same regions in China. The local groups are often established based on the specific areas or dialects they use in China. For example, in Hong Kong, the clans from Shanghai had a strong regionalism and formed their organisations in competition with the local Hongkonger businesses. This distinction is possible due to the mutual unintelligibility among different Chinese dialects. As such, the local population, in general, cannot understand the dialects spoken by different clans from other areas of China. The same can be said of the Chinese immigrants to Singapore in the early 1960s to 1990s. Many Chinese immigrants came from Southeast China, such as Fujian and other parts of China. Similarly, clans and organisations are formed based on their origins. However, the author noted that the interviewees mentioned that this relationship is much weaker now. This can also be said in Hong Kong and Taiwan, where the local official languages such as Cantonese and English (Hong Kong) and Mandarin Chinese (Taiwan) have become the main languages, therefore, standardised communication. As such, this base of Guanxi is waning in influence when compared to an earlier time. This is also expected from an institutional perspective as formal institutions take a stronger hold; informal institutions such as membership-based on origin are likely to have less influence.

Kinship

Kinship is another strong base for Guanxi. Jobs and opportunities are more likely to be given to immediate kin. Another unusual perspective of this base is that people who share the same surname are more likely to gain favours. However, this is getting less important as the possibility of changing surnames and travels made this selection less relevant.

Workplace

The workplace is another major of cultivating Guanxi. Years of working together provided opportunities to establish or strengthen Guanxi people often get to know one another intimately. This source is common in other countries, such as the alumni or ex-employee network.

Friendship

The last base for Guanxi is based on friendship. Friendship is often a base to further existing relationships. This often does not equate to Guanxi, as Guanxi is often the criteria by which friendship can be established on.

Disadvantages

It is now clear that Guanxi's nature is formed from a close-knitted group. However, a significant disadvantage can also form the basis of patron-client relations. As a result, it creates challenges for businesses whose members are obligated to repay favours to members of other businesses when they cannot sufficiently do so. A guanxi network may also violate bureaucratic norms, leading to corporate corruption.

The boundary between business and social lives can sometimes be ambiguous as people tend to rely heavily on their closer relations and friends. This can result in nepotism and cronyism in the workforce being created through Guanxi, as it is common for authoritative figures to draw from family and close ties to fill employment opportunities instead of assessing talent and suitability. Regulators understand the inherent disadvantage of the Guanxi network as such policies were created to combat unfair discrimination against members outside of the network.

Managerial Implications - Finding the Middle Way

Guanxi undoubtedly remains the main obstacle for new businesses looking to get into the Chinese market. This is, however, achievable, given the appropriate strategy. Doing business in China and building Guanxi is like a catch-22 problem–to build Guanxi, an existing Guanxi network is needed. This poses obstacles for many foreign businesses wanting to do business in China. For example, Hong Kong is a much easier base to begin a business and often acts as a gateway to China. For example, the Hong Kong administration operates based on the common law system, which is like that in the UK. It also requires much less Guanxi to establish new businesses and conduct transactions. The same can be said for Singapore, as well as it operates in a similar model attracting foreign investors. As such, the business environments of Hong Kong and Singapore constitute a blend of East and West, which makes them the prime candidates for breaking into the China market. However, the strategy to build Guanxi remains a long-term approach that can be done in several ways.

General Knowledge of China

Guanxi has been seen above as a form that emphasises the closeness of relationships between business partners. The first step is to have general knowledge of China and its culture. Often the Chinese language is needed to reduce the foreignness of the business wanting to get into this market. A general understanding of history and cultural attributes also helps businesses. This can assist in establishing an immediate connection to a new Chinese contact.

Formal Introduction

Often Chinese businesses prefer to do business with existing networks. As such, it is important to be introduced to the key networks. For example, Hong Kong is a much friendlier location to conduct business as the working language is English and has less emphasis on the network. That can be leveraged into future networks and business in mainland China. It can also help if the business is part of a trade organisation that facilitates a network for international trade flows, such as the China-Britain Business Council or associations for other geographies. In general, the higher the social status your connection has, the more successful you are likely to be at being introduced to the right people and key decision-makers.

The Effort, Gift-Giving Culture and Entertainment

The biggest difference between Western and Chinese ways of gaining new business is perhaps the need to wine and dine. It has become almost essential for new businesses to give the gift to secure any meaningful relations. This is often done by gifting personal gifts and hosting entertainment parties and dinners. It is not surprising that this is often not allowed in many companies under Western governance, such as the "no gift" policy. However, this is seen as part of doing business and can raise ethical issues depending on the relationship between the patron and client. The gift-giving etiquette can be complicated depending on the specific geography and the prevailing regulatory environment. For example, the Chinese official policy in 2021 is that giving gifts is illegal as it can be considered a form of bribery. However, this continues to be done in a lower-level business where hosting dinners or personal gifts is still acceptable.

Conclusion - The Rise of China and its Implications

Throughout this chapter, we have argued that Guanxi and other characteristics are autonomous products that were produced as a form of informal institutions.

This informal institution is a blend of traditional values and the prevailing formal institutions, such as laws and regulations at the time. Therefore, a strong implication here is that institutions will change. The study tried to sketch the rapid changes in the Chinese economy from the 1970s to the present. The accompanying intuitions have shifted from a Communist / Marxist ideology to a market-based one. The question then remains, what does the rise of the Chinese economy mean for the rest of the World? Two points stand out 1) the Guanxi network is likely to reduce gradually as globalisation and online businesses dominate, and 2) the re-recognition of Chinese identity among a trend of the surging identity of being East Asian.

The traditional Guanxi network, sorted by origins, dialects and regions, is likely to diminish. This is inevitable as globalisation has reduced the differences between cultures. More so for existing Chinese organisations created based on their local identity. New modern transport infrastructure in China means it is common to travel to remote provinces whenever required. The distance has since reduced greatly between different local regions. The use of Guanxi has not disappeared but rather taken in a different form. It has less emphasis on the origins and more on the commonalities. For example, research from Dahles (2004) has found that ethnic Chinese people often gain an advantage when conducting business in China, whether they are from Hong Kong or Singapore (which are foreign to mainland Chinese businesses due to different legal jurisdictions and culture). Ethnic ties continue to dominate but not necessarily based on the local regions they come from but rather the fact that they are also *Chinese* – this is a change that has shifted from regionalism to a broader concept of ethnicity for foreigners who would like to conduct business in China. There is also a shift toward individual relations beyond the family and the ethnic group favour professional and institutional linkages. This is reinforced by the fact that many younger Chinese citizens have studied abroad with that. They have brought overseas relationships into China, thus reducing the dependency on regional and ethnic identities.

A second trend is also emerging, and this is to do with self-identification outside of China. The rise (or re-rise) has led many ethnic Chinese in Southeast Asia to re-identify themselves as Chinese. There have been significant permeant and ethnically Chinese populations in Southeast Asia since the 19th century. Due to local politics and the prevailing nationalist policies at times (such as in Indonesia in the early 2000s, Vietnam throughout much of the late 20t century etc.), ethnic Chinese in those countries are re-understanding their history. Many see China as a rapidly emerging market and flaunt their ethnic background (Tong, 2014, p.142). Due to the increasing importance of the Chinese markets, schools are also encouraged to teach Mandarin Chinese in nearby countries such as Thailand, Malaysia, Korea,

Indonesia etc. If economic growth continues, this trend is likely to continue. Like all entrepreneurs, Chinese businesses also prioritise profitability first, but ethnic and cultural affinities can often facilitate good relationships. This chapter has shown the economic basis of analysing the constituent of such a relationship.

While the foremost consideration of many Chinese businessmen in deciding on investments is profitability and economic opportunities, cultural affinities can facilitate effective personal and business relationships with the China Chinese. Being Chinese has become a form of ethnic networking, exploiting ties with co-ethnics with the China Chinese to do business.

References

Acs, Z.J., Estrin, S., Mickiewicz, T. & Szerb, L. (2018). Entrepreneurship, institutional economics, and economic growth: an ecosystem perspective. *Small Business Economics, 51,* 501–514. https://doi.org/10.1007/s11187-018-0013-9

Bardhan, P. (1989). The new institutional economics and development theory: A brief critical assessment. *World development,* 1389-1395.

Barzel, Y. (1997). *Economic Analysis of Property Rights.* Cambridge: Cambridge University Press. https://doi.org/10.1017/CBO9780511609398

Coase, R., & Wang, N. (2012). *How China become Capitalist.* Palgrave Macmillan.

Dahles, H. (2004). Venturing across Borders: Investment Strategies of Singapore—Chinese Entrepreneurs in Mainland China. *Asian Journal of Social Science, 32*(1), 19-41.

Djankov, S. (2016). The Doing Business Project. *Journal of Economic Perspectives,* 247–248.

Ellickson, R. C. (1991). *Order without Law: How Neighbors Settle Disputes.* Harvard University Press. https://doi.org/10.2307/j.ctvk12rdz

Feeny, D., Berkes, F., McCay, B.J. Acheson, J. M. (1990). The Tragedy of the Commons: Twenty-two years later. *Human Ecology,* 18, 1–19. https://doi.org/10.1007/BF00889070

Gray, H. (2016). Access orders and the 'new'new institutional economics of development. *Development and Change,* 51-75.

Hardin, G. (1968). The tragedy of the common. *Science,* 1243-1248.

Hodgson, A. (2017). Reperceiving the Future. *World Futures Review, 9*(4), 208-224. https://doi.org/10.1177/1946756717729511

Holcombe, C. (2017). *A History of East Asia.* Cambridge University Press.

Kahn, R.L. (1979). Aging and Social Support. In: Riley, M.W. (Ed.), *Aging from Birth to Death: Interdisciplinary Perspectives* (pp.77-91), Westview Press.

Ménard, C., & Shirley, M. (2005). *Handbook of new institutional economics.* Dordrecht: Springer.

Nabli, M. K., & Nugent, J. B. (1989). The new institutional economics and its applicability to development. *World Development,* 1333-1347.

Niehans, J. (2018). Transaction Costs. In *The new Palgrave dictionary of economics* (pp. 13782-13787). Palgrave Macmillan. https://doi.org/10.1057/978-1-349-95189-5_1682

North, D. C. (1990). *Institutions, institutional change and economic performance.* Cambridge University Press. https://doi.org/10.1017/CBO9780511808678

North, D. C. (1993). The new institutional economics and development. *Economic History*, 1-8.

Prasetyo, P. E., & Kistanti, N. R. (2020). Human Capital, Institutional Economics and Entrepreneurship as a Driver for Quality & Sustainable Economic Growth. *Entrepreneurship and Sustainability Issues*, 7, 2575-2589. https://doi.org/10.9770/jesi.2020.7.4(1)

Roland, G. (2016). *Development economics.* Routledge.

Silin, R. (1976). *Leadership and values.* Harvard University Press.

Tamanaha, B. (2015). The knowledge and policy limits of new institutional economics on development. *Journal of Economic Issues*, *49*(1), 89-109. https://doi.org/10.1080/00213624.2015.1013881

Tong, C.K. &Yong, P.K. (2014). *Guanxi* Bases, *Xinyong* and Chinese Business Networks. In Tong, CK. (Ed.), *Chinese Business*. Springer. https://doi.org/10.1007/978-981-4451-85-7_3

Tong, C.K. (2014). The Rise of China and Its Implications. In: Tong, CK. (Ed.), *Chinese Business*. Springer. https://doi.org/10.1007/978-981-4451-85-7_8

Yong, C. T. (2014). Guanxi Bases, Xinyong and Chinese Business Networks. In C. Tong, *Chinese Business - Rethinking Guanxi and Trust in Chinese Business Networks*. Singapore: Springer.

Zhou, Q. (2020). *Property Rights and Changes in China.* Springer. https://doi.org/10.1007/978-981-15-9885-2

Chapter 3

Managing Cultural Differences: An Ethnographic Case Study of Cameroon

Yvonne Kamegne
Towson University, USA

Joyram Chakraborty
Towson University, USA

Abstract: Cultural factors are an extremely sensitive topic that poses many opportunities and pitfalls. Cross-cultural studies help individuals to understand better and manage cultural differences. Conducting a flourishing business across cultural boundaries requires a deep understanding of a foreign culture. From a high-tech perspective, one's cultural background is tied to the user experience of products or systems being used, implying that people from different cultures understand and use technologies differently. It is essential to comprehend how cultural elements impact the product's design, user experience (UX), and user interaction with the product, and how to properly incorporate these elements in the product design. This chapter provides a better understanding of the relationship between culture, business, and technology and a perspective on cross-cultural approaches in user interface design. It can assist organizations, academia, researchers, and students in better understanding, managing, designing, and interacting with people from different cultural backgrounds. Cameroon will be investigated as a case study.

Keywords: Culture, Technology, Cross-cultural design, Ethnography, Cameroon, Cultural Models

***

Introduction

The mammoth innovation of technology provides different benefits to users as they interact with these technologies. As the world moves toward a more diverse society, it is essential to understand how cultural values affect the user interaction with different products. Technologies, websites, and mobile platforms allow the worldwide distribution of products and services. A suitable designed user interface (UI) enhances the performance and appeal of these platforms, as well as the success of the commercialization of products and services.

Product designers are often wedged in a bubble and make assumptions about another culture's behaviors or habits. These assumptions, which can often be wrong, impact the product's success and financial revenues. A simple example is Apple, one of the biggest tech companies worldwide, with a US market share of 61% (LawyersTech, 2021). Nevertheless, Apple's iPhone market share is only 2.7% in India, and 4.66% in Central African countries, such as Cameroon. One of the reasons for low market shares in these countries is related to the fact that Apple overlooks cultural differences when designing for these foreign markets. Instead of designing for localization (adapting the product to meet each locale's language, culture, and other requirements). Apple designs for internationalization (design of a product so that it can be adapted to various cultures without modifications). In India, services such as Siri, Apple Pay and Apple Map are inaccurate and must be explicitly designed for Indian users.

Another example is eBay's downfall in Japan due to a failure to understand cultural differences between Japanese and American users. For instance, Japanese users were required to submit credit card information during signup, causing a high percentage of abandonment of eBay's website. Additionally, eBay's UI was a translation of eBay's US version without consideration of cultural differences.

Cultural differences highly impact the UX, UI, e-commerce, trust, advertising, technology adoption and communication of a product. The product will not meet needs and expectations if it does not fit a user's cultural background. The research of a product's design is often conducted on observations. However, the results of design requirements in one culture do not automatically apply to other cultures because the traditions, behaviors, values, and beliefs of users in one culture are different from those in other cultures. This chapter investigates cultural differences to provide designers with valuable references for designing successful customized products and overcoming cross-cultural issues. Furthermore, the chapter reports traditional ethnographic research with Cameron as a case study, as the results can be precious for businesses or investors interested in this market.

Literature Review

Culture

Culture can be very confusing; it can have different meanings, and people can understand it in numerous ways. Culture shapes people and gives them a sense of who they are. It bonds individuals, gives them a distinctive identity, and serves as the foundational value of one's life. Culture can be described as specific features and knowledge of a particular group of people, encompassing values, symbols, languages, religions, beliefs, cuisine, social habits, music, and arts (Lebron & Mendez, 2013). One of the most famous definitions of culture comes from (Hofstede, 2011), who defines culture as the collective programming of the mind that distinguishes the members of one group of people from others.

Achieving a successful cross-cultural design can be a challenging task. Designers may design products that best fit their needs but cannot guarantee performance leverage unless the user utilizes them effectively. Cultural elements are beyond the usability of a product or system. They include the functions and features and the user's expectations, motivations, and feelings. These traits influence the UX when interacting with the product. Culture plays a significant role in technology design and usage, and the review of cultural dimensions raises many issues about UI design. Designers intend to develop interfaces that trigger a pleasant emotional reaction in order to generate an enjoyable memory. However, emotions are subjective and diverse because of cultural differences.

Barber and Badre (1998) described cultural markers as the elements that are most dominant and preferred within a specific cultural group, and they are specific to a given culture. They can be colors, symbols, languages, norms, values, religious beliefs, and artifacts. They directly impact a user's perception and satisfaction. Colors have different meanings in distinct cultures. In Cameroon, for example, red represents blood, whereas in Canada, red represents hope and prosperity. Thus, a company using a website to promote services for Cameroonian users may want to avoid the use of red, which could be associated with criminality. On the other hand, Canadian companies may want to use red to attract Canadian customers, as red has a positive implication in Canada.

The Impact of Culture on Technology

Technology is essential in daily life activities; it can be incorporated into all aspects of people's mundane life, including entertainment, travel, and education. Successful product adoption depends on its design and the user's preference. Cultural factors determine user preferences for products, and a product consistent with a user's cultural preference would be more appealing

(Reinecke & Bernstein, 2013). Most technologies are developed within the western culture and are culturally biased. Therefore, such technologies are not entirely usable for non-western cultures (Chakraborty, 2013). Cultural elements have different signification in different cultures; what may seem usable for one culture may not be perceived as usable by another. Cultural preferences vary among users, and usability features should also be reflected in a cultural context. Cultural biases and user preferences are part of a user's characteristics, so designers should further consider cultural markers.

Numerous studies have investigated the impact of cultural elements on technology acceptance, user experience, and usability. One such study provided evidence that products are more efficient and users perform better if the product is designed to match their cultural profile (Santoso & Schrepp, 2019). Furthermore, the authors highlighted that the user's subjective cultural profile had an impact on the adoption of particular technologies for some typical tasks.

Hall and Hall (1990), whose work is discussed later in this chapter, described culture as an Iceberg. Like an iceberg, culture is comprised of visible cultural elements above the water and invisible cultural elements submerged by the water. Hence, culture has some observable aspects (e.g., language, food, dressing style, dance, etc.) and other aspects that can only be assumed (e.g., relationship, dating, authority, religion, etc.). Designing technologies for external cultures requires a deep understanding of cultural elements in order to be able to identify accurate user requirements, and cultural dimensions should be deemed throughout the design of technologies.

Theoretical Framework

As designers are shifting away from a "one size fits all" UI design, cross-cultural studies and design issues will need more consideration, and designers must implement guidelines to assist them in the design process. Better knowledge and understanding of cultural dimensions related to UI elements can assist designers. Understanding one's culture is very complex; designers cannot just rely on the internet (e.g., Google or Wikipedia) and expect to get accurate information about a foreign culture. Theoretical foundations of cultural models can help designers and researchers better understand cultural differences. The three cultural frameworks discussed in this chapter are the Onion Model of Culture, the Iceberg Model, and the Hofstede Model of National Culture.

The Onion Model of Culture

The onion model of culture is a cultural model developed by Fons Trompenaars (Merk, 2003). It encompasses three layers: the outer layer, the middle layer, and the inner layer. The outer layer consists of symbols and artifacts of a culture, such as clothes, music, or food. The middle layer defines norms and values and shapes the way people in a particular culture behave. Privacy and material success are considered values one finds important in life. The third layer is the inner layer; it is implicit and describes how people adapt to their environments. It encompasses fundamental principles such as traditions, religions, and personal values and defines the basic assumptions of a society. Trompenaars uses seven dimensions to explain this cultural model:

1. Universalism vs Particularism: Do people place values on rules or laws?

2. Individualism vs Communitarianism: Do people believe in personal achievement, or is the group greater than the individual?

3. Affective vs Neutral: Do people display their emotions or hide them?

4. Specific vs Diffuse: Do people separate work from personal life?

5. Achievement vs Ascription: Do people have to prove themselves to receive status, or is it given to them? Are people valued for what they do or for who they are?

6. Time perception/Sequential vs Synchronic cultures: Do people do things one at a time or numerous things at once?

7. Internal vs outer direction: Do people aim to control their environment or collaborate with it?

The Iceberg Model

The Iceberg model was established in 1976 by Edward T. Hall, who suggested that culture was similar to an iceberg. He highlighted that culture has two components: only about 10% of culture is easily visible to others, while the rest of the 90% of internal culture is hidden below the surface (Hanley, 1999). The internal culture is learned while growing up, unconscious, and challenging to change. The external culture is the visible part; it is the way people live and interact with each other. These visible elements are explicitly learned, conscious, and modifiable. Hall outlines three cultural dimensions:

1. Perception of space: The physical distance that is perceived as comfortable. It is the physical space between people as they interact with each other.

2. Context of communication (High and low context): How a message is conveyed, whether the communication is implicit or explicit. High-context cultures, such as those found in Latin America, Asia, and Africa, tend to be more indirect and expect the person they are communicating with to decode the implicit part of their message. Body language is particularly important, sometimes even more important than actual

words spoken (Hall & Hall, 1990). Low-context cultures such as the United States tend to be explicit and direct in their communications.

3. Perception of time (Polychronic vs Monochronic Cultures): In polychronic cultures, people tend to multitask. Human interaction is valued over time and material things, leading to reduced concern for getting things done on time. Monochronic cultures tend to do one task at a time and prioritize planning and time management.

The Hofstede Model of National Culture

The Hofstede model is a cross-cultural communication and comparison showing the impact of culture on the values of its members (Hofstede, 2011). It described six dimensions of national culture as follows:

1. Power distance (PDI): The extent to which the less powerful members of an organization recognize and expect that power is distributed unequally. PDI suggests that a society's level of inequality is endorsed by the followers as much as by the leaders. Low power distance cultures such as the US value equality and do not expect orders from subordinates before taking positive actions and encourage innovation. High power distance cultures, such as France and India, accept inequality in power and wealth.

2. Individualism vs collectivism: Individualism in cultures implies loose bonds where everyone is expected to look after themselves or their immediate family. They place individual social-economic interests over the group. Individualist cultures such as the US and Canada tend to be more innovative and therefore more willing to adapt to new products or UI features. Collectivist cultures such as Japan place a higher value on group goals (Rinne et al., 2012). Most African and Asian countries, such as Nigeria, Nepal, Cameroon, and Brazil, are categorized as collectivist.

3. Masculinity vs femininity: In a cultural context, masculinity and femininity refer to gender roles, not physical characteristics. This dimension outlines the traditional assignment to masculine roles of assertiveness, competition, and toughness and feminine roles of orientation to home and children, and tenderness. Women in feminine countries have the same modest, caring values as men, and men and women are expected to be modest. In masculine countries, women are somewhat assertive and competitive. Masculine cultures such as Mexico, Italy, and Japan place a high value on achievement, tasks, money, performance, and purposefulness, while more feminine cultures such as the Netherlands and Sweden focus on relationships, helping others, and

preserving the environment. For instance, this dimension can have implications for a cross-cultural design, as masculine cultures may prefer a UI design that enables them to quickly control and navigate through the interface. Such UI will provide graphics, sound, and animation used for utilitarian purposes. Feminine culture, on the contrary, tends to prefer more emotional, aesthetic UI and unifying values to gain attention and appeal (Marcus, 2013).

4. Uncertainty avoidance (UA): Refers to a society's tolerance for uncertainty and ambiguity. It indicates the extent to which culture makes its members uncomfortable or comfortable in unstructured situations and how they deal with unpredictable futures. Countries such as the US, and Canada, scoring low on UA, tend to be tolerant of uncertainty and feel relatively secure. Whereas countries high on this factor, such as France, Germany, or Belgium, constantly avoid uncertainty and work to create a sense of control.

5. Long-term vs short-term orientation (LTO vs STO): LTO refers to values such as perseverance, prudence, and having a sense of shame. On the other side, STO aims to reciprocate social obligations, respect for tradition, personal steadiness, and stability. LTO cultures include China and Nigeria.

6. Indulgence vs Restraint: Indulgence stands for a society that allows free gratification of basic and natural human desires related to enjoying life and having fun. Restraint stands for a society that controls the gratification of needs and regulates it through strict social norms. Thus, an indulgent culture sees freedom of speech as an essential concern.

Based on Hofstede's cultural studies, UA has been deemed as the most influential cultural dimension in determining technology adoption. UA is the extent to which members of an organization within a society feel threatened by uncertain situations (Hofstede, 2011). People from cultures with a low UA index are more tolerant of risk and are more willing to try new things. Thus, Members of a low UA society do not hesitate to accept new technology or try a new UI design.

The Hofstede model of culture is the most quoted in cross-cultural research; it provides insights into cross-culture fundamentals and is helpful in being more effective when interacting with people from different cultural backgrounds. To illustrate Hofstede's cultural model, comparisons of cultural dimensions between India and Germany and between Cameroon and the US retrieved from Hofstede (2022) are shown below:

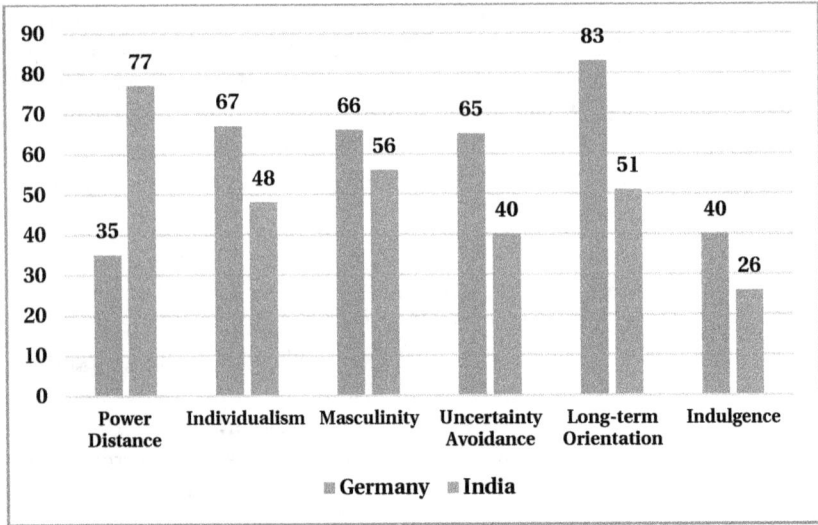

Figure 3.1: Comparison of Germany and India's Cultural Dimensions

Power Distance: Germany is among the lower power distant countries with an index score of 35, which implies that it is a highly decentralized society. Leadership is challenged to show expertise and is best accepted when it is based on knowledge. India's score implies that they accept inequalities among people and embrace hierarchy in society.

Individualism: As a highly individualist culture, Germans believe in self-actualization. They encourage the ability to solve problems or accomplish goals independently without relying on assistance. India is a society with both collectivistic and individualistic characteristics. The collectivist side means that individuals are expected to act for the better good of their defined in-group. The religious belief that every individual is responsible for his/her life and the outcome is the Individualist side can be observed in Hinduism (Rana, 2018).

Masculinity: Germany is a masculine society in which performance is highly regarded and demanded at an early age. Germans have much self-esteem and a high degree of assertiveness and determination. Similarly, India is a masculine culture, with a large gap between the value of men and women. They are driven by competition, success, and achievement.

Uncertainty Avoidance: Germans prefer avoiding uncertainty and structure and proper organization. Businesses, rules, regulations, and contracts are essential. On the other hand, Indians tend to be more open to unstructured ideas and situations. Thus, the tolerance for the unexpected is high; things do not have to go as planned.

Long-term orientation: Germany is a very pragmatic culture. Individuals believe that truth depends on the situation, context, and time. They adapt easily to changing conditions and have a strong tendency to save and invest. India's score indicates that they are more prudent.

Indulgence: A score of 40 implies that German culture is restrained in nature. Individuals in German society perceive that social norms restrain their actions and therefore feel wrong about indulging themselves. India's low scores indicate that Indians are pessimistic and do not enjoy leisure time.

Since Cameroon was a country not included in Hofstede's data set, it was not possible to have a precise graph to display the comparisons of Cameroon and the US cultural dimensions. Nevertheless, the comparison of Hofstede's cultural dimensions is discussed below.

Power Distance: Cameroon scores 54 on the PDI, implying that Cameroonians endorse a level of inequality in their society. The different distribution of power justifies that power holders have more benefits and are wealthier than the less powerful in society (Djamen et al., 2020). On the other side, the US scores low on the PDI, meaning that they are less dependent on hierarchy and promote equality.

Individualism: Cameroon, like many African countries, is a collectivist culture. Individuals encourage solidarity, responsibilities are shared, and accountability is collective. In contrast, the US is an individualist society with a high score of 91. The expectations are that individuals should only look after themselves and their immediate relatives and not rely too much on authorities for support.

Masculinity: Cameroon's culture is a masculine one with a focus on equity. Society is driven by competition and performance. The US is also a masculine society characterized by values such as money, success, power, and individual achievement.

Uncertainty Avoidance: Cameroonians score high on the UA index. Thus, implying that they prefer to avoid ambiguous situations. They are not comfortable with uncertain situations and prefer rules and laws to conduct safer business. Social and economic life in Cameroon is unstable, which can be seen from the unreliability of transportation and the higher education system not being a guarantee of employment. In the US culture, individuals embrace innovation and change.

Long-term Orientation: Cameroon is a pragmatic society; individuals can adapt to different situations and tend to save and invest. The US's score means they are considered a short-term-oriented culture with a strong tendency to save and invest. Americans are practical. Performance in organizations is measured on a short-term basis, encouraging individuals to strive for quick and effective results in the workplace.

Indulgence: Cameroon is a restrained society and somewhat reserved. Individuals control how they satisfy their needs and believe that social norms limit their actions. In contrast, the US society is reflected by the slogan "Work Hard, Play Hard". They promote gratification and fun.

UI Design

UI design applies to different devices such as computers, mobile phones, tablets, and all electronic devices. It focuses on the look, the style, the content, and other design elements to make the interface interactive and usable. Over the past years, designers and researchers have identified and defined a set of UI components, the essential entities of UI. A user interface that encompasses these components is efficient and usable. A list of UI components is outlined below (Marcus, 2005):

- *Metaphors.* They are the fundamental concepts conveyed via words, images, sounds, and tactile experiences. Metaphors help users understand, remember, and enjoy the entities and relationships of computer-based communication systems.

- *Mental Models.* They are a user's thought process about the system and how it works. They are also called user or cognitive models.

- *Navigation.* The movement through the mental models, that is, through the UI.

- *Interaction.* Interaction elements handle interaction, such as a mouse or interaction using a keyboard.

- *Appearance.* It encompasses all the essential attributes, that is, visual, auditory, and tactile attributes.

In addition, Shneiderman (1998) developed a set of golden rules as a guide for designing usable UIs. They include striving for consistency, enabling frequent users to use shortcuts, offering informative feedback, designing dialogues to yield closure, offering error prevention and simple error handling, permitting easy reversal of actions, supporting internal locus of control, and reducing short-term memory load. These golden rules are the foundation of designing usable UIs. Nevertheless, they omit to consider cultural differences and mainly focus on universal design.

UI Design and Culture

As people embrace diversity, culture plays a critical role in UI design, and a broader range of users will accept the design that implements culturally relevant features. The initial step toward cultural adaptability is to find out how to adapt the UI to the cultural needs of the user. A user may adapt to an interface that fails to respect his/her cultural background, while another user may choose to reject the interface.

The perceived usability of a website increases when it is initially designed in a user's native language. English-speaking countries represent about 8% of the world's population, and nearly 75% of internet users are non-English speakers. However, this cultural factor is still overlooked. The translation should happen not just in terms of language but also in terms of cultural content. The design of the UI must fit certain cultural aspects, which in turn influence the user's acceptance or rejection of a product (Czaja et al., 2019). Some cultural elements to consider when doing cross-cultural design are outlined below (Fernandes, 1994):

- *Nationalism:* The fundamental components of a culture, such as icons, colors, or symbols. Each of these components can have a different meaning in different cultures. Designers must use them appropriately.

- *Language:* Some countries use various dialects. Thus, it is important to do research on the local language and incorporate the nuances of the language to build engagement and understanding.

- *Time:* Date and time formats vary from culture. It should be reflected in the UI.

- *Currency:* Currencies and exchange rates vary highly around the world.

- *Symbols:* They have different significance in different cultures. Designers must suitably use them.

- *Units of Measure:* Countries have distinct metric systems. Cameroon and most French-speaking countries use KG (kilogram), while the US uses pounds. Designing a website for cooking recipes can have a different outcome in another culture because of the different metrics.

- *Beliefs:* Unpleasant or offensive images and objects or symbols considered taboo in one culture can be considered normal in another.

- *Esthetic:* Cultures have their look and feel. These could be the symbolic use of colors. Without taking them into account, a UI's visual design can seem irrelevant to a user or convey unsought messages.

- **Names:** In Cameroon, individuals go by their last name, followed by their first name. In the US, it is quite the opposite. Such details can confuse a user during the registration step, thus affecting the UX.

Oh and Moon (2013) define Culture Centered Design (CCD) as a design process focusing on the user and his cultural conditions. They highlighted that the goal of the CCD process is to ensure that design choices are focused on cultural relevance, functionality, and usability. The awareness of one's culture-dependency is a good starting point for a successful cross-cultural design. Three important perspectives to consider in CCD include the hierarchical structure of culture, the aspects of diversity, and its relevance to UI design (Gould et al., 2003). When discussing cultural diversity, it should be clear at which level and aspects of the culture are being discussed, as well as the issues pertinent to UI design.

It is quite apparent that users have different requirements and preferences correlated to their cultural background. For example, US's low PDI means that Americans do not accept the unequal distribution of power but endorse equality. Thus, in e-commerce design, users will most likely prefer a UI that is easily navigable and rich in information about the product and quality because users of such cultures do not like to be controlled. They would instead make their own buying decisions based on information provided on the websites. On the contrary, a culture that scores high on PDI, such as India or Cameroon, accepts the unequal distribution of power. They tend to prefer a UI design that focuses on the visuals of products. Because they agree to the unequal distribution of power, they trust and want the seller to choose a product. Only a few important navigations can be displayed, and the UI design should be made easy for the user to select quickly from the options presented.

Methodology

Understanding individuals from different cultures are crucial to anyone desiring to conduct business across cultural boundaries. Different types of empirical research (e.g., experimental research, field study, interview, focus group, survey, diary study, ethnography, contextual inquiry) can be applied to better understand humans and how they engage with technology. For this chapter, an ethnographic study has been performed.

Ethnography is a qualitative research method in which the **researcher observes and interacts with participants in their natural habitats or** their cultural context (Gobo, 2008). The researcher usually becomes part of the society, builds trust with its members, and wants to deeply understand the culture that is being observed. While design ethnography can be referred to as ethnography used to understand user requirements, traditional ethnography focuses on the broader purpose of understanding culture and context in a holistic way. Design ethnography can often be substituted with terms like user-centred design, human-centred design, participatory design, end-user customization, and qualitative methods, and focuses on building empathy to understand users and their contexts (Wood & Mattson, 2019).

The same ethnographic research does not apply to different cultures. One cannot conduct the same study for Cameroonians, Tanzanians, Indians, or Congolese, because these countries have different cultures and lifestyles. Ethnography looks at languages, symbols, economy, rules, norms, systems, traditions, shared meanings and much more within a specific culture, and each of these elements varies from one culture to another. Ethnography is not limited to the social life or economy of a culture; it encompasses the study of other factors such as religion, gender roles, education, authority, law, behavior, currency, relationship, interaction with technology, etc., to get a thorough picture of a specific culture. Moreover, the outcomes of ethnographic research for distinct cultures are ultimately different.

Case Study: The Cameroonian Culture

Sub-Saharan Africa is a large region in size, population, and cultural heterogeneity. Populations in these member countries have different cultures, attitudes, behaviors, and communication. With a population of 26 million habitants, Cameroon is a developing country with a GNP (PPP) of 96.53 billion dollars and a GDP per capita of $1,470 (The World Bank, 2022). French and English are the two official languages of Cameroon, though French is widely used for most activities. An ethnographer fluent in either French or English will be able to gather data on the daily activities and interact with the residents more effectively. An interpreter could be helpful, as language is imperative in constructing realities. Nearly 71% of Cameroonians are of the Christian faith, 25% are of the Islamic faith, and the remaining population is of other non-major faith backgrounds.

Social Life

Though Cameroon is more of a restrained culture, inhabitants in big cities such as Douala and Yaoundé tend to plan time for fun and entertainment. This can be reflected by shopping malls, such as Douala Grand Mall, movie theatres, fancy restaurants, and nightclubs in the city. Inhabitants in urban areas are modernized; they relate themselves to the western lifestyle and often stay busy with fun activities (travel, vacation, sport, concert spa, etc.) during leisure time. Wealthy people in the country can easily afford such lifestyles. People usually migrate to urban areas to seek a modernized lifestyle. Residents of small cities, such as Bafoussam, Maroua, Bafia, or Buea, have a slower way of life. As a collectivist culture, the country is oriented toward extended families. Individuals like to socialize while following a sense of distance. Personal space tends to be less between members of the same gender, friends, and family.

The Economy and Business

Cameroon is a growing market with a lot of opportunities to invest in and conduct business. Cameroonians are perceived as being polite, respectful, and hard-working. One should expect a slower way of life and a lack of punctuality in keeping appointments. Cameroonians favor an indirect style of communication and tend not to directly say what they think in order to avoid being offensive. The workdays are Monday through Saturday, and business hours can range from 8 am to 5 pm during weekdays and from 8 am to 12 pm on Saturdays.

A successful career is very important to Cameroonians. International business and trade are highly valued and respected. Cameroonians' millennials and generation z are investors, open-minded innovators, and enthusiastic users of innovative technologies. Penetration of technology is less available in rural areas. Nevertheless, technology is imported without consideration of cultural differences between the country of export and the country of import, and wealthy Cameroonians utilize technology designed in western cultures. Furthermore, the country is a suitable place for investment due to its abundance of natural resources. For those looking forwards to doing business in Cameroon, it is possible to get a visa at the Cameroonian Airport in Douala or Yaoundé upon arrival. However, to be on the safe side, it is better to get a visa in advance at the Cameroon Embassy of the Country of origin. Investing in Cameroon is beneficial since investors can transfer more than 75% of their profits to their home country. Companies can be in the form of a sole proprietorship, partnership, public limited companies, private limited companies, and limited liability companies.

Conducting Business in Cameroon

Cameroonians usually initiate business relationships by establishing personal rapport, mutual respect, and trust. When meeting in person, greetings usually happen by shaking hands, and it is important to use a person's honorific title and surname when conversing. Government authorities may be addressed as "Excellence" without using their surname. Business communication is quite formal and follows the rules of protocol. Punctuality is not very common, but patience and perseverance are necessary to do business in Cameroon. The Cameroonian currency is the Franc CFA, which is pegged to the Euro (one Euro is worth 654 CFA). Currency fluctuation and exchange rate should both be considered, as they impact businesses, imports, exports, and transactions. The country is still a cash-heavy economy. Most business transactions involve more cash. However, e-payment systems are growing, and more businesses are using electronic credit and debit cards. Emerging online payment systems and electronic payment platforms allow Cameroonians to buy and sell online using local payment methods. Furthermore, International financial businesses such as Visa, MasterCard, American Express, and Discover process payments between merchants, and card-issuing banks enable Cameroonian users locally and around the world to effectuate e-transactions. Nevertheless, e-commerce remains slow because shipping methods and address infrastructures are not quite reliable. Poor infrastructures, rapidly changing taxes, and regulatory regimes that lack transparency can be challenging to businesses attempting to enter the Cameroonian market.

Political Issues

The political state of the country is sometimes unstable, with the ongoing anglophone crisis that began in 2016. The crisis is taking place in the Southern region (Anglophone region), where hundreds of civilians have been killed as protesters seeking independence for the country's minority, the Anglophone regions. The government military aggressively responded to the crisis, often targeting civilians, destroying homes, and killing hundreds of people across the southern region. Furthermore, the Islamist armed group Boko Haram and their Nigerian troops have been waging war in some regions of the country, intending to enforce an Islamic state. The African Union, the United Nations, and the European Union have been involved in resolving this issue.

Major Challenges in Ethnographic Study

Being an ethnographer is not easy, as it involves several challenges that the researcher would have to overcome. The main challenges in ethnographic studies are outlined below.

- The Hawthorne effect is described as a phenomenon in which participants behave differently because they know they are being observed (Payne & Payne, 2004). Human nature is complex. Participants may be deceiving the ethnographer because they are unsure of his intentions, or they might want to provide a positive view of themselves, their culture, and their society. For instance, if someone is aware that guests will be visiting their home soon, they might be more inclined to clean it before, which wouldn't necessarily be an accurate representation of their daily experience. In general, Cameroonians tend to be more influenced by outsiders. They will likely alter their behaviors to provide a better image of themselves.

- *Poor infrastructures*. Cameroon is a developing country with poor infrastructure, such as poor electricity and internet access, along with slow connection rates with a low bandwidth of 340 gigabytes. Electricity and water can be scarce in some regions; however, access varies widely between urban and rural areas. These could hinder and slow down the research process.

- *Punctuality*. A lack of punctuality became a habit for Cameroonians. For instance, an individual will schedule an appointment for 2 pm but will not show up until 4 pm. This does not just apply to social occasions. Even in the corporate world, business practitioners do not respect punctuality. Foreigners may find this lack of punctuality rude and unorganized. This habit has quite been normalized in the Cameroonian culture.

- *Religious and gender issues*. These could pose challenges where a male ethnographer could be denied access to an all-female Madrasa (Islam-centered school). Moreover, the ethnographer's background, gender, ethnicity, culture, and age could distinctly facilitate or obfuscate the ethnographer's possibilities of conducting successful research.

- *Cultural shock*. A foreigner travelling to Cameroon is moving to a different culture and must learn the new language, adapt to a different lifestyle and culture, and figure out how things work in the host country (e.g., what is the process for getting a new phone line, or for contacting an apartment rental service such as Airbnb). These can be very challenging and stressful, provoking a cultural shock. This can be described as a feeling of disorientation, and distress, resulting from the stress that occurs during the first weeks or months of immersion in a foreign culture (Ward et al., 2020). During this time, it is common to be frustrated and to have difficulty communicating and adapting to a foreign culture. However, the shock eventually passes.

- *Time-consuming and costly*. The role of an ethnographer requires him to build rapport with participants and make them comfortable around him to ease the process of studying them. Eventually, he must spend months or even years observing how participants live and understanding their culture. Furthermore, recruiting costs, relocation costs, travel expenses, as well as the cost associated with running the dataset can be very high.

- *Difficulty in choosing a representative sample*. In most ethnographic research, just a portion of culture is studied attentively because it is impossible to observe and talk to everyone. Thus, only a sample of the population is selected. Selecting who will be in the sample can be a tough task.

- **Language obstacles.** An external ethnographer who is presented with the option of working with a translator can face some issues; these can include a lack of confidentiality of conversations and the risk of misinterpretations and misunderstandings.

Possible Outcomes

Successful ethnographic research requires the ethnographer to adapt to different cultures and overcome several challenges. How an ethnographer deals with them defines the success or failure of the study. The bulleted list below outlines potential guides for overcoming the challenges mentioned above.

- To overcome the Hawthorne effect, the ethnographer should establish rapport and build trusting relationships through conversations with participants, as this improves communications and helps the ethnographer become accepted in society. By doing this, he can acquire accurate and useful information from conversations. The ethnographer needs to create empathy with participants. The Hawthorne effect is one of the greatest challenges an ethnographer can face, and he needs to be aware of this challenge to be prepared in advance.

- Regarding poor electricity, a generator would be helpful in Cameroon in case of electricity outages, as it keeps power running. As for poor water, public fountains provide water to individuals in need. To overcome poor internet connections, the ethnographer might have to subscribe to the best internet provider in the country, which is currently Orange Cameroon. Furthermore, tips like reducing unnecessary connections and turning off ads could improve internet connection.

- Having to deal with a Cameroonian who constantly shows up late to scheduled appointments can become frustrating. The ethnographer will have to be flexible and proactive. If one has an appointment and the other is running late, he should use time wisely and maybe perform other tasks. Patience and perseverance will be required.

- Religious and gender issues are common and almost inevitable in societies. An ethnographer can choose to work with a partner of the opposite sex in case he is not allowed to enter a Madrasa. Furthermore, he should be aware and ready to manage cultural biases by communicating, remaining open-minded, building awareness, avoiding generalization, and educating. Additionally, the collaboration of a local and a foreign ethnographer to enrich the ethnographic research could be beneficial because the participants' views of the ethnographer can affect their behavior, as well as the potential for building rapport.

- Relocation and adaptation challenges are common for anybody transitioning to a different culture. Before relocating, the ethnographer must gather essential information about how things operate in a foreign country (apartment rental, car rental, mobile and internet services, etc.) to smooth the transition process. Once arrived in a foreign country, it will take some time to adapt. But the cultural shock will pass.

- One of the major drawbacks of ethnography is that it requires a considerable amount of money and time in fieldwork. The ethnographer should be patient and positive as it takes time to develop trusting relationships and fit in a foreign society. Additionally, it is important to be prepared to spend a lot of time abroad. The ethnographer can also intend to get support from his family or relatives if needed, as well as emotional and financial support from the company and coworkers.

- Choosing who will be part of a probability sample is not an easy task. An ethnographer can rely on purposive or judgment sampling, which is the deliberate choice of a participant due to the qualities the participant possesses. Participants are selected based on criteria deemed critical to the research interest (Etikan et al., 2016). For instance, salesmen would be the focus if the research involves sales practices. Other sampling techniques, such as convenience, random and stratified sampling, can be considered.

Discussion

Culture has a strong impact on business and product design. One cannot expect to conduct business with a different culture without having good knowledge of that culture. Since various cultural dimensions influence user preferences, it is important to gain insights into a culture to better understand how they perceive certain design elements. Let's further consider the Apple example mentioned above. Apple iPhones have not been able to succeed in the Indian market because the company failed to accurately understand Indian culture. Iphone's virtual assistant (Siri) does not understand many words of Indian origin and often struggles with Indian accents (Broussard, 2018). This is in contrast to Google Assistant and Amazon's Alexa, which perform better in India and other cultures because they are designed to work with several different dialects and variations in speech. Moreover, Philips, one of the major manufacturers of consumer electronics and household appliances of the world, has different website designs for different cultures (China, Saudi Arabia, USA), and Facebook's UI design for some Arabian countries is different from the original Facebook UI design. These are examples that emphasize the importance of localization to better fit market conditions and lower cultural barriers. Many global firms are challenged by a diverse environment in their homeland, which only becomes more complex as they step across cultural boundaries. It is the degree to which they can manage cultural differences that determine their level of success.

Cross-cultural barriers have hindered the successful design of technologies in Africa. Cross-cultural design goes beyond users' involvement in the product's design phases. Understanding user requirements is the primary step toward designing successful products. Cross-cultural design is even more complex because understanding a foreign culture without stereotypes can be very challenging. Cultural dimensions or internet research can provide insight into a specific culture, but the accuracy of these insights is questionable.

Ethnographic studies are essential as they provide the opportunity to gather reliable data, develop a realistic understanding of cultural patterns in different cultural settings, and provide direction toward a successful cross-cultural design. For instance, in ethnographic research conducted in Itacoatiara, Brazil and Kigali, Rwanda, the study revealed that having cultural familiarity provides better opportunities in which researchers are most likely to gather valuable data for product design (Wood & Mattson, 2019). Data collected from each country provided different results and revealed different needs in terms of user requirements and allowed ethnographers to gather useful information for product design. The study also revealed several challenges, such as language fluency and the need for an interpreter or non-respect for time-bound, which should be considered before conducting an ethnographic study in a different culture.

Cameroonian users often struggle with products designed in western countries because the features implemented in these products do not fit the Cameroonian market. For example, a company investing in a food delivery business in Cameroon will fail because the country does not have a reliable or accurate address system. For this reason, the use of a GPS navigation system is almost useless in Cameroon. It is important to understand people to make their life better with a product. Designers from western countries have different experiences than those from the Middle East or African countries and are unfamiliar with the culture, language, or norms of the location where the product they are designing will be used. Thus, information about users gathered through ethnographic research becomes significantly valuable.

Future Work

Future research patterns should involve expanding cross-cultural studies to specific cultural groups to better understand their needs and wants. Emphasis could be given to overlooked cultural groups of users such as India, Nepal, Cameroon, Ivory Coast, Congo, etc., who use technologies predominantly designed for western cultural groups. Research can also be extended to other developing countries, which could benefit from UI designs tailored to fit their needs, as there is a huge potential to gain more insight from further studies in these specific countries.

In addition, the authors see a potential to conduct further research studies with an extended focus on design ethnography to gain deeper insights valuable in understanding the Cameroonian market in terms of technology acceptance and preference and design products specifically tailored to fit Cameroonian locals.

Conclusion

A shift toward a more diverse society gives individuals and businesses more opportunities to interact with and learn about diverse cultures. Nevertheless, cultural diversity presents challenges because the opposing culture can often be misjudged, biased, or misunderstood. Cultural barriers and stereotypes heavily affect business and product design due to the diverse nature of culture. Cross-cultural design approaches are often based on quantitative studies of different cultures through online surveys, usability testing, or international surveys. Such analysis can have limitations, such as non-response bias or uncertainty over the validity of the data. In contrast, empathic approaches, such as ethnographic studies, can provide strong insight. Product designers with cultural knowledge and understanding ultimately have a distinct advantage over user requirements, while other designers will make assumptions to fill in gaps in their understanding of user requirements. Such assumptions can lead to the design of less effective products.

Cameroon is a country with a lot of opportunities for investment. However, conducting business in Cameroon requires an understanding of the culture, which goes above and beyond internet research, reading articles, watching documentaries, or going through reveals of ethnographic studies of other cultures; it is important to grasp the difference between perception and reality. For instance, people are sometimes amazed and unaware that Cameroonians can speak French and English fluently or that Cameroon does not have automated transport systems because they perceive what life in Cameroon could be like. This paper is an eye-opener, but one needs to be open-minded and merge with and interact with the opposite culture to understand that culture better. Ethnographic research can provide insight into aspects of life, including norms, perception, religion, time-bound, etc., and illuminate what goes unspoken within a culture. Alas, one cannot apply findings from an ethnography conducted in Congo or Rwanda to Cameroonian users and vice versa because every culture has distinct and unique characteristics.

Managing cultural differences means unplugging globalization and plugging in the locals to eliminate cultural barriers and understand cultural differences. As the Onion Model of Culture implies, culture has to be peeled like an onion to be fully understood, and one has to invest time and energy to discover the hidden layers and reach the core.

References

Barber, W., & Badre, A. (1998). Culturability: The merging of culture and usability. *Proceedings of the 4th Conference on Human Factors and the Web, 7*(4), 1-10. https://www.usj.edu.lb/moodle/stephane.bazan/obs_interculturelle/Barber%20and%20Badre.pdf

Broussard, M. (2018, January 30). *Indian iPhone Users Discuss Apple's Poor Services Performance: 'Apple Maps is a Joke'*. MacRumors. https://www.macrumors.com/2018/01/30/indian-iphone-users-apple-maps

Chakraborty, J. (2013). Cross Cultural Design Considerations in HealthCare. In: Kurosu, M. (eds.) *Human-Computer Interaction. Applications and Services* (pp. 13-19). Springer. https://doi.org/10.1007/978-3-642-39262-7_2

Czaja, J., Boot, W., Charness, N., & Rogers, W. (2019). *Designing for Older Adults: Principles and Creative Human Factors Approaches*. CRC Press. https://doi.org/10.1201/b22189

Djamen, R., Georges, L., & Pernin, J. L. (2020). Understanding the cultural values at the individual level in central Africa: A test of the cvscale in Cameroon. *International Journal of Marketing and Social Policy (IJMSP)*.

Fernandes, T. (1994). Global interface design. *Proceedings of Conference Companion on Human Factors in Computing Systems* (pp. 373-374). https://doi.org/10.1145/259963.260509

Gobo, G. (2008). *Doing ethnography*. Sage. https://dx.doi.org/10.4135/9780857028976

Gould, E. W., Honold, P., Kurosu, M., Melican, J., Marcus, A., & Yu, L. A. (2003). Culture issues and mobile UI design. *Proceedings of CHI'03: Extended Abstracts on Human Factors in Computing Systems* (pp. 702-703).

Hall, E. T., & Hall, M., R. (1990). *Understanding Cultural Differences, Germans, French and Americans*. Intercultural Press.

Hanley, J. (1999). Beyond the tip of the iceberg. *Reaching Today's Youth, 3*(2), 9-12.

Hofstede, G. (2011). Dimensionalizing cultures: The Hofstede model in context. *Online readings in psychology and culture, 2*(1), 2307-0919.

Hofstede Insights. (2022). *Hofstede Insights: Organizational, Culture, Consulting*. Hofstede-insights. https://www.hofstede-insights.com/

International Hydropower Association (2022). *Country profile: Cameroon*. IHA https://www.hydropower.org/country-profiles/cameroon

LawyersTech (2021). 9 reasons why iPhone is not successful in India. https://www.lawyerstech.com/why-is-apple-iphone-not-so-successful-in-india/

Lebron, A., & Mendez, A. (2013). What is culture? *Merit Research Journal of Education and Review, 1*(6), 126-132.

Marcus, A. (2005). User interface design and culture. *Usability and internationalization of information technology, 3*, 51-78.

Marcus, A. (2013). Cross-cultural user-experience design. *Proceedings of SIGGRAPH Asia 2013 Courses, 8*, 1-31. https://doi.org/10.1145/2542266.2542274

Merk, V. (2003). Communication across Cultures: from cultural awareness to reconciliation of the dilemmas. *SSRN Electronic Journal*. http://dx.doi.org/10.2139/ssrn.464720

Oh, J. M., & Moon, N. (2013). Towards a cultural user interface generation principles. *Multimedia tools and applications, 63*(1), 195-216.

Payne, G., & Payne, J. (2004). *Key concepts in social research*. Sage.

Rana, M. (2018). Cultural Variations in Organizations of India and United States: A Comparative Study. *International Journal of Arts and Commerce, 7*(1), 16-28.

Reinecke, K., & Bernstein, A. (2013). Knowing What a User Likes: A Design Science Approach to Interfaces that Automatically Adapt to Culture. *MIS Quarterly, 37*(2), 427–453. http://www.jstor.org/stable/43825917

Rinne, T., Steel, G. D., & Fairweather, J. (2012). Hofstede and Shane Revisited: The Role of Power Distance and Individualism in National-Level Innovation Success. *Cross-Cultural Research, 46*(2), 91–108. https://doi.org/10.1177/1069397111423898

Santoso, H.B., & Schrepp, M. (2019). The impact of culture and product on the subjective importance of user experience aspects. Heliyon, *5*(9), e02434. https://doi.org/10.1016/j.heliyon.2019.e02434

Shneiderman, B. (1998). *Designing the User Interface*. Addison-Wesley.

The World Bank. (2022). *International Comparison Program, World Bank*. The World Bank. https://data.worldbank.org/indicator/NY.GNP.MKTP.PP.KD

Ward, C., Bochner, S., & Furnham, A. (2001). *The psychology of culture shock*. Routledge.

Wood, A. E., & Mattson, C. A. (2019). Quantifying the effects of various factors on the utility of design ethnography in the developing world. *Research in Engineering Design, 30*(3), 317-338.

Chapter 4

Harnessing Cultural Intelligence in Cross: Cultural Business and Management

James Phelan

Veterans Health Administration, The Ohio State University,
Columbus, USA

Abstract: Cultural Intelligence (CQ) is vital in a modern and global-oriented cross-culture business and management environment. Apart from awareness and theoretical constructs, business leaders and field-level experts need practicality to harness CQ for optimal functioning in cross-cultural business. This information is also vital for students as they prepare for the global business workforce. Based on a comprehensive overview of the literature, this chapter will provide students, managers, and field-level experts with practical ideas and measures they can use to improve their performance in a cross-cultural work environment. While CQ has strong theoretical underpinnings, drawing out practicality is vital for a thriving and prosperous business environment. This chapter will better equip managers, field-level practitioners and students to practice CQ. Readers will also benefit as they learn about various measures which they can utilize to gauge their practice of CQ and work towards sharpening and improving their skills.

Keywords: cultural intelligence, cultural quotient (CQ), CQ practicality, cross-culture business and management, business culture, cultural competency

***

Introduction

Practicality in cross-cultural business involves experience and active application, along with knowledge of the theory. It is important to have an understanding of how the theoretical foundation of cultural intelligence, or "cultural quotient" (CQ), drives practicality. Simply put, CQ is "the capability to function effectively in intercultural settings" (Van Dyne et al., 2012, p. 295). CQ is comprised of cognitive and metacognitive, behavioral, and emotional/

motivational components (Earley & Ang, 2003; Van Dyne et al., 2012) and adheres to a multiple intelligence framework (Sternberg, 1988). The purpose of this chapter is to progress from the theory of CQ, elevate to CQ practical methods, and inform managers, students, and field experts of the importance of these practical methods in a cross-cultural environment in ways that can improve collegial relations and, ultimately, improve customer service and increase productivity.

In terms of background, this chapter became necessary as the overview revealed that more education about the practicality of CQ was needed. The objective, therefore, is to provide a comprehensive tool that readers can use that will help them increase competency about how to grow, use and measure CQ.

Method

The contents of this chapter are informed through an overview of published literature. For the overview, the relevant literature was abstracted from several electronic databases, including Google, Google Scholar, WorldWideScience.org, OVID, and EBSCOhost, using keywords associated with CQ. A sensitive approach was used to maximize the number of retrieved articles. The year of publication was not used as a limiting factor for the searches.

Background

CQ helps business partners improve collegial relations, ultimately leading to enhanced customer service and workflow. It is important to learn and practice CQ early in the academic environment to better prepare for the modern global workforce. Research has shown that students who receive cross-cultural training demonstrate improved workplace communication, customer service, and cultural self-awareness; this was particularly true with a sample of Australian students (Bean, 2008).

It is important to understand CQ because communication is vital in managing business workflow. Behaviors, values, attitudes, beliefs, practices, and ideas that are appropriate in one culture or region may not be so in another. For example, while self-promotion might be considered acceptable in one part of the world, in many other parts, it may be considered conceited and unacceptable (Molinsky, 2018). Identifying and understanding differing cultural viewpoints can help create room for flexibility. Understanding what kinds of communication are expected improves businesses' chances of communicating successfully (Molinsky, 2018). As challenging as it may be, CQ is important in cross-cultural business and management because communication is key to collaboration and getting the results business partners desire (Lovelace, n.d.). Cohesion and a sense of having one's culture respected enable them to feel connected. Employees who feel connected are more productive and less likely to leave their organization (Stallard et al., 2015).

Theoretical Framework

Cultural Intelligence stems from the multiple loci of intelligence frameworks. While some are supportive of a unitary factor of intelligence, more popular views support multiple intelligence theory. Multiple loci of intelligence theory stem from cognitive-contextual theory. Sternberg (1988) considers intelligence as triarchic in that we can think in novel ways that are creative, analytic, and practical.

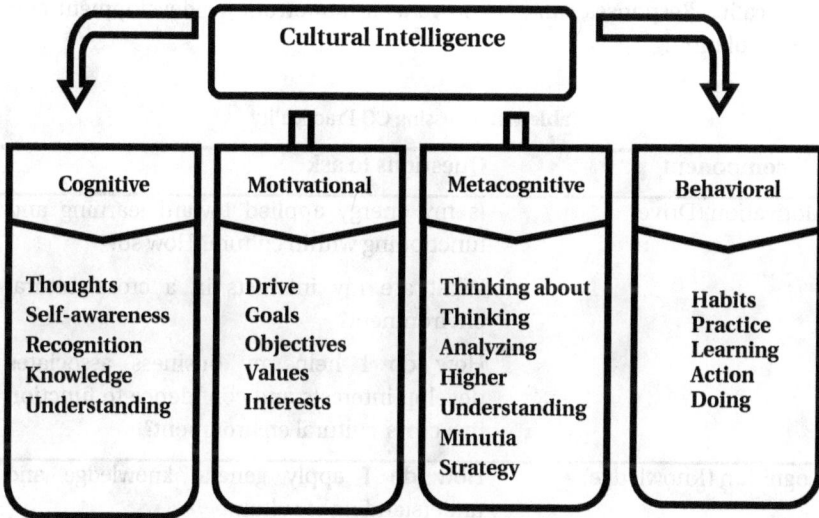

Cultural Intelligence			
Cognitive	**Motivational**	**Metacognitive**	**Behavioral**
Thoughts Self-awareness Recognition Knowledge Understanding	Drive Goals Objectives Values Interests	Thinking about Thinking Analyzing Higher Understanding Minutia Strategy	Habits Practice Learning Action Doing

Figure 4.1: Cultural Intelligence Framework

Earley and Ang (2003) built upon Sternberg's multiple loci framework on intelligence and argue that intelligence is not merely about cognitive ability, which is how one understands differences and similarities, but also about motivation and behavior. Besides cognitive ability, Ang and Van Dyne (2008) discuss other CQ capabilities, such as the CQ drive, which is a motivational level that shows a person's interest and confidence in functioning in a cross-cultural environment; CQ strategy, which is the metacognitive level for which a person plans for and remains aware of cross-culture; and CQ action or behavior, which displays a person's flexibility and skills in a cross-cultural context (see *figure 4.1* for an illustration). Overall, discussion, review, and research pertaining to CQ are robust (Ang et al., 2011; Ng et al., 2012).

Practical Implications

Practicality is vital to fostering cultural competency or "the ability to do the same task efficiently and repeatedly with superior performance" (Roy, 2019, p. 52). The following sections display practical ideas that can help harness CQ in cross-cultural business and management.

Assessing CQ Practicality

It is important to assess CQ practicality. Table 4.1 contains a helpful self-assessment to help gauge how individuals handle the four components of CQ practicality. Responses can help serve as a framework for development and growth planning.

Table 4.1: Assessing CQ Practicality

CQ component	Questions to ask
Motivation (Drive)	Is my energy applied toward learning and functioning within culture? How so?
	What are my interests in a cross-cultural environment?
	How do I help my business associates develop interests and confidence to function in a cross-cultural environment?
Cognition (Knowledge)	How do I apply general knowledge and understanding of culture?
	Using the metrics outlined in the "Measuring CQ" section, what is my understanding of CQ?
Behavior (Action)	What are my actions and interactions within my cross-culture environment?
	What changes can I make?
Metacognition (Monitoring)	How do I monitor my thoughts about cross-culture and apply these?
	What have I learned from this monitoring and how can I apply it in cross-cultural environments?

Budgeting

It is vital that businesses use a line-item approach to CQ. Many businesses devote attention to diversity, equity, and inclusion (DEI) programs in the workforce (Graham, n.d.); for these, cross-cultural competency (3C) can be part of the process. Bucher (2008) provides examples of how people have implemented CQ in the workplace to bring about bottom-line results. This text is also good for students as it provides several "megaskills" to help build CQ.

Conversations

Conversations about cross-culture are important. These conversations can be embedded into the business environment. Some examples include roundtables, where everyone shares their ideas. Building cohesion via talk-and-listen sessions can help foster growth and acceptance of each other's differences and similarities.

Counter-Stereotypic Training (Negation)

The *Kirwan Institute for the Study of Race and Ethnicity* found that another approach for implicit bias mitigation is negation, where individuals are trained to reject stereotypical activity. It was found that saying "no" to stereotypical behavior is one thing, but better than that is saying something more meaningful such as "That's wrong!" Negation can be role-played in workgroups to help practice these principles.

Feeling Connected

Workplace connections build trust and comradery. As Stallard et al. (2015) stated,

> One of the most powerful and least understood aspects of successful organizations is how employees' feelings of connection, community, and unity provide a competitive advantage. Employees in an organization with a high degree of connection are more engaged, more productive in their jobs, and less likely to leave for a competitor. They are also more trusting and cooperative; they are more willing to share information with their colleagues and therefore help them make well-informed decisions.

When workers and employees feel they belong and are included and accepted, there will generally be higher employee engagement, increased productivity, reduced conflict, improved relationships, enhanced levels of learning and performance, decreased stress, better health, and more resilience, trust, and happiness (Kinne, 2020).

According to Stallard et al. (2015), "The work context has six specific needs: respect, recognition, belonging, autonomy, personal growth, and meaning" (p. 4). When respect, recognition, and belonging are met, workers feel connected to each other. Autonomy and personal growth are task mastery needs, which affect how connected workers feel about the work they are doing, while meaning is an existential need. Attending to the following needs in a cultural context generally helps improve work performance:

Respect

Building CQ requires instilling respect. Workers need to be around people who are courteous and considerate. The authors point out that people who are patronizing, condescending, or passive-aggressive will only stress people out and keep them from thriving.

Recognition

People get energized when they work with others who recognize and voice their task strengths; otherwise, they will feel emotionally and physically drained. Thus, workgroups should seek ways to recognize others in various ways, which include praise and different kinds of rewards.

Belonging

When one feels that they belong, they also feel more resilient when things get difficult. One way to establish a sense of belonging in the workgroup is by helping others through hard times and showing care and empathy. One exercise is to send encouraging messages or cards to others.

Autonomy

People need the freedom to do their work. Therefore, people must allow each other the opportunity to be autonomous. Most people do not work well when being micromanaged or are slowed down by bureaucracy. This stalls production since it creates doubts in workers' minds and forces them to question everything they do. Managers should create work queues that support both creativity and autonomy.

Personal Growth

Personal growth happens when people are engaged in a task that is a good fit for their strengths and provides the right degree of challenge. Workers should experience a flow of change to a degree that challenges them and inevitably invigorates them. Workgroups should continually seek ways to help workers achieve personal growth. Personal Growth and Development plans can help workers build confidence and advance standards. These plans work best when they include goals that are measurable and obtainable (Wallis, 2020).

Meaning

Finding meaning is an existential need and is important to workgroups because when people are energized, they put additional effort into their work. "When our work has meaning, we feel a sense of significance" (Stallard et al., 2015, p. 4). Building meaning into cross-cultural workgroups involves honoring the strengths of culture within the workgroup. A good exercise is to have workers write/verbalize the meaning of culture in the workplace.

Flexibility

According to Kolovou (2020), it is important to raise awareness of cross-cultural differences and make necessary adjustments. The author notes that it is not as much about knowing the right answers as it is about asking the right questions. This author suggests that cultures differ across the globe and are based on high and low contexts. Low-context cultures tend to focus on following rules, practicing fairness, using more words, and valuing individual goals. They tend to use direct communication. Examples of low-context cultures are US and German cultures, where feedback is generally open, and people tend to say what's on their minds without inhibition. However, to an outsider or high-context culture, this might seem impersonal.

High-context cultures focus more on teams and relationships, implicit and indirect communication, and subtle messages; often, lengthy conversations are more common, and individuals might find it difficult to say "no" as it might seem impolite. For example, we might find a high-context culture in India and Greece. High-context cultures are typically group-oriented and trade individualist goals for shared values.

Context is important to keep in mind when dealing with cross-cultural business. Further, it is important to realize that not all cultures emphasize individualized goals and that team recognition might be valued more highly. According to Kolovou (2020), people must be flexible and aware of differences in communication styles and values. The author further adds that one must know their preferences yet be prepared to flex and adjust to meet goals. Kolovou (2020) recommends a four-step approach:

1. Assess the situation (in other words, know the culture).

2. Strategize the approach (know how to respond appropriately to others' needs and be flexible).

3. Take action (practice CQ).

4. Evaluate how things have gone and be willing to adjust when necessary.

Feedback

It is important to strategize how to receive feedback from high-context cultures (Kolovou, 2020). As an example, the author claims that she won't ask high-context people what they thought of her content; instead, she will ask what they found to be the three major takeaways. The reason for this is that some cultures don't give direct answers reflecting displeasure with performance; conversely, with her method, she can get meaningful feedback indirectly in the form of the major takeaways that would be warmly suggested.

Further Evaluation

Kolovou (2020) gives a good example of evaluating a business interaction. In the given example, she knows that her client is of a low-context culture and is direct, which is culturally appropriate. So, she:

- Asks a few open-ended questions.
- Asks about specific feedback on work processes and ideas for improvement.

When the meeting is over, she:

- Evaluates how the performance appraisal and interaction with the client went.
- Asks the client a few days later if she has any additional thoughts about their discussion or if she has further questions about the potential job move.
- Continues to get a feel for interactions with the new office staff.
- Considers arranging social hours or lunches.
- Finds a close confidante in the workplace, possibly someone who understands this culture and can help her assimilate.
- Assesses the ongoing relationship.
- Asks herself questions: Did I communicate openly? Did I express myself openly? Did I get the positive result that I wanted?

The scenario is simple but a good example to demonstrate a cross-cultural CQ mindset. If she can look at the strengths and weaknesses and then act and evaluate, she will learn from these experiences and become a more efficient leader.

Incentives

Alon et al. (2018) suggest that employers consider rewarding employees who improve their own CQ (Alon et al., 2016) and include CQ in their workplace by offering opportunities for upward career mobility. The inclusion of CQ might serve as a prerequisite for upward career mobility:

> Managers need to openly and consistently communicate the company policy of providing development opportunities and rewards for those who improve their CQ in expected ways. The expected reward may indeed act as an incentive for employees to adopt the intended behavior. (p. 10)

Ingroup Membership

Another practice to implement is making sure that all members feel included. The "one team" mentality should be instilled in all workgroups. Research shows that ingroup membership is "a particularly appealing practical approach to reducing bias, as positive associations seemed to be conferred as part of ingroup membership" (Scroggins et al., 2016, p. 219).

LESCANT Model

Global teams that harness their diverse perspectives and talents have better outcomes than those that don't. However, communicating across cultures can present some challenges. The LESCANT model, developed by Victor (1992), helps individuals and teams think through the cultural issues that can come up in cross-cultural business communication. LESCANT stands for:

Language

Cultures vary based on language; even countries can have regions that differ in language. According to Victor (1992), these factors can vary depending on attitudes about language and how people speak in ways that others can understand. The use of interpreters can influence the interpretation of the message, thereby impacting the relationship. Individuals and teams can apply flexibility if they get a correct assessment. Behaviors that are acceptable in one country/region may be inappropriate in another. Thus, understanding what kind of communication is expected helps to improve the chances of communicating more successfully.

Environment

The environment factor includes the physical surroundings of culture and includes things such as land, weather, size, density, populations, green mentality, food, and topography. For example, if a business associate is concerned about green initiatives, it is best to know how to tread effectively in this situation.

Social Organization

Social organization refers to how society is put together and includes things such as education, religion, class systems and family and roles. It is important to understand the social organization when working in a cross-cultural context because social issues may present themselves, and it is important to be sensitive and aware of cultural differences in social organizations.

Context

According to Lovelace (n.d.), context in cultures can vary. Following are some examples of context and what they represent:

- **Enthusiasm:** Refers to how much emotion or energy one is expected to show.
- **Formality:** Refers to how much deference and respect one is permitted to show.
- **Assertiveness:** Refers to what is the acceptable extent one can speak his or her mind.
- **Self-promotion:** Refers to whether it is acceptable to boast or not.
- **Personal Disclosure:** Refers to how appropriate it is to reveal personal information in a particular situation.

Understanding context allows for the opportunity to effectively understand where people are coming from and to practice and engage in flexibility.

Authority

In some cultures, authority (power and decision-making) is hierarchical, while in others, it is lateral. It is important for individuals and teams to understand the authoritative styles of the cultures they are working with. This is especially important as it could affect relationships and sales.

Non-Verbal communication

Non-verbal communication deals with those nuances that appeal to the senses, especially sight. Like verbal communication, non-verbal communication can imply flexibility. Thus, understanding what kinds of communication are acceptable helps to improve the chances of communicating more successfully. Take the example of the US and India: In the US, enthusiasm is moderately high and is generally expected, whereas in India, it is relatively low. In terms of assertiveness, in the US, it is culturally acceptable to be viewed as a go-getter, but in other countries, this may be seen as aggressive and not showing composure.

Time

It's important to understand how others deal with time and how they schedule their activities, and how they organize daily activities. For example, in the Middle East, people may move a little slower, and in some parts of Europe and the US, there is a high emphasis on tight schedules. Neither of these approaches is necessarily better than the other. Business is conducted in both cultures; it's just done differently. Figuring out the time orientation of a culture prior to interaction can increase effectiveness.

According to Lovelace (n.d.), the LESCANT model provides considerations for communicating in cross-cultural teams. If individuals and teams have questions about how others think or feel, they should plan to ask them. "[A] team is only as strong as [its] ability to effectively communicate across cultural boundaries" ("Cross-cultural communication Within Teams" section).

Other Models

In addition to The LESCANT model, other models can also be helpful. The Framework for Cultural Intelligence consists of the following parts: knowledge, strategic thinking, motivation, and behaviors. These are laid out as the ABCs of CQ (Schmitz, 2012):

Acquire (knowledge)

Once a person is aware that they are unfamiliar with different cultures, it is therefore important to leverage intercultural training. This resonates well with the cognitive aspect of CQ. A question to ask is: "What is needed to learn about CQ?"

Build (Strategic Thinking)

After acquiring knowledge about interculture, it is important to know how it is practiced and ask oneself how it can be used. This resonates well with metacognition.

Contemplate (Motivation and Ability to Work with Others)

This part deals with how to reflect or step back and analyze one's own biases, judgments, or microaggressions. A question to ask is: "How do I deal with my bias about a culture that is different from my own?"

Do (Perform)

This part deal with practicing what has been thought about and acquired. Schmitz (2012) shares that "Culturally intelligent leaders are like chameleons in social environments, changing their behaviors to mimic their surroundings" (section 3.2).

Newsletters

Newsletters can help inform workers about cultural trends and opportunities. They can be an avenue to communicate and foster new ideas and can facilitate acknowledgement of culture and wellbeing. Content creation and dissemination are important in supporting a cause. If a business has an existing newsletter, it would be helpful for them to seek out ways to enhance its cross-cultural effectiveness. If a business does not have a newsletter, then implementation would be a good step to help foster an improved cross-cultural environment.

Social Forums

Companies can hold organized and informal forums or summits that allow for cultural diversity interchange, for example, having one culture share its customs in a show-and-tell session or over a special meal. These social forums provide a great opportunity for storytelling and can be held during working hours, on lunch breaks, or over a weekend in the form of a retreat. Moreover, with some creativity, these forums can also be conducted virtually.

Sojourns

Doing business from one's own homeland and interacting with others is one thing, but physically being in a business partner's homeland is an entirely different experience and can help gain superior CQ. Businesses should make ways for partners to sojourn in each other's country to provide an opportunity to learn the culture and embrace it more broadly.

Teaching and Integrating Cultural Metacognition

The following sections (Modeling, Feedback, and Schemas) are taken from Phelan (2018):

> Metacognition is awareness of one's own thinking. It involves regulating, monitoring, and adjusting thoughts and strategies as one learns cross-cultural skills. The goal for educators is to enable students to move their cognitive knowledge to a higher level of metacognition, where they are active, self-monitoring, goal-directed, and embrace an internal locus of control over their own learning. The three basic

framework strategies for fostering metacognition are connecting new information to former and current knowledge; selecting deliberate thinking strategies; and planning, monitoring, and evaluating the process (Baker, 2010; Dirkes, 1985).

Following are some practical tools/strategies that can inform cultural metacognition:

Modeling

Modeling is an effective way to learn. Teachers and business leaders play vital roles in affecting both the learner and the learning environment. The classroom and field provide the opportunity for educators and leaders to model cultural metacognition skills, which can have a significant impact on students.

Feedback

Mor et al. (2013) also recommend the use of performance feedback as a way to develop awareness and planning habits. Feedback helps show students the areas where their metacognitive strategies might benefit from more training or harnessing.

Monitoring

Teaching students to monitor their cognitive processes is an important step toward building cultural metacognition practice. There are several ways to enhance students' monitoring techniques.

Monitoring involves continually checking for understanding. In terms of practice, students should be taught to self-monitor their cultural understanding by reflecting on their biases, awareness, sensitivities, inclusiveness, and relationship to business outcomes.

Educators should start by introducing self-awareness and self-monitoring skills. Students and educators should discuss key strategies for learning how to self-monitor. These sessions can include group activities designed to help students think about these new skills and apply them in practical ways. For example, after initial sessions designed to teach self-monitoring skills, students could participate in staged groups that incorporate various cultural scenarios. One student could be staged as someone from a majority culture who interacts with others who portray persons from a minority culture. After a few rounds of interactions, students can report back their experiences and how the use of self-monitoring was applicable in the scenarios.

Another skill is monitoring one's own macroaggressions and microaffirmations. Microaggressions are small events or subtle acts of disrespect, which are often hard to prove, sometimes covert, and often unintentional, but may lead to the perception of discrimination or harassment (Sue et al., 2007). Conversely, microaffirmations are micro messages that convey inclusion, respect, trust, and genuine willingness to see others succeed (Rowe, 2008). Microaffirmations may lead to a more productive and efficient work environment where all members feel valued and enjoy work. Research also shows that these "small" messages have power for insiders and outsiders (Wong et al., 2014). For example, when a person with higher status acknowledges someone at a meeting, that acknowledgement influences others to also think more highly of the acknowledged person.

Schemas

Schemas (knowledge structures) are sets of propositions or mental constructs that create generalizations and expectations about categories of objects, places, events, activities, and people. According to Earley and Peterson (2004), metacognition is critical for developing shared schemas. Research has shown that when certain schemas are applied in an intercultural-communication context, it could cause misunderstandings in the process. From implicit schema, explanations are derived for contradictory behavior to go with our schemas (e.g., if a professor is late, students might think some emergency has arisen; however, if the professor is consistently late, students may decide he is an inadequate professor). One way of thinking about schemas is by working in intercultural teams where participants can learn, assess, and strategize.

Understanding Personal Bias

It is important to learn about implicit bias, which according to the *Kirwan Institute for the Study of Race and Ethnicity*, is the unconscious attitudes and stereotypes people hold about different groups of people that influence their actions (Staats et al., 2017). The institute offers free public education on understanding the origins of implicit associations and how to uncover personal biases and learn strategies for addressing them. Going over the "Implicit Bias Review" (Staats et al., 2017) and completing learning modules provided by the institute with workgroups can help increase understanding of biases and mitigation strategies.

Workshops

Workshop-based programs can enable facilitators and workgroups to develop experiences that help build cross-cultural competencies and increase CQ. Further, field guides and training manuals can provide materials such as agendas, schedules, and practical exercises needed to run effective workshops (Dolan & Kawamura, 2015).

Case Study

At one point, the Chinese government decided that China wasn't ready for Amway's direct-sales model. Eva Cheng, executive vice president for Amway Asia, drew on cultural intelligence to convince Amway executives to adapt their business strategy to align with the Chinese government's priorities yet remain true to the non-negotiable strategies of Amway. Not only did China change its policy on direct selling, but the Asian arm of Amway began to shape Amway's business practices in the USA. Amway recognized the "value of a long-term approach and worked deliberately to build trust and local ownership among all markets" both at Amway's home office and abroad.

Amway places importance in China on helping distributors build sustainable businesses through intense training and codes of conduct. Despite controversies, Amway is often cited as the model for ethical direct selling around the world and sets itself apart from pop-up illegal pyramid schemes.

Managers with high CQ are more likely to negotiate effectively with Asian officials and companies. "Many Chinese insiders believe the high-pressure negotiation tactics used by Western leaders erode their opportunities in China." So, if organizations want to do business with China, it is important to gain trust and that the purpose of the work also is good for the culture and its people. It takes CQ to manage that (Case study from SHRM, 2015, p. 14).

CQ is also needed when approaching new markets in nations that value natural remedies and require trust. Amway India has added a new category with the launch of "Chyawanprash" by Nutrilite, which strengthens its immunity-supporting portfolio (The Economic Times, 2021). Again, it takes CQ to manage that, especially when high- and low-contextual nations work together (Kolovou, 2020).

Measuring CQ

It is important to evaluate the cultural or personal differences that may be enhancing or limiting one's own potential to interact in a multicultural business environment. Getting an accurate picture requires gauging cognitive, relational, and behavioral differences along various dimensions where cultural gaps are most common; this helps assess those areas. The following assessment tools can be helpful, the majority of which were also reviewed in Phelan (2018):

Cultural Intelligence Scale (CQS)

The CQS is a 20-item scale that measures drive, knowledge, strategy, and action CQ and possesses good metric properties with applied and empirical potential (Van Dyne et al., 2008). Later, Van Dyne et al. (2012) proposed a second-order 11-factor structure and convergent discriminant validity of the sub-dimensions.

The *Cultural Intelligence Center* provides several self-assessments that measure 4 CQ capabilities and 13 CQ sub-dimensions. Pre- and post-assessments allow for comparisons over time. This feedback also includes an action plan (Cultural Intelligence Center, n.d.).

Multicultural Personality Questionnaire (MPQ)

The MPQ was originally a 91-item survey but then reduced to 40 items (MPQ-SF). The results help to determine one's attitudes and behavior in a variety of cross-cultural contexts (Van der Zee & Van Oudenhoven, 2000).

Assess Yourself 2: Cultural Awareness Self-Assessment

The Assess Yourself 2: Cultural Awareness Self-Assessment is a 10-item scale to self-measure cultural awareness and has been adapted from the Cultural Awareness Self-Assessment Form 3. I CANS (Integrated Curriculum for Achieving Necessary Skills and can be retrieved from: http://highered.mheducation.com/sites/dl/free/0072563974/87090/ch02.html)

Cross-Cultural Adaptability Inventory (CCAI)

The CCAI is a 59-item inventory that can help determine individuals' or groups' strengths and weaknesses in 4 cross-cultural areas. Results can help students and the workforce improve their effectiveness and build a corporate culture that embraces diversity and inclusion (Emamjomehzadeh, 2012; Kelley & Meyers, 1993).

Cultural Competence Self-Assessment Checklist

The Cultural Competence Self-Assessment Checklist is a self-assessment tool that is available in the free domain by the Central Vancouver Island Multicultural Society and is designed to explore individual cultural competence. Its purpose is to help participants consider their skills, knowledge, and awareness of themselves in their interactions with others. Its goal is to assist them to recognize what they can do to become more effective while working and living in a diverse environment (Central Vancouver Island Multicultural Society, n.d.).

The Cultural Competence Checklist: Personal Reflection

The Cultural Competence Checklist was developed by the American Speech-Language-Hearing Association to heighten awareness of how professionals view clients/patients from culturally and linguistically diverse (CLD) populations (American Speech-Language-Hearing Association, 2010).

Implicit Association Tests (IAT)

Another way to evaluate awareness is by using the IAT to help gauge personal implicate bias (see https://implicit.harvard.edu/implicit/takeatest.html). These tests have documented the existence of bias on various dimensions of diversity (e.g., gender, race, ethnicity, age, skin tone, sexual orientation) and cultures/contexts. These tests measure and compare response times to identify unstated biases, which is a great way to increase awareness. The underlying theory is that people respond more accurately and quickly to associations that fit with their own implicit social cognitions, that is, those acquired associations that are largely involuntary (Banaji & Greenwald, 2013; Greenwald et al., 1998). A comprehensive toolkit developed by the American Bar Association to teach practical ways of dealing with implicit bias could be an excellent tool for educators and employers to adapt.

Business Cultural Intelligence Quotient (BCIQ)

The BCIQ measures several CQ items on several dimensions and shows good psychometric properties and predictive power (Alon et al., 2016). The BCIQ can help workgroups identify high-potential CQ employees to improve their intercultural skills. The instrument could also help to assess the weaknesses and strengths of workers in each of the CQ dimensions in order to design the most effective training programs.

Diagnosing Your Cultural Intelligence Assessment Tool

This assessment tool allows assessing the three facets—cognitive, physical, and emotional/motivational—of one's own cultural intelligence and facilitates learning of one's relative strengths and weaknesses (Earley & Mosakowski, 2004). A six-step practical model can be followed based on the results of the tool: 1) examine strengths and weaknesses, 2) focus on improving weaknesses, 3) practice exercises to help build mastery, 4) organize resources to support efforts, 5) coordinate plans with others and reassess, and 6) get 360-degree feedback.

Intercultural Adjustment Potential Scale (ICAPS-55)

The ICAPS-55 helps predict the degree to which a person will successfully adjust to working effectively in cross-cultural environments. The ICAPS-55 can help determine one's strengths and weaknesses in order to help build cultural competency (Matsumoto et al., 2007).

Research Considerations

Future research should focus on the practicality of harnessing cross-cultural business relationships that is both qualitative and quantitative. Although the research on CQ is rich (Ang et al., 2007; Ang & Van Dyne, 2008; Ang et al., 2011; Ng et al., 2012), specific research dedicated to practical aspects is scant. Findings from research in educational and cognitive psychology show that CQ has a substantial influence on individual performance. As also discussed earlier, some of the research studies examine CQ skill as it applies to academic settings; however, studies of other contexts, such as cross-cultural settings, are needed (Phelan, 2018). Vich (2015) recommends that researchers should extend their examination of individual effects to the effects in workgroup relationships. Research is evolutionary, and the formats for measurement vary and should be improved to include performance-based measures (Ang et al., 2015).

Given earlier findings, Mor et al. (2013) hypothesized that cultural perspective-taking (i.e., considering how another's cultural background shapes behavior in each context) facilitates intercultural coordination and cooperation. Manipulation that boosts cultural perspective-taking would benefit individuals who score low in dispositional cultural metacognition. Along these lines, future research could examine the cultural metacognition effects of assigning students scoring higher on cultural metacognition to negotiate or work on class assignments with students scoring low on cultural metacognition.

As I have stated previously (Phelan, 2018), a better understanding of CQ calls for additional research and exploring the ability to accurately detect culture-specific congruent or incongruent norms, which may require the development of metacognitive habits in tandem with cognitive CQ. Additionally, more research is needed to expand on the theory that links cultural diversity with creativity, as findings suggest that conditions that allow collaboration of different cultures help increase creativity (Chua et al., 2012). Finding out what dynamics in teamwork lead to effective intercultural creative collaboration requires more research with multicultural teams. Expanding organizational research with diverse social and communicative networks and considering what innovations are needed to advance business is recommended.

Narrative research can be effective in determining communication expectations. The research built on narrative works by Gertsen and Søderberg (2011) could enable further study of how to adjust and learn while communicating across cultures, to build mutual understanding, respect, and trust that could advance business practice.

Also stated previously (Phelan, 2018), it is important to know how to build on the work of others, such as Chua et al. (2012), who found that individuals' perceptions of colleagues' reliability and competence probably do not hinge as much on the quality of their interactions as they do on their affective feelings toward their colleagues. Intervention research is needed to find out how to build affective feelings among those involved in cross-cultural business.

Conclusion

Cultural intelligence is not just a cognitive drive but also motivational, behavioral, and metacognitive. Putting CQ into practice is important in fostering "doing" rather than merely "thinking" and helps to develop an effective cross-cultural business environment. This chapter addressed several practical strategies for harnessing CQ in cross-cultural business and management. The idea is that students and practitioners will be able to use these strategies to not only create a better understanding of CQ but also practice them.

Cultural intelligence has strong theoretical underpinnings, and practicality is vital for a thriving and prosperous business environment. It was the intention that the readers walk away better equipped to practice CQ and benefit from learning, and hopefully use in the future, the various measures to gauge the practice of CQ and work towards sharpening and improving their skills.

Future research should focus on harnessing cross-cultural business relationships while looking at what works and how to broaden those enactments. Ideally, research should be both qualitative and quantitative to gain a broader understanding.

Declaration: Sections on Teaching and Integrating Cultural Metacognition, Measuring CQ, and Research Considerations, all or in part are used by permission from IGI Global.

References

Alon, I., Boulanger, M., Elston, J. A., Galanaki, E., Martínez de Ibarreta, C., Meyers, J., Muñiz-Ferrer, M., Vélez-Calle, A. (2018). Business cultural intelligence quotient: A five-country study. *Thunderbird International Business Review,* 60(3), 237–250. https://doi.org/10.1002/tie.21826

Alon, I., Boulanger, M., Meyers, J., Taras, V., Tung, R., & Ralston, D. (2016). The development and validation of the business Cultural Intelligence Quotient. *Cross*

Cultural and Strategic Management, 23(1), 78–100. https://doi.org/10.1108/CCS M-10-2015-0138

American Speech-Language-Hearing Association. (2010). Cultural competence checklist: Personal reflection. http://www.asha.org/uploadedFiles/Cultural-Competence-Checklist-Personal-Reflection.pdf

Ang, S., & Van Dyne, L. (2008). *Handbook of cultural intelligence.* M.E. Sharpe.

Ang, S., Van Dyne, L., Koh, C., Ng, K. Y., Templer, K. J., Tay, C., & Chandrasekar, N. A. (2007). Cultural intelligence: Its measurement and effects on cultural judgment and decision making, cultural adaptation and task performance. *Management and Organization Review, 3*(3), 335–371. https://doi.org/10.11 11/j.1740-8784.2007.00082.x

Ang, S., Van Dyne, L., & Rockstuhl, T. (2015). Cultural intelligence: Origins, conceptualizations, evolution, and methodological diversity. In M. J. Gelfand, C. Chiu, & Y. Hong (Eds.), *The handbook of advances in culture and psychology* (pp. 273–323). Oxford University Press.

Ang, S., Van Dyne, L., & Tan, M. L. (2011). Cultural intelligence. In Sternberg, R. J., & Kaufman, S. B. (Eds.), *The Cambridge handbook of intelligence* (pp. 582–602). Cambridge University Press.

Baker, L. (2010). Metacognition, In, P. Peterson, E. Baker, & B. McGaw (Eds), *International Encyclopedia of Education* (3e) (pp. 204-210). Elsevier. https:// doi.org/10.1016/B978-0-08-044894-7.00484-X.

Banaji, M. R., & Greenwald, A. G. (2013). *Blind spot: Hidden biases of good people.* Delacorte Press.

Bean, R. (2008). *Cross-cultural training and workplace performance.* National Centre for Vocational Education Research. https://files.eric.ed.gov/fulltext/ ED503402.pdf.

Bucher, R. D. (2008). *Building cultural intelligence (CQ): Nine megaskills.* Pearson.

Central Vancouver Island Multicultural Society. (n.d.). *Cultural competence self-assessment checklist.* http://rapworkers.com/wp-content/uploads/2017 /08/cultural-competence-selfassessment-checklist-1.pdf

Chua, R. Y. J., Morris, M. W., & Mor, S. (2012). Collaborating across cultures: Cultural metacognition and affect-based trust in creative collaboration. *Organizational Behavior and Human Decision Processes, 118*(2), 179–188. https://doi.org/10.1016/j.obhdp.2012.03.005

Cultural Intelligence Center. (n.d.). *Cultural intelligence self-assessments.* https://culturalq.com/products-services/assessments/cqselfassessments/

Dirkes, M. A. (1985). Metacognition: Students in charge of their thinking. *Roeper Review, 8*(2), 96–100. https://doi.org/10.1080/02783198509552944

Dolan, S. L., & Kawamura, K. M. (2015). *Cross cultural competence: A field guide for developing global leaders and managers.* Emerald.

Earley, P. C., & Ang, S. (2003). *Cultural intelligence: Individual interactions across cultures.* Stanford University Press.

Earley, P. C., & Mosakowski, E. (2004, October). Cultural intelligence. *Harvard Business Review, 82*(10), 139–46. https://hbr.org/2004/10/cultural-intelligence

Earley, P. C., & Peterson, R. S. (2004). The elusive Cultural Chameleon: Cultural Intelligence as a new approach to intercultural training for the global manager. *Academy of Management Learning and Education, 3*(1), 100–115. https://doi.org/10.5465/AMLE.2004.12436826

Emamjomehzadeh, S. J., Damirchi, Q. V., Zamanzadeh, D. & Sharifi, S. (2012). The cross-cultural adaptability among university facilities. *Interdisciplinary Journal of Contemporary Research in Business, 3* (19), 205-212.

Gertsen, M. C., & Søderberg, A. (2011). Intercultural collaboration stories: On narrative inquiry and analysis as tools for research in international business. *Journal of International Business Studies, 42*(6), 787–804. https://doi.org/10.1057/jibs.2011.15

Graham, N. (n.d.). The why behind DEI: How diversity, equity, and inclusion initiatives benefit business. *Workhuman.* https://www.workhuman.com/resources/globoforce-blog/the-why-behind-d-i-how-diversity-and-inclusion-initiatives-benefit-business

Greenwald, A. G., McGhee, D. E., & Schwartz, J. L. K. (1998). Measuring individual differences in implicit cognition: The implicit association test. *Journal of Personality and Social Psychology, 74*(6), 1464–1480. https://doi.org/10.1037//0022-3514.74.6.1464

Kelley, C. & Meyers, J. E. (1993*). Cross-Cultural Adaptability Inventory manual.* National Computer Systems.

Kinne, A. (2020, July 22). Back to basics: What are career milestones? *Workhuman.* https://www.workhuman.com/resources/globoforce-blog/back-to-basics-what-are-career-milestones

Kolovou, T. (2020, February 21). *Developing cross-cultural intelligence: Working across cultures: A path of discovery.* LinkedIn Learning.

Lovelace, D. (n.d.). *Communication within teams.* LinkedIn Learning. https://www.linkedin.com/learning/communication-within-teams/how-high-performing-teams-communicate?u=70115025

Marmer, R. L., Ridgeway, D. A., Sherman, C. E., Bass, H., & Epps, J. (n.d.). *Implicit bias task force toolkit PowerPoint instruction manual ABA section of litigation.* Academic Press.

Matsumoto, D., LeRoux, J. A., Robles, Y., & Campos, G. (2007). The Intercultural Adjustment Potential Scale (ICAPS) predicts adjustment above and beyond personality and general intelligence. *International Journal of Intercultural Relations, 31*(6), 747–759. https://doi.org/10.1016/j.ijintrel.2007.08.002

Molinsky, A. (2018). *Boost your cultural intelligence* [Video file]. https://valo.skillport.com/skillportfe/main.action?assetid=141695

Mor, S., Morris, M. W., & Joh, J. (2013). Identifying and training adaptive cross-cultural management skills: The crucial role of cultural metacognition. *Academy of Management Learning and Education, 12*(3), 453–475. https://doi.org/10.5465/amle.2012.0202

Ng, K.-Y., Van Dyne, L., & Ang, S. (2012). Cultural intelligence: A review, reflections, and recommendations for future research. In A. M. Ryan, F. T. L. Leong, & F. L. Oswald (Eds.), *Conducting multinational research: Applying organizational psychology in the workplace* (pp. 29–58). American Psychological Association.

Phelan, J. E. (2018). Research, theories, and pedagogical practices of cultural metacognition in cross-cultural business education. In C. G. Maheshkar & V. Sharma (Eds.), *Handbook of research in cross-cultural business education* (pp. 115–139). IGI Global. https://doi.org/10.4018/978-1-5225-3776-2.ch006.

Rowe, M. (2008). Micro-affirmations and micro-inequities. *Journal of the International Ombudsman Association, 1*(1), 1–9.

Roy, D. (2019). The adaptation of cross-cultural competence. *Training Industry, 13*(1). https://www.nxtbook.com/nxtbooks/trainingindustry/tiq_2 0191112/index.php#/p/52

Schmitz, A. (2012). *Leading with cultural intelligence*. Saylor Academy. Retrieved from https://saylordotorg.github.io/text_leading-with-cultural-intelligence/index.html

Scroggins, W. A., Mackie, D. M., Allen, T. J., & Sherman, J. W. (2016). Reducing prejudice with labels: Shared group memberships attenuate implicit bias and expand implicit group boundaries. *Personality and Social Psychology Bulletin, 42*(2), 219–229. https://doi.org/10.1177/0146167215621048

Society for Human resource Management (SHRM). (2015). Cultural intelligence: The essential intelligence for the 21st century. SHRM Foundation. Retrieved from https://www.shrm.org/hr-today/trends-and-forecasting/special-reports -and-expert-views/Documents/Cultural-Intelligence.pdf

Staats, C., Capatosto, K., Tenney, L., & Mamo, S. (2017). *Implicit bias review*. https://kirwaninstitute.osu.edu/

Stallard, M. L., Pankau, J., & Stallard, K. P. (2015). *Connection culture*. ATD Press.

Sternberg, R. J. (1988). *The triarchic mind: A new theory of human intelligence*. Viking Press.

Sue, D. W., Capodilupo, C. M., Torino, G. C., Bucceri, J. M., Holder, A. M., Nadal, K. L., & Esquilin, M. (2007). Racial microaggressions in everyday life: Implications for clinical practice. *American Psychologist, 62*(4), 271–286. https://doi.org/10.1037/0003-066X.62.4.271

The Economic Times. (2021, June 13). *Amway plans to invest Rs 170 crore over the next two to three years in India*. Retrieved from https://economictimes. indiatimes.com/news/company/corporate-trends/amway-plans-to-invest -rs-170-crore-over-the-next-two-to-three-years-in-india/articleshow/83480 060.cms?utm_source=contentofinterest&utm_medium=text&utm_campaig n=cppst

Van der Zee, K.I., & Van Oudenhoven, J.P. (2000). The Multicultural Personality Questionnaire: A multidimensional instrument of multicultural effectiveness. *European Journal of Personality, 14*(4), 291–309.

Van Dyne, L., Ang, S., & Koh, C. (2008). Development and validation of the CQS: The cultural intelligence scale. In S. Ang & L. Van Dyne (Eds.), *Handbook of cultural intelligence: Theory, measurement, and application* (pp. 16–38). M.E. Sharpe.

Van Dyne, L., Ang, S., Ng, K. Y., Rockstuhl, T., Tan, M. L., & Koh, C. (2012). Sub-Dimensions of the Four Factor Model of Cultural Intelligence: Expanding the conceptualization and measurement of cultural intelligence. *Social and Personality Psychology Compass, 6*(4), 295–313. https://doi.org/10.1111/j.17 51-9004.2012.00429.x

Vich, M. (2015). The emerging role of mindfulness research in the workplace and its challenges. *Central European Business Review, 4*(3), 35–47. https:// doi.org/10.18267/j.cebr.131

Victor, D. A. (1992). *International business communication.* HarperCollins.

Wallis, A. (2020). *How to create a personal growth and development plan.* Southern New Hampshire University. Retrieved July 21, 2021 from https:// www.snhu.edu/about-us/newsroom/2018/07/personal-development-plan

Wong, G., Derthick, A. O., David, E. J. R., Saw, A., & Okazaki, S. (2014). The what, the why, and the how: A review of racial microaggressions research in psychology. *Race and Social Problems, 6*(2), 181–200. https://doi.org/10.100 7/s12552-013-9107-9

Chapter 5

Breaking the Borders: An Overview of Cultural Intelligence

Rupa Rathee

Deenbandhu Chhotu Ram University of Science and Technology, India

Madhvi Lamba

Deenbandhu Chhotu Ram University of Science and Technology, India

Abstract: Cultural Intelligence, a term that came into the limelight in 2002, has an extreme significance in cross-cultural interaction. As expatriates move into the international market, diversity doesn't limit itself to demographic but rather extremely high demographic diversity; they also experience experiential and cognitive diversity where the importance of cultural intelligence becomes necessary. Cultural intelligence is a cultural capability that can be inculcated through formal education and training. It helps in cross-cultural adaptation and adjustments. Why is it important to adjust cross-culturally? It has a major impact on the performance and effectiveness of the expatriates. This chapter emphasizes breaking the borders: an overview of cultural intelligence, which talks about the importance of cultural intelligence, sources and precursors of cultural intelligence, formal education and training to enhance cross-cultural adjustments and the role mindfulness can play in cultural intelligence. This study is entirely based on exploratory analysis.

Keywords: Cultural Intelligence (CQ), Expatriates, Culture, Mindfulness, social, Individual

***

Introduction

The terminology 'Cultural Intelligence' or 'Cultural Quotient (CQ)' was introduced in 2002; it is gaining popularity nowadays (Fang et al., 2018). CQ fascinates the interest of many researchers because it is associated with impactful functioning in a culturally diverse work environment. It is a different factor and is mainly studied in multicultural contexts (Bernardo &

Presbitero, 2018). What does CQ actually mean? The idea of CQ is based on the contemporary theories of intelligence. It simply means the capability of individuals to manage effectively at the international level (Guðmundsdóttir, 2015). In a world where everything is connected globally, employees, managers, expatriates and others are involved in cross-cultural interactions. Their capability to interconnect with people of diverse cultures is termed CQ. The empirical research in CQ began around 2008 and focuses on the methods to develop CQ in people nowadays (Fang et al., 2018).

Values and norms are necessary facets of a person because they direct the individuals about what is valued in the social environment. CQ is a multidimensional construct because CQ means the interaction between diverse individuals; these interactions are known as cross-cultural interactions. The diverse nature says there is a difference between individuals, regardless of race, ethnicity or nationality. CQ tries to understand inter-individual differences. By understanding these differences, the ability to adapt these differences effectively to a new cultural environment can be developed (Guðmundsdóttir, 2015).

Why do organizations invest so much in such a trait as "cultural intelligence"? The reason behind the vast amount of cross-cultural interaction is globalization. Many organizations are transforming their businesses and expanding to international markets, but it all depends on an expatriate's transfer of knowledge from their home country to the host country (Guðmundsdóttir, 2015). Many organizations and management give so much importance to this trait because they require expatriates to manifest their entire knowledge, potential, energy and confidence in CQ to accomplish the task effectively and efficiently despite their origin. CQ exhibits why some people work and interact so wonderfully in international markets other than those who don't possess this quality (Chen, 2015). The reason behind this is that people with CQ are culturally aware, and intercultural training has enhanced the awareness of these individuals and sensitizes them to cultural differences (Fischer, 2011). They can adjust cross-culturally well, which means they have psychological comfort and are well acquainted with the numerous facets of the international environment during expatriation (Hu et al., 2019).

Literature Review

Intelligence is a broad term, and many researchers proposed the g-theory, the theory of general mental ability. Those who believe in this theory generally don't follow the theory of multiple intelligence. CQ is also considered one of the facets of the theory of multiple intelligence, emotional intelligence, and social intelligence (Crowne, 2014). CQ is "the capability of an individual to function effectively in situations characterized by cultural diversity" (Ang & Dyne, 2008, p. 3; Fang et al., 2018).

Eight definitions of CQ have been given by Thomas et al. (2008), which vary from one another, amongst which his definition describes CQ as "a system of interacting knowledge, linked by cultural metacognition that allows people to adapt to, select, and shape the cultural aspects of their environment" (Thomas et al., 2008, p. 126; Fang et al., 2018). CQ enables people to "look beyond their own cultural lens" (Earley, 2002, p. 285; Fang et al., 2018). Is the difference between CQ, social intelligence and emotional intelligence (EQ) possible? Indeed, Yes. How? CQ considers diverse culture, whereas EQ and social intelligence doesn't look around the cultural aspect (Earley, 2002; Fang et al., 2018). CQ is associated with EQ, but the major thing is that CQ begins where EQ ends (Earley & Mosakowski, 2004).

CQ is quintessential as it is related to the effective functioning where the culture is diverse (Bernardo & Presbitero, 2018). It is quintessential to answer the difference between intelligence and intelligent behaviour before answering this question. Intelligent behaviour is an outcome of intelligence. The different behaviours can be demonstrated in different cultures even after having the same mental process. That is why intelligence carries supreme importance in "cultural intelligence", as it is necessary to have the attributes of intelligence in order to be culturally intelligent (Thomas et al., 2008).

The conceptual building of CQ is based on the triarchic intelligence theory of Sternberg, which talks about the functioning of individuals in different situations or experiences. The role of cognitive, behavioural and motivational capabilities matters in the individual's functioning (Bernardo & Presbitero, 2018). Let's understand the triarchic intelligence theory. According to Sternberg's theory, there are three types of intellectual abilities: a) analytic, b) creative, and c) practical. Analytic abilities allow individuals to examine, assess, elucidate, and compare. Creative abilities help problem-solving as those who possess the ability to create, design, discover and develop. Practical abilities enable individuals to implement problem-solving processes (Howard et al., 2001). This theory is an amalgamation of three sub-theories: a) contextual sub-theory, b) componential sub-theory, and c) two-facet sub-theory. The contextual sub-theory is associated with the intended adjustment to the external environment, shaping and forming an appropriate external environment for the individuals. This sub-theory talks about the intelligence to deal with the external environment. The componential sub-theory defines the mental mechanism, which is essential for learning, arranging, executing and assessing intelligent behaviour. It talks about critical intellect. The two-facet theory deals with both the kind of intelligence, i.e. internal as well as external intelligence (Sternberg, 1984).

Cultural adjustments seem to be important in order to adapt new environment. It is quintessential to adapt new environment (Guðmundsdóttir, 2015) in order to prevent oneself from cultural shock. When individuals need to learn and adapt to a wide range of cultural norms, standards, ethics and taboos in a new environment, then there is a possibility that individuals may experience a generalized trauma. That trauma is described as cultural shock. In order to prevent individuals from cultural shock, intercultural training becomes important (Earley, 1987).

Methodology

This study explores the sources from where the CQ arises. It also provides insights into the various dimensions of CQ to understand it in a better manner. This paper brings all four factors together which form CQ and also explains the precursors of the CQ. Ways to enhance CQ are explained by various training and simulation methods.

A number of papers from reputed journals have been reviewed to understand these facets of cross-cultural intelligence and how they can be improved.

Sources of CQ

According to Earley & Mosakowski (2004), the individual's head, body and heart are where CQ resides. Head enables individuals to remember other countries' customs, norms, beliefs and taboos.

For instance, an Indian joins a multinational company as an expatriate in America and doesn't know much about American culture. It will be difficult for the individual to adapt to the new environment or culture. The culture of the countries varies, and so does the culture of India and America. America is a monochronic country, whereas India is a polychronic country. The USA is low context-oriented, whereas India has high context culture (Madhavan, 2016). So, in order to adjust to a new environment successfully, an Indian must be aware of the American culture. To be aware of American culture, one must know the beliefs, norms, customs and taboos in an individual's head. The body can reflect your gestures' customs, norms and beliefs (Earley & Mosakowski, 2004).

For instance, the language of space in the Edward Hall model defines the reflection of gestures very well. Japanese and Asian are not comfortable getting touched even in business, whereas Arabs and Latin Americans are fine with it (Madhavan, 2016). If an Arabian tries to contact an Asian in close physical proximity, the Asian might be uncomfortable. Confronting all the obstacles and getting back towards developing the capability to adapt to a new culture comes under the heart (Earley & Mosakowski, 2004).

CQ is not restricted to one type of knowledge but is based on multiple understandings. It involves the understanding of comprehensive and detailed information and its applications. It also involves understanding and managing the thinking and learning of individuals. Understanding and managing the thinking and learning of individuals come under metacognition and cognition (Thomas et al., 2008). Studies (e.g., Guðmundsdóttir, 2015) show that a higher level of normal adaptation is associated with high meta-cognitive and motivational CQ. The rising levels of interrelated adjustments are associated with the high meta-cognitive and motivational CQ. A high level of work adjustment is also associated with the meta-cognitive CQ.

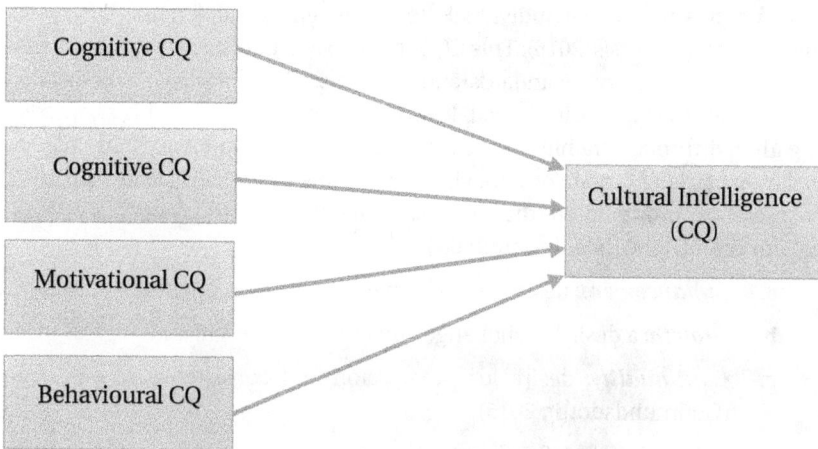

Figure 5.1: Constructs of Cultural Intelligence

There are four major constructs of CQ (Guðmundsdóttir, 2015; Fang et al., 2018):

1. Metacognitive CQ
2. Cognitive CQ
3. Motivational CQ
4. Behavioural CQ

1. *Metacognitive CQ* is defined as "an individual's level of conscious cultural awareness during cross-cultural interactions" (Ang & Dyne, 2008, p. 5; Fang et al., 2018). It enables individuals to adjust, adapt and form the cultural facets of their surroundings (Thomas et al., 2008). The meta-cognitive level requires individuals to be mindful in order to discern and expound on a particular event (Bergh & Plessis, 2016). It is a mental process adopted by individuals to obtain and recognize the cultural understanding of the host country. Observing, planning and altering mental models related to cultural standards are associated with meta-cognition (Guðmundsdóttir, 2015).

2. *Cognitive CQ* is defined as "knowledge of norms, practices and conventions in different cultures that have been acquired from educational and personal experiences" (Ang & Van Dyne, 2008, p. 5; Fang et al., 2018). The cognitive level requires expertise to recognize the cultural phenomenon. Cognition incorporates the procedures of knowing, covering the entire range of mental functioning, which can be used in obtaining apprehension about something. Regarding CQ, cognition stands for the understanding of the basic principles of interactions used in a cross-cultural environment, that is, basic cognitive compositions and substructures to succour individuals to make sense to differentiate between things (Bergh & Plessis, 2016). This CQ is composed of the knowledge associated with the host country's standards and practices. The knowledge is associated with various host countries' social, legal and economic factors. This knowledge is gathered through training, education and personal experiences. In order to make expatriates capable enough to use this knowledge and construct responses appropriate to the culture, three primary motivators are used: enhancement, growth and continuality.

a.   ***Enhancement:*** desire to have a pleasurable emotion about oneself;

b.   ***Growth:*** a desire to challenge and enhance oneself; and

c.   ***Continuality:*** desire for progression and consistency in one's life (Guðmundsdóttir, 2015).

3. *Motivational CQ* is defined as the "capability to direct attention and energy towards learning about and functioning in situations characterized by cultural differences" (Ang & Van Dyne, 2008, p. 5; Fang et al., 2018). Individuals can learn and act in a culturally diverse environment (Guðmundsdóttir, 2015). People with high intensity of motivational CQ are curious to perceive and learn about the societal norm to adjust to a new culture. There are two major constituents of motivational CQ: a) intrinsic motivation and b) self-efficacy. Intrinsic motivation considers the interaction with other people from a different culture as beatitude. Self-efficacy is the trust and ability to guide and exert efforts to accomplish the interaction in an intercultural environment even when the situation is not so easy (Peng et al., 2015).

4. *Behavioural CQ* is defined as the "capability to exhibit appropriate verbal and non-verbal actions when interacting with people from different cultures" (Ang & Van Dyne, 2008, p. 6; Fang et al., 2018). It comprises body language, tones and gestures (Engle & Crowne, 2013). It is a behaviour in which an individual engages and can adopt and adapt behaviours appropriate according to the new culture (Guðmundsdóttir, 2015).

Precursors of CQ

There are various precursors of CQ (Fang et al., 2018):

- Big Five Personality Trait
- Personality
- Intercultural Experience
- Language Ability and International Orientation
- Context-dependence
- Social Intelligence
- Spanning
- Self-monitoring
- Identity
- Cultural Boundary
- Polyculturalism and Multiculturalism

Big Five Personality Trait

On a broader level, personality is nothing but a pattern of an individual's behavioural, emotional, mental and temperamental traits. The Big Five Factor, or OCEAN model, which stands for Openness, Conscientiousness, Extraversion, Agreeableness and Neuroticism, is one of the popular models of personality (Durupınar, 2011). People open to new experiences are artistic, creative, broad-minded, culture-oriented and intelligent. People with high conscientiousness performed better at work than low conscientious people. Agreeable people are soft-hearted, amiable, altruist, cooperative and flexible. Highly emotionally stable people are calm and can manage their temper in their daily routines. People who score high in extraversion are assertive, enthusiastic, bold, and sociable. The OCEAN model is an important model because it is one of the stable models which bifurcate the personality into five different traits. Various types of research have shown a strong association between work behaviour and OCEAN Model (Ang et al., 2006). Outcomes stated that conscientiousness and extraversion were affirmatively associated with the metacognitive CQ. Agreeableness was positive, while emotional stability was negatively associated with the behavioural and overall CQ. Openness to experience was positively associated with all four dimensions of CQ (Fang et al., 2018; Ang et al., 2006).

Intercultural experience

Past studies show that those who had stayed abroad as students or expatriates, even for a short time, have higher CQ than those who visited as tourists on vacations (Engle & Crowne, 2013). Exposure to a multicultural environment relates to higher metacognitive and overall (Fang et al., 2018) CQ.

Identity and social intelligence were positively associated with metacognitive CQ, while language ability and orientation towards international culture (Fang et al., 2018) are affirmatively associated with overall CQ. Identity can be bifurcated into different types. It can be personal, religious or multi-ethnic. Ethnic identity was an affirmative predictor of cognitive CQ, while religious identity was a negative predictor (Fang et al., 2018).

Polyculturalism and multiculturalism were affirmatively associated with the overall CQ. Cultural boundary spanners had high CQ in all aspects. Self-monitoring was affirmatively associated with overall CQ, while the perceived promotion was affirmatively related to the metacognitive and motivational CQ. Language ability and international orientation were affirmatively associated with the overall CQ (Fang et al., 2018).

Cross-Cultural Training Programs

The training programs are categorized into two parts:

1. Based on the participation of employees (low, medium or high)

2. The focus of the intervention (aim to transform behaviour, affect or cognition).

Intercultural training can be of two types (Fischer, 2011):

1. Lecture method

2. Experiential method

1. Lecture Method: The lecture method is described as the one in which participants are passively given lectures based on culture-related topics (Fischer, 2011).

Advantages:

a. It is cost-effective;

b. The nature of the participants is non-threatening;

c. The probability of transmitting the information in a short period in terms of quantity is high; and

d. The acceptance of information by the participants is high.

Disadvantages:

a. Due to the passive nature of the lectures, participants might be less involved. Therefore, a lack of active engagement can be witnessed.

b. Lack of active engagement can lead to less effective lectures.

2. Experiential Method: Experiential methods can be of different types. Role plays, simulation games, and behaviour modification training are part of experiential training methods. The following two experiential methods are discussed in brief.

1. BaFa-BaFa
2. Excel

1. BaFa-BaFa: BaFa-BaFa is an intercultural (Fischer, 2011) simulation game (face-to-face) introduced by Dr. R. Garry Shirts in 1974. This technique helps in enhancing the cross-cultural competence of the participants, such as intercultural awareness and adaptability to the new environment (Fischer, 2011), by making them understand the effect of culture on the behaviour of people and organizations.

How can this simulation technique be used?

The contestants are bifurcated into two groups. They are taught about complex values, behavioural standards and styles of communication which will let them know how to behave in a culture other than their own culture. Then two individuals from different cultures interact with each other using the cultural scripts they have learnt. The individuals encounter a cultural shock, barriers associated with communication and the general experience of interaction with other people from different cultures with non-identical cultural standards. This activity is challenging and requires a high level of emotional involvement. The reason behind this is the differences in cultural norms, and participants can't easily decipher another group's values and behaviours, which leads to communication breakdown. At the end of the session, contestants share their reactions, points of view and sentiments. Subsequently, the emphasis is on sharpening contestants to the power of social standards and permitting the members to question their social standards, assumptions and identity (Fischer, 2011).

The BaFa-BaFa has three versions:

1) For high schools, charities and universities
2) For middle school age (RaFa-RaFa)
3) For business and government agencies- Professional version

This training method can be used in ("BaFa' BaFa',"):

a. Diversity and inclusion training;
b. Management training;
c. Classes of Sociology;

d. Preparing (Peace Corps, missionaries and military) to travel to different cultures; and

e. Staff and professionals of medical and educators.

2 Excel: It is training that modifies behaviour. This theory focuses on the inculcation of key sociocultural competencies that will help individuals survive and negotiate in a new culture. Sociocultural competencies can be participation in group discussions, making contact and expressing disagreement. Sociocultural competencies can be participation in group discussions, making contact and expressing disagreement. This theory works on the principle of social learning theory. It involves learning through observations.

In this training method, participants develop a cultural map, also called a behavioural map which helps them to negotiate in new surroundings.

This training method can be used to enhance the following:

a) Social efficacy.

b) Social interaction skills.

Evidence shows that the combination of lecture and experiential training is more appropriate than any individual training method. This is because it provides an equilibrium between participants' active engagement and the training's aim (behaviour, affect or cognition) (Fischer, 2011).

Cultural competence is a quintessential skill set (Fischer, 2011). The number of expatriates is increasing nowadays. Whether the expatriates in the given assignment will succeed depends upon the individuals' cross-cultural adjustment skills (Guðmundsdóttir, 2015).

The intercultural training programs are bifurcated by considering five comprehensive perspectives (Earley, 1987):

1. Documentary programs: exposure of individuals to a new culture with the help of other countries' written material (history, economy, geography and culture).

2. Culture assimilator: individuals are exposed to the new culture with critical incident techniques.

3. Preparation of the language of the target country.

4. Sensitivity training: Rising self-awareness of individuals.

5. Experience in the field: Expose the individuals to the glance of the culture of other countries in their own country.

Earley (1987) also defined the onsite and offsite methods of intercultural training and suggested that sending individuals to new cultures can help them adjust flexibly to the new environment.

Role of Mindfulness in CQ

Mindfulness is a Buddhist meditation practice (Hülsheger et al., 2013; White, 2014). In psychology, mindfulness is described as paying attention to the experiences that individuals experience from moment to moment without any judgment (White, 2014). There are three attributes important to mindfulness: a) empathy, b) open-mindedness, and c) using all the senses. How is mindfulness associated with the CQ? Mindfulness is about being attentive in the present moment (Hülsheger et al., 2013), and motivational CQ is about being attentive to learn about cultural differences (Fang et al., 2018). Hence, what becomes quintessential is to develop a capability to integrate the old and new cultural knowledge, which can provide a better glance towards the similarities and dissimilarities of the culture, enabling individuals to develop new behavioural routines that can help to meet the demands of the different cultural settings. The three attributes are also associated with CQ cognition (Kaufman & Hwang, 2012).

Behavioral ability also plays an important role in CQ, and generating appropriate behavior is very important. Behavioral ability can be generated by an appropriate combination of knowledge as well as mindfulness. Many researchers show that picking up appropriate behaviour in an intercultural environment is an added advantage that may lead to an affirmative attitude (Thomas, 2016). The training associated with mindfulness is vital as it helps reduce stress, enhances awareness, and provides clarity and insights into the context of emotions and thoughts. Empathy training can also be used for employee training which further impacts the behavioural ability of the employees (Kaufman & Hwang, 2012).

CQ is not a one-time process. It takes a lot of time to be produced. So, when knowledge is combined with mindfulness, it generates behaviour and then again, the same process is followed to generate behavioural ability, which is quintessential in a cross-cultural environment (Thomas, 2016).

Cross-Cultural Adjustments

The personality of expatriates has an impact on cross-cultural adjustments. Motivational CQ is affirmatively associated with cross-cultural adjustment, and psychological comfort is associated with behavioral CQ. Motivational CQ and behavioral CQ make a major impact on whether an expatriate would be able to manage in a new country or not (Kumar et al., 2008). The general estimation of the time individuals need to adjust to the new cultural surrounding is six months. However, this time can vary as per the conditions. The conditions can be time taken to acquire a new language, previous experiences in an international context, cross-cultural training, the family's ability in the new surroundings and cultural novelty.

Cross-cultural transformations can be bifurcated into two parts:

a) Psychological

b) Sociocultural

Psychological adjustments are defined as the degree of comfort or ease perceived within new surroundings.

Sociocultural adjustments: Sociocultural adjustments are located within the behavioral domain. It is the capability to fit in or interact effectively in a new cultural environment (Guðmundsdóttir, 2015).

As diversity is increasing in Western countries, citizens and the young workforce must be prepared to accept the differences better. Intercultural training helps individuals deal with the differences that occur due to the differences in cultures (Fischer, 2011). It is a process that enhances the individuals' abilities to adjust to a cross-cultural environment. The main aim of intercultural training is to make individuals capable of dealing with uncertain events in another country. It further helps decrease conflicts arising due to uncertain situations (Earley, 1987).

Conclusion

CQ is a term coined lately but plays a significant role in the lives of expatriates. Over time, the demand for CQ has increased among expatriates. CQ is awareness of the culture, norms, standards, values and taboos of a country where an expatriate is going so that the individual can adjust well to a new environment. CQ is vital in a cross-cultural environment. Cross-cultural interactions are increasing daily, and the work environment is becoming dynamic. Without CQ, it won't be easy to deal with people of diverse cultures. People do not only vary in demographic compositions; rather, diversity can also be seen in experiences and cognition and to deal with such diversity, CQ plays a vital role. Though there are many precursors of CQ, like intercultural experiences, big five personality traits, language ability, self-monitoring, polyculturalism and multiculturalism, there are four significant constructs of CQ: meta-cognitive, cognitive, motivational and behavioral CQ. The precursors are somehow affirmatively or negatively associated with the CQ. When individuals come across new cultures without awareness, they may encounter a cultural shock.

Intercultural training can reduce cultural shock. Intercultural training makes individuals aware of other cultures by enhancing their knowledge or with the help of various simulation activities. Cross-cultural training and simulation techniques help to overcome the issues like cultural shocks. Techniques like lectures, experiential methods, BaFa-BaFa and Excel are explained, which helps defeat issues associated with cultural shock. Moreover, mindfulness can play a critical role in enhancing the CQ of individuals. Development of behavioural capability can allow expatriates to adjust better to a cross-cultural environment. It has been seen that individuals who received intercultural training were more capable of adjusting to other cultures than individuals who didn't receive the training. Cross-cultural training help in adapting to the differences of the individuals and allows people to survive in new surroundings. Cross-cultural transformations are necessary when one goes in order to accomplish foreign assignments. It cannot be done in one go, but such methods and techniques allow expatriates to cope with cross-cultural adjustment and adjust to other environments where they go for a foreign assignment.

References

Ang, S., & Van Dyne, L. (2008). Conceptualization of cultural intelligence: Definition, distinctiveness, and nomological network. In S. Ang, & L. Van Dyne (Eds.), *Handbook of cultural intelligence: Theory, measurement, and applications* (pp. 3–15). Sharpe.

Ang, S., Van Dyne, L., & Koh, C. (2006). *Personality Correlates of the Four-Factor Model of Cultural Intelligence. Group & Organization Management, 31(1), 100–123.* https://doi.org/10.1177/1059601105275267

Bergh, R. V. D. & Plessis, Y. D. (2016). *The Role of Cognitive and Meta-Cognitive Cultural Intelligence in The Adjustment Experiences of SIE Women.* European Academy of Management, Paris.

Bernardo, A. B. I., & Presbitero, A. (2018). Cognitive flexibility and cultural intelligence: Exploring the cognitive aspects of effective functioning in culturally diverse contexts. *International Journal of Intercultural Relations, 66,* 12–21. https://doi.org/10.1016/j.ijintrel.2018.06.001

Chen, A. S. (2015). International Journal of Intercultural Relations CQ at work and the impact of intercultural training: An empirical test among foreign laborers. *International Journal of Intercultural Relations, 47,* 101–112. https://doi.org/10.1016/j.ijintrel.2015.03.029

Crowne, K. A. (2012). The relationships among social intelligence, emotional intelligence and cultural intelligence. *Organization Management Journal, 6(3),* 37–41. https://doi.org/10.1057/omj.2009.20

Durupinar, F., Pelechano, N., Allbeck, J. M., Gudukbay, U., & Badler, N. I. (2011). How the Ocean personality model affects the perception of crowds. *IEEE computer graphics and applications, 31(3),* 22–31. https://doi.org/10.1109/MCG.2009.105

Earley, P. C. (1987). Intercultural Training for Managers: A Comparison of Documentary and Interpersonal Methods. *Academy of Management Journal, 30*(4), 685–698. https://doi.org/10.5465/256155

Earley, P. C. (2002). Redefining interactions across cultures and organizations: Moving forward with cultural intelligence. *Research in Organizational Behavior, 24,* 271–299. https://doi.org/10.1016/S0191-3085(02)24008-3.

Earley, P. C., & Mosakowski, E. (2004). Cultural Intelligence. Retrieved from https://hbr.org/2004/10/cultural-intelligence

Engle, R. L. & Crowne, K. A. (2013). The impact of international experience on cultural intelligence: an application of contact theory in a structured short-term programme. *Human Resource Development International, 17*(1), 30–46. https://doi.org/10.1080/13678868.2013.856206

Fang, F., Schei, V., & Selart, M. (2018). International Journal of Intercultural Relations Hype or hope? A new look at the research on cultural intelligence. *International Journal of Intercultural Relations, 66.* https://doi.org/10.1016/j.ijintrel.2018.04.002

Fischer, R. (2011). Cross-cultural training effects on cultural essentialism beliefs and cultural intelligence. *International Journal of Intercultural Relations, 35*(6), 767–775. https://doi.org/10.1016/j.ijintrel.2011.08.005

Guðmundsdóttir, S. (2015). Nordic expatriates in the US: The relationship between cultural intelligence and adjustment. *International Journal of Intercultural Relations, 47,* 175–186. https://doi.org/10.1016/j.ijintrel.2015.05.001

Howard, B. C., McGee, S., Shin, N., & Shia, R. (2001). The triarchic theory of intelligence and computer-based inquiry learning. *Educational Technology Research and Development, 49*(4), 49–69. https://doi.org/10.1007/BF02504947

Hu, N., Wu, J., & Gu, J. (2019). Cultural intelligence and employees' creative performance: The moderating role of team conflict in interorganizational teams. *Journal of Management & Organization, 25*(1), 96–116. https://doi.org/10.1017/jmo.2016.64

Hülsheger, U. R., Alberts, H. J. E. M., Feinholdt, A., & Lang, J. W. B. (2013). Benefits of mindfulness at work: The role of mindfulness in emotion regulation, emotional exhaustion, and job satisfaction. *Journal of Applied Psychology, 98*(2), 310–325. https://doi.org/10.1037/a0031313

Kaufman, S. R., & Hwang, A. (2012). The Role of Mindfulness in Cultural Intelligence (CQ). *Pace Pacing and Clinical Electrophysiology, 2003,* 87601–87619.

Kumar, N., Rose, R. C., & Ramalu, S. (2008). The Effects of Personality and Cultural Intelligence on International Assignment Effectiveness: A Review. *Journal of Social Sciences, 4*(4), 320–328. https://doi.org/10.3844/jssp.2008.320.328

Madhavan, S. (2016). *Cross cultural management- Concepts and Cases (2e).* Oxford University Press.

Peng, A. C., Van Dyne, L., & Oh, K. (2015). The Influence of Motivational Cultural Intelligence on Cultural Effectiveness Based on Study Abroad: The Moderating Role of Participant's Cultural Identity. *Journal of Management Education, 39*(5), 572–596. https://doi.org/10.1177/1052562914555717

Sternberg, R. J. (1984). Toward a triarchic theory of human intelligence. *Behavioral and Brain Sciences, 7*(2), 269–287. https://doi.org/10.1017/S0140 525X00044629

Thomas, D. C. (2016). Domain and development of cultural intelligence: The importance of mindfulness. *Group & Organization Management* 31(1), 78–99. https://doi.org/10.1177/1059601105275266

Thomas, D. C., Elron, E., Stahl, G., Ekelund, B. Z., Ravlin, E. C., Cerdin, J. L., & Maznevski, M. (2008). Cultural intelligence: Domain and assessment. *International Journal of Cross Cultural Management, 8*(2), 123–143. https://doi.org/10.1177/1470595808091787

White, N. (2014). *Mechanisms of Mindfulness: Evaluating Theories and Proposing a Model* (Unpublished master's thesis). Victoria University of Wellington, New Zealand. https://researcharchive.vuw.ac.nz/xmlui/bitstream /handle/10063/3377/thesis.pdf?sequence=2

Chapter 6

Business Management Theories: Relevance and Implications in Cross-Cultural Business World

Tarika Nandedkar

Institute of Business Management and Research

(IPS Academy), Indore, India

Amit Kumar

Institute of Business Management and Research
(IPS Academy), Indore, India

Abstract: Every decade acknowledged the formulation and introduction of business management theories proposed by researchers, academicians, and psychologists. Management theories and models have been developed to strengthen entrepreneurs for efficiently handling cross cultural issues and effective decision making, covering the different dimensions of the business world. Researchers analyze the relevance and importance of these models and theories from time to time. The present chapter includes four business management theories, viz. *Scientific Management Theory, System Management Theory, Theory X and Y,* and *Contingency Management.* The chapter explains these theories concerning the current business environment and discusses its relevance in the cross-cultural world. With the help of popular management theories, modern management techniques, contingency management, handling of cross-cultural issues, resources planning, and decision making have been discussed concerning the current dynamic world.

Keywords: Management Theories, Socio-cultural, Cross-Cultural Issues, System Management, Scientific Management, Theory X, Theory Y, Contingency Theory

***

Introduction

Business Management

Business management refers to the activities of planning, organizing, and coordinating resources for smooth business operations and decision-making. It is an art and science of managing an organization in such a manner that can deliver predicted results. Business management is a broader term due to rapidly emerging complexity and difficulties in the modern business world. Workable strategies may help businesses overcome unusual problems and ensure foreseen growth (Salkar, 2021). Management experts believe that business management combines all activities essential to run a business efficiently and ensure optimum use of available resources. Activities like-product development, management of funds, marketing & promotion, internal coordination, resource allocation, and infrastructure maintenance. In short, it attempts to coordinate all the essential business activities required for goal achievement (Conerly et al., 2021). Therefore, experts have identified five essential functions: Planning, Organizing, Staffing, Directing, and Controlling.

Business Management in Modern World

Cross-border business operations increased the need for scientific business management to handle global business issues. The universal approach of 'management sciences' makes it rational and comprehensive. There is a vast scope of management in the modern business world due to business diversity, cross-cultural integration, sharing resources, moving technology, and others. Rapidly increasing business capacity created multifold challenges for the entrepreneurs for which efficient management tools and techniques are needed for human management, machine management, production management, marketing management, operation management, and SCM management (Deekay, 2020). Business management helps meet various objectives, viz., economic, human and overall business objectives of the firm. A dynamic marketing environment brings new challenges to businesses which have a lasting effect on the business if not settled within the time limit. It seeks efficient managers and leaders to cope with the rapidly changing environment and carry the business on a progressive route. Globally, business management systems are being used that help firms in tactical planning and its implementation (Reeves et al., 2020). Formulate policies, set guidelines and do strategic planning for efficient business execution across different territories. Hence, business management models and theories gained immense importance in today's competitive business world.

Defining Popular Business Management Theories

Undoubtedly, machines play a significant role in business, but humans are very much required at every level until they can think and make decisions themselves. Decisions often need to be taken based on intuition, experience, and the situation wherein previous data is irrelevant or doesn't provide relevant input for the right decision-making. However, human-based decisions are always right, not always true. Therefore, a mixed approach is usually adopted by leaders for decision-making. Experts believed that comprehensive decision-making contributes a lot to the business's success; hence, entrepreneurs take help of different business management theories. Some very popular theories are being discussed briefly.

Table 6.1: Business Management Theories

	Theory	Author
1.	Scientific Management Theory	Frederick W. Taylor
2.	System Management Theory	Ross Ashby
3.	Contingency Management Theory	Fred Fiedler
4.	Theory X and Theory Y	Douglas McGregor

Scientific Management Theory

It's a well-known theory about the strategic use of employees' energy and skill set to improve organizational excellence. The theory of management concentrates upon synthesizing efficient workflow in the organization and deals with enhancing employees' productivity (Kanigel, 1997). Labor productivity improvement was the focus area for which the author rigorously worked. There was a monotonous practice across the industries, forcing employees to work hard, which did not bring expected results, but stress. F. W. Taylor, who gave this theory, propounded that forcing people in the workplace for hard work cannot bring results; however, one should focus on simplifying the task so that employees can understand that quickly and be willing to do that (Metzgar, 2004). This is called work simplification, which helps firms optimize their output by motivating people through scientific techniques. Scientific management theory introduced a practice named 'fair day's wage for fair day's work', which became popular worldwide. It also helped to improve the relationship between employees and employers. The author also stressed the use of technology to perform routine tasks. The basic principles of this theory are:

- Task-specific supervisors should be used to give direction to respective employees.

- Separate planning should be done for a specific task.

- There should be fatigue and time study to measure the output of individual employees.

- Improvising machines & tools, working environment and time for higher output.

- Use the scientific method of hiring, training and motivating employees.

- Use incentive mechanisms to boost employees' motivation.

System Management Theory

The approach of system management theory covers the human relationship in the workplace. It believes that the success of an organization depends upon various internal factors like interrelationship, interdependence, coordination, trust, empathy, and synergy (Taylor, 2008). The theory treats an organization as a system that includes various parts that interact to form an efficient organization. System theory carries an interdisciplinary approach that brings all the elements of an organization together to form a united organization (Alchon, 1992). Various elements have been identified like **subsystems**– various subsystems work with a composite system to form a unified group directed towards the one goal, **flow of energy**– organizational energy flow from the workforce, technology, information, and material, **synergy**–includes the output of the organization and compare it with total output (Cooke, 2003). According to this theory, an organization may have an 'open or close' system. An open system interacts with all the elements of its environment regularly and establishes harmony (Knights & Roberts, 1982). It integrates efforts at all levels to achieve organizational goals with minimal effort. A closed system stays isolated from its environment and acts as a self-contained unit. It is not rational and is non-adaptive (Thompson & Mchugh, 2002).

Contingency Management Theory

Contingency management theory includes three essential elements likely to affect its operations and way of doing activities. The three elements are- leadership style, organization size, and technology in use. In this approach, the author reveals that leadership style is crucial because a leader directs his/her team to achieve organizational goals. Leadership traits excel the organization's system by providing accurate guidance with continuous motivation. A leader must be understandable, flexible and adaptive to change to meet the situation's demand and ensure the highest performance. Next is 'organization size'; size matters a lot because size decides the way of management. Management approaches cannot be the same in small and big organizations. The size, resource allocation, requirement of human resources, and technology have to be decided. The size of the organization has a direct influence on its operation. The third important element is 'technology'. Technology plays a crucial role in the modern world and reflects the firm's competitiveness. According to the author, technological infrastructure and the technology in use decide a firm's operational efficiency. Altogether, all three elements contribute significantly to efficiently managing the firm and improving efficiency.

Theory X and Theory Y

The theory believes that employees get satisfaction from the work he does or just do his task to earn livelihood without getting any satisfaction or motivation. The theory depends upon these two assumptions and points out the two exclusive management styles. Participative management and authoritarian management. In an organization where employees reflect lower level of passion and dedication for their work, we can say the management style adopted in that firm is 'authoritarian'. This is what 'Theory X' speaks about: employees hold a pessimistic approach and do not work efficiently until they get incentives. Employees' behavior becomes casual and unprofessional due to authoritarian leadership; here, the superior become 'the boss', not a leader. Whereas 'Theory Y' focuses on a participative management style in which a superior becomes a 'leader' rather than a 'boss'. In this situation, employees show a higher level of participation, motivation and work-related dedication. High enthusiasm and willingness to work are the main characteristics of this theory. The world has gained a lot from this theory, the all across the world, organizations adopt this management style as per their structure, goals and resources. Optimistic work behavior can be initiated using these theories, extended cooperation, a collaborative approach, and a trust-based relationship.

Relevance of Management Theories in the Cross-Cultural Business World

Globalization has evolved the world as one market without any boundary that has helped firms to explore global demand and opportunities. Cross-border transactions have increased, and migration of employees, experts, and technical people started happening (Basabe & Ros, 2005). Today, the work floor includes diversified people working together for a common goal. Workplace diversity is expected in the industries (Helen, 2013; Maheshkar & Sharma, 2018; 2021). Undoubtedly, cross-border transactions brought prosperity to the firms, but various challenges have also stood up, which are complex and critical in nature (Oyserman & Lee, 2008). One of the prominent challenges before firms in this global era is *cross-cultural issues* that arise from workplace diversity. Experts believe that contemporary management techniques can give ease of handling such issues in the organization (Waddell et al., 2013). So, before understanding the importance of management theories in handling cross-cultural issues, one must understand the concept of 'cross-culture' (Nisbett & Miyamoto, 2005).

> Cross-culture refers to the differences that occur due to nation, ethnicity, background etc. In a broader sense, cross-culture combines people from different religions, languages, ethnicity, and values. It has increased due to globalization and economic integration for trade, research, and economic cooperation.

Researchers worldwide have continuously studied cross-cultural environments to understand the possible issues that arise and determine the efficient techniques to handle them. Cross-cultural issues produce many obstacles and introduce multi-facet problems to the firms operating at the global level (Kopp, 2021; Maheshkar & Sharma, 2018; 2021). Cross-cultural research compares employees' socio-cultural characteristics, which may significantly impact work culture, organizational operation and interpersonal relationships. Employees' performance, behavior and attitude are influenced by cultural integration at the workplace, and if not controlled in time, it may become a severe problem (Ember, 2007).

Significance of Management Theories to Handle Cross-Cultural Issues

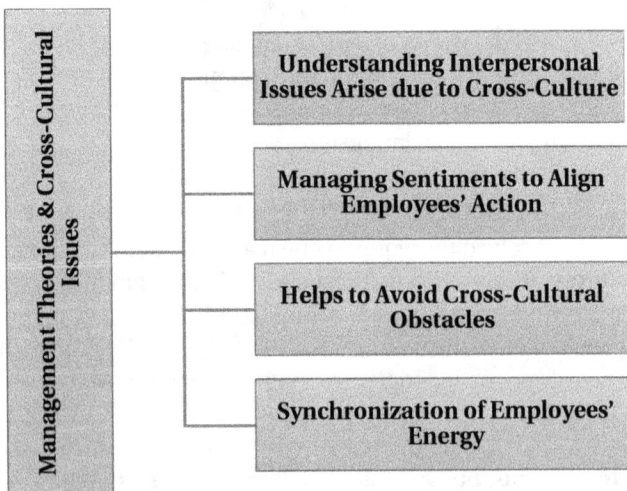

Figure 6.1: Relevance of Management Theories to Manage Cross-Cultural Issues

Management theories work efficiently to handle issues arising out of cultural, interpersonal, and personality differences. Some of the essential functions that management theories perform to handle cross-cultural issues in the organization are discussed above.

1. Understanding Interpersonal Issues Arise due to Cross Culture

Management theories rationally develop a sense of smelling interpersonal issues arising due to employee cultural differences. It also helps to understand the differences with due causes, making it easier for the manager to resolve the matter then and there (Boden, 2008). Management theories cover multi-angles to analyze the workplace configuration and related consequences. Cultural diversity is widespread in the workplace due to globalization and the merger of corporate entities. It increases the conflict of interest, attitude and opinion amongst religious and ethnic groups. Data shows huge implications on organizational performance and effectiveness. Hence, leaders always refer to popular business management theories and models to handle such situations and make the rational decision (Neuliep, 2014).

2. Managing Sentiments to Align Employees' Action

Actions derive from human emotions and sentiments that ultimately occur due to cultural and religious beliefs. Often these beliefs enter into conflicts with others' reliefs & faith and lead to disputes. Disputes due to differences in religion go a long way and hurt the organization's system. In this context, experts found various management models and theories carry appropriate solutions without hurting anyone's sentiments or emotions. With the help of these theories, leaders can implement the plans and materialize the strategies to help them control the chaos in the workplace (Romani & Claes, 2014).

3. Helps to Avoid Cross-Cultural Obstacles

Management theories work upon systems and procedures that align employees' efforts towards the final goal achievement without letting them affect the work culture and system. It acts as a firewall that does not allow any socio-cultural noise to influence workplace culture, ethics and operation. It establishes a robust intercultural environment where collaborative learning and cooperation extend amongst the employees. Today, in the modern business world, catering to employees' needs, sentiments and values is a potential challenge that can only be handled through effective management systems/theories (Cristopher, 2015).

4. Synchronization of Employees' Energy

Cross-cultural issues dilute workplace harmony and significantly reduce efficiency. Firms that follow management theories and adopt efficient models can protect themselves from loss of human energy and efforts due to workplace disputes arising from religious and cultural differences. Cultural issues influence team togetherness and reduce cooperation amongst the members. It also splits team efforts into small bites that cannot help the organization to achieve its objectives. The culturally divergent group usually loses its capacity, energy and capabilities, increasing the organization's problems (Hofstede, 2010).

Literature Review

Business models/theories have evolved to eradicate management issues critical to ensure business success in today's competitive market (Peric et al., 2017). Firms come across many challenges, which are very common across the industries. They look for optimum solutions with high predictability of business success. Various business models have derived from actual business situations with optimistic solutions to specific problems (Amit & Zott, 2015). For example, the ANSOFF matrix, a business model, depicts the product and market-related strategies under specific conditions. On the other hand, the BCG matrix, a four-quadrant matrix, helps leaders to formulate product-related strategies under particular market condition (Arend, 2013). However, business management theories never get away from critics, but still, carry immense importance in the business world. Experts believe that business model/theories have not been defined clearly for a specific business issue or problem, but it carries a widespread approach and provides comprehensive thought to the decision-makers for sustainability (Abdelkafi & Tauscher, 2016). Various theories/models have been developed from the industry's real problems, and suggestions have been made to optimize success even in a critical time. The primary focus of business management models is to provide a rational approach towards business problems with predictable solutions. It gives direction to explore optimum solutions with the highest success rate (Bocken et al., 2015). Today, the market sustainability of any business depends upon the business model being followed in the organization.

Business management theories facilitate actions and practices that ensure competitive position and long-run sustainability (Cucculelli & Bettinelli, 2015). It gives direction to handle divergent market environments with workable business strategies (Dahan et al., 2010). Businesses get a competitive advantage and generate desired profit from well-organized and controlled business practices (Demil & Lecocq, 2010). Success does not mean high profit and market leadership but stakeholders' satisfaction and a favorable market image. Popular businesses are not profit-driven but value-driven, creating significant differentiation from others (George & Bock, 2011). Brands which are value driven are known forever and gain customer trust. Business models are not just a set of practices or guidelines but a business holly book that clearly mentions dos and don'ts (DaSilva & Trkman, 2014). A good business model gives self-sustainability with a competitive position. All the business management theories signify tools and techniques for a successful business model and reinventing the lost business opportunities (Cavalcante et al., 2011).

Research Question and Method

Whether or not business management theories carry real meaning in today's dynamic and technological business world? Whether it is workable? Furthermore, what are its implications with respect to real business problems? The study focuses on four distinct and very popular business management theories: *scientific Management Theory, System Management Theory, Contingency Management Theory and Theory X & Theory Y*. The primary task of the study is to collect evidence supporting these theories' success in the real world. Also, determine each theory's key factors at which it concentrates to facilitate solutions to business problems. The descriptive research method elaborates the research question with the help of literature support and essential factors on which these theories focus. The research is purely a review study that provides insights into the usability of these business management theories for handling cross-cultural issues in the real world. It also analyzes researchers' views on its implications for handling real business problems and critical decision-making.

Analysis - A Fact-Finding Exercise

Analyzing Concept and Key Factors of 'Scientific Management Theory'

Scientific management theory was propounded by Frederick Winslow Taylor, an engineer by profession. He observed efficiency loss in production houses that leads to low-profit margin and minimum use of resources (Taylor, 2008). His primary focus was to scale up business productivity by focusing on employees' performance with limited resources (Turan, 2015). The theory emphasizes the scientific method of motivation, resource allocation and managing wastage. It was a new way of managing an organization through a scientific approach and was widely accepted by the firms because its principles helped avoid biases based on religion, culture, language, color, and other factors. There were four primary factors on which scientific management theory was based, and these factors were also known as the 'basic principles' of the theory.

Table 6.2: Key Factors of Scientific Management Theory

F-1	Work Standardization
F-2	Equal Division of Work and Responsibility
F-3	Scientific Selection
F-4	Develop Mutual Collaboration

1. Work Standardization: It refers to the scientific analysis of job specifications and accordingly identifies the team to complete it without concerning the religious or cultural background of the employees. Work standardization ensures task harmony and significantly reduces the burden on employees. It advocates using standardized tools and methods to improve the quality of work above cultural background. Taylor stressed the concept of the right man at the right place for the right job for organizational excellence and productivity without concerning the cultural attributes of employees.

2. Equal Division of Work and Responsibility: Taylor did not mean that work should be distributed amongst the worker in equal quantity, but he said work should be distributed rationally based on the nature of the job and employees' competency level. It means the nature of work must determine and choose the right man to perform it without concerning personal relationship, religion or culture. By doing this, an organization can achieve work excellence and significantly minimize the cost of operation. Strategic tasks should be allotted to highly experienced employees so that they can use their experience for successive decision-making.

3. Scientific Selection: Taylor emphasized the scientific selection method for employee selection, not based on cultural characteristics. The theory talks about the scientific method of selection, which means employee selection must be based on innovative techniques like analyzing the requirement, identifying the technicality features, matching the employees' skills and evaluating the qualification for the suitable post rather than religion or culture of employees. He propounded a variety of methods for employee selection which are unbiased.

4. Develop Mutual Collaboration: This concept was based on the interpersonal relationship between employees and the management. Mutual collaboration was found crucial by Taylor for effective management and increased productivity. According to him, workplace collaboration improves interpersonal communication, reduces personal grudges based on culture, religion or language, and develops feelings of belongingness.

These four principles back the entire theory, but a few more factors were later added to the theory to offer complete solutions to manufacturing firms, as exhibited in figure 6.2.

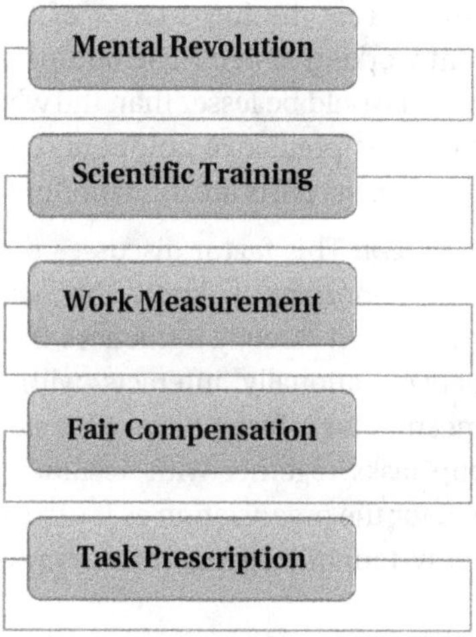

Figure 6.2: Other Important Factors of Scientific Management Theory

Key Factors of 'System Management Theory'

System management theory was well accepted by the industries and implemented to harmonize the internal management system (Mele et al., 2010). The theory was proven advantageous to the firms and improved their efficiency by using basic principles of scientific system management. It overlooks employees' socio-cultural aspects and puts them into a rational system based on scientific assumptions. The theory believes that an organization is a combination of various systems that must be aligned and well connected for efficiency building. It emphasizes strong connections between departments and collaborative functioning (Chikere & Jude, 2015). System management theory helped the firms establish an error-free network connecting each system element and interacting efficiently (Mullin, 2005). There is no place for religious ethics and values in this type of system. It treats all the employees equally based on the organization's norms and system. System theory helped firms to eliminate biased cultures and reduce cross-cultural conflicts. It also suggested a scientific way to analyze job-related requirements and appropriately fill them with the most eligible people without getting influenced by their culture or religion. Essential factors (components) of system management theory are:

C1-Subsystem: Sub-system refers to the small parts of the whole system that work together for the firm's smooth function. Each subsystem is critical for success and efficient functioning. System management theory discusses each subsystem's interconnectedness, forming a competent organizational structure.

C2-Synergy: This factor reveals the importance of the synchronization of a subsystem for an efficient working system. The author believed that sum of all the parts of the organization would be lesser than the whole. Hence, the synergy between each element ensures predictive output and better control. A system cannot work effectively until all its parts are interconnected and synchronized.

C3-Open and Closed System: This factor discusses the nature of the system, i.e. open or closed. It is important to know the nature of the system for organizational success because it directly influences the probability of success. An open system is active, rationally interacts with its environment, and establishes a close connection for information exchange. Good communication helps in taking up group tasks together with accuracy and speed. Whereas a closed system is not good for the organization as it carries weak communication and connectivity. Hence, system management theory promotes an open system for successive management.

C4-System Boundary: According to this concept, each subsystem has its boundary, which restricts its functioning to move across it and protect its sovereignty. It helps to keep the inner system secured from its external environment. The author believed that this boundary plays an essential role in maintaining harmony amongst them and keeping each subsystem alive.

Key Factors of 'Contingency Management Theory'

The theory provides firms with a situation-based management approach that allows taking distinct decisions to manage the current situation efficiently. The contingency approach to management includes circumstances-oriented decision-making because it doesn't focus on one technique but allows the most appropriate action according to the current situation. The world has recognized it as an effective tool for dynamic leadership in a competitive world. It has broadened the scope of management by emphasizing group effectiveness for the overall efficiency enhancement of the organization (Shala et al., 2021). It is believed that the corporate world has gained a lot from the contingency management approach.

Table 6.3: Basic Principles of Contingency Management Theory

1.	There is no perfect method or way to manage an organization
2.	Decisions are situation based
3.	Co-worker scale (LPC) to measure leadership orientation
4.	Leader-Member-Follower Relationship

Key Factors of 'Theory X and Theory Y'

The theory has taught the world how to identify the personality of managers as well as employees (Kevin, 2008). According to theory X, employees with low aspiration, low ambition, low motivation, focus on lower needs, and safety cannot deliver high performance. Even they cannot contribute much to the organization's success (Aydin, 2012). McGregor, the author, propounded that theory X management style firm can improve its operations by identifying the employees whose primary interest is in 'safety & psychological needs' than social or self-esteem needs (Russ, 2011). On the other hand, theory Y identify employees who are desperate to work, self-motivated, well-committed and capable enough to identify the best solutions for problems (Jenab & Staub, 2012). Such a kind of personality carries the inherent nature of working rather than reluctantly working (Islam & Eva, 2017). Over the years, industries have gained immense expertise through this theory and succeeded in building a potential workforce (Aydin, 2012). The basic principles of Theory X and Theory Y are as follows:

Principles of Theory X

- People tend to avoid working whenever it is possible.
- Employees show a lack of ambition and desire to take up responsibilities and prefer to be directed.
- Employees are reluctant to show creativity to solve a problem rather than wait for others to do it.
- Low motivation due to limited needs.
- Resist for change.
- Employees of this nature tend to be self-centred.

Principles of Theory Y

- Employee performance depends upon favorable working conditions.
- Employees usually are self-directed, motivated and creative.
- Employees are committed to their responsibilities which results in high quality and productivity.
- Employees are creative.
- Willing to handle tasks and take up responsibilities on their own.

Conclusion

Business management theories played a crucial role in enhancing industrial productivity worldwide and helped firms manage their resources efficiently through scientific principles of management rather than cultural influence. These theories have eliminated the social approach of management, which leads to social-cultural issues. Cross-cultural issues have long-range implications for organizations. Hence, such theories played an important role in improving efficiency by reducing incidents of cross-cultural conflicts. As the study focused on four distinct management theories, a conclusion is being made separately for each one and pointing out their best outcome. The theory *Scientific Management Theory* has been widely used for industrial research and investigation. The theory has broadened the scope of scientific methods and systems in manufacturing firms to optimize their production and managerial skills. Various concepts have been developed that have transformed business management techniques. Industries have learned about 'work standardization' that helped in ensuring workplace harmony, 'optimum work distribution' that helped in getting maximum output from each employee, 'scientific selection technique' that helped in selecting the 'right man for the right job', and 'methods of developing mutual collaboration' that helped in improving organizational culture and workplace prosperity. Years have been spent to excel in these principles and proven their implications in the real world. Hence, scientific management theory still has immense significance for industry excellence.

The second theory, the System Management Theory, revolutionizes the industrial working system by clearly mentioning the principles of a scientific system implementation for organizational excellence. It has given the fundamental principles for an internal management system which helps to establish well structured, controlled and dynamic system. The theory gives the key criteria to enhance system efficiency, which can deliver higher output with low discrepancies. It primarily focused upon four important components, viz. '*Subsystem, Synergy, Open & closed System and System Boundary*'. In each component, the author pointed out a key factor of an efficient management system. 'subsystem', given the concept of the nuclear part of the whole system, contributes significantly to smooth functioning. 'Synergy', given the concept of synchronization of each tiny part of the system for predictive output and efficient working. 'Open & closed system' talked about the nature of the organization's resource management system. Based on the observations, it can be stated that an open system is always better for the firms than a closed system that does not allow a collaborative approach, lacks coordination, poor cooperation and closed centric approach. 'System Boundary', given a foreign entity's concept of system security. It does not mean a system should be 'closed', but dynamic enough can protect its exclusiveness while exchanging dialogues and instructions from other departments.

The third theory, Contingency Management Theory, gives the concept of derived decision-making based on the current business situation. It has given the fundamental approach to understanding the important elements of a situation and form efficient decisions. Manager can take dynamic decision to handle the situation which is uncertain and unpredictable. The management approach in this theory is given the philosophy of situation-oriented decision-making rather than a predetermined set of actions. It has given the concept of dynamic leadership to the modern industrial world. The theory gives valuable principles to the world like- 'there is no perfect method to manage an organization' it has promoted dynamic decision making based on situation's demand and circumstances, 'decisions are situation based' firms should not go monotonously but go rationally. 'Co-worker scale to measure leadership orientation' given the philosophy of modern measurement method, which helped to determine leadership effectiveness. Moreover, the last principle is the 'leader-member-follower relationship' that gives fundamental tips for managing the relationship between leader-member-follower.

'Theory X & Theory Y' introduced the industrial world with the personality types of humans. It helped to predict employees' performance based on their personality traits. It is a great tool to identify the employee's approach toward his/her task. With the help of this theory, industries have identified the people who fall into both categories and conducted appropriate training programs to boost their energy. According to theory X, in every organization, certain people are reluctant, rigid, resist change, slow to give creative ideas and avoid taking up responsibilities. Whereas some people show extraordinary energy, are willing to take responsibilities, and are self-motivated and creative for their job. Industries have learned to identify these people to take necessary action and improve organizational performance.

Reference

Abdelkafi, N. & Täuscher, K. (2016). Business models for sustainability from a system dynamics perspective. *Organization & Environment, 29,* 74-96. https://doi.org/10.1177/1086026615592930

Alchon, G. (1992). Mary Van Kleeck and Scientific Management. In Nelson, D. (Ed.), *A mental revolution: scientific management since Taylor* (pp. 102-129). *Ohio State University Press.*

Amit, R. & Zott, C. (2015). Crafting business architecture: The antecedents of business model design. *Strategic Entrepreneurship Journal, 9,* 331-350. https://doi.org/10.1002/sej.1200

Arend, R. J. (2013). The business model: Present and future—beyond a skeumorph. *Strategic Organization, 11*(4), 390–402. https://doi.org/10.1177/1476127013499636

Aydin, O. T. (2012). The Impact of Theory X, Theory Y and Theory Z on Research Performance: An Empirical Study from A Turkish University. *International Journal of Advances in Management and Economics,1*(5), 24-31.

Basabe, N., & Ros, M. (2005). Cultural dimensions and social behavior correlates: Individualism-collectivism and power distance. *International Review Social Psychology*, 18(1), 189-225.

Bocken, N. M. P., Rana, P., & Short, S. (2015). Value mapping for sustainable business thinking. *Journal of Industrial and Production Engineering*, 32, 67-81. https://doi.org/10.1080/21681015.2014.1000399

Boden, J. (2008). *The Wall Behind China's Open Door: Towards Efficient Intercultural Management in China.* ASP Editions.

Cavalcante, S., Kesting, P., & Ulhøi, J. (2011). Business model dynamics and innovation: (re)establishing the missing linkages. *Management Decision*, 49, 1327-1342. https://doi.org/10.1108/00251741111163142

Chikere, H. & Jude, N. (2015). The Systems Theory of Management in Modern Day Organizations - A Study of Aldgate Congress Resort Limited Port. *International Journal of Scientific and Research Publications*, 5(9).

Conerly, T. R., Holmes, K., & Tamang, A. L. (2021). *Introduction to Sociology (3e).* OpenStax.

Cooke, B. (2003). The denial of slavery in management studies. *Journal of Management Studies, 40*(8), 1895-1918. https://doi.org/10.1046/j.1467-6486.2003.00405.x

Cristopher, E. (2015). *International Management and Intercultural Communication: A collection of case studies (Volume 1).* Palgrave Macmillan.

Cucculelli, M. & Bettinelli, C. (2015). Business models, intangibles and firm performance: Evidence on corporate entrepreneurship from Italian manufacturing SMEs. *Small Business Economics*, 45, 329-350. https://doi.org/10.1007/s11187-015-9631-7

Dahan, N. M., Doh, J. P., Oetzel, J., & Yaziji, M. (2010). Corporate-NGO collaboration: Co-creating new business models for developing markets. *Long Range Planning*, 43, 326-342. https://doi.org/10.1016/j.lrp.2009.11.003

DaSilva, C. M., & Trkman, P. (2014). Business model: What it is and what it is not. *Long Range Planning*, 47, 379-389. https://doi.org/10.1016/j.lrp.2013.08.004

Deekay (2020). *What is the Scope of Management in Today's Business?* DailyOjo Articles. http://dailyojo.com/articles/what-is-the-scope-of-management-in-todays-business.html

Demil, B., & Lecocq, X. (2010). Business model evolution: In search of dynamic consistency. *Long Range Planning, 43*(2-3), 227-246. https://doi.org/10.1016/j.lrp.2010.02.004

Ember, C. R. (2007). Using the HRAF Collection of Ethnography in Conjunction With the Standard Cross-Cultural Sample and the Ethnographic Atlas. *Cross-Cultural Research, 41*(4), 396–427. https://doi.org/10.1177/1069397107306593

George, G. & Bock, A. J. (2011). The business model in practice and its implications for entrepreneurship research. *Entrepreneurship Theory and Practice*, 35, 83-111. https://doi.org/10.2139/ssrn.1490251

Helen, D. (2013). *International Management: Managing across Borders and Cultures.* Upper Prentice Hall.

Hofstede, G. (2010). *Cultures and Organizations: Software of the Mind (3e).* McGraw-Hill Education.

Islam, M. S., & Eva, S. A. (2017). Application of Mcgregor's Theory X and Theory Y: Perception of Management toward the Employees in the Banking Industry of Bangladesh. *The International Journal of Business & Management,* 5(11), 135-145.

Jenab, K., & Staub, S. (2012). Analyzing Management Style and Successful Implementation of Six Sigma. *International Journal of Strategic Decision Sciences,* 3(3), 13-23, https://doi.org/10.4018/jsds.2012070102

Kanigel, R. (1997). Taylor-made. *The Sciences,* 37(3), 18-23.

Knights, D., & Roberts, J. (1982). The power of organization or the organization of power?. *Organization Studies,* 3(1), 47-63.

Kopp, C. M. (2021). Cross Culture. Investopedia Business Essentials. https://www.investopedia.com/terms/c/cross-culture.

Maheshkar, C., & Sharma, V. (2018) (Eds.). Cross-cultural Business Education: Leading Businesses around the Cultures. In *Handbook of Research on Cross-Cultural Business Education* (pp. 1-35). IGI Global. https://doi.org/10.4018/978-1-5225-3776-2.ch001

Maheshkar, C., & Sharma, V. (2021) (Eds.). Cross-cultural Business Education: Leading Businesses around the Cultures. In *Research Anthology on Business and Technical Education in the Information Era* (pp. 677-711). Business Science Reference. https://doi.org/10.4018/978-1-7998-5345-9.ch038

Mele, C., Pels, J., & Polese, F. (2010). A Brief Review of Systems Theories and Their Managerial Applications. *Service Science,* 2, 126-135. https://doi.org/10.1287/serv.2.1_2.126

Metzgar, C. R. (2004). The principles of scientific management/The one best way: Frederick Winslow Taylor & the Enigma of Efficiency. *Professional Safety,* 49(2), 49.

Mullin, L. J. (2005). *Management and organizational behavior* (7e). Prentice Hall.

Neuliep, J. (2014). *Intercultural Communication: A Contextual Approach* (6e). Sage.

Nisbett, R. E., & Miyamoto, Y. (2005). The influence of culture: Holistic versus analytic perception. *Trends in Cognitive Sciences,* 9(10), 467-473.

Oyserman, D., & Lee, S. W. (2008). Does culture influence what and how we think? Effects of priming individualism and collectivism. *Psychological Bulletin,* 134(2), 311-342.

Peric, M., Durkin, J. & Vitezic, V. (2017). The Constructs of a Business Model Redefined: A Half-Century Journey. *Sage Open,* 7(3). https://doi.org/10.1177/2158244017733516

Reeves, M., Wesselink, E., & Whitaker, K. (2020, July 1). *The end of bureaucracy, again?* BCG Henderson Institute. https://bcghendersoninstitute.com/the-end-of-bureaucracy-again/

Romani, I., & Claes, M. T. (2014). Why critical intercultural communication studies are to be taken seriously in cross-cultural management research? *International Journal of Cross Cultural Management,* 14(1), 127-132. https://doi.org/10.1177/1470595813507156

Russ, T. L. (2011). 'Theory X/Y assumptions as predictors of managers' propensity for participative decision making. *Management Decision*, 49 (5), 823-883.

Sager, K. L. (2008). An Exploratory Study of the Relationships between Theory X/Y Assumptions and Superior Communicator Style. *Management Communication Quarterly, 22*(2), 288–312. https://doi.org/10.1177/0893318908323148

Salkar, R. (2021). The Importance and Future Scope of Management & Strategy in Today's Market. https://www.consultantsreview.com/cxoinsights/the-importance-and-future-scope-of-management--strategy-in-today-s-market-vid-490.html

Shala, B., Prebreza, A. & Ramosaj, B. (2021). The Contingency Theory of Management as a Factor of Acknowledging the Leaders-Managers of Our Time Study Case: The Practice of the Contingency Theory in the Company Avrios. *Open Access Library Journal, 8*, 1-20. https://doi.org/10.4236/oalib.1107850

Taylor, W. F. (2008). *The Principles of Scientific Management.* Digireads Publishing.

Thompson, P., & Mchugh, D. (2002). Management and Control. *Work organizations* (2e), Palgrave.

Turan, H. (2015). Taylor's "Scientific Management Principles": Contemporary Issues in Personnel Selection Period. *Journal of Economics, Business and Management*, 3(11), 1102-1105.

Waddell, D., Jones, G.R., & George, J. (2013). *Contemporary Management (3e).* McGraw-Hill Education.

Chapter 7

Online Group Buying Behavior: A Comparison of USA, China and Indian Markets

Rachna Bajaj
Freelance Consultant

Gaurav Gupta
Christ University, Delhi-NCR, India

Rachna Bansal
Sharda University, India

Abstract: Online group-buying (OGB) is a new market and has gained much academic and practitioners' attention. It is an arrangement that facilitates discounts on various products and services on a daily basis but with the condition that a minimum number of buyers would make the purchase. The design is to utilize the power of purchasing in bulk to avail the benefit as a customer or supplier from the transaction. Group-buying has always been a widespread practice among customers- like students forming a group to negotiate with coaching institutes to get coaching at discounted rates, ladies forming a group called kitties with the shopkeepers to get discounted suits etc. This concept originated in the United States, and it has since been successfully embraced by China. The chapter aims to analyze the current scenario and future scope of OGB in the Indian Market. The study also contrasts the difference in OGB behavior of consumers in the market settings of the USA, China and India. The main focus of this chapter is to study social-demographic and psychographic features of online group-buying users, as well as likenesses and variances in their shopping habits, attitudes and motivations for this kind of purchase, decision-making factors, and the type of products and services that are usually purchased and used. The chapter has observed that Chinese consumers are more inclined to purchase from group-buying websites than their US counterparts, as consumers in collectivistic cultures are more likely to be attracted by group appeals and engage in group purchases than consumers in individualistic cultures. In India, group buying is popular for daily essentials, kitchen utensils, cosmetics and food items, and real estate. The chapter has enormous implications for businesses to assist managers in promoting online group buying in various product categories, using modified marketing strategies to meet different cultural requirements. For the US market, to enhance perceived trust, marketers should emphasize the credibility of the group-buying platform and consumer satisfaction as a company's main role. For this, there should be a blog for consumer reviews and a question-and-answer section for interactive communication among existing customers, potential buyers and buying platform's customer service (Tsai & Zhang, 2016). Marketers should facilitate an app-based shopping experience in the Chinese market because people are more prone to use mobile phones than laptops (Hossain & Rahman, 2021).

Keywords: Online group-buying (OGB), Cross-Culture buying behavior, Indian Market, USA, China

***

Introduction

Increased use of the internet during the Covid-19 pandemic has influenced the shopping behavior of people. Another reason for an increase in online shopping is that people prefer shopping online instead of going to malls or retail stores to contain the spread of coronavirus. Online group buying is also gaining momentum among customers. Online group-buying websites are platforms where a group of people can come together to buy products at discounted prices. Online group-buying is a new form of marketing for promotional borders. It offers a lower, more affordable pricing, with a daily discount scheme for a wide range of services and products. The global online group-buying market is expected to proliferate in the coming years. After 2020, the market is likely to grow with key players' rising adoption of new marketing strategies. North America, particularly the United States, will continue to play a critical role that cannot be overlooked. Any modifications made by the United States could have an impact on the growth trend of Online Group-buying. The market in North America is expected to expand significantly in the future years. The progress of the Online group-buying Market in 2021 would be significantly different from the previous year and the OGB Market will see a tremendous increase in compound annual growth rate (CAGR) over the next five years. With the introduction of advanced technology and the presence of major players in this region, the market is expected to have adequate expansion.

Online group buying was popular, in the early years of this century, also. The expanded use of broadband technology, along with a shift in consumer behavior, explains the current rapid expansion (Oppenheim & Ward, 2006). Consumers, stimulated by the recession and reduced purchasing power, utilize the internet to band together and strengthen their position against sellers all in the hopes of obtaining volume discounts. This new trend is trying to cope with the economic crisis by turning it into benefit with the newer version of E-commerce. In such a trade, people come together to negotiate a better price or to create better sale condition by removing geographical boundaries. According to Kauffman & Wang (2001) this is an innovative way of generating economies of scale. Web-based group-buying is already prevalent in the B2B (business-to-business) market and the B2C (business-to-customer) market, where buyers and sellers are confident that, it can lead to higher profits. In this concept, group-buying websites play the role of intermediary between sellers (producers, retailers, service providers) and buyers (customers) (Stulec & Petljak 2010). Marketers must understand their customers and how they make purchasing decisions, whether using a traditional system or an e-commerce platform (Hollensen, 2004). Therefore, the main objectives of this chapter are, to determine social-demographic and psychographic features of online group-buying users, as well as likenesses and variances in their shopping habits, attitudes and drives for this kind of purchase, decision making factors, and the type of products and services that are usually purchased and used. Globally there are 60 group-buying companies (Top Group Buying Startups, 2022). To date, there is a limited number of studies available on this topic and the phenomenon of OGB is not sufficiently explored. This indicates a need to analyze and explore the current scenario and future scope of OGB. One purpose of this chapter is to assess the extent to which culture influences the purchase decision of online group buyers. This study also sets out to investigate the current scenario of online group-buying in different markets like USA, China and India.

Theoretical Underpinning

E-commerce technology has evolved into a strategic imperative for businesses (Al-Mashari, 2002). E-commerce grew significantly until the early 1990s, when the internet became commercialized and the World Wide Web was used widely. The growth of e-commerce is inextricably linked to the growth of the Internet (Turban et al., 2006). With the growth of e-commerce, online group-buying (OGB) has become a popular shopping model. A big number of customers gather together online and undertake collective buying to benefit from price discounts as a group, which is known as online group-buying (Cheng & Huang, 2013, Erdoğmuş & Čiçek, 2011).

In 2008, a website in the United States, Accompany.com created online group-buying, which has since grown to become one of the fastest growing OGB websites. As according to Cheng and Huang (2013), and Shiau and Luo (2012), OGB is extremely popular and successful in the United States and Europe during 2010 and 2011. By the end of 2010, online group-buying had worked with over 18 countries' enterprises (Xu, 2011). According to a CNN report from 2010, OGB is also experiencing rapid growth in Asia (CNN, 2010).

Traditional e-commerce patterns such as business-to-business (B2B), business to employees (B2E) and business-to-customer (B2C) were not applicable to OGB (Turban et al., 2006). OGB is a new e-commerce business model that follows a business-to-team (B2T) structure (Kai et al., 2013). An emerging market, according to Li et al. (2010), is a country that shares certain characteristics with a developed market but is not one. Emerging markets have seen significant economic growth and have made bigger contributions to global growth - Brazil, Russia, India and China which are known as the BRIC countries, are the four largest emerging markets. China became the world's largest regional emerging market at the start of 2010 (Li et al., 2010). Since 2010, China has seen an increase in the popularity of online group-buying; OGB has a large market potential in China (Dong et al., 2012; Kai et al., 2013). The first Chinese OGB website went live in January 2010, and there are now over 1215 group-buying websites in China (Network World, 2010). The population of OGB customers has reached 18.75 million by the end of 2010, according to data issued by the China Internet Network Information Center (CNNIC, 2011). The OGB market's overall transaction value was expected to exceed RMB980 million (US$147.6 million) (Network World, 2010). The Chinese name for online group-buying is "Tuangou," which means "group-buying" or "collective buying" (Xu, 2011). Meituan, Nuomi, Lashou, Aibang, and Juhusuan are some of the most popular rising group-buying companies in China, and they are all in severe competition with one another (Dong et al., 2012). Group-buying is also known as collective buying, where goods and services are offered at reduced prices only if the minimum number of buyers applies for the same. Online group-buying is becoming popular once again after the pandemic due to increased usage of the internet and marketers bringing innovations for the sites and consumers. Group-buying is being popular for daily essentials, kitchen utensils, cosmetics, food items, educational loans, real estate, and consumer products.

Factors/Personality Traits of Customers Across Cultures Affecting OGB Decisions

There are several factors which influence the buying decision of consumers around India, China and USA. These factors/personality traits are as discussed below:

Reciprocity

It has a positive relationship with customers' buying decision-making in OGB. Its impact on Chinese customers' online group-buying decision-making is high. Reciprocity means to get new information about a product and service while buying at a given price which may confirm quickly the buying intention and influence other customer's buying intention as well (Shiau & Luo, 2012). Hsu & Lin (2008) explained how other customer's previous and live comments help the current customer to make a final decision about the transaction in online group buying. That's why it is more important to have customer feedback and share their participation experience which may help other customers to decide whether to purchase or not in OGB.

Loyalty

According to Gao (2014), loyalty is not found amongst Chinese customers regarding the usage of a particular online group-buying website. Even the group members do not participate in the same groups again in collective buying.

Trust

If a customer relies on a particular seller in online group-buying, that affects positively on customers buying intention. Shiau & Luo (2012) explained trust as a belief on seller's uprightness towards their customers. Customers can rely on the promises made by the sellers. Trust provides the security to participants in online group-buying about the fair deals of the website /seller. Hence, trust avoids uncertainty about online shopping (Becerra & Korgaonkar, 2009).

Price

Low price or discounted prices always attract customers in online group-buying (Erdoğmuş & Čiçek, 2011), hence it affects customers' online purchase decision making (Cai & Xu, 2008). Besides, in case of unavailability of proper information about the goods, customers' decision making is influenced by the low-priced goods (Pi et al., 2011).

Website Design

According to the study by Gao (2014), website design has a positive association with the customers' online group-buying intention. The convenient website design facilitates the customers to scroll all the relevant information easily while making a purchase decision (Liao, Palvia & Lin, 2006). The website design should be such which provides all the information precisely.

Apart from these, various personality traits also impact group-buying behavior. In OGB, one has to start the purchase process by selecting a product, discussing with the seller, and referring the product to others to form a group to avail the discounted product at bargained price. Such initiation is affected by personality traits only (Yang & Lester, 2005).

Hossain & Rahman (2019) explained that extroversion, agreeableness, and conscientiousness stimulate customers' online group-buying behavior, but neuroticism and openness to experience are not that pertinent in the OGB framework. Some of the studies identified extroversion and neuroticism more related to online transactions (e.g., Olsen et al., 2016; Ross et al., 2009). Amichai-Hamburger et al. (2002) says that introverts and neurotics use more internet may be to avoid their loneliness and mental stress by staying online (Ryan & Xenos, 2011). The people for whom it is difficult to make connections are more comfortable with the internet shopping by hiding their actual identity (Ehrenberg et al., 2008). But this does not mean that introverts and neurotics are more likely to purchase in online group-buying because in the OGB framework one has to discuss with other group members and reveal their identity. Bosnjak et al. (2007) suggested that these people rather prefer to use B2C e-commerce platform instead of OGB. Venkatesh et al. (2014) exhibited that extroverted people are regular customers of e-government portals rather than introverted people. In OGB, members have to share the benefit with all other group members, so they have to be altruist like thinking for the benefit of all without expecting anything in return. But Hossain & Rahman (2019) observed agreeableness as a negative predictor in OGB behavior. Because customers while shopping on OGB sites are more concerned in availing the discount for themselves than for other group members.

In OGB, *conscientiousness* is a very important attribute. This trait directs people to thoroughly search for the information before making a purchase in online group buying. These people look for the item on various sites and wait for the best deal to make a final purchase. So, shopping on OGB site requires systematic planning and analysis. Usually, the products and deals are available on OGB sites for a limited time period, so it entails group members to organize and plan before the deal ends. Hence, *conscientiousness* has a positive impact on OGB behavior (Hossain & Rahman, 2019). Current studies do not suggest the trait "openness to experience" as an influence in customers' OGB behavior, but in the future with advancements in the technology and more usage of social media, openness to experience may become demanding personality trait (Hossain & Rahman, 2019).

Comparison of OGB Behavior in India, China and USA

Online Group-buying in China

Group-buying is the latest catchword in China e-commerce, with the hash tagged term collecting 4.7 billion views on Weibo (Williams, 2020) But it's not the first time that group-buying is gaining popularity in China, it's a trend which gained popularity in USA and China a decade ago. Numerous local players such as A and Dianping hopped on this trend a decade ago, emulating the US-based online marketing company Groupon. In 2010, Alibaba had also formed a group-buying platform named Juhuasuan. Eventually the sector collapsed, but the collective buying trend has returned – with a new competitive perseverance (Williams, 2020). Subsequently many big companies started launching services to target this segment of consumers. In 2018, Alibaba added Pingou to its prevalent Juhuasuan. JD.com also worked on the group-buying program and ultimately launched a devoted group-buying app Jingxi the succeeding year. In the interim, another app came into market in July 2018 by online retail website Suning. Pinduoduo, initiated in 2015 is now China's 3rd e-commerce operator after Alibaba and JD.com (Williams, 2020). In recent years, these companies have prospered in anticipation of the evolution of consumers trapped in their homes during a pandemic and their love for word-of-mouth and social shopping, transforming lone desktop shoppers into exciting shoppers (Williams, 2020).

China's eagerness for group-buying can be devoted to the country's exceptional take on the trend. In an interview given to Jing Daily, Miranda Shek, head of international corporate affairs at the Pinduoduo, described that during the platform formation, there was a desire to digitally mimic offline shopping (Williams, 2020). "We created the feeling of being in a mall with your friends and enjoying the sensation of window shopping and sharing goods by replicating it online," she said. Now consumers can share their purchases with friends via posts to build networks and communities. They can even produce and host their own sales event for any product. Host offers friends to purchase along with them, buyer target is met, and hence discounted price is availed. This facilitates online shopping for even older generations who were uncomfortable with online shopping but can trust their families and friends (Williams, 2020).

Company employed tactics which worked for the Chinese consumers and the trend for Online group-buying is booming again in China. Group-buying and WeChat-based social commerce surpass 90% of the global market and the pandemic has increased the number of consumers who understand and use social commerce as a new way of shopping and making it part of their daily lives (*Social Commerce – The Virtual Shopping Stroll with Friends*, 2021).

As a first mover, Pinduoduo has set new standards. Pinduoduo platform has engrossed social media and e-commerce directly into its business model. One of its key assets is group-buying. Pinduoduo has grown into China's third-largest e-commerce platform, within 3 years of its launch. It offers group-buying deals at reduced prices and incentivizes users to share good bargains among their friends and family on social media. In this case, customers can enjoy the heavy discounted product price and earn the commissions if their friends join the group-buying deal and positively place orders (Admin, 2021).

Specifics about Chinese Consumers

The following are the few points which highlight the cultural and personality traits of Chinese consumers which affect their OGB behavior and how OGB sites should incorporate these to become successful in China.

1. Chinese consumers are more inclined to purchase from group-buying websites than their US counterparts. It may be supported by the concept that consumers in collectivistic cultures are more likely to be attracted by group appeals and engage in group purchases than consumers in individualistic cultures. (Zhang & Tsai, 2015)

2. In China, group-buying website offer a great range of proposals, products and deals and hence facilitate more options for unique and unusual products to Chinese male consumers who exhibit a greater need of uniqueness (Tsai & Zhang, 2016).

3. In China, people tend to participate in Online group-buying to signal assimilation with other fellow shoppers in the group whom they perceive as like-minded person simultaneously looking for the unique deals exclusive to OGB channel (Tsai & Zhang, 2016).

4. Chinese consumers' OGB behavior is affected by system quality i.e., if an online group-buying website is safe and if it ensures consumers that in case of any transactional dispute the website will provide full support to resolve such issues, then consumers get greater satisfaction (Hossain & Rahman, 2021)

5. Chinese consumers prefer online group-buying websites with ease of use where search for the product, group forming, checkout and payment are easy (Hossain & Rahman, 2021).

6. Chinese consumers are more prone to using mobile phones than laptops, so group-buying websites should facilitate application-based shopping which is compatible with the mobile phones (Hossain & Rahman, 2021).

7. Chinese consumers are more concerned about the product quality than their US counterparts (Hossain & Rahman, 2021).

8. There are certain personality traits which affects the OGB Behavior, such as extrovert people prefer buying in groups than introvert Chinese consumers (Hossain & Rahman, 2021).

9. Chinese consumers are becoming more individualistic which has come to knowledge from one of the studies that customers shopping on OGB sites are more interested in obtaining the discounts for themselves than for the other group members though they belong to the collectivist society (Hossain & Rahman, 2021).

10. For an OGB business to operate successfully in Chinese culture, they need to target opinion leaders and socially active people as potential initiators. These initiators can influence the purchase Behavior of the other group members (Hossain & Rahman, 2021).

11. Chinese consumers looking for more details trust those OGB sites which provide thorough information about the product and the vendor along with the customer reviews (Hossain & Rahman, 2021).

12. The impact of brand consciousness on OGB decisions is stronger in Chinese consumers as they are more concerned with face image (Tsai & Zhang, 2016).

Online Group-buying in India

Group-buying was much popular in 2010 when sites like Snapdeal, My Dala, Koovs, Deals and You, Dealivor and Grabbon emerged as a sub-segment in E-commerce in India. They expected much growth in this sector in India than in the USA as people showed interest in bulky discounts when shopping collectively. But later in India, these sites suffered and had to shut down their business. But still, in lower-middle-class families in India, there is a Behavior around committees and kitties, so Grofers mimicked that Behavior online ('Group-buying' to contribute, 2018). Under their plan, if there are several people ready to buy a particular product, Grofers will offer them better prices. They introduced an online group-buying store "share to save" and this initiative helped them in attracting more consumers. The company saw increasing revenues in their financial statements.

In India, group-buying is not only popular for daily essentials, kitchen utensils, cosmetics and food items but in real estate also. But to sustain in this market, copycat models will not survive, companies need to differentiate their model from others concerning brand positioning, type of deals and audience targeted (Sharma, 2010).

Gyan Dhan is one of the examples of group-buying in India. An innovative group-buying plan has been launched by Gyan Dhan i.e., Gyan Dhan Allied. It is India's first education funding negotiation plan which helps students to bargain interest rates with the lenders in a group (*India Education Diary*, 2021). Gyan Dhan Allied facilitates the gathering of students for bargaining interest rates and then they can utilize strong buying power to lower the interest rates. It's similar to the situation that when you buy veggies or fruits in bulk from a grocery store, Gyan Dhan Allied members can get lower rates when they are part of the group than if they have to apply for a loan individually. At a particular time, students can evaluate the negotiated interest rates of different plans and select the one which suits their needs.

Another example of the group-buying model in India is DealShare (Sarkar, 2021), a social commerce startup established in 2018 by Vineet Rao, Sankar Bora, Sourjyendu Medda and Rajat Shikhar, targets the middle- and lower-income groups of India in smaller towns and cities. This platform provides various categories of consumer products at a much-discounted price to the non-metro cities. Earlier a decade ago, online buying was limited to tier-1 cities only. With the pervasive usage of smartphones and reduced data prices, online shopping is becoming popular in tier 2 and tier 3 cities also. WhatsApp is being used by 95% of Indians every day, which motivated DealShare to start messaging-based platforms for online group shopping (Abrar, 2021).

Indians are always attracted by discounts and bargained prices. Focusing on this attribute DealShare has introduced this online shopping model which facilitates consumers to purchase in bulk to get overwhelming discounts from the sellers. DealShare is bringing innovations and offering a mind-blowing shopping experience to its nascent internet users. Its business is also rising with a $200 million annual GMV. DealShare has established a leading community group-buying network. Its app is used by consumers more than 40 times a month which makes it one of the most appealing e-commerce applications. It has a network of more than 1000 small business owners.

People are being forced to stay indoors due to this pandemic. So, people are using social media to stay connected with friends and families. Social E-commerce companies are taking advantage of this situation to set up their online marketplace. Another startup CityMall, an online group-buying gateway founded in 2019 trades in multiple ranges of products at discounted prices. It has a network of over two lakh customers and twenty thousand sellers. Likewise, Mall91 initiated the 'Mohalla network' to sell a wide range of products from clothing to electronics to home furnishings. It was founded in

2018, as a social group-buying e-commerce platform. The platform's unique selling point (USP) is video-based social shopping and displaying product catalogues in vernacular languages with WhatsApp-based checkouts, and it already has a presence in over 2000 smaller cities and villages. Mall91 has over 15 million downloads, with users spending an average of 10 minutes on the app (Sarkar, 2021).

Online group-buying in the USA

Groupon is a foremost renowned group-buying website born in the USA in 2008; subsequently Group-buying websites came into existence all over the world rapidly (Jiang & Deng, 2014). These are the few examples of the companies in USA marketing their efforts to attract consumers using innovative schemes under this model.

Amazon: Amazon was founded by Jeff Bezos in 1994 and it's headquartered in Washington, United States. The company is specialized in e-commerce, cloud services, digital streaming and intelligent systems. It keeps on announcing its great sale week, or weekend to increase the traffic on their website.

Groupon: It was founded in Chicago, the United States in 2008 by Andrew Mason, Eric Lefkofsky and Brand Keywell. Customers can get the new deals every day on Groupon. It has a network of local companies. It has a strong customer base.

LivingSocial: It was founded by Eddie Frederick and team headquartered in Washington, United States. LivingSocial is an online group-buying brand where users can buy and promote the activities. This company offers deals on daily basis and occasionally for buying in bulk to make profit and customer base.

The online group-buying brands are entering into new topographies through mergers and acquisitions and becoming competitive through consolidations. OGB has become an efficient marketing strategy to achieve a large consumer base and become an entrenched player in the market.

The following are the few points which highlight about the cultural and personality traits of US consumers which affect their OGB Behavior and how OGB sites should incorporate these to become successful in United States.

1. The US consumers OGB intention is affected if they notice group-buying websites reliable and fulfilling their promises and commitments (Tsai & Zhang, 2016).

2. US consumers who considers themselves as opinion leaders participate in online group buying (Tsai & Zhang, 2017).

3. US consumers are more concerned about the vendor quality so the online group-buying websites should provide transparent information about the vendor (Hossain & Rahman, 2021).

4. US consumers hunt for others opinion before making an online group-buying transaction to avoid uncertainty. Moreover, American OGB sites present less information about the product and focuse more on the deals (Tsai & Zhang, 2016).

5. United States has a high trust social system where people being strangers can trust each other and work collectively for the combined benefits and shared purposes. (Ward et al., 2014). In OGB, the group-buying website is more reliable if consumers trust other group member's objectives and their reviews/feedback. Hence, U.S consumers seem to be more interested in group-buying sites than their Chinese and Indian counterparts.

Marketing Strategies

As a suitable marketing strategy, companies should incorporate the element of social commerce in their E-commerce platform. It can save on expensive advertisements (*E-commerce lessons,* 2019). This trend promotes shopping together in an online shop and avail benefits from discounts for group-buying. Groupify, a berlin-based start-up is working on the same platform by providing a shop page where users get an opportunity to invite two friends by sending them an encrypted link via WhatsApp or Messenger. The system recognizes the group via the response to the link and discounts the buying for all three. A blog is available to discuss the shopping experience (Schulz, 2019).

There is a huge scope for shopping on Insta which is in the infancy stage in the countries like India. And after the pandemic, a shift from E-commerce to social commerce is also gaining attention and more strategic moves are required by the companies to be unique and attract consumers. Social commerce in India is still small at only $1.5 -2 billion (Tandon, 2021).

After the pandemic, more people are moving online and discovering new ways of shopping, so group-buying over the internet has more potential. Companies like WhatsApp and Instagram are stamping too, as is a clench of startups such as Meesho, Mall91, Shop101, Dealshare, and Bulbul (Tandon, 2021).

There are 60 group-buying companies globally and let's have a look at the most famous ones:

Pinduoduo: It's an e-commerce platform that allows users to participate with friends for the deals. It works with the Wechat app and deals in various categories like food, baby products and cosmetics. It was founded in 2015 in Shanghai, China.

Qoo10: It is an e-commerce marketplace for daily deals, group buying and auctions. It deals in various items like watches, clothes, electronics and sculpture items. Qoo10 was established in 2010 in Singapore.

BuyWithMe: It is a group-buying website that provides daily deals for various activities like Spa, restaurants, health clubs and bars in the local city. It was founded in 2009 in New York City, United States.

Mall91: It is a community platform for the consumer products like clothes, jewellery, electronics, home decor and cosmetics. It uses social group-buying for accumulating demand. It was founded in 2017 in Delhi, India.

KitaBeli: It's an app-based group-buying platform for multiple categories such as food, home appliances, cosmetics, mother and baby care products etc. It was originated in 2020 in Jakarta, Indonesia.

CityMall: An online group-buying gateway founded in 2019 at Gurugram (India). This platform trades in multiple ranges of products like beauty and home furnishings at discounted prices. It has a network of over 2 lakh customers and 20000 sellers.

ShopG: This allows users to group with their friends and avail discounts for products ranging from electronics, grocery items, beauty & personal care accessories, kitchenware, home decor products, and more. It is an online retailer established in 2018 in Bangalore, India.

Facily: It's an app-based shopping platform for android users. This platform provides group-buying for products like beauty products, electronics, drinks, smartphones and headsets etc. It was established in 2018 in Sao Paulo Do Potengi, Brazil.

Lashou: This is a daily deal website that offers discounts if a minimum number of people show their interest in purchasing a product. Deals are offered in categories like hotels and travel. It started in 2010 in Beijing, China.

Grupanya: This is a group-buying website offering daily deals on restaurants, spas, beauty centres and more. It was founded in 2010 in Istanbul, Turkey.

These are the few key points which marketers should keep in mind while promoting in different cultures:

1. For the US market, to enhance perceived trust, marketers should emphasize the credibility of the group-buying platform and consumer satisfaction as a company's main role. For this, there should be a blog for consumer's reviews and a question-and-answer section for interactive

communication among existing customers, potential buyers and buying platform's customer service (Tsai & Zhang, 2016).

2.   For the Chinese market, the popularity of the deals should be highlighted. Apart from this, a segmentation strategy can be implemented for Chinese male consumers to promote unique and unusual products (Tsai & Zhang, 2016).

3.   In the Chinese market, advertisers should endorse uniqueness in their promotional strategies to persuade consumers with a strong desire to differentiate. Even the group-buying sites should be positioned as trendsetting and distinguishing shopping platforms appealing to consumers with unique tastes (Tsai & Zhang, 2016).

4.   In the Chinese market, marketers should facilitate app-based shopping experience, because people are more prone to use mobile phones than laptops. (Hossain & Rahman, 2021)

5.   In the American market, OGB sites become popular only if it has positive and reliable feedback from other group members. So, marketers should promote blogs, feedback and through social networking sites to gain trust from the consumers. (Ward et al., 2014)

6.   In the American market, a risk-free environment should be promoted by the online group-buying websites to attract US consumers (Tsai & Zhang, 2016).

7.   For newly established OGB sites, they should strategically promote name brand products at discounted prices to stand differently in the competitive Chinese OGB sites as it will attract more Chinese consumers, but this penetration strategy will not work with US consumers (Tsai & Zhang, 2016).

Conclusion

The idea lying behind group-buying is that buyers come organized to a seller about buying a specific product in bulk. Purchasing in bulk usually facilitates negotiated prices by working collectively. It is not only the discounted price that persuades group-buying but this trade makes possible the dealings that won't happen without this group-buying approach. Buying in groups isn't a new notion but it's prevalent for many years. One example is buying of household solar power by the local households being together as a group to negotiate with the installers. This system is beneficial for both parties' buyers and installers. It is gainful for the installer to provide the service in a local area where there are multiple buyers.

Group-buying deals are helpful for marketers to manage the consumer traffic on quiet days such as deal on spa activity on a particular weekday to avoid the rush on weekends. Marketing cost is also lower if the deal is offered to a group. Group-buying is all about relationships -between the buyers as co-workers, between seller and buyer and between seller and middlemen that represent the group. To engross with buying groups, you need to manage these relationships effectively.

Based upon the above study, businesses should keep on modifying their marketing strategies to suit the different cultural requirements, as they should focus upon the unique products or deals to attract Chinese consumers and make their sites more reliable by providing detailed information to keep their American consumers and provide heavy discounts and ease of access to capture Indian counterparts. In India, there is a huge scope of online group buying. Moreover, pandemic has also changed the mindset of people towards online shopping due to increased use of internet and phones. Hence marketers should keep on bringing innovations in the deals and services to capture massive segment.

References

Abrar, P. (2021, July 8). *E-commerce firm DealShare's valuation crosses $455 mn after raising $144 mn.* Businessstandard.Com. Retrieved March 2, 2022, from https://www.business-standard.com/article/companies/e-commerce-firm-dealshare-s-valuation-crosses-455-mn-after-raising-144-mn-1210708 00679_1.html

Admin-Demo. (2021). *Social Commerce – the virtual shopping stroll with friends.* Just Style. Retrieved October 12, 2021, from https://www.just-style.com/comment/social-commerce-the-virtual-shopping-stroll-with-friends

Al-Mashari, M. (2002). Electronic commerce: A comparative study of organizational experiences. *Benchmarking: An International Journal.*

Amichai-Hamburger, Yair, Galit Wainapel, and Shaul Fox. "On the Internet no one knows I'm an introvert: Extroversion, neuroticism, and Internet interaction." *Cyberpsychology & behavior* 5, no. 2 (2002): 125-128.

Becerra, E. P., & Korgaonkar, P. K. (2009). Hispanics' information Search and Patronage Intentions Online. *Journal of Electronic Commerce Research, 10*(2).

Bosnjak, M., Galesic, M., &Tuten, T. (2007). Personality determinants of online shopping: Explaining online purchase intentions using a hierarchical approach. *Journal of Business Research,* 60(6), 597–605.

Cai, S., & Xu, Y. (2008). Designing product lists for e-commerce: The effects of sorting on consumer decision making. *Intl. Journal of Human–Computer Interaction, 24*(7), 700-721.

Cashmore, P. (2010, April 15). *Group buying: A Billion-dollar web trend?* CNN. Retrieved October 15, 2021, from http://www.cnn.com/2010/TECH/04/15/cashmore.group.buying/index.html.

Cheng, H. H., & Huang, S. W. (2013). Exploring antecedents and consequence of online group-buying intention: An extended perspective on theory of planned behavior. *International Journal of Information Management, 33*(1), 185-198.

CNNIC. (n.d.). Retrieved October 15, 2021, from http://www.cnnic.cn/hlwfzyj /hlwxzbg/dzswbg/201208/P020120827473850053431.pdf

Dong, B., Peng, W., & Zhou, Y. (2012, June). The credit evaluation system for marketers of online group buying. In *2012 Fifth International Joint Conference on Computational Sciences and Optimization* (pp. 85-88). IEEE.

E-commerce lessons from China: How group buying pays off. SmartBrief. (2019, April 4). Retrieved October 12, 2021, from https://www.smartbrief.com/original/ 2019/04/e-commerce-lessons-china-how-group-buying-pays-0

Ehrenberg, A., Juckes, S., White, K.M., &Walsh, S. P. (2008). Personality and self-esteem as predictors of young people's technology use. *Cyberpsychology & Behavior,* 11(6), 739–741.

Erdoğmuş, I. E., & Čiçek, M. (2011). Online Group Buying: What Is There for The Consumers? *Procedia - Social and Behavioral Sciences, 24,* 308–316. https://doi.org/10.1016/J.SBSPRO.2011.09.138

Gao, L. (2014). *Customers' online group buying decision-making in emerging market: A Quantitative Study of Chinese online group buying* (thesis).

'Group buying' to contribute 25-30 PC of revenues in FY19: Grofers - et retail. ETRetail.com. (2018, October 6). Retrieved October 12, 2021, from https://retail. economictimes.indiatimes.com/news/food-entertainment/grocery/group-buying-to-contribute-25-30-pc-of-revenues-in-fy19-grofers/66094584.

Hollensen, S. (2004). Global Marketing. England.

Hossain, M. A., & Rahman, S. (2021). Investigating the Success of OGB in China: The Influence of Personality Traits. *Information Systems Frontiers, 23*(3), 543–559. https://doi.org/10.1007/s10796-019-09968-0

Hsu, C. L., & Lin, J. C. C. (2008). Acceptance of blog usage: The roles of technology acceptance, social influence and knowledge sharing motivation. *Information & management, 45*(1), 65-74.

India Education Diary (2021, September 15). *Gyandhan launches Gyandhan Allied – India's first group buying plan for Abroad Education Loans.* India Education | Latest Education News | Global Educational News | Recent Educational News. Retrieved March 2, 2022, from https://indiaeducationdiary. in/gyandhan-launches-gyandhan-allied-indias-first-group-buying-plan-for-abroad-education-loans/

Jiang, X., & Deng, S. (2014). Optimal strategy for selling on group-buying website. *Journal of Industrial Engineering and Management, 7*(4), 769–784. https://doi.org/10.3926/jiem.1153

Kai, C., Xiaofan, W., Qiuying, Z., & Huanhuan, L. (2013). An Exploratory Study of Influence Factors about Consumers Online Group Buying Intention. *Journal of Applied Sciences, 13*(8), 1370-1375.

Kauffman, R. J., & Wang, B. (2001). New buyers' arrival under dynamic pricing market microstructure: The case of group-buying discounts on the internet. *Journal of Management Information Systems, 18*(2), 157-188.

Leading Online Group buying brands. Verified Market Research. (2021, July 26). Retrieved October 13, 2021, from https://www.verifiedmarketresearch. com/blog/leading-online-group-buying-brands/.

Li, C., Sycara, K., & Scheller-Wolf, A. (2010). Combinatorial coalition formation for multi-item group-buying with heterogeneous customers. *Decision Support Systems, 49*(1), 1-13.

Liao, C., Palvia, P., & Lin, H. N. (2006). The roles of habit and web site quality in e-commerce. *International Journal of Information Management, 26*(6), 469-483.

Olsen, S. O., Tudoran, A. A., Honkanen, P., & Verplanken, B. (2016). Differences and similarities between impulse buying and variety seeking: A personality-based perspective. *Psychology & Marketing, 33*(1), 36-47.

Oppenheim, C., & Ward, L. (2006). Evaluation of web sites for B2C e-commerce. *Aslib Proceedings, 58*(3), 237–260. https://doi.TsauTsaiorg/10.1108/000125306 10701022

Pi, S. M., Liao, H. L., Liu, S. H., & Lee, I. S. (2011). Factors influencing the behavior of online group-buying in Taiwan. *African Journal of Business Management, 5*(16), 7120-7129.

Ross, C., Orr, E. S., Sisic, M., Arseneault, J. M., Simmering, M. G., & Orr, R. R. (2009). Personality and motivations associated with Facebook use. *Computers in human behavior, 25*(2), 578-586.

Ryan, T., & Xenos, S. (2011). Who uses Facebook? An investigation into the relationship between the Big Five, shyness, narcissism, loneliness, and Facebook usage. *Computers in human behavior, 27*(5), 1658-1664.

Sarkar, S. (2021, July 16). *DealShare, a social commerce startup, is using the community group-buying model to cater to the online shopping interests of consumers belonging to smaller Indian towns and cities*. Dutch Uncles. https://dutchuncles.in/discover/dealshare-promoting-the-community-group -buying-model/

Schulz, K. (2019, December 23). *Shopping in a collective – Social commerce is evolving into social group buying*. Dmexco.Com. Retrieved March 7, 2022, from https://dmexco.com/stories/shopping-in-a-collective-social-commerce-is-evolving-into-social-group-buying

Sharma, S. (2010, August 27). *Group buying ventures are here to stay in India? entrepreneurs and investors talk on the current opportunities and challenges in this space*. YourStory.com. Retrieved October 12, 2021, from https://yourstory. com/2010/08/group-buying-ventures-are-here-to-stay-in-india-entrepreneurs-and-investors-talk-on-the-current-opportunities-and-challenges-in-this-space/ amp

Shiau, W. L., & Luo, M. M. (2012). Factors affecting online group buying intention and satisfaction: A social exchange theory perspective. *Computers in Human Behavior, 28*(6), 2431-2444.

Social commerce – The virtual shopping stroll with friends. (2021, March 2). Just-Style.Com. Retrieved March 7, 2022, from https://www.just-style.com/ comment/social-commerce-the-virtual-shopping-stroll-with-friends/

Stulec, Ivana, and Kristina Petljak. (2010). Moc grupne kupovine. *Suvremena trgovina* 35 (6): 22–25.

Tandon, S. (2021, May 4). *Social Commerce gets closer to being 'formal'*. mint. Retrieved October 12, 2021, from https://www.livemint.com/industry/retail /social-commerce-gets-closer-to-being-formal-11620156344574.html

Top Group Buying Startups. (2022, January 14). Tracxn.Com. Retrieved March 7, 2022, from https://tracxn.com/d/trending-themes/Startups-in-Group-Buying

Tsai, W. H. S., & Zhang, J. (2016). Understanding the Global Phenomenon of Online Group Buying: Perspective from China and the United States. *Journal of Global Marketing, 29*(4), 188–202. https://doi.org/10.1080/08911762.2016 .1138565

Turban, E., King, D., Lee, J. K., & Viehland, D. (2006). Electronic Commerce: A Managerial Approach.

Venkatesh, V., Sykes, T. A., & Venkatraman, S. (2014). Understanding e-government portal use in rural India: Role of demographic and personality characteristics. *Information Systems Journal, 24*(3), 249–269.

Ward, P. R., Mamerow, L., & Meyer, S. B. (2014). Interpersonal trust across six Asia-Pacific countries: testing and extending the 'high trust society' and 'low trust society' theory. *PloS one, 9*(4), e95555.

Williams, G. A. (2020, September 2). *What can luxury learn from group buying?* Jing Daily. Retrieved October 13, 2021, from https://jingdaily.com/ what-can-luxury-learn-from-group-buying/.

Xu, F. (2011, August). A comparative study of online group-coupon sale in USA and China. In *2011 2nd International Conference on Artificial Intelligence, Management Science and Electronic Commerce (AIMSEC)* (pp. 1806-1809). IEEE.

Yang, B., & Lester, D. (2005). Gender differences in e-commerce. *Applied Economics, 37*(18), 2077-2089.

Zhang, J. J., & Tsai, W. H. S. (2015). United We Shop! Chinese Consumers' Online Group Buying. *Journal of International Consumer Marketing, 27*(1), 54–68. https://doi.org/10.1080/08961530.2014.967902

Zhang, J., & Tsai, W. S. (2017). What Promotes Online Group-Buying? A Cross-Cultural Comparison Study between China and the United States. *Journal of Promotion Management, 23*(5), 748–768. https://doi.org/10.1080/10496491. 2017.1297986

Chapter 8

Greenhouse Effect: The Driver for the Convergence in the Cross-Cultural Business Ethics

Rauno Rusko

University of Lapland, Finland

Abstract: This chapter considers the cross-cultural effects of the joint global features, such as the greenhouse effect and global warming (or Covid-19). The analyses are based on the content analysis of the articles on the greenhouse effect and global warming from the magazines in the different continents of the world. Outcomes show the convergence of attitudes and rhetoric in cross-cultural business ethics due to the greenhouse effect. Terminology (in English) was very similar all over the world. Articles revealed uniform attitudes around the world to cut global warming. National nuances were minor, and these few nuances were based on the reflections of global warming, national conditions and domestic policy. Especially the international reports about the greenhouse effect and global warming were introduced similarly across the world. Also, the need to reduce greenhouse emissions was accepted in the headlines and general content of the articles. Actually, none of the studied articles denies global warming. Furthermore, several articles noticed similarities or linkages between the greenhouse effect and Covid-19. The studied articles were written in English, which might have effects on these uniform results.

Keywords: cross-cultural business ethics, global warming, greenhouse effect, convergence, divergence, attitudes, corporate social responsibility.

***

Introduction

The contemporary global business environment is turbulent. Also, the changes between different cultures and groups in society are turbulent. There are several local, national and global drivers that have divergent or convergent effects on the cross-cultural business environment. However, seminal business and management studies provided by Michael Porter (1990) in *Competitive Advantage of Nations* and Kenichi Ohmae (1990) in *The Borderless World* express the role of countries and cultures differently. Porter (1990) emphasizes the importance of a national home base in business, but Ohmae (1990) sees similarities between different nations and cultures.

Actually, it is important to understand these global convergent trends, such as consumer cultures or other joint tendencies, which have global effects on everyday living and business. Consumer culture is one potential driver for convergent cross-cultural business and management practices, but not the only one. Also, several other international phenomena, such as tourism and travelling, digital technology, global epidemics (e.g. Covid-19) or global warming and the greenhouse effect, might have convergent effects on cross-cultural business attitudes and management practices. Covid-19 is an example of a short-term tendency or reality, and global warming is an example of a long-term tendency, which is globally similar, but it meets the diversified cultural and national contexts. There are similar global manifestations to the business practices, but still some small divergent nuances among cultures and nations in the struggle against global warming – or Covid-19 epidemics, for instance. In other words, various cultures and nations, in spite of different backgrounds, take similarly into account global warming in their societal and business attitudes, and the general effects of the awareness of global warming on business ethics are nearly uniform.

According to Scherer and Palazzo (2008), the world has several cross-national problems and accidents, such as environmental disasters (Tchernobyl, global warming, overfishing of oceans, loss of biodiversity, etc.), global diseases (bird flu, mad cow disease etc.) and social problems (drugs, organized criminality, terrorism etc.), which do not halt at national borders but affect the lives of people who become aware that their traditional nation-state institutions have become unable to protect them from harm. They argue that "political corporate social responsibility" (CSR) can be understood as a movement of the corporation into environmental and social challenges such as human rights, global warming, or deforestation (Scherer & Palazzo, 2008). CSR, which is a popular way of acting and thinking in business, takes wide care of the threats of natural changes and business ethics. This study focuses on CSR, business ethics, greenhouse effects and cross-cultural business environment together. The focal point is in the connection between the greenhouse effect and cross-cultural business ethics, but not especially in the concept of CSR.

This study leans on textual comparative content analysis. It describes and analyses expressions about global warming and the greenhouse effect in public documents, actually articles in magazines, from across the world, taking into account six continents: Europe, Asia, Africa, North America, South America, and Australia.

After the introduction follows the theoretical part of the chapter, which contains the greenhouse effect in scientific business and management discussions, discussions of business ethics and cross-cultural discussions in management, then the method and research material are introduced. After that are outcomes with general findings and the greenhouse effect and reflections on cross-cultural business ethics. Finally, this chapter contains conclusions, references and an appendix.

Literature Review

This subsection introduces literature about the triangle of cross-cultural business and management Greenhouse effect (global warming), and business ethics. The literature about business ethics and CSR (Corporate social responsibility) is multifaced. Furthermore, cross-cultural business and management is a topical and popular theme of research in the field of management. In addition, the greenhouse effect or global warming is one of the most popular topics not only in everyday discussions but also among scientific literature in nearly all disciplines. In this sense, the effects of global warming on public and scientific discussions resemble the effects of contemporary Covid-19 epidemics all over the world. Practically the linkage between these two phenomena is thin, however. The literature, which is focused on both global warming and Covid-19, expresses the effects of Covid-19 on global warming due to lockdown actions in societies (Boretti, 2020; Krecl et al., 2020; Yang et al., 2020). Some discussions see these two phenomena as similar to the threat of nuclear war. That is, Covid-19, nuclear war and global warming are "lessons for our vulnerable world" (Muller & Nathan, 2020).

Deliberation on Cross-Cultural Management

Two important business researchers, Michael Porter and Kenichi Ohmae, have demerged perspectives on national borders and cultures in business. Porter (1990) emphasizes the importance of countries in international business. According to Porter, successful international firms are based on geographical clusters and home bases. Thus, the different local conditions are important in the creation process of the business diamond models. Ohmae (1990), however, expresses the importance of cultural convergence in international business. Even before the expansion of the internet and other digital connections, Ohmae claimed that cultural similarities are more and more important among customers due to rising education levels all over the world. Similar consumer cultures all over the world might have stronger effects on international management and business than local cultural characteristics, such as religion or nation.

Cross-cultural management has several definitions with nuances in the literature. Some researchers, such as Holden (2002), emphasize this context knowledge management. Holden (2002) see also that cross-cultural management might be a sub-discipline of international management and management practice. It offers tools to handle cultural differences seen as sources of conflict or miscommunication (Søderberg & Holden, 2002). However, Søderberg and Holden (2002) express the need to understand cross-cultural management in a new way, which focuses on the complexity of intra- and inter-organizational connections and identities in a globalizing business context.

Several cross-cultural studies consider some basic perspectives, such as Schein's model of organizational culture and Hofstede's cultural dimensions (Derr & Laurent, 1989; Holden, 2002; Feldman & Msibi, 2014). Schein's model of organizational culture contains observable and non-observable elements having three levels in organizational cultures: artifacts and behaviours, espoused values and assumptions. Only artifacts are visible to the people who are not part of the culture. Espoused values are the organization's stated values and rules of behavior in official philosophies and public statements of identity. Shared basic assumptions are well integrated, difficult to recognize, and they are deeply embedded, taken-for-granted behaviours (Schein, 1980). Hofstede's cultural dimensions theory is a framework for cross-cultural communication showing the effects of a society's culture on the values of its members and how these values relate to behavior (Adeoye & Tomei, 2014). These dimensions of national culture are 1) Power distance index (PDI): distance between less powerful members and powerful. A lower degree of PDI means that people question authority and attempt to distribute power; 2) Individualism vs. collectivism 3) Uncertainty avoidance 4) Masculinity vs. femininity 5) Long-term orientation vs. short-term orientation 6) Indulgence vs. restraint (Hofstede, 1991).

This chapter is not restricted to these seminal studies of cross-cultural management. Of course, these studies of Schein and Hofstede have been taken into account, but the focus is on the practical manifestations of cross-cultural business and management actions, discussions and attitudes in the context of the greenhouse effect and global warming.

Greenhouse Effect in the Scientific Business and Management

Business ethics covers several subthemes, such as environmentalism, corporate social responsibility and good and polite business practices (Hoffman, 1991). Business ethics does not have a good definition, or actually, there are too many various definitions. According to Lewis (1985), typical definitions of business ethics refer to the rightness or wrongness of behavior, but the problem is that not everyone agrees on what is morally right or wrong, good or bad, ethical or unethical. Furthermore, these definitions are highly at abstract levels (Lewis, 1985). Actually, Trevino and Weaver (1994) noticed that there are two fields of business ethics, normative business ethics, which is quite abstract and empirical business ethics, which is relatively concrete.

Business ethics has several nuances and attitudes. A very typical perspective is based on a somehow reverse definition of business ethics. Actually, "missing" business ethics. One of the basic assumptions in business ethics seems to be that people in business are somehow "morally insufficient" (Jones et al., 2010). Also, Donaldson and Fafaliou (2003) have similar perspectives. According to them, business ethics, corporate social responsibility and corporate governance movements have been developed "as responses to a growing sense of corporate wrongdoing". Furthermore, business ethics and corporate social responsibility are linked with sustainable development and the greenhouse effect (Moon, 2007).

Some of the latest contemporary studies about business ethics and corporate social responsibility express the role of business and marketing education and the possibilities to improve the attitudes of the students. Hopkins and colleagues (2021) studied the attitudes toward marketing ethics of the students before and afterward of the lectures. Blanco-González et al. (2021) examined, among others, the connection between higher education and business ethics. In the education of business ethics, the role of the natural environment is linked with the natural conditions of the area. In Oceania, for example, where the threat of global warming is concrete due to concerns about water security and rising sea levels, the natural environment is very important (Gustavson, 2011).

The greenhouse effect and global warming is not a new topic in scientific discussions. Already 1985 was an international conference that warned that increasing concentrations of carbon dioxide and other greenhouse gases in the atmosphere could raise the global temperature higher than ever before in recorded history (Mintzer, 1987). Thus, these discussions have been topical for nearly 40 years. The general problem is not limited to one or some countries, but it is global. Therefore, the greenhouse effect provides a good starting point to investigate cross-cultural dimensions in the discussions of this problem.

The greenhouse effect is linked with energy in the world. According to Hu (2005),

From thermodynamics, the global warming problem is an 'energy balance' problem. The heat (energy) accumulation in the earth and its atmosphere is the cause of global warming. This accumulation is mainly due to the imbalance of (solar) energy reaching and the energy leaving the earth, caused by the 'greenhouse effect' in which the CO2 and other greenhouse gases play a critical role; so that balance of the energy entering and leaving the earth should be the key to solve the problem.

However, some early studies were skeptical about characters of the greenhouse effect, such as the role of fossil fuels. Even the question "Could reducing fossil-fuel emissions cause global warming?" has been asked by Wigley (1991). According to Wigley, when fossil fuel is burned, both carbon dioxide and sulphur dioxide are added to the atmosphere. Actually, sulphur dioxide, by producing sulphate aerosols, may cause a cooling effect (Wigley, 1991). Generally, the focal point in the discussions of global warming and the greenhouse effect is energy.

Some management and business studies, which focus on the greenhouse effect, consider industrial or sectoral perspectives. These perspectives of the greenhouse effect in the industries are generally twofold: either they consider problematic industries, such as oil and coal industries, and their activities to improve the environmental effects of these, in this sense harmful, industries, or they focus on new branches, which have aimed to generally diminish global warming and greenhouse effect, such as the industries producing or using renewable energies. That is, their main focus is based on tackling the greenhouse effect of the developed technology, which is possibly suitable for several uses in business.

The oil industry is one of these first-mentioned themes. Jaworska (2018), for instance, studies discourses of climate change in corporate social responsibility (CSR) and environmental reports produced by major oil companies from 2000 to 2013. According to Jaworska (2018), the oil industry seems to accept that climate change does exist and needs to be tackled or combatted. However, there is little discussion about the causes of climate change or discussions using expressions such as 'potential' and 'eventual', implying a degree of doubt in the link between greenhouse gas emissions and climate change. Jaworska (2018) says that, in this way, causes that obviously link climate change with the oil industry are conveniently 'talked down'.

Hybrid cars, for example, represent the latter cases. Seitz et al. (2007) focused on Asia and hybrid cars in their study. Furthermore, the purpose of the study was to measure the awareness of global warming in addition to attitudes toward hybrid cars in Asia, especially in Singapore. Generally, there was a great demand for cars in Singapore among young people, but they have low awareness of corporate social responsibility. Most respondents in the study of Seitz et al. (2007) knew basic information about global warming, and over half had little knowledge regarding hybrids and their role in reducing global warming. They see that marketers need to raise awareness of hybrid cars, communicating both environmental and economic benefits.

More generally, management discussions consider the reactions and tools of the firms to participate in the global game against the greenhouse effect. These perspectives have provided new concepts, such as carbon management practices (CMP). According to Lee and Klassen (2016), the firms have very different reactions in adopting and implementing CMPs in response to the global warming issue. The results of their study indicate that perceived business uncertainty decreases the adoption of CMPs, organizational learning and lean production capabilities strongly facilitate the adoption and implementation of CMPs, and lean production capability positively moderates the impacts of business uncertainty on the adoption of CMPs (Lee & Klassen, 2016).

However, the use of CMP does not necessarily ensure significant improvements in the firms. According to Doda and colleagues (2016), they find only little compelling evidence that commonly adopted corporate carbon management practices are reducing emissions. They noticed three possible reasons for it. First, corporate carbon data and management practice information have not been reported in a standardized way. Second, the delay between the application of corporate carbon management practices and their impact on emissions performance. In addition, carbon management practices are not sufficiently impact-oriented (Doda et al., 2016). Scientific CMP discussions cover several branches, such as farming (Liu et al., 2019; Mills et al., 2020), tourism (Stefan, 2010) and forestry (Yang et al., 2020), among others.

Method and Research Material

This study leans on content analysis, which focuses on the articles of magazines, where the content is based on the greenhouse effect and/or global warming. There are articles from all continents of the world (excluding the Antarctic). The amount of population has effects on the analyzed number of articles from different continents: the largest amount from Asia and the smallest amount from Australia, together with 23 analyzed articles (see Appendix 1). These articles have to fulfill the following criteria:

1. They are written in English;

2. They focus on the greenhouse effect and/or global warming;

3. They are available on the Web;

4. They are the latest (or nearly the latest) articles on the greenhouse effect/global warming. Practically nearly all of them were published during Summer 2021 or Autumn 2021.

In addition to content analysis, this chapter follows the principles of the case study strategy. The studied articles are examples of the greenhouse effect discussions in different parts of the world. Due to the large geographical area of this study, the case study analysis is based on secondary data. In the management discussions, secondary data has been used to provide the representative features of the studied theme (e.g., Rusko, 2014).

The analysis considered only national (or continental) magazines which are written in English. This might have effects on the general content of these magazines. In several countries and continents, English is not the main language. The fact that the magazine is written in English reflects some implications: it is not directed to the "ordinary" or the "main" people of the area. This is not the problem in Northern America (especially in USA and Canada), Great Britain or in Australia, but the other parts of the world. This study is aimed to be multinational, and therefore the share of the material about these English-speaking countries is not over-emphasized. Furthermore, uniform language has effects on the content of the studies articles in the magazines. Especially the magazines which are written in English and which are not published in the English-speaking area might be directed to the international public. Thus, they are not mainly directed to the local people of the area.

The Outcomes

General Findings

This subsection introduces some examples of the contents of the articles in the magazines when they view greenhouse effects and global warming from each continent of the world. The aim is not to compare these contents here, but the next subsection analyses this material focusing on the reflections of the content on cross-cultural business ethics. The language used in the articles, that is, English, has some effects on the results: In many nations, most of the citizens do not understand English, and the content of the articles might be directed mostly to the international audience.

There are in the world seven continents: Asia, Africa, North America, South America, Antarctica, Europe, and Australia, but this chapter investigates only six of them, excluding Antarctica. Asia has 51 countries and about 60 percent of the population in the world. Africa contains 54 countries and about 17 percent of the population in the world. North America has 38 countries; the largest ones are the United States, Canada and Mexico, and about 7.6 percent of the population in the world. South America contains 12 countries and 5.6 percent of the population in the world. Europe has 51 countries and nearly 10 percent of the population in the world. The continent of Australia contains three countries and about 0.5 percent of the population in the world.

National articles, which focus on the greenhouse effect and global warming, emphasize several similar themes and perspectives all over the world, such as the target of global warming is to be kept below 1.5 °C. Furthermore, they use the same sources in their content. Especially international reports, such as the IPCC report and the IEA report, are important sources of these articles, and even the main message of these reports is the same in these articles (Articles 12,14,15,18,19 and 22). Only some of the articles focus on financial themes (Articles 3 and 16). Three out of 23 articles view Covid-19 in the context of global warming and the greenhouse effect (9, 20 and 23). It is interesting that the problems of coal have been expressed only in Chinese articles (Articles 5 and 7) and oil in one Norwegian article (22).

National Findings: Greenhouse Effect and Reflections on Cross-Cultural Business Ethics

Indian articles, which focus on the greenhouse effect and global warming, often consider international reports and introduce the most important results them. These articles emphasize, for example, forecasted movements of people within their own countries in the case of six regions (Latin America; North Africa; Sub-Saharan Africa; Eastern Europe and Central Asia; South Asia; and East Asia and the Pacific), (Article 1), or effects of global warming in the USA (Article 3). However, Indian today also introduces some national studies about the financial effects of global warming, such as 'carbon risk premium'. IIT Guwahati and IIM Bangalore researchers have found a 'carbon risk premium' in stock returns, which establishes links between the carbon footprint of polluting companies and the long-term risks of investing in them (Article 2).

The studied Chinese articles have more national nuances compared with Indian articles. These articles emphasize the large problematic role of coal in the economy of China. However, Article 4 considers global warming, but the main focus is on one old Chinese character, which has several (alternative) meanings of natural conditions in different historical periods. Most of the studied Chinese articles, which are written in English, express the aims of China to cut greenhouse emissions. On the main page of News China magazine, global warming and the greenhouse effect has a remarkable role: In the changing headline (Cover Stories), 3 out of 4 themes focus on global warming. These headlines contain articles which view: "Coal hard truth", that is, "reaching China's carbon emissions target before 2030, means a painful adjustment period lies ahead for its coal-rich provinces" (Article 5); "Green revolution", where "senior climate change official Li Gao talks about the progress China has made toward the goals of peaking carbon emissions and achieving carbon neutrality" (Article 6); and "Climate for change", which introduces ambitious goals of China "to cut its carbon emissions. But given its heavy investment in coal power, which fuels the country's economic growth, a path to carbon neutrality or even carbon peaking has yet to emerge" (Article 7). Article 5, for example, considers partly also the themes of domestic or local policy: Inner Mongolia produces coal for other parts of China, and it consumes energy three times related to its region's total economic output. The authorities have to change the situation in the near future in this region.

Some of the studied Japanese articles introduce similar roadmaps in the path of green economy as Chinese articles. Article 8 contains details about the "Sustainable Recovery: TIME TO ACT" conference of the Tokyo Metropolitan Government (TMG), which is "laying down the roadmap for Tokyo to spearhead a global charge towards environmental sustainability" (Article 8). Article 10 also considers the national effects of greenhouse effects: the shortage of snow in the local Snow-festival, but also the wide economic effects of global warming in several sectors of Japan, and finally, the possibilities in Japan to change the direction. According to Article 10, Japan is one of the fortunate countries to have vast biodiversity and different weather patterns from Hokkaido to Okinawa. Furthermore, Article 10 expresses that there "can be national strategies in place to help species move northward, by replanting corals or seaweed and thus giving them a small push". Article 9 compares Covid-19 to global warming: they have several similar features, such as "it sees no borders, cares naught for your wealth nor the color of your skin, and none will be spared its repercussions" and "It is worse, much worse than you think." Article 9 ponders with the continuous comparisons to effects of Covid-19, how Japan can become more energy efficient in the future.

The analysis of African magazines concentrated on Africa Business Magazine because it focuses on the whole continent of Africa, emphasizing the themes of management and business. However, the results were relatively general: the themes of the articles consider the whole world with the items such as the reports of IPCC (Intergovernmental Panel on Climate Change), where the article contains details about the estimated climate changes (Article 12); or the possibilities to slash greenhouse gas emissions in transportation and power generation with the help of renewable methanol fuel (Article 11). This article is based on the international Renewable Methanol Report, which was prepared for the Methanol Institute (in the USA). Furthermore, among African articles was a paper, which has the following headline: "Mining and Metals Companies Accelerate Focus on Sustainability"

(Article 13). This article contains details about environmental cooperation between French and British firms, and it is written in India.

Generally, plenty of English articles in the magazines, which focus on the greenhouse effect and global warming, have been written in North America, especially in the USA. In this chapter, the number of articles from North America is comparable to the population of this area. The contents in the analyzed articles of the USA resemble the articles from the rest of the world: they are based on international reports about global warming and greenhouse effects (Articles 14 and 15). Article 15 emphasizes that

> Global temperatures will likely exceed the 1.5C limit set by the Paris climate agreement within the next 20 years unless swift and drastic action is taken to reduce greenhouse gas emissions, according to a comprehensive assessment of climate science by the Intergovernmental Panel on Climate Change (IPCC), the world's leading authority on the subject.

Article 14 is based on the same IPCC report. Article 16 asks, "What if we could accelerate decarbonization and the removal of carbon dioxide from the air, achieving global climate targets, all without saddling future generations with trillions of dollars of debt?" The article introduces the ideas of researchers in Oxford who have developed an idea for dealing with greenhouse gas emissions as if they are financial debt (Article 16).

Canadian article (Article 17) focuses on natural catastrophic events and their effects on the insurance business. This article emphasizes local conditions and admits that the effects of global warming on the insurance business are difficult to evaluate. However, "certain areas of the country are at higher risk of flooding, fires and other extreme events, and premiums are priced accordingly" (Article 17).

Articles 18 and 19 introduce the content of magazines in South America. The headline of Article 18 is "Brazil set to be devastated by climate change". This article also introduces the IPCC report, which "shows how rising sea levels, floods, and droughts will impact the country if emissions continue to rise". Also, Article 19 (Buenos Aires Times) considers the content of the same IPCC report.

Analyses cover three articles in the magazines from Europe: from Great Britain (Article 20), Germany (Article 21) and Norway (Article 22). Article 20 (The Guardian) considers both Covid-19 and global warming in the same article. The content of the article is mainly focused on British domestic policy though the themes are global. Article 20 contains the thought that "Boris Johnson should set out plans to provide Covid-19 vaccinations to all developing countries to achieve a global climate deal, Labor's shadow business secretary, Ed Miliband, has urged". According to the headline of Article 21 (The European), "Decarbonization startups raise hope for corporate sustainability, says GlobalData". This article focuses on the theme: "The need for a reduction in emissions has led to an increase in the number of innovative startups helping to make processes a little greener". The introduced environmental innovations of Article 21 are from German, Iceland and USA, among others. Article 22 concentrates on Arctic oil drilling and express that "there can be no new oil and gas projects in the Arctic if global warming is to be kept below 1,5 °C," according to the report of IEA.

Article 23 from Australia considers at same time Covid-19 and global warming. Covid-19 has (temporary) positive effects on nature, which this article expresses. Article 23 has some kind of astrological or mythological background though it considers these two themes above properly.

Conclusions

The analysis of the articles in magazines about the greenhouse effect and global warming provided certain cross-cultural outcomes. Outcomes confirm the ideas of Ohmae (1990). Differences between the contents of the articles about the greenhouse effect and global warming from different parts of the world are minimal. All over the world, the same international reports of the greenhouse effect have been introduced using the same information and even the same words. There are no remarkable cultural differences in the message of the greenhouse effect and global warming. Even the articles, which show new cases of environmental innovations and improvements, contains mainly example from other countries. Thus, the outcomes show the convergence of attitudes in cross-cultural business ethics due to the greenhouse effect. It is possible to conclude that the greenhouse effect will unify the discussions of business ethics in the branch of environmentalism: the terminology is the same; the national aims of the environmental policy are parallel with each other. Articles all over the world are based on long-term orientation and some kind of (positive) collectivism, that is, some kind of "we together" attitude. However, articles do not find solutions for global warming, and they mainly only notice the development and the need to cut greenhouse gas emissions in the long run. Some of the articles even noticed that new, already-decided coal energy investments would speed up the (local) development. One exception is article 16 from the USA, which introduced new ideas invented by Oxford to construct economic intensives to cut greenhouse emissions.

Another frequent feature in several articles is the comparisons or linkages between Covid-19 and the greenhouse effect/global warming. These two phenomena have been noticed to have similarly wide global effects, and, furthermore, Covid-19 had (temporal) effects, which partly slowed down global warming.

Cultural differences between the articles, which focused on the greenhouse effect, are difficult to find. Surprisingly there were only a couple of articles that focused on domestic policy (Article 5 from China and Article 20 from Great Britain). The reasons for these themes are different: in China, the very high coal-intensive energy production in some regions and in Great Britain, this might be explained by the topical BREXIT situation. One of the Chinese articles considers the (historical and mythological) importance of one Chinese character associated with contemporary global warming. Also, studied Australian article about global warming has some mythological nuances.

Though the fact that chosen language in this study (English) has effects on the results, the outcomes confirm that global phenomena, such as the greenhouse effect/global warming (or Covid-19), will narrow the cross-cultural differences in the world. Especially international reports about the greenhouse effect have similar large effects on public attitudes toward environmentalism and nature all over the world. However, it is important that these phenomena are discussed in the national context in order to confirm the environmental activities against the greenhouse effect and global warming.

References

Adeoye, B. & Tomei, L. (2014). *Effects of information capitalism and globalization on teaching and learning.* IGI Global. https://doi.org/10.4018/978-1-4666-6162-2

Blanco-González, A., Del-Castillo-Feito, C., & Miotto, G. (2021). The influence of business ethics and community outreach on faculty engagement: the mediating effect of legitimacy in higher education. *European Journal of Management and Business Economics, 30*(3), 281-298. https://doi.org/10.11 08/EJMBE-07-2020-0182

Boretti, A. (2020). Covid 19 impact on atmospheric CO2 concentration. *International Journal of Global Warming, 21*(3), 317-323.

Derr, C.B. and Laurent, A. (1989) The Internal and External Career: A Theoretical and Crosscultural Perspective. In Arthur, M.B., Hall, D.T., & Lawrence, B.S. (Eds.), *Handbook of Career Theory* (454-471). Cambridge University Press.

Doda, B., Gennaioli, C., Gouldson, A., Grover, D., & Sullivan, R. (2016). Are corporate carbon management practices reducing corporate carbon emissions?. *Corporate Social Responsibility and Environmental Management, 23*(5), 257-270.

Donaldson, J., & Fafaliou, I. (2003). Business ethics, corporate social responsibility and corporate governance: a review and summary critique. *European Research Studies Journal, 0*(1-2), 97-118.

Feldman, A., & Msibi, S. (2014). Influence of cross-cultural leadership on organizational culture: Arcelormittal, Newcastle, a South African perspective. *African Journal of Hospitality, Tourism and Leisure, 3*(1), 1-9.

Gustavson, R. (2011). Business ethics as field of teaching, training and research in Oceania. *Journal of business ethics, 104*(1), 63-72.

Hoffman, W. M. (1991). Business and environmental ethics. *Business Ethics Quarterly, 1*(2), 169-184.

Holden, N. (2002). Cross-cultural management: A knowledge management perspective. Pearson.

Hopkins, C. D., Ferrell, O. C., Ferrell, L., & Hopkins, K. H. (2021). Changing Perceptions of Marketing Ethics and Social Responsibility in Principles of Marketing. *Journal of Marketing Education, 43*(2), 244–259. https://doi.org/10.1177/0273475321995553

Hu, E. (2005). The core of the global warming problem: energy. *International Journal of Global Energy Issues, 23*(4), 354-359.

Jaworska, S. (2018) Change but no climate change: discourses of climate change in corporate social responsibility reporting in the oil industry. *International Journal of Business Communication, 55*(2), 194-219.

Jones, C., Parker, M., & ten Bos, R. (2005). *For Business Ethics.* Routledge. https://doi.org/10.4324/9780203458457

Krecl, P., Targino, A. C., Oukawa, G. Y., & Junior, R. P. C. (2020). Drop in urban air pollution from COVID-19 pandemic: Policy implications for the megacity of São Paulo. Environmental Pollution, *265*(B), 114883. https://doi.org/10.1016/j.envpol.2020.114883

Lee, S., & Klassen, R. D. (2016). Firms' Response to Climate Change: The Interplay of Business Uncertainty and Organizational Capabilities. *Business Strategy and the Environment, 25*(8), 577-592. https://doi.org/10.1002/bse.1890

Lewis, P. V. (1985). Defining 'business ethics': Like Nailing Jello to a Wall. *Journal of Business ethics, 4*(5), 377-383.

Liu, Y., Ruiz-Menjivar, J., Zhang, L., Zhang, J., & Swisher, M. E. (2019). Technical training and rice farmers' adoption of low-carbon management practices: the case of soil testing and formulated fertilization technologies in Hubei, China. *Journal of Cleaner Production,* 226, 454-462. https://doi.org/10.1016/j.jclepro.2019.04.026

Mintzer, I. (1987). A matter of degrees. The potential for limiting the greenhouse effect. *Bulletin of Science, Technology & Society, 8*(3), 344–344. https://doi.org/10.1177/027046768800800375

Moon, J. (2007). The contribution of corporate social responsibility to sustainable development. *Sustainable development,* 15(5), 296-306. https://doi.org/10.1002/sd.346

Muller, J. E., & Nathan, D. G. (2020). COVID-19, nuclear war, and global warming: lessons for our vulnerable world. *The Lancet,* 395(10242), 1967-1968. https://doi.org/10.1016/S0140-6736(20)31379-9

Ohmae, K. (1990/1999). *The borderless world.* Harper Business.

Porter, M.(1990). *Competitive Advantage of Nations.* Harvard Business Review.

Rusko, R. (2014). Mapping the perspectives of coopetition and technology-based strategic networks: A case of smartphones. *Industrial Marketing Management,* 43(5), 801-812. https://doi.org/10.1016/j.indmarman.2014.04.013

Schein, E. H. (1990). Organizational culture. *American Psychologist,* 45(2), 109–119. https://doi.org/10.1037/0003-066X.45.2.109

Scherer, A. G., & Palazzo, G. (2008). Globalization and corporate social responsibility. Globalization and Corporate Social Responsibility. In Crane, A., Matten, D., McWilliams, A., Moon, J. & Siegel, D.S. (Eds.), *The Oxford Handbook of Corporate Social Responsibility* (pp. 413-431). Oxford University Press.

Seitz, V., Razzouk, N., & Nakayama, C. (2007). Leading the Fight Against Global Warming: Hybrid Cars in Emerging Markets. Proceedings of International Research Conference Change Leadership in Romania's New Economy (p. 89). California State University of San Bernardino, USA.

Søderberg, A.-M., & Holden, N. (2002). Rethinking Cross Cultural Management in a Globalizing Business World. *International Journal of Cross Cultural Management,* 2(1), 103–121. https://doi.org/10.1177/147059580221007

Stefan, G. (2010). Carbon Management in Tourism: Mitigating the Impacts on Climate Change (1st ed.). Routledge. https://doi.org/10.4324/9780203861523

Trevino, L. K., & Weaver, G. R. (1994). Business ETHICS/BUSINESS ethics: One Field or Two?. *Business Ethics Quarterly,* 4(2), 113-128. https://doi.org/10.23 07/3857484

Wigley, T. M. L. (1991). Could reducing fossil-fuel emissions cause global warming?. *Nature,* 349(6309), 503-506. https://doi.org/10.1038/349503a0

Yang, L., Wang, N., Chen, Y., Yang, W., Tian, D., Zhang, C., Zhao, X., Wang, J., & Niu, S. (2020). Carbon management practices regulate soil bacterial communities in response to nitrogen addition in a pine forest. *Plant and Soil,* 452, 137-151.

Yang, Y., Ren, L., Li, H., Wang, H., Wang, P., Chen, L., Yue, X., & Liao, H. (2020). Fast climate responses to aerosol emission reductions during the COVID-19 pandemic. *Geophysical Research Letters,* 47(19), e2020GL089788. https://doi. org/10.1029/2020GL089788

Appendix 1

Articles referred in the analysis (All accessed in September 19, 2021)

Asia

Associated Press. (2021, September 13). Climate change could see 200 million move by 2050: Report. India Today. http://www.indiatoday.in/science/story /climate-change-could-see-200-million-move-by-2050-report-1852475-202 1-09-13 [**Article 1**]

Desk, I. T. W. (2021, July 26). IIT Guwahati, IIM Bangalore find link between carbon footprint of polluting companies and long-term investing risks. India Today. https://www.indiatoday.in/education-today/news/story/iit-guwahati-iim-bangalore-link-between-carbon-footprint-of-polluting-companies-investing-risk-1832844-2021-07-26 [**Article 2**]

Associated Press. (2021a, July 5). Summer swelter trend: West gets hotter days, East hot nights. India Today. https://www.indiatoday.in/science/story/us-heatwave-canada-heat-dome-climate-change-global-warming-1824055-2021-07-05 [**Article 3**]

Weijia, H., & Yunfei, T. (2020, February). On the Character. The World of Chinese. https://www.theworldofchinese.com/2020/02/on-the-character-%E9%A3%8E/ [**Article 4**]

Dawei, X. (n.d.). Coal Hard Truth. News China. www.newschinamag.com/newschina/articleDetail.do?article_id=6767&section_id=34&magazine_id=69 [**Article 5**]

Tian, X. (n.d.). Green Revolution. News China. www.newschinamag.com/newschina/articleDetail.do?article_id=6766&section_id=34&magazine_id=69 [**Article 6**]

Tian, X. (n.d.). Climate for Change. News China. www.newschinamag.com/newschina/articleDetail.do?article_id=6765&section_id=34&magazine_id=69 [**Article 7**]

McElhinney, D. (2021, July 13). Tokyo on Sustainability: Time To Act Conference Takeaways. Tokyo Weekender. https://www.tokyoweekender.com/2021/02/the-tokyo-metropolitan-government-on-sustainability-time-to-act-conference-key-takeaways/ [**Article 8**]

McElhinney, D. (2020, August 5). What the Covid-19 Pandemic can Teach Japan about Climate Change. Tokyo Weekender. https://www.tokyoweekender.com/2020/07/covid-19-pandemic-japan-climate-change/ [**Article 9**]

Petkoska, Z. (2020, August 4). How Climate Change Is Directly Affecting Japan. Tokyo Weekender. https://www.tokyoweekender.com/2020/04/how-climate-change-is-directly-affecting-japan/ [**Article 10**]

Africa

Africa Business (2020, August 30). Renewable Methanol Fuel Slashes Greenhouse Gas Emissions in Transportation and Power Generation. https://africabusiness.com/2019/02/14/renewable-methanol-fuel/ [**Article 11**]

Africa Business (2021, August 9). https://africabusiness.com/2021/08/09/global-warming-unequivocally-human-driven-at-unprecedented-rate-ipcc [**Article 12**]

Dsouza, N. (2021, July 15). Mining and Metals Companies Accelerate Focus on Sustainability. https://africabusiness.com/2021/07/15/mining-and-metals-companies-accelerate-focus-on-sustainability/ [**Article 13**]

North America

Downes, S. (2021, August 9). inc.com. http://www.inc.com/sophie-downes/climate-change-united-national-ipcc-environment-report-global-warming.html [**Article 14**]

Hart, R. (2021, October 12). *'Code Red For Humanity': Humans Driving 'Unprecedented' Climate Change, U.N. Report Finds.* Forbes. https://www.forbes.com/sites/roberthart/2021/08/09/code-red-for-humanity-humans-driving-unprecedented-climate-change-un-report-finds/ [**Article 15**]

Vetter, D. (2021, July 9). *Could This Revolutionary Idea Pay Our Climate Change Debt And Supercharge CO2 Reductions?* Forbes. https://www.forbes.com/sites /davidrvetter/2021/07/09/could-this-revolutionary-idea-pay-our-climate-change-debt-and-supercharge-co2-reductions/?sh=6d7f64ec640a [**Article 16**]

Law, J. (2022, September 23). How climate change is affecting your home insurance. MoneySense. https://www.moneysense.ca/spend/insurance/home-insurance/how-climate-change-affects-home-insurance/ [**Article 17**]

South America

TBR Newsroom. (2021, August 9). *Brazil is set to be devastated by the effects of climate change.* The Brazilian Report. https://brazilian.report/environment/ 2021/08/09/devastated-climate-change/ [**Article 18**]

Buenos Aires Times (2021, August 13) UN report: Human role in global warming overwhelming and 'unequivocal'. www.batimes.com.ar/news/world/un-human-role-in-global-warming-overwhelming-and-unequivocal.phtml [**Article 19**]

Europe

Harvey, F. (2021, September 19). Ed Miliband: honour promises on jabs to poor countries to save Cop26 deal. The Guardian. https://www.theguardian. com/environment/2021/sep/18/ed-miliband-honour-promises-on-jabs-to -poor-countries-to-save-cop26-deal [**Article 20**]

The European Editor. (2021, April 23). Decarbonisation startups raise hope for corporate sustainability, says GlobalData. The European Magazine. https:// the-european.eu/story-23845/decarbonisation-startups-raise-hope-for-corporate-sustainability-says-globaldata.html [**Article 21**]

Staalesen, A. (2021, May 20). The Arctic leaders that sit down to discuss climate must abandon plans for oil drilling. The Barents Observer. https://thebarents observer.com/en/climate-crisis/2021/05/arctic-leaders-sit-down-discuss-climate-must-abandon-plans-oil-drilling [**Article 22**]

Australia

Living Now (2020, May 4). May 2020 Stargazer – Uranus in Taurus – Stella Woods. LivingNow Magazine. https://livingnow.com.au/may-2020-stargazer/ [**Article 23**]

Chapter 9

Cultural Cosmopolitanism: Blurring the Lines of Cultural Demarcation

Deepti Sinha
CHRIST (Deemed to be University), India

Sachin Sinha
CHRIST (Deemed to be University), India

Abstract: A cataclysmic churning of human and non-human ingredients has been in operation for a fairly long time. Men, machinery, materials and money have been traversing the globe across latitudes and longitudes. This has resulted in metamorphosing the globe into one big melting pot, a phenomenon which can be summed up as 'globalization'. In an increasingly unified and integrated global economic order, the continuance of cultural differences creates many inherent contradictions. Due to the emergence of this new cultural pattern, a sense of contradistinction is disappearing. In global or cosmopolitan culture, the sense of physical or geographical distance is diminishing. Local traditions and practices are getting blurred, and the uniqueness of national cultures has become rather ubiquitous. The typical modern-day consumer has acquired a cosmopolitan outlook and can conveniently be called a cosmopolitan consumer. He is equipped with an evolved sense of global sensibility, emotional citizenship of the world and a broad-based, universal outlook on life. His tastes, preferences and lifestyle aspirations match the global standards of excellence. The objective of this chapter is to understand the idea of culture, multiculturalism, and glocalization and to finally arrive at the concept of a cosmopolitan consumer.

Keywords: Culture, Globalization, Multiculturalism, Cosmopolitan Consumer

***

Introduction

As per the data of 2020, the most popular film on Netflix was 'Extraction', which was filmed in the locales of Bangladesh, and starred Australian actor Chris Hemsworth while the plot revolved around rescuing an Indian boy. The film garnered a viewership of about 99 million people across the world. Can there be anything more globalised and more multicultural?

A wide array of meanings can be ascribed to the widely used word 'culture'. Different people view culture from different perspectives (Taylor, 1871). The Cambridge dictionary defines culture as the way we lead our life. It particularly includes the behavioral practices that we follow collectively and the value systems to which we subscribe collectively.

Sociologists and anthropologists, academicians and researchers, politicians and performing artists – they all might have their own respective perspectives of culture, their own colored views of culture. But, if one were to attempt a widely accepted definition, culture could simply be called a collection of control mechanisms (O'Reilly & Chatman, 1996).

According to the Center for Advanced Research on Language Acquisition, culture is a collection of commonly owned and practiced behaviors, collective configurations of our cognition and comprehension, which we acquire through social learning (Carla.umn). And, this planet of ours, the only one presumably with a humongous human population pulsating on it, is crisscrossed with these lines of control mechanisms, these lines of the cross-cultural divide. As per Hofstede (1984), "Culture is the collective programming of the mind which distinguishes the members of one category of people from another." (p. 51).

Historically, culture has been both a differentiator and an integrator – differentiating groups of people from each other and integrating the members within each group. Culture has always been the cohesive glue that has bound its adherents to each other and also kept one set of adherents from another set. So, it is culture that created "us" and "them". It is culture that demarcated the Eastern Hemisphere from the Western Hemisphere. It is culture that exalted one section of humankind and berated another, eulogized one kind of people and looked down upon another.

Of course, in the beginning, there was no culture, only geography. People were geographically distant and different from each other. With the passage of time, the geographical diversity translated itself into cultural heterogeneity. So, it was "us living here" and "they living there". And this continued for ages. Cultures and sub-cultures kept on crystallizing themselves, and regions of the world kept becoming more and more different from each other and ditto with people. But then, somewhere in the journey of evolution and cycle of civilization, the counter-currents set in. Maybe somewhere in the second half of the previous century, a new process of cultural conversion – 'interconversion' actually – set in. A heightened awareness and also a greater appreciation of each other's distinctive cultural characteristics began happening, leading to an amalgamation of mindsets, a convergence and coalescence of cultures, sub-cultures cross-cultures.

All cultures share some basic characteristics. Culture is *acquired and learnt* over time. It is not something that is biologically inherited. It is learnt through the process of enculturation. Also, culture is a set of *shared beliefs* amongst the members of a group, community, society, region or country, constituting the internal mental component of culture. Despite it being the commonly shared beliefs, culture carries within itself the hues of cross-cultural influences. It consists of *symbols, signs and artifacts* which could be arbitrary and may carry different interpretations in different cultures. Art, currency, language, attire, etc., are all part of this symbolism. These constitute the external material component of culture. Culture is not an isolated idea. It is *holistic* in nature. In order to understand a culture, one must understand all parts of it. Last but not the least, though relatively permanent, culture is *dynamic.* Cultures interact and change, but the process of change is gradual and evolutionary and not revolutionary. The cause for the change of culture is to better adapt to the changing dynamics of the environment. Moreover, if one part of culture changes, it creates a kind of ripple effect and causes the entire culture to change sooner or later.

This chapter intends to highlight the movement from the very basic idea of understanding culture, the concept of multiculturalism, and then moving onto intermingling of cultures, blurring the differentiating lines of culture and eventually arriving at the concept of cosmopolitan culture and cosmopolitan consumer.

Cultural Heterogeneity or Multiculturalism

Culture differs from country to country and, therefore, poses a problem for corporations since they have to formulate their marketing strategies to fit the host country's culture in order to win over customers. Since culture is a combination of values, beliefs and attitudes, what works in one country may not work in another. The 'tradition' part of culture is one of the most important aspects of cultural differences, mainly so for food and beverage companies, since eating habits vary across different countries and cultures (Hill, 2007). In fact, multiculturalism helps in establishing a kind of cultural rainbow, which together create a hue of colors while still maintaining their individuality. Multiculturalism can be interpreted in multiple ways, depending on the lens of the discipline through which we are looking at it. Sociologists refer to it as 'ethnic pluralism', which is the generally accepted meaning of this term. The phenomenon of multiculturalism manifests itself when small constituent units of a much larger cultural group retain their distinctive cultural sub-identities, which are duly acknowledged and accepted by the majoritarian, predominant culture, on the condition that the ethos of the parts does not run counter to the ethos of the whole. It is like the co-existence of many microcosms within one macrocosm (Reynolds & Fletcher, 2008). Multiculturalism also entails the prevalence of inequitable power distribution and dynamics across the cross-section of cross-cultural identities because of the deviation of these cross-cultural groups from the superordinate 'norms' (Clayton, 2020; Maheshkar & Sharma, 2021, 2018).

It entails a state of affairs in which groups and sub-groups and communities and sub-communities tend to look inwards in an attempt to assert and re-re-assert their particular and specific identities. But at the same time, there are waves and currents of globalization sweeping across these particular and specific identities, as a result of which they are in a constant state of flux (Appadurai, 1996). And these waves and currents force the groups and sub-groups to redefine and re-invent their identities. Of course, this redefinition and reinvention of cultural identity take place at the surface and peripheral level while the core remains the same (Ritzer, 2010). This is comparable to the way the outer layers of the onion can easily be peeled off, leaving the core intact. Global and cross-cultural influences remain confined to the marginal cultural identity while the central cultural identity remains, by and large unaffected. This leads to a state of cultural co-existence in which the 'indigenous' and 'imported' identities dwell together.

Culture also plays an important role for companies when it comes to understanding the behavior and decision-making of consumers.

Cultural Market Segmentation

Market segmentation can easily be understood as the act of identifying distinct groups and sub-groups with distinctly identifiable needs and wants and tastes and preferences in the large mass of the customer population. The members of these identified customer groups and sub-groups generally give the same responses to marketing stimuli. Market segmentation helps marketers approach markets with focused efforts and energies rather than dissipating them across a broad-based mass market.

The advent of market segmentation can be likened to Creation itself. It's almost like God saying, "Let there be segments!" And there were segments. Not only segments but sub-segments, fragments, niches and the like, so much so that every individual became a market in himself. Cultural segmentation is about understanding customer conduct in the context of social traditions, attitudes and behaviors embedded in the community to which they belong.

The whole concept of culture is quite wide and rather difficult to comprehend. Companies have to take cultural differences into consideration, differences such as language, religion, social standing and demographics. If the company has the information and knowledge it needs, the entry process and the cultural shock will be less painful. Mode of entry is also a vital factor for companies. For instance, what mode of entry is the best to use for the chosen market, and how to combine the mode of entry process with cultural differences? Researchers have previously been conducted in the fields of emerging markets, culture, and marketing, as well as a mode of entry, by Hofstede (1984a), Hollensen (2007), Jonscher and Summerfield (1994), in addition to several others.

Cultural market segmentation could become complex due to cultural differentiation, which involves different languages, different values and different attitudes (Harris et al., 1999). When doing business in a foreign market, communication is essential, and the three factors mentioned above hugely influence the communication process. A business relationship or deal can easily be damaged because of misunderstandings that are based on cultural differences.

The all-encompassing impact of culture is more than evident when we see things from the perspective of the four broad bases of market segmentation. The cultural characteristics of consumers are conditioned to a great extent by the market segment to which they belong. From the point of view of demographic market segmentation, the cultural composition of city dwellers would be very different from village folk. Demographically speaking, the cultural identity of affluent consumers would be quite distinct from that of non-affluent consumers. There are strong cultural underpinnings of different psychographic market segments. Also, the behavioral segmentation of markets has marked cultural dimensions to it (Boykin, 2017).

Intermingling of Cultural Cross-Currents

A cataclysmic churning of human and non-human ingredients has been in operation for a fairly long time now. Men, machinery, materials and money have been traversing the globe across latitudes and longitudes for a fairly long time now. This has resulted in metamorphosing the globe into one big melting pot (Ritzer & Malone, 2001), a phenomenon which can be summed up as 'globalization'. Consequently, a lot of ideological heat has also been generated, even giving birth to multiple controversies surrounding these ideological differences (Bird & Stevens, 2003). The very notion of 'globalization' has become subject to multiple interpretations and contradictory connotations. The opinion seems to be divided between seeing globalization as a unitary phenomenon and viewing it as an outcome of multiple causes. It can also be said that researchers have not been able to capture the entire panorama of globalization in all its hues and shade.

Authors like Acosta and Gonzalez (2010) have compared globalization to a river with a number of tributaries, viz., ideological, political, cultural and social. Ideological globalization is all about the interchange and exchange of ideas and ideological beliefs; political globalization caters to the development and growing influence of international organizations such as the UN or WHO. It also signifies the governmental actions at an international level. Cultural globalization stands for the interpenetration of cultures which, as a consequence, means nations adopt the principles, beliefs and customs of other nations, losing their unique culture to a unique, globalised supra-culture, and social globalization refers to the intermingling of communities across the borders.

There has been no end to the raging debate on globalization viewed as it has been from the lenses of geopolitics, international economics and other academic and intellectual disciplines. The ongoing debate on globalization is actually of a quite recent origin. In addition to that, it still remains to be established if ideas like Americanization and McDonaldization can be equated with globalization or not (Latouche, 1996). We should be mindful of the fact that globalization should not be perceived as Americanization simply because the flow of cultural influences is a two-way traffic. The American 'brand' of cultural influences might be stronger in impact and intensity, but America is also at the receiving end of cultural imports from other parts of the world. Also, we must understand that globalization should not come to mean the McDonaldization of the globe. Of course, the people of the world at large, as global citizens, are acquiring a cultural commonality, but that does not necessarily imply that we as a society of consumers are becoming 'standardized and predictable', which is the basic premise of McDonaldization.

The Two Sides of Globalization

The onslaught of globalization on regional and local cultural identities can be both productive and counter-productive, leading to both beneficial and hazardous outcomes (Cowen, 2002). Cultural heterogeneity and homogeneity are not contradictory; rather, they are complementary to each other. Globalization is responsible for bringing differentiation in culture (cultural differentiation), an amalgamation of two or more cultures (cultural convergence) and creating a mixed culture with constituents contributed by multiple cultures (cultural hybridization). Cultural convergence can be understood in terms of people across the world giving the same IMDb rating to the same series on Netflix, discussing the same hot couture and same fashion trends in Lakme India Fashion Week or Cannes Film Festival, or

Gordon Ramsay reviewing Indian cuisine on the beaches of Australia. The prevalence of fusion music or fusion dance forms can best explain cultural hybridization. A popular Sri Lankan song was recently translated and sung in more than 100 languages. All these versions of new cultures could be termed as 'Global Culture' or 'Cosmopolitan Culture'.

In an increasingly unified and integrated global economic order, the continuance of cultural differences creates many intra-contradictions. Due to the emergence of this new cultural pattern, a sense of distinction is disappearing. In fact, the very definition of culture as 'something that defines the boundary or creates identity' is losing its relevance. In global or cosmopolitan culture, the sense of physical or geographical distance is diminishing. Local traditions and practices are getting blurred, and the uniqueness of national cultures has rather become ubiquitous. Cultural coalescence and fusion should not be taken as a utopian scheme of things. Variety is the spice of life.

Too much cultural commonality can tend to diminish our uniqueness as human beings belonging to diverse cultural and sub-cultural streams. It can also lead to a loss of product differentiation and ultimately to a dull and drab modern-day avatar of mass marketing. Cultural commonality is the writing on the wall. The boundaries and barriers that were used for demarcating consumer classes are doing a vanishing act. India, which prided itself in being the epitome of cultural homogeneity, has now become a culturally heterogeneous nation both within its borders and beyond. Let us take a few cases in point. There used to be festivals in India that were the sole proprietorship of particular states. Can we deny the fact that Chhath in Bihar, Durga Puja in West Bengal, Rath Yatra in Odisha, Navaratri in Gujarat and Ganesh Utsav in Maharashtra, previously preserved as cultural copyright by their respective states, have not only become pan-Indian in complexion but have also crept across the national borders? To take things to a higher plane, are we not witness to Diwali being celebrated in the White House in Washington, DC, and, reciprocally, the Halloween 'spirit' catching up fast with Indian yuppies now?

And things do not end here. There is now an increasing trend toward the intermingling of creative currents across the globe. Crossover cinema is both the cause and effect of this phenomenon. The world has come a long way from Richard Attenborough's 'Gandhi' to Rakesh Roshan's 'Kites'. There used to be movies made by foreign filmmakers that featured Indian actors, and then came movies made by Indian filmmakers that used foreign artists. Now, there are both. There are Hindi movies made with an overseas viewership in mind, and James Cameron is a household name in India. Subtitles or no subtitles, dubbing or no dubbing, movies, or for that matter, entertainment products of all kinds, today are addressing an international audience, transcending all possible cognitive barriers, echoing a universal sentiment that can be expected to be understood and appreciated everywhere. 'Spiderman 3', dubbed in Bhojpuri, and 'Slumdog Millionaire' bear ample testimony to the fact that we are living in a cosmopolitan cinematic cauldron.

India has not only influenced other cultures but has also been influenced by them. If there has been an 'Americanization' of Indian culture, there has also been the 'Indianization' of American culture.

Glocalization

A large number of global companies have deployed the strategy of going 'glocal,' and it has worked to their advantage. These marketers, who can be called 'glocal' marketers, follow a fusion approach. While on the one hand, they try to follow a globally thought-out standard prototype for their products, which helps in keeping their unit cost of production low. On the other hand, they try to customize their positioning and communications in sync with the local cultures and ethos. One case in point is McDonald's, which tries to balance its global product offerings with the local food habits and taste buds, like offering vegetarian burgers to Indian customers, owing to the fact that a sizeable section of the population in this country is vegetarian (Boykin, 2017).

Glocalization is all about thinking 'global' and acting 'local' – when we blend the international product with the local flavor to cater to the needs and wants of the host country's population. Let us take, for instance, the characteristics of the conventional Indian consumer. Haven't they gone for a toss? We were once a predominantly 'saving' nation. Aren't we fast becoming a 'spending' nation? The ethics of the issue notwithstanding, this is the fact of the matter. Impulse purchase was never part of our national consumer character, but aren't we now willing to shell out a fortune at the drop of a hat in case a particular window display catches our fancy? Another case in point. Traditionally, Indian consumers were temperamentally brand-loyal for monetary reasons or otherwise. Indian buyers used to patronize particular points of purchase. All that is fast becomes history. We have now become grossly experimental switchers and would now not like to 'hold on' to anything. Unheard of in India in the sixties, seventies and eighties, replacement buying is now the norm. The term 'consumer durables' is in search of a definition itself. In terms of value systems, these elements come to us from the Western world.

But somewhere in this mad frenzy for pandering to the microscopically specific tastes and preferences of consumers, fuelled by the efforts of multinational marketers to 'glocalize' their product portfolios, a new kind of mass marketing has started emerging. It's actually a paradox. In the process of identifying different, newer and better bases of market segmentation at the global level, somehow, the very concept of market segmentation has become redundant. Everything that was once local, regional or geographically confined has acquired a national, if not global, character.

Consumer Metamorphosis – The Blurring Lines

Consumer behavior, as they say, is all about buying and being, or the other way around. So when 'being' is fast becoming homogenized, can 'buying' be far behind? Consumer mindsets, product choices, brand preferences, buying tendencies, purchase frequencies, usage rates, and almost all possible dimensions of buyer behavior are falling into a pattern, a cosmopolitan pattern.

Consequent to people moving across the cultural equator for work or for permanent residential relocation, acculturation in some form or other is bound to happen and is also peremptory for the successful transaction of global trade and business. Globalization actually creates and provides a platform for the cultures of the world to converge and coalesce so that the world order can operate as a proper blend of heterogeneity and homogeneity (Featherstone, 1995).

The idea of 'translocal fusion' is fast gaining ground along the length and breadth of the world. This concept entails that countries and cultures obviously resist the influx of 'other' countries and cultures into their soil, but these 'invasive' forces are strong enough to override this resistance. But, at the same time, these 'invasive' forces are not strong enough to completely annihilate the identity of the indigenous cultures. This leads to a strong synthesis of global and local cultural streams as if the two have been blended together in a mixer-grinder of sorts. An entirely new variant of culture is born, which is neither global nor local in its fundamental texture (Ritzer, 2010). The mechanisms of homogenization and heterogenization come into play with equal force (Robertson, 2001).

The Amalgamation of Occidental and Oriental Mindsets

The social norms, customs, beliefs, and ethical values followed in the west are referred to as 'Occidental,' and those of the east are called 'Oriental'. As opposed to the past, in the present-day globalised world, people are less governed by their regional or local 'personality' and are more influenced by their individualistic selves, extensions of which are their family (Wang, 2015). The point to be underscored here is that the once-very-clearly-defined (though imaginary) vertical equator that used to divide the globe into two cultural hemispheres – eastern and western has almost disappeared. We now have occidental lifestyles with oriental values, and vice-versa, although this is stretched to ludicrous lengths sometimes. A Hindu NRI bride opting for the typical white Christian bridal outfit and a Hollywood celebrity couple getting their marital rites solemnized by a Hindu priest in Varanasi is no longer fiction. It's no longer 'aping'; it's just being.

These consumer trends are actually pointers to the 'big picture'. In the penumbra of this very much visible 'cosmopolitan consumer,' we can easily spot the relatively hazy silhouette of the 'cosmopolitan citizen'. It's actually a 'meeting of minds' in the truest sense of the term. The political map of the world can no longer delineate the psychographics of the nations of the world. Americans and Europeans are becoming more and more group-oriented, whereas individualism is on the rise in Asian societies. Ancient Indian scriptures and Chinese philosophy have established the supremacy of sorts in the Western mind space, while our part of the world is voraciously devouring the stuff dished out by modern-day evangelists from the US. In academic circles, while 'they' are raving about Kautilya and Sun Tzu, 'we' are busy extolling the virtues of Tom Peters and Stephen Covey. And again, it's not just about finding thought anchors in each other's domain; it's also about thinking just like each other. Diaspora has become a fixed demographic feature in today's global cultural contours.

'Once upon a time', chronically ill (and financially fit) Indian patients used to take refuge in sanatoria at exotic international locations (Switzerland, for instance) to regain their lost health. Today, India happens to be a favorite health-tourism destination for people from across the world. Conversely, India used to be a global cynosure for students from far and wide (Nalanda and Taxila are still names to reckon with), while American academia is the Mecca of pupil pilgrims today. There is a cross-section of foreign nationals constituting the student population of most of the premier educational institutions in most of the developed countries of the Western world.

This intermingling of cultural currents of such macroscopic proportions has produced results of a very microscopic nature also. Let's take our sensory sensibilities as a case in point. There used to be a time when certain delicacies were the culinary cultural characteristic of certain countries or communities alone. Not any longer. For instance, how Chinese is Chinese food today or how Italian is Italian? This transcontinental acclimatization has had a very subtle but very telling effect on our taste buds. The native tongue, so to say, governed undoubtedly by the native mind, has now come to acknowledge a number of alien entities as native.

Cosmopolitan Consumer: The Genetically Modified Breed

This sensory conditioning has also traversed to the crevices of our cognition. The age-old historically-ingrained psychological paradigms are undergoing a metamorphosis of sorts. Traditionally, India was a country where interpersonal relationships were characterized by stability and solidity. The institution of marriage was supposedly sacrosanct and came with 'lifetime validity'. Aren't we witnessing a cultural cataclysm in India today wherein we have become consciously comfortable with alarmingly high divorce rates? Haven't we almost effortlessly come to 'accept' live-in relationships as 'acceptable' in our country (cemented further by legal endorsement in a state like Maharashtra)? The merits and demerits of these phenomena notwithstanding, can we actually deny their existence?

Let us take another perspective on things. Acknowledgement of authority and a subconscious spirit of subordination were an integral part of the Oriental value system, be it families or workplaces. Aren't we seeing the emergence of a complete generation of rebellious youngsters – children and employees alike? Have the conventional control systems not become dysfunctional? Have they not lost much of their steam, if not all of it? Be it familial dynamics or organizational behavior, every band of the Indian sociocultural spectrum is dominated by an increasingly high level of mental violence, something that 'was not' indigenously produced by us. To take things to another level of analysis, maybe we can say that we are now into 'import substitution' of the so-called 'foreign' materials, namely, an aggressive and abrasive outlook on life, a highly consumption-driven, materialistic lifestyle, and so on – crops that supposedly did not grow on Indian soil traditionally. We have become, in a way, a genetically modified breed that has started thinking the 'other' way.

The ancient work ethic of 'lifetime employment' once prevalent in Japan, one of the torch-bearers of Eastern culture, has actually become extinct. Very much extant in our own country also till the end of the eighties, it has ceased to exist here also. Frantic job-hopping is now the hallmark of the yuppie work culture, with employers also promoting this by going in for 'temping' or handing out only temporary jobs to job-seekers. And let's not stereotype this as an 'invasion' by Western marauders. It's also not a crossover. It's actually a makeover – a makeover that is happening in most of the countries of the world and waiting to happen in others; a makeover that is happening on both sides of the cultural equator of the globe; a makeover that is making a molten mass of the entire populace of this planet.

The typical modern-day *cosmopolitan consumer* is different from ever before. He is equipped with an evolved sense of global sensibility, an emotional citizenship of the world and a broad-based, universal outlook on life. His tastes, preferences and lifestyle aspirations match the global standards of excellence. He can very easily and effortlessly relate to the cultural currents emanating from the world beyond the frontiers of his home country.

The entire concept of the cosmopolitan consumer can be very well delineated through the consumer adoption model of Schiffman & Kanuk (2010). This model charts the journey of consumer adoption on a continuum, which can broadly be divided into four phases (Quadrants). It is a matrix mapped between the degree of cosmopolitan orientation and the degree of local orientation. The first category of consumers exhibits a high degree of parochialism and has a strong 'local' orientation. They are strongly biased in favor of lifestyles and consumption patterns which are in sync with their local culture. A slight variance from these consumers are the ones who have a parochial mindset, but they are not tied down by any trappings of local orientation (third Quadrant). The consumers falling in the second Quadrant are the ones who have a cosmopolitan outlook, but at the same time, they are also entangled by a strong attachment to their local roots. And finally, the first Quadrant comprises consumers who combine within themselves a high degree of both cosmopolitan outlook and global orientation.

Cosmopolitan consumers are characterized by a breadth of mental horizons. They are keen to learn and adopt new ideas which are alien to their indigenous culture. They are not averse to affiliating with people belonging to a cultural milieu in which they did not grow up. They exhibit a high level of tolerance for diversity. This tolerance for diversity extends well into their ready acceptance of products from diverse cultures belonging to diverse parts of the world. And this tolerance and acceptance get translated into a conscious consumption experience.

Conclusion

The study of consumer behavior is an attempt to understand the interplay between people and products. This interplay is actually a set of complex complementary relationships. Whether people of a particular kind prefer products of a particular kind or whether using products of a particular kind makes people follow a particular life pattern will always remain a moot question. But the proliferation of global products has created a generation of cosmopolitan consumers, and these global products themselves are an offshoot of the hybridization of cultural identities. The whole idea of global consumer culture is rather associated with economic globalization, which can be described as an increasingly homogenized culture of consumption lived by consumers worldwide and enabled through the provision of standardized global products and reinforced by global (mass-)media (Scheibel, 2021).

The message for the modern marketer is loud and clear. The aforementioned molten mass of humanity is the bull's eye, albeit too large a one. It would not be an exaggeration to say that the marketers of tomorrow would actually be clones of each other for the simple reason that they would be dealing with consumers who would be clones of each other. Life indeed comes full circle. The super-saturation of customized marketing has led to the reincarnation of mass marketing. And the focal point of this new wave of marketing is the cosmopolitan consumer.

References

Acosta, O., & Gonzalez, J. I. (2010). A Themodynamic Approach for the Emergence of Globalization. In Deng, K. G. (Ed.), Globalization - Today, Tomorrow. IntechOpen. https://doi.org/10.5772/10223

Appadurai, A. (1996). *Modernity at Large: Cultural Dimensions of Globalization.* University of Minnesota Press.

Bird, A.W., & Stevens, M.J. (2003). Toward an emergent global culture and the effects of globalization on obsolescing national cultures. *Journal of International Management, 9*(4), 395-407. https://doi.org/10.1016/j.intman.2003.08.003

Boykin, G. (2017, November 21). *What Impact Does Culture Have on Market Strategy and Segmentation?* Your Business. https://yourbusiness.azcentral.com/impact-culture-market-strategy-segmentation-26371.html

Clayton, J. (2020). Multiculturalism. In Kobayashi, A. (Ed.), *International Encyclopedia of Human Geography (2e)* (pp. 211-219). Elsevier. https://doi.org/10.1016/B978-0-08-102295-5.10296-3

Cowen, T. (2002*). Creative Destruction: How Globalization is Changing the World's Cultures, Princeton*. Princeton University Press.

Featherstone, M. (1995). *Undoing Culture: Globalization, Postmodernism and Identity.* Sage.

Harris, P. R., Moran, R. T. & Moran, S. V. (1999). *Managing cultural differences. Global leadership strategies for the 21st century (6e)*. Elsevier/Butterworth-Heinemann

Hill, C.W.L. (2007). *International Business Competing in the Global marketplace (6e)*. McGraw-Hill/Irwin.

Hofstede, G. (1984a). National cultures and corporate cultures. In L.A. Samovar & R.E. Porter (Eds.), *Communication Between Cultures*. Wadsworth.

Hofstede, G. (1984). *Culture's Consequences: International Differences in Work-Related Values* (2e). Beverly Hills CA: SAGE Publications.

Hollensen, S. (2007). *Global Marketing* (6e). Pearson.

Jonscher, C. & Summerfield, A. (1994). Prospects for Western Food Companies in Central and Eastern Europe. *British Food Journal, 96*(1), 4-9. https://doi.org/10.1108/00070709410061041

Latouche, S. (1996). *The Westernization of the World.* Polity Press.

Maheshkar, C., & Sharma, V. (2018) (Eds.). Cross-cultural Business Education: Leading Businesses around the Cultures. In *Handbook of Research on Cross-Cultural Business Education* (pp. 1-35). IGI Global. https://doi.org/10.4018/978-1-5225-3776-2.ch001

Maheshkar, C., & Sharma, V. (2021) (Eds.). Cross-cultural Business Education: Leading Businesses around the Cultures. In *Research Anthology on Business and Technical Education in the Information Era* (pp. 677-711). Business Science Reference. https://doi.org/10.4018/978-1-7998-5345-9.ch038

O'Reilly, C.A., & Chatman, J.A. (1996). Culture as social control: corporations, cult and commitment. *Research in Organizational behaviour, 18*, 157-200.

Reynolds, C. R. & Fletcher-Janzen, E. (Eds.) (2008). Pluralism, Cultural. *Encyclopedia of Special Education.* https://doi.org/10.1002/9780470373699. speced1627

Ritzer, G. & Malone, E. (2001). Globalization theory: Lessons from the exportation of McDonaldization and the new means of consumption. In G. Ritzer (Ed.), *Explorations in the sociology of consumption.* Sage.

Ritzer, G. (2010). *Globalization: A Basic Text.* Wiley.

Robertson, R. (2001). Globalization Theory 2000+: Major Problematics. In G. Ritzer & B. Smart (Eds.), *Handbook of Social Theory.* Sage.

Scheibel, S. (2012). *Against all odds: Evidence for the 'true' cosmopolitan consumer.* [Masters Dissertation, London School of Economics and Political Science]. MEDIA@LSE. https://www.lse.ac.uk/media-and-communications /assets/documents/research/msc-dissertations/2011/63.pdf

Schiffman, L. G. & Kanuk, L. L. (2010). *Consumer Behaviour* (10e). Pearson.

Taylor, E. (1871). *Primitive Culture.* Putnam's Son.

Wang, Y. (2015). Globalization and Territorial Identification: A Multilevel Analysis Across 50 Countries. *International Journal of Public Opinion Research, 28*(3), 401-414. https://doi.org/10.1093/ijpor/edv022

Chapter 10

Reproduction of Paternalism: A Neo-Institutionalist Perspective on Power Relations in Domestic Private Enterprises in China

Xiaodan Zhang

York College, City University of New York, USA

Abstract: The chapter studies managerial practice in domestic privately-owned enterprises (DPEs) that have newly developed under the market reforms in China. This research finds that managers in DPEs adopted many labor-controlling strategies and methods that the state-owned enterprises used under the socialist system before the reforms. This observation depicts a more colorful picture of Chinese DPEs than its fixed image as sweatshops. The observation also raises questions regarding the assumption that managerial practice will automatically change along with economic structural changes. In this case, the author presents the managerial isomorphism from a neo-institutionalist point of view that takes into consideration the impact of interactions between macro-structural change, ideological continuity and micro-human practice on enterprise management. Based on ethnographic studies, the chapter examines these interactions and argues that the persistent paternalist ideology that influences the formation of power relations in DPEs is reproduced in the interactional process.

Keywords: Private Enterprises, Management, Paternalistic Ideology, Paternalism, Power Relationship, China

***

Introduction

A domestic private enterprise in today's China is defined as a firm, a company, or a factory owned by an individual or individuals who are Chinese citizens

(Tsui et al., 2006:5). As a result of the development of the market economy, domestic private enterprises (DPEs) started emerging in the last two decades of the twentieth century and were continuously booming especially in the first decade of the twenty-first century in China. The DPEs' contribution to China's economic growth has become increasingly important and indispensable. According to Cao and Huang (2004), by 2001, the total number of private enterprises was 1.323 million, and the total number of employees was 31.703 million (p.2). In only five years, there were 29.3 million private businesses (including private industrial enterprises), employing over 200 million people and accounting for 49.7 percent of the GDP (Tsai, 2007, p.3). These numbers are fast-growing in the second decade. At the end of 2017, DPEs' contribution to GDP was raised to 60%. In addition, their contributions to new employment were 90% and to tax revenue more than 50% (Zhang et al., 2019). Data gathered by McKinsey & Company in 2021 shows that the share of Chinese urban employment supported by private enterprises quadrupled from just 18 percent in 1995 to 87 percent in 2018, and exports created by the private sector also more than doubled from 34 to 88 percent.[1]

This chapter, however, is not about the causes of the DPEs' emergence and development. It is about the following observation from the author's research on DPEs: privately owned enterprises, particularly regarding labor control mechanisms, adopt many managerial strategies and methods popular in state-owned enterprises (SOEs) under the socialist system before the economic reforms launched more than forty years ago. More intriguing is that, with SOEs, DPEs share similar managerial rhetoric about relations between owners/managers and workers. Those managerial strategies, methods, and rhetoric, along with the newly implemented, so-called "modern management," have inevitably constructed a similar paternalistic type of power relations in DPEs as it was and still is observed in SOEs.

This observation challenges our knowledge and assumptions about DPEs, at least on the following two fronts. Firstly, DPEs are notoriously known as sweatshops with despotic management and abusive labor conditions. DPEs often exemplify the naked capitalist exploitation of cheap labor, a critical factor in China's rapid economic success. The benevolent aspect of a paternalist model, which is defined by Farh and Cheng (2000) as "a style that combines strong discipline and authority with fatherly benevolence and moral integrity couched in a personalistic atmosphere," is undoubtedly inconceivable as this well-known image of DPEs is often presented in scholarly works as well as in mass media. What was actually going on?

---

[1] https://www.statista.com/chart/25194/private-sector-contribution-to-economy-in-china/ (Sept. 2, 2021)

Secondly, it is a puzzle about this unchanged way of managing enterprises and controlling labor. Since the reforms have changed economic and political paradigms, domestic private enterprises face different structural conditions from what the SOEs encountered under a socialist planning economy. Under the changed structural conditions, why do managers (many of whom are also owners) in DPEs still use the same controlling methods to stimulate workers' incentives or enforce their compliance to maximize production output?

This chapter addresses these two questions by applying a neo-institutionalist perspective, which understands people's actions and reactions through an angle that differs from either a structural approach or a cultural approach alone. In the following sections, after reviewing the literature, theoretical framework, and methodology, the author presents the ethnographic stories from seven DPEs. The discussion of the empirical cases targets the relations between changes and continuity in people's practices, between compatibility and conflicts in managerial ideology, and between new social conditions and the reproduction of the paternalistic management style. The main argument is that the DPEs' managerial imitation of the socialist SOEs is the product of combined influences from dominant ideologies, institutional rearrangement as well as people's constant meaning-making through daily practices.

Literature Review

Since the economic reforms embarked in the late 1970s, joint ventures and domestic private-owned enterprises have been the new additions to the previously existing state-owned and collectively owned industrial organizations. As different ownerships often indicate differences in state coordination, budget constraints, profit maximization, and other business conditions (Liao, 2009), it is often treated as an important causal variable that impacts managerial styles, especially in management studies (Xia & Walker, 2015; Wong, 2018). Scholars tend to associate economic and humanistic managerial styles with foreign companies and joint ventures but despotic styles with DPEs (Wang et al., 2007; Nan, 2013).

Quite a number of empirical studies, however, reveal the patterns of authority relations that go beyond a sweatshop model in DPEs (e.g., Lin, 2006) and the paternalistic style of leadership is instead prevalent (Farh et al., 2006, Lau & Young, 2013; Xiong et al., 2021). Since paternalism, characterized by strong authority, benevolence and moral leadership (Chen, 1995; Cheng et al., 2004; Aycan et al., 2013; Lee et al., 2018), is viewed as part of the Chinese Confucianist tradition as opposed to modern management, the cultural approach is popular in explaining persistent paternalism. It emphasizes the unchanged cultural beliefs that sustain the unchanged managerial style. (Farh et al., 2006; Qin, 2011; Wang et al., 2012; Wong, 2018; Bian & Shuai, 2020;

Xiong et al., 2021) This explanation is certainly plausible. It catches our attention to the culturally distinctive patterns, being sensitive to cultural nuances, and understanding different pathways to modernization (Pye, 1985).

Some research findings also show that reality seems more complicated than a simple paternalistic model. They noticed that many DPEs implemented the so-called modern management systems as their SOE and FIE (foreign invested-enterprise) counterparts did after the economic reform (Zhu et al., 2010) when paternalist management was also observed at the same time (Wang et al., 2012; Lau & Young, 2013). Treating the Western style of modern management and Chinese Confucian paternalistic management as a dichotomy (Lau & Young, 2013; Aycan et al., 2013; Xiong et al., 2021), researchers directly question how two ideologically distinct governance models may integrate into one coherent and workable framework (Lau & Young, 2013). Others propose an elective affinity between market rationality and *guanxi* favoritism in China's organizational governance structure and suggest the two do not necessarily reject each other (Bian & Shuai, 2020; Wang et al., 2012).

These insightful researches leave some crucial questions unanswered: Why do certain cultural beliefs have such strong endurance that they survive different political and economic systems while others have faded? Do new ways of thinking and acting never influence the old ones, especially due to the fact that the new ways seem more adequate to the current capitalist economic order? If paternalism is not completely the opposite of modern managerial spirit, how shall we explain the evident conflicting principles between the two, and where can we find their compatible spot? The cultural approach seems to treat cultural influence as a default factor and thus neglects a complicated process in which conflicts and compatibility between people's new and old perceptions take place in their belief systems and therefore direct their practices, especially when a radical structural change occurs.

Theoretical Framework

To understand the seemingly complicated managerial practice in the Chinese DPEs, this paper utilizes a neo-institutionalist approach that goes further than the cultural explanation. As DiMaggio and Powell (1991) claim, new institutionalism emphasizes the process of institutional legitimation and reproduction. They point out that in this process, despite the cultural elements, including taken-for-granted beliefs and widely promulgated rules, humans are not "cultural dopes." Instead, as "knowledgeable agents," when confronting changing reality, their cognitive constraints shape their choices and inform actions; in turn, their daily practices actively enrich their knowledge reservoirs. In other words, they actively think and act by building on what they already know and can do while learning new ways (Scott, 2002).

This theoretical framework can be applied to both Chinese managers' and workers' choices of actions and reactions. Mean-making is important for both rulers and the ruled. Constantly facing competing ideas and value systems, especially under a significant social structural change, people automatically find a compatible spot that either appears to maintain consistency in their minds or helps them manage any inconsistency. This chapter attempts to dissect how new ideas and existing ideas, especially in relation to people's culturally informed cognition, interplay under social structural changes in China and how this interplay reproduces paternalistic, authoritarian relations. This approach allows us to view the possible elective affinity (Weber, 1946, cited from Bian & Shuai, 2020) not as a static entity but as a dynamic process in which structural changes interplay with human actions to form interesting managerial models.

Research Methods

Table 10.1: Seven Domestic Private Enterprises

	Locations	Year*	Employees	Products	Markets
Company A	Wenzhou	1985	500	Cable	Domestic
Company B	Wenzhou	1984	1000	Voltage adapter	Domestic/ International
Company C	Guangzhou	2002	100	Oil processing	Domestic
Company D	Guangzhou	1993	600	Stainless steel	Domestic
Company E	Shanghai	2005	80	Printing	Domestic
Company F	Shanghai	2006	70	Honing pipe	Domestic
Company G	Beijing/Suzhou	1997/2007	50/36	Cardboard	Domestic

* It indicates the time that a company was established.

Seven DPEs for the research project were selected randomly, although with the consideration of regional representations. Both Wenzhou and Guangzhou are the areas in which DPEs first emerged as early as the 1980s. DPEs in Shanghai are relatively late boomers. Two enterprises in each of the three cities are chosen, including a seventh case to see whether regional differences have any significant impact on managerial ideology and practice since regional differences in China often reflect differences in social development in terms of economy, politics and culture. The seventh company had two production sites, one in Beijing and the other in Suzhou, a city next to Shanghai. As shown in Table 1, there are differences in size and time length of business among the seven cases. The possible influences of these differences are also examined in the article.

The author spent about one week each in Company **A** (making cables) in Wenzhou and Company **C** (processing restaurant kitchen refuse to extract oil for industrial use) in Guangzhou. In these two companies, the author interviewed both managers and workers. In the DPEs the author visited, all owners are general managers (总经理). Below general managers, there are deputy general managers, department managers and workshop managers. Owners/general managers were interviewed in four of the seven companies. In the two companies in Wenzhou and the stainless-steel company in Guangzhou, their deputy, assistant and workshop managers were interviewed as the owners/general managers were not available. The author was allowed to observe productions on the shop floor. For the printing company in Shanghai (Company **E**), the author was also allowed to observe the shop floor activities only for one day. For the other four companies, besides interviews with managers, the author was allowed to tour some of the workshops. There was another company the author planned to visit in Shanghai. At the last minute, the owner/general manager changed his mind and did not feel comfortable having a researcher come over. Instead, I interviewed both the deputy general manager Mr. Wang and a worker he selected at Mr. Wang's home. The interviews are used in the paper and the company is referred to as the eighth one: Company **H**.

In addition to these seven companies, the author also conducted interviews with managers and workers in other companies, mainly in Shanghai and Kunshan, in 2012 and 2014. The data presented in the article were collected from the above-mentioned observations and interviews, all conducted from 2008 to 2014. The author found that the regional differences in terms of local economic development and cultures had no impact on managerial styles; the size and time length of the business for each particular enterprise in three different regions caused slight variations in terms of relations between owners/general managers and workers. As the owners/general managers more likely knew workers in person in smaller-sized enterprises that had run in a shorter period of time, specific strategies to cultivate workers' compliance were different from larger-sized counterparts with longer time. In general, there was no difference among the companies in terms of the relations between the state, local government and enterprises. This means most DPEs functioned in a similar institutional and ideological framework.

One of the common problems regarding doing fieldwork in Chinese companies is caused by managers' own hesitation about having an independent researcher enter their factories. Generally, owners and managers do not like people to do research on their companies if they do not think the companies would directly benefit from the research. If a researcher is referred through a personal connection with a manager, conducting interviews with managers is relatively easier, but permission to production sites is always difficult to get for many conceivable reasons. Even if managers allowed the researcher access to the shop floor, as some of them did to the author, the unspoken agreement was that the researcher did not stay there too long. This is an obstacle for a researcher to understand how productions were actually carried out and what kind of labor relations was formed through daily interactions among different players at the micro level. The lack of extended shop floor participant observation also makes it difficult for the researcher to verify what the managers said in interviews was in concordance with what they actually did. The author did sense during the interviews that her own identity as a sociologist from one of the American higher education institutions could be an unfavorable influence on the research. As most of the managers were aware of the Western concerns over human rights issues in China, they might only tell the researcher things they thought she would like to hear or approve. Their hesitation to have researchers enter the workshop could be partially viewed as their awareness of the distance between their practice and their ideas, consciously or unconsciously. Thus, rather than using the interviews to prove their practices without other necessary conditions for verification, this author treats most of their statements as rhetoric that reflects their perceptions of ought-be power relations. Their words are put into a large social context to understand why they had made such statements during the interviews with a researcher from the United States. The author also sought written records as references to the information gathered through ethnographical investigation. Special attention is paid to the conflicts in their thoughts as well as in their practice.

Taking into consideration the methodological limitations, the author expects the paper makes the following theoretical contributions: (1) to understand how the human choice of actions and reactions are conditioned by the interplay between new and old ways of thinking in correspondence with social structural changes; and (2) to understand how cultural continuity and change are influenced by the trajectory of human actions in correspondence with the conflict and compatibility of ideas.

Research Findings

Relations among DPEs, the State and Local Governments

The relations between the state and enterprises have changed after the economic reforms. One of the most conspicuous changes is the decentralized administrative control from the state over enterprises regarding production, employment and distribution. Enterprises, on the other hand, have the autonomy to decide what to produce, how much to produce, whom to hire, how many to hire and how much to pay for labor.

However decentralized decision-making is, the Chinese state remains a powerful player in the arena through a few institutional rearrangements. Mainly since the 1990s, the state's control over private enterprises has been carried out mostly through taxation, legislation, and other policy makings. The Labor Law, which has been revised once, and the Trade Union Law, which has been revised twice, are legal measures not only directly related to labor's interest but also understood as aiming at protecting workers whose vulnerability was a result of the dismantling of the lifetime job security and the launch of an overcrowded labor market. Local labor bureaus and trade unions at every administrative level were dispatched to supervise the implementation of these state apparatuses. The Labor Arbitration Committees (LACs), a revived institution, allowed workers to file grievances. If there are other administrative ways that the state and local governments could use to control SOEs, from my observations, legal measures and the above-mentioned government institutions are among the most direct and institutionalized governmental control mechanisms over DPEs after the market reforms.

The owners and managers in DPEs the author talked to did say that they all took the Labor Law seriously. The deputy manager, Mr. Zhou from Company G, told the author that he studied the new version of the law ten times on his own, besides watching tutorial programs on TV. Mr. Zhou also stated that the company tried hard to follow the law regarding insurance and vacation days. Company E's the owner/general manager claimed that he had to follow the law, although it reduced his profits by 10%-20%. While being asked what made them comply, they all admitted that they just wanted to "avoid trouble" (避免麻烦). One of the managers, Mr. Yang, in Company **A,** told the author that a worker claimed injury compensation even though he was not injured by work-related matters. The company found it out after the payment, but to "avoid trouble," the company decided not to rescind the money. It was not a significant amount to the company and whether it was a work-related injury or not was actually debatable. In a previous study this author did in 2000, some managers who were contacted by the LACs also claimed that they would rather "buy peace" instead of be dragged into negotiations mediated by the LACs.

There are two layers while DPEs deal with governments. One layer is with the central government (the state), and the other involves connections with local governments. Generally, "avoiding trouble" means that private owners and managers try hard to avoid confrontation with local governments and government officials since they seem to have a lot more to lose than their workers. In the first decade of the reforms, many private owners started businesses through all kinds of personal connections with government officials at different levels, and some officials themselves might be the investors behind a particular private business (Wank, 1999; Wright, 2010). In the second decade, the importance of personal connections with government officials is diminished for an owner to start a private business. That does not mean a private owner could afford not to "cultivate a good relationship" (搞好关系) with those who have the power to directly determine whether one's business goes smoothly with a green light or not. Mr. Chen, the owner/general manager of Company C, said that he did not really involve in the daily management of his company. Besides thinking of technological development and market shares, he spent 50% of his time cultivating all sorts of "social relationships" with local officials from different government departments that dealt with private enterprises. The company had only ten employees in the beginning and now has 70 employees after five years. While the shop floor workers in the company were mostly migrants from rural areas, the office workers were mainly recommended by the local government officials. While visiting Company C, the author was invited to a dinner party held by the company's managers for the local village leaders. This kind of informal dinner party was frequently held to build "good relationships".

Local government officials are also eager to build "guanxi" (network) with private owners for various reasons. One of the differences between SOEs and DPEs is that the state or local government has no administrative power to appoint its personnel or staff members. Since most DPEs are still considered "family business", a common practice is that the owner/general managers often hire their own relatives and personal friends to be their managerial assistants. Local government officials are involved in the hiring process informally. That is to arrange for their own relatives and friends to work in DPEs. To DPEs' owners and managers, this is considered a way to cultivate relationships with the local officials. There is a mutually understood reciprocity. A few DPEs started hiring professional managers, but those managers often had a hard time firing incompetent personnel that had personal ties with owners. The deputy general manager of Company C, Mr. Li, told me that one of the headaches he had to bear was hiring people recommended by local officials personally. He said, "You cannot really fire them even if they are not that competent and cannot get along with people." He claimed that the company's chief engineer was such an example.

Mr. Tong from Company E expressed similar ideas in a different way, "We cannot afford to offend (得罪) local officials. Who doesn't have some faults (小辫子) in conducting business? If you offend the local officials, they could make small faults become big ones." Mr. Lu and Mr. Zhou, the owner and manager of Company **G,** agreed with Mr. Tong while being told what Mr. Tong said about the local government officials. We cannot verify whether what they said was true and certainly do not believe every official was corrupted, but we can clearly observe the complicated interdependent relationship between private owners/managers and local government officials.

This kind of interdependent relationship is sustained by shared interests as well. None of the factories the author visited strictly followed the work hour limit set by the Labor Law. In other words, workers worked much more than forty hours a week, and the overtime certainly exceeded the thirty-six-hour limit stipulated in the law. This practice was not only legitimized by the belief that working more and thus earning more was what workers wanted but also supported by local government officials who always emphasized their particular local conditions whenever the author raised the issue with them. We can conclude that even regarding the laws, local governments have their own discretions. With support from local governments, enterprises do not always comply with laws and regulations. Although private owners and managers are afraid of "trouble", they also hope for their luck since local supervision is not always rigid in every legal area. The local governments' concern about their GDP and private owners' concern about profits is the common ground for the interdependent relationship formed within the system and for the local maneuvers of the institutional reorganization arranged by the central government.

The maneuver enhances the interdependent relationship, which is not only limited to the local government level. Along with the development of DPEs, the Communist Party started wooing private owners and entrepreneurs to become party members. Of course, the Party has only eyed the owners of those large-scale and successful enterprises. This practice is similar to a phenomenon in Chinese history called "zhao-an" (招安). "Zhao-an" refers to the central government that entitled the leaders of peasant rebellion within the official rank system. It served the purpose of quelling the rebellion as well as absorbing the political and military forces from the rebellion. The party-state today wanted to recruit private owners into the Communist Party, supposedly a working-class party. For example, the owner of Company B was a party member and a representative of the People's Congress. The policy and practice entail the control over private owners who become more and more independent in the economic arena, which may increase the possibility that they form an independent political force against the state. The inclusion makes private owners willing to focus on generating profits under a "harmonious environment" controlled by the party-state.

Besides wooing private owners to join the Party, another way to contain private owners in the system is to give them various kinds of honorable titles through government-sponsored rewards. Such titles include "Outstanding Entrepreneurs", "The Most Meritorious Entrepreneurs", and "Outstanding Young Entrepreneurs". For example, Mr. Yu, the owner/general manager of Company A, won "The Most Meritorious Entrepreneurs" four times. The political capital accumulated through those honorable titles certainly reinforced Mr. Yu's connection with the government, which can be turned into a positive force for the development of his company. If the connection with the government officials for economic capital, information, and protection is indispensable for private owners to set up a private enterprise at the beginning of the reforms, the development of the business cannot be successful without these resources from the governments in the late period. The more successful the enterprises are, the more actively those private entrepreneurs involve themselves in the current political and economic systems and become part of the establishment.

Adopted Managerial Control Methods

Modern management was implemented in all seven DPEs the author visited. So was Company **H**, told by its manager in the interview. The size of a company determines how rigorously the formal rules are followed. In addition, the longer the private companies are in business and the larger the companies become, the more control methods commonly used in former SOEs would be adopted. These methods include: building and relying on a group of so-called "backbone" employees, organizing production competitions, soliciting suggestions from employees, and setting entertainment facilities within the company compounds.

Backbone employees refer to those who are expected to have personal loyalty to their employers in exchange for political or material favors in an SOE. Those employees are either appointed or considered potential candidates for lower management positions. This feature was vividly captured in Walder's path-breaking study of the SOEs before the reforms (1986). Walder calls it clientelism, characterized by the particular ties based on exchanges of material and political favors with submissive loyalty between managers and a group of "activists" in SOEs. This exchange principle was also clearly understood by managers and their "backbones" in DPEs. Managers often cultivated their particular ties with "backbone" employees based on this principle. For example, the manager Mr. Zhou from Company G, said in the interview that one of the employees was from the earthquake area in Sichuan Province in May 2008. Since he was considered the "backbone" of the company, the management gave the worker extra 500 *yuan*[2]. According to Mr. Zhou, the worker was very grateful. The author asked to speak to the worker. With the managers sitting next to us, the worker said that he was indeed grateful and could only work harder for the company to repay the managers' kindness. 500 *yuan* are not a big amount, but the gesture seemed taken seriously by both sides. Assuming that this type of exchange was effective for extracting loyalty, some managers in larger companies also extended favors to all employees. In Company A, the managers went to visit employees with financial difficulties during the Spring Festival every year. Usually, 500-1000 *yuan*, called "subsidy money" (补助), would be given to these employees at a small ceremony held by the general manager. Mr. Zhang, the union director, thought, "This is one of the ways to enhance 'the cohesion in enterprises' (企业凝聚力)." Employees also received small gifts for their personal occasions, such as birthdays, weddings and funerals.

Different from former SOEs, though, most of the DPEs used this control method without a political propensity toward the Communist Party-State described in Walder's book. In Company A, there was a loyal follower of the Falun Gong, the cult organization firmly quelled by the party-start for years. He constantly dissipated the Falun Gong doctrines among workers and claimed that the Communist Party would be short-lived. Both managers and workers knew that his activities were illicit, but no one reported him to the authority. On the contrary, he was not only a team leader but also selected as a model worker by the company. After he invented a production method that saved the company about 104,000 *yuan*, the general manager decided to name the method after him. Reportedly, he said[3], "I am only a common worker. But the general manager used my name to denominate the method. It rarely happens in other companies. I consider it a great honor. It is as important as my life." Despite being "the enemy of the state" as a Falun Gong follower, he was considered a "backbone" employee of the company.

Company size seems to be an important variable in influencing the managerial choice of control strategies. In the smaller companies, the relationship tended to be more personal. In Company **C**, despite implementing

---

[2] The exchange rate in 2008 was that 1 US dollar (USD) equals 6.84 Chinese *yuan* (CNY).

[3] Published on the company's website.

formal management with rules and regulations, the managerial control was partly done through informal networks. The operation manager and accountant were the owner/general manager's relatives. One of the shop floor managers, who had worked for the company since it started, developed a personal loyalty with the owner. After becoming the backbone, he himself was also able to bring in a few of his own relatives to work in the company.

In Company **A**, a relatively bigger company, foremen and machine operators were treated as "backbones." They received higher payments in the form of wages and bonuses. They were also union representatives in the company. The managers not only mainly relied on those "backbone" workers for accomplishing production tasks but also expected their support if any resistance occurred. During the Annual Workers and Staff Representative Meeting in 2008, these representatives did raise many suggestions regarding workers' pay and benefits; but the general manager certainly encountered neither confrontation nor further negotiation after he rejected some of their suggestions that required him to pay more (e.g., reimbursement of yearly transportation cost for workers going back home).

The method to solicit "Rationalization Proposals" (合理化建议) from workers used in SOEs in the past was also favored by some companies. Both Company A and D set "Suggestion Boxes" (意见箱) for workers to leave their comments and suggestions. In Company **A**, the general manager made 2009 an "Innovation Year" and encouraged workers to be technologically creative and innovative based on their work experience. In the first half of the year, the management already collected 56 proposals and 112 suggestions (published on the company's website).

Other methods from SOEs, such as themed production campaigns, personal consultation (思想工作) and selection of model workers, were also used to boost workers' morale. In addition, one more adoption from the SOEs by the management of DPEs is worth elaboration. It is to set up entertainment facilities for employees. Among the seven companies, except Company **A**, **E** and **F**, all four other companies provided workers dormitories. Companies **B** and **D** were two big companies. While talking to me, the managers emphasized that their dormitory rooms were all equipped with TV sets. Both companies offered their workers new apartment buildings near the factories, which I did see myself. According to Mr. Li, the deputy general manager of Company D, workers paid 150 *yuan* a month for the food and board for a room of four people. There were two fish ponds, one ping pong room, one basketball court, and one soccer field. A computer room and a small convenient store were subcontracted to some employees to run. The company union periodically organized production competitions, sports, and other entertaining activities (e.g., tug of war) among workers. Company B did about the same. In addition, at the time of my visit, according to the union director, the company was buying air-conditioners for the dorm rooms. Company A was building a dormitory house for its workers at the time of the author's visit. Reportedly, the general manager paid attention to the food quality in its canteen, one of the issues raised by the union representatives. After he heard the complaints about the quality of the rice, the general manager ordered a change the next day. The company union director also told me that the union often organized holiday parties and sports competitions.

Mr. Wang from Company H told the author about the similar living conditions in his company. The company charged workers 150 *yuan* per month for a room of three or four people. In the dorm building, on the first floor, located the canteen and convenience store, ping pong room, pool table, and mahjong room; on the second and third floors, TV, KTV sets and computers with internet connections could be found. Again, the author could not verify what Mr. Wang said since she was not allowed to visit the company; the significance of his report, however, lies more in his attempt to make meaning out of these facilities than in practice itself. Like other managers being interviewed, he believed these nice gestures built a benevolent boss image for the owners/general managers. Workers were expected to work harder for nice bosses to return the favors.

These control methods can be viewed as an effort to deal with a high turnover rate and keep the most skillful and experienced employees in the companies. Arguably, these managerial methods were neither Chinese creation nor their privilege to use. In connection with the rhetoric of modernity and paternalism, which we will discuss in the next section, it is important that we understand the practice in a particular ideological context, which is probably straightly Chinese.

Managerial Rhetoric in Modernity and Paternalism

What is seldom mentioned in previous research is the ideological tie built through the interaction between the governments and private entrepreneurs. The official rhetoric of modernity and paternalism noticeably influences the managerial discourse in DPEs.

Adopting modern management from the West started as early as the dawn of the reforms. Many training programs on the topic were organized, and many SOE managers were sent to this kind of program abroad. Modern management is a synonym of the Western managerial techniques that are supposedly the best in managing production and human resource. Under the banner of "modern management," production norms were tightened, rules associated with punitive measures, usually in monetary forms, were set, and performance evaluation of workers was institutionalized in many SOEs and joint ventures. These changes were supposedly aimed at erasing the "irrationality" in former SOEs, which allegedly had low production efficiency and pampered workers before the economic reforms.

For DPEs, as briefly mentioned in the last section, the adoptions of these regulations are various. For many early birds who started the business in the 1980s, especially in Wenzhou and Guangzhou areas, the factories were most in the form of family workshops. Modern management was not relevant. But, through the years of capital gains and organizational expansion, many family workshops are turned into large-scale enterprises such as Company A and B in Wenzhou. It becomes necessary for this kind of DPEs to adopt the techniques that are supposed to enable them to manage their business better. For example, Companies A, B and many others hired professional managers. Companies F and G were newcomers. The owners/general managers of the two companies were college graduates who studied modern management on their own. They no longer run family workshops from the beginning; instead, they set their business organizations based on modern factory models.

However, the adoption was never merely out of necessity. Modern management, from the beginning, has been part of the modernity discourse that the state has created and promoted to legitimize the reforms. Many private owners, especially the second-generation owners/general managers who inherited the family business from their fathers, were eager to shed their family workshop label and rebuild the business image as a modern enterprise. Company B's owner/general manager started his small workshop with a few of his relatives. Besides getting himself an MBA in 2000 after becoming a famous entrepreneur, he hired professional managers for the company. The general manager Mr. Yu, who had an MBA degree in Company A, was the second son of the previous owner. After taking over the family business from his father, he tried to enhance managerial power at different levels with a detailed description of bureaucratic duties and regulations. People in the company told the author that it was he who set the card-punch system to monitor the daily punctuation of his employees. The modern managerial control, as well as modernity discourse, legitimizes their firm and grips absolute authority over the labor force.

On the other hand, building a harmonious society and advocating for a so-called "humanized management" (人性化管理) are part of the dominant discourse promoted in the state-controlled media. Humanized management is understood as treating workers with care and empathy. All the owners and managers being interviewed seemed to take it in, at least verbally. They emphasized they were building a harmonious relationship with their workers. When doing so, they did have their own interpretation and purposes for the implementation of the so-called "humanized management."

Mr. Chen of Company **C** thought it was important to be a good boss. When being asked to define what kind of bosses would be considered good ones, he said, "To take care of your subordinators is important. Only then could you expect their loyalty." "Loyalty" is indeed a word repeatedly used by different managers in conversations with the author. In Company **A**, it was told that the general manager often emphasized self-willingness and loyalty. He connected the company's interest with its employees to hope for voluntary effort.

To be a "good boss," caring and benevolent, was believed as one of the conditions for drawing loyalty. As discussed in the last section, one of the necessary ways to show management's care was to offer good living conditions. The other way to do so was to word any small gesture as favors bestowed upon employees who might not be considered backbone workers. In Company **E**, the owner/general manager, Mr. Tong, told the author,

> I did match-making for a couple in the factory. The woman got pregnant before the marriage. Her family asked the man to pay 15,000 yuan for the wedding. The man could not afford, and the woman had to consider abortion if they were unable to get married. I asked the man how much savings he had. He said 8,000. I said, OK, then, I lent you 7,000 without interest. I would deduct a few hundred from your salary each month. They were very grateful to me.

Small companies such as Mr. Tong's often did not provide dorm rooms, let alone entertainment facilities and fringe benefits. Involving workers' private affairs and helping them in non-financial ways seem important to accumulate "social capitals" for owners and managers. Noticeably, the owners and managers often verbally emphasize their caring part in this kind of favor-giving. Mr. Tong also said,

> The other night I took a walk on the street outside the company. I saw a few young workers of mine were also on the street. They were drunk. I told them it is so hot these days and you need enough sleep for tomorrow's work. If you are injured, I have to pay, and you have to suffer the pain. It is not good for anybody. (I asked Mr. Tong how they reacted to his comments.) Not much reaction. I don't even know whether they would listen to me. But I am just like their father. I have the responsibility to educate them. They are, on the other hand, like grown-up children who may not listen to their father's advice anymore.

Tong thought of himself as those young workers' father, a role he believed coexisted with his role as a "good boss." On the other hand, he claimed that the government, not he, should be the "father" who was supposed to care for workers' welfare. In his mind, the government did not do its job but dumped it, especially on private enterprises, because "everyone believed that private owners were the richest." "However," he also said, "no one knows how hard I worked. The government forced me to be the father of my employees." He told the following story:

> A man and a woman started a flirtatious fight. The man broke the woman's arm by accidence. The woman's parents came from the countryside and asked me to compensate the woman's medical bill of nearly 20 thousand because they argued it happened on the shop floor. I refused since I didn't think this was a job-related injury. They reported to the labor bureau. The bureau asked me to pay one-third. The reason was not that they agreed that it was a job-related injury. They only asked me to buy the peace. I cannot afford to offend the people of the government. We are under their control for many things. If I insisted that I was right and refused to pay, they might find other ways to punish me for my disobedience to them. No company is completely spotless. It is easy for the government if it does want to make trouble for you.

What is interesting here is his interpretation. On the one hand, he believed that the party-state *should* be the father of his workers, which means taking care of their welfare. Forced to follow the Labor Law that resulted in fewer profits for him, he thought he became the appointed "father" with reluctance. On the other hand, he internalized his fatherly role that exchanges caregiving for absolute authority over his subordinators. In addition, if taking care of workers' welfare is the government's duty as a father, he voluntarily took the other part of the fatherly duty as his own, namely educating his subordinates to be adequate for a capitalist system coated with modernity discourse. Most of the private owners/general managers being interviewed shared this kind of belief and mentality. As most of the managers the author interviewed were men, one female manager of a privately-owned advertising company in Shanghai entitled herself to the caring mother of her employees despite the fact that she did facial plastic surgery to make her look at least ten or fifteen years younger than her actual age.

Discussions

Change and Continuity in Managerial Practices

The economic reforms initiated by the Chinese Party-State have certainly brought tremendous changes to the country and its people time and again. One of the most conspicuous changes is in the restructured relations among the state, management of the industrial companies, and workers throughout the years. Rather than the direct state intervention in production and labor control, the state and local governments now play intermediate roles between business owners/managers and workers through institutional rearrangements to resume their control over these two important social groups (Zhang, 2009) and prevent either from developing into independent political forces.

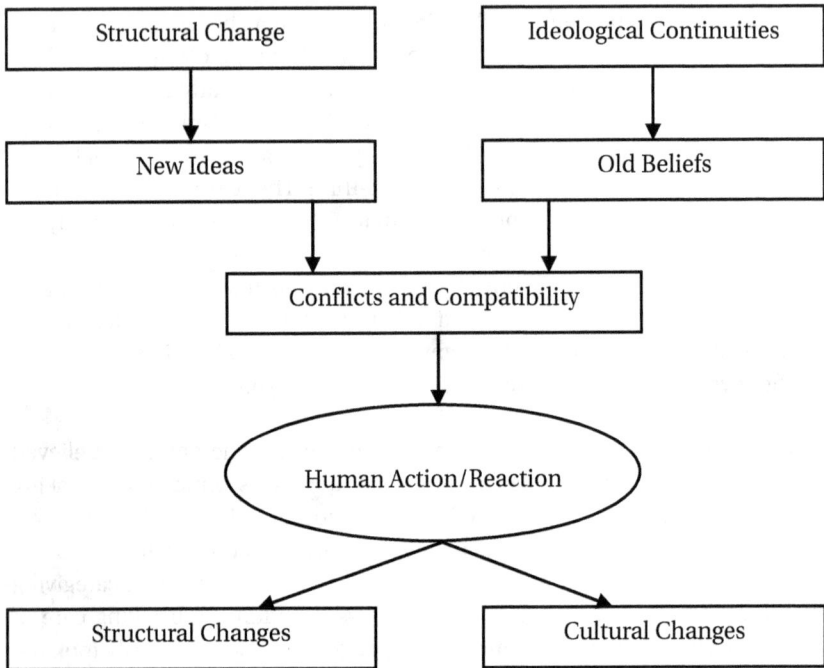

Figure 10.1: Process of Changes and Continuities

For DPEs, profit-making becomes the ultimate goal not only for survival but also driven by the innate value system of any business. The so-called "modern management," promoted by the state, is believed to provide the best means to achieve this goal. Chinese companies, including newly developed domestic private enterprises, have adopted "modern management," this time not from the Soviet as it did in the 1950s but directly from the West.

While implementing modern management from the West, the companies, big or small, have also utilized some strategies and methods from the former state-owned enterprises, as discussed in this chapter. The messages those strategies and processes try to convey are that owners and managers care about their employees if they are loyal to the companies and willing to comply voluntarily. Obviously, the continuity of the governing principles here is primarily based on the belief in the effective exchanges between benevolent gestures from the superiors and voluntary compliance from the subordinators. The state itself also establishes its own legitimacy of the rule by creating such an ideological context. Both fatherly authority and benevolence are emphasized through two equally essential but appearing conflicting discourses: modernity and paternalism.

Compatibility and Conflicts in the Managerial Ideology

Tsui and Lau find "the integration of Western and Eastern management styles and ways of doing business" in the new reform era in China (Tsui & Lau 2002). We notice that this type of integration happens more and more in Eastern and in many Western countries. Despite the awareness of the integration, however, without much discussion on how the two styles are actually integrated, most of us seem to pay attention more to the dichotomy of the Western and Eastern Models than to the compatibility of the two. Especially in the Chinese case, modernity and paternalism are viewed as separately representing two kinds of power relations between owners/managers and workers: impersonal bureaucracy vs. personal ties. This author argues that the two types of power relations may be conceptually different, but, in practice, people do find the compatible point of the two, which is the absolute authority granted to enterprise owners/managers by both managerial principles.

The research findings presented in this chapter suggest that DPE owners/managers took from the so-called "modern management" two core tenets: 1) maximizing profits while minimizing the cost and 2) centralized absolute managerial power. To them, this style of ruling was not necessarily contradictory with paternalistic ideas that emphasize absolute managerial power just the same. In other words, they did not use the two styles to complement each other as how integration is usually understood; instead, in the particular ideological and institutional context, they found modern management adequate to enhance their power as a father figure. They used the modernity discourse in a way to fulfill this father figure's educational duty: being "modern" means being deferent to the orders of business organizations, which are sometimes deliberately personified by the organizations' owners and managers.

The compatibility is, however, not always seamless. Acknowledging the natural combination of the new and old beliefs and norms that guide owners and managers' intention to be "benevolent" on the one hand, we notice that, in practice, not every DPE either could afford the welfare or be willing to be financially "generous" in offering the welfare on the other. Maximizing profits with low cost as another core tenet of "modern management" would make owners/managers perceive any monetary "benevolent gestures" as an extra expense, especially if the business is small and has just started. Those owners/managers often find ways to win a reputation of being a "nice" boss who takes care of his employees. One of the strategies is to make meaning out of every small financial help either by holding some ceremonies while rendering the help or by spreading moral persuasions associated with their actions. In other words, they spare no effort to interpret their gestures as being kind and caring. In the end, not only do they make themselves believe they are genuinely concerned with their employees' well-being, but they also expect their nice gestures, no matter how small they might be, will be reciprocated with loyalty, voluntary compliance, and impetus in production. The poor labor conditions, long working hours and other violations of the Labor Law are thus justified in their mind. This kind of meaning-making is well connected with profit-making. It also corresponds to the mainstream ideology and discourses.

Reproduction of Paternalism under the New Social Conditions

One of the central issues in organization studies is about what effective incentive schemes and other managerial strategies are the best to motivate employees toward greater cooperation and increasing production effort. This chapter argues that we need to take into consideration the dominant ideology that shapes the belief systems of rulers (such as the state, owners and managers) and governs what schemes and strategies they decide to use. In the Chinese case, after the economic reforms, the dominant ideology is paternalism, which is reproduced through new institutional arrangements and new discourses that reflect current social conditions and development stages.

The reconstruction has been taking place at both macro and micro levels. The players, while learning new ways, often think and act on what they already know and can do. In addition, the ongoing reality teaches them that coercion alone is not the best way to enhance absolute power. That can explain why the state, as a leading player in the reconstruction discussed previously, woos successful DPE owners to the Communist Party or includes them in the People's Congress controlled by the Party. It also presents itself as workers' protector by issuing or revising the relevant labor laws and regulations. The local governments often follow the state's policy lines, but the conflicting behaviors manifested in the weak implementations of those laws and regulations. Many local government officials and DPE owners are also eager to develop their personal relationships with each other.

Practice within business organizations follows this power relation model but has its own complication. The above-discussed findings suggest sizes of the companies and their length of business seem correlated with each other. Along with the development of the scale for most DPEs throughout the years, two seemingly opposite things could happen: on the one hand, the relationship between individual owners/managers and their workers becomes less personal; on the other, the paternalistic ways of management are enhanced through tightening the rules over production as well as over labor discipline while extending certain kinds of welfare to workers as a whole.

Conclusion

The ethnographic study in this chapter provides a detailed account of both rule-based and norm-based managerial controls in Chinese domestic privately-owned enterprises. It puts forward a more complicated picture that shows several layers of reality. By examining the intriguing relations between the state/local governments and DPEs, and between two different kinds of managerial styles along with two seemingly conflicting managerial narratives through a neo-institutionalist explanatory lens, the author argues that the DPEs' managerial imitation of the socialist SOEs is the product of combined forces from dominant ideologies, institutional rearrangement as well as the cultural meaning-making through daily practices and negotiation. Compared with a structural approach that often overlooks people's culturally informed cognition and a cultural approach that focuses only on the impact of persistent traditional belief systems, this neo-institutionalist approach directs our attention to a more dynamic process in which new ideas in response to the new structural conditions interplay with previously existing ones; the interplay, therefore, shapes the choice of actions and reactions both managers and workers made.

The chapter discusses the value conflicts and compatibilities between so-called Western and Eastern control mechanisms and rhetoric and how people actively find the consistent spots among different ideas as well as manage the inconsistencies in a unique way when product making and profit making are the legitimate principles behind their actions. Consequently, the chapter opposes a dichotomic understanding of different value systems and attempts a more insightful comprehension of how and why paternalist management is reproduced. Although we still use the concept of "paternalism" to characterize the current managerial style, we know that Western and Eastern ideas are already intertwined behind the new practice.

References

Aycan, Z., Schyns, B., Sun, J., Felfe, J., & Saher, N. (2013). Convergence and divergence of paternalistic leadership: A cross-cultural investigation of prototypes. *Journal of International Business Studies*, 44, 962-969.

Bian, Y. & Shuai, M. (2020). Elective affinity between guanxi favouritism and market rationality: Guanxi circles as governance structure in China's private firms. *Asia Pacific Business Review, 26*(2), 149-168.

Cao, J. & Huang, Q. (2004). System transition, management upgrade, and growth of private enterprises: Huafeng group corporation sample of Zhejiang Province. *The Chinese Economy, 37*(6), 7-27.

Chen, C., Li, Z., Su, X., & Sun, Z. (2011). Rent-seeking incentives, corporate political connections, and the control structure of private firms: Chinese evidence. *Journal of Corporate Finance, 17*, 229-243.

Chen, M. (Ed.). (1995). *Asian management systems*. Routledge.

Cheng, B., Chou, L., Wu, T., Huang, M. & Farh, J. (2004). Paternalistic leadership and subordinate responses: Establishing a leadership model in Chinese organizations. *Asian Journal of Social Psychology, 7*(1), 89-117.

Farh, J. & Cheng, B. (2000). A cultural analysis of paternalistic leadership in Chinese organizations. In J. T. Li, A. S. Tsui & E. Weldon (eds.), *Management and organizations in the Chinese context* (pp. 84-130). MacMillan Press.

Farh, J., Cheng, B., Chou, L., & Chu, X. (2006). Authority and benevolence: employees' response to paternalistic leadership in China. In Tsui, A. S., Bian, Y. & Cheng, L. (eds.), *China's domestic private firms: Multidisciplinary perspectives on management and performance* (pp. 230-260). M.E. Sharpe.

Lau, K. & Young, A. (2013). Why China shall not completely transit from a relation based to a rule based governance regime: A Chinese perspective. *Corporate Governance: An International Review, 21* (6), 577-585.

Lee, J., Jang, S. & Lee, S. (2018). Knowledge sharing with outsiders in emerging economies: Based on social exchange relations within the China context. *Personnel Review, 47*(5), 1094-1115.

Liao, C. (2009). *The governance structures of Chinese firms: Innovation, competitiveness, and growth in a dual economy*. Springer.

Lin, Y. (2006). The sweatshop and beyond. In Tsui, A. S., Bian, Y. & Cheng, L. (eds.), *China's domestic private firms: Multidisciplinary perspectives on management and performance* (pp. 82-96). M.E. Sharpe.

Nan, R. (2013). Chinese private enterprises' management innovation. *Asian Social Science, 9* (4). https://doi.org/10.5539/ass.v9n4p51

Powell, W. & DiMaggio, P. (Ed.). (1991). *The new institutionalism in organizational analysis*. University Chicago Press.

Pye, L. W. (1985). *Asian power and politics*. Belknap Press of Harvard University Press.

Schlevogt, K. (2002). *The art of Chinese management: Theory, evidence, and applications*. Oxford University Press.

Scott, R. (2002). The changing world of Chinese enterprise: An institutional perspective. In Tsui, A. S. & Lau, C. (eds.), *The management of enterprises in the People's Republic of China* (pp. 59-78). Kluwer Academic Publishers.

Tang, J. & Ward, A. (2002). *The changing face of Chinese management*. Routledge.

Tsai, K. S. (2007). *Capitalism without democracy: The private sector in contemporary China*. Cornell University Press.

Tsui, A. S. & Lau, C. (Ed.). (2002). *The management of enterprises in the People's Republic of China.* Kluwer Academic Publishers.

Tsui, A. S., Bian, Y. & Cheng, L. (Ed.). (2006). *China's domestic private firms: Multidisciplinary perspectives on management and performance.* M.E. Sharpe. Walder, A. (1986). *Communist neo-traditionalism: Work and authority in Chinese industry.* University of California Press.

Walder, A. (1989). Factory and manager in an era of reform. *China Quarterly,* 118, 242-264.

Wang, C., Tee, D. & Ahmed, P. (2012). Entrepreneurial leadership and context in Chinese firms: A tale of two Chinese private enterprises. *Asian Pacific Business Review,* 18(4), 505-530.

Wang, X., Bruning, N. & Peng, S. (2007). Western high-performance HR practices in China: A comparison among public-owned, private and foreign-invested enterprises. *International Journal of Human Resource Management,* 18 (4), 684-701.

Wang, Y. (2018). Trust, job security and subordinate-supervisor guanxi: Chinese employees in joint ventures and state-owned enterprises. *Asia Pacific Business Review,* 24(5), 638-655.

Wank, D. (1999). *Commodifying communism: Business, trust, and politics in Chinese society.* Cambridge University Press.

Wright, T. (2010). *Accepting authoritarianism: State-society Relations in China's reform era.* Stanford University Press. Xia, F. & Walker, G. (2015). How much does owner type matter for firm performance? Manufacturing firms in China. *Strategic Management Journal,* 36, 576-585.

Xiong, M., Wang, C., Cui, N. & Wang, T. (2021). The influence of clan culture on business performance in Asian private-owned enterprises: The case of China. *Industrial marketing management,* 99, 97-110.

Zhang, H., Ding, D., & Ke, L. (2019). The effect of R&D input and financial agglomeration on the growth private enterprises: Evidence from Chinese manufacturing industry. *Emerging Markets Finance & Trade,* 55, 2298-2313.

Zhang, X. (2009). Trade unions under the modernization of paternalist rule in China. *Working USA: the Journal of Labor and Society,* 12, 193-218. Zhong, Q. (2011). Models of trust-sharing in Chinese private enterprises. *Economic Modelling,* 28, 1017-1029.

Zhou, X., Cai, H & Li, Q. (2006). Property rights regimes and firm behavior: Theory versus evidence. In Tsui, A. S., Bian, Y. & Cheng, L., *China's domestic private firms: Multidisciplinary perspectives on management and Performance* (pp. 97-119). M.E. Sharpe.

Zhu, J. & Delbridge, R. (2021). The management of second-generation migrant workers in China: A case study of centrifugal paternalism. *Human Relations,* 1872672110329. https://doi.org/10.1177/00187267211032948.

Zhu, Y., Webber, M. & Benson, J. (2010). *The everyday impact of economic reform in China: management change, enterprise performance and daily life.* Routledge.

Chapter 11

Implications of Cross-Cultural Diversity in Global Virtual Teams

Arti Sharma

Jindal Global Business School, India

Sushant Bhargava

Indian Institute of Management (IIM) Jammu, India

Abstract: Globalization and technological innovations have diluted geographical boundaries. Organizations are working tirelessly across different nations and time zones through global virtual teams (GVTs). These teams are comprised of culturally diverse members from different geographies working together through common technological platforms, mostly temporarily on a common goal. Having cross-cultural diversity as an implicit defining characteristic, GVTs are exposed to both merits and demerits associated with a diverse workforce in an organization. This becomes more pertinent as organizations continue to employ GVTs extensively at different levels. Addressing this, in this chapter, we propose a framework for the interplay of GVTs across different dimensions of diversity at different levels or organizations. In that process, we also bring forth the challenges and opportunities arising due to cross-cultural diversity for GVTs. Accordingly, the implications and conclusions have been discussed.

Keywords: Cross-Cultural Diversity, Global Virtual Teams, GVTs, GVT Challenges, GVT Opportunities

***

Introduction

Increasingly, organizations are relying completely on the adoption of Information and communication technologies (ICTs) to manage the workforce across the globe, specifically the global virtual teams (Pauleen & Yoong, 2001; Rice & Leonardi, 2014). The global pandemic due to COVID-19 necessitated the transition of traditional businesses to virtual platforms and led to major business disruptions, prominent in the digitization of all business operations. Thus, GVTs are the need of the hour than merely a choice and have to be handled efficiently to contribute maximum within an organisation. Subsequently, all the organisations adopted ICT-based remote working to restrict the spread of the coronavirus (Dwivedi et al., 2020), making global virtual teams an essential part of evolving workforce (Chamakiotis et al., 2021).

Global virtual teams (henceforth GVTs) refer to a group of people working together towards a common goal and spanning across organizational boundaries and different time zones using technology-enabled communications (Maznevski & Chudoba, 2000). The members of GVTs are dispersed in different geographies and rarely meet in person during the duration of the entire project (Cordery et al., 2009). Being embedded in different countries, the GVTs are comprised of members from different cultures with diverse characteristics and different languages to work for a unified purpose (Goettsch, 2014).

The influence of a wide variety of cultural factors, for instance, ethnicity, and organizational and national culture attributes to the manifestation of cross-cultural diversity in GVTs. Diversity in a cross-country context refers to the mutual recognition, acceptance, and bridging of differences among individuals and businesses across different nations and ethnicities (Portes & Vickstrom, 2015). This richness of diverse attributes in GVTs has both merits and demerits, leading to differential effects on the dynamics and performance of GVTs (Taras et al., 2019). GVTs are advantageous to organizations in providing access to a large skill set with minimum development cost and recused locational constraints (Chin, 2013; Dondanville & Stafford, 2006). Additionally, these facilitate the instant exchange of information working across flexible work schedules (Adamovic, 2018; Zivick, 2012), thus, becoming a sought-after solution that can enhance lateral communication, employee participation, and organizational performance (Shachaf, 2008). Despite these advantages, GVTs pose numerous operational challenges, specifically due to language barriers, negligible in-person interactions, and loss of vocal and nonverbal cues during communication (Jimenez et al., 2017).

In essence, a GVT is exposed to a wide range of diversity of team members, comprising demographic, geographic, socio-cultural, and economic, to name a few (Townsend et al., 1998). The diversity literature characterizes these differences as distinct dimensions, namely, primary or surface-level and secondary deep-level attributes (Stahl & Maznevski, 2021). The primary dimension of diversity refers to the surface-level characteristics of individuals that are readily visible or observable, such as age, gender, and race, while the secondary dimensions refer to the deep-level characteristics that are less visible or non-observable such as attitudes, beliefs, affect, and values (Barsade et al., 2000; Harrison et al., 1998; Harrison & Klein, 2007).

Research in cultural diversity is skewed towards its manifestation due to primary dimensions (Fleury, 1999; Wright & Noe, 1996; Zakaria, 2000; 2019). For instance, Scholars have demonstrated that language barriers hinder adequate understanding within a team and hamper the team's functioning (Klitmøller & Lauring, 2013). Furthermore, the language barrier is argued to trigger the social categorization processes, thereby affecting team collaboration (Lauring, 2008). For the first time, Stahl et al. (2010) emphasized both primary and secondary dimensions to study cultural diversity and indicated the interplay of both dimensions. Still, there is a dearth of research to explore and understand the interplay of these two dimensions with few exceptions (Taras et al., 2019).

Addressing this gap, we attempt to contribute to the less explored aspect in GVTs research by discussing the interplay of dimensions of cross-cultural diversity in the context of global virtual teams. We present the framework findings for the dyadic, team, and organizational levels of implementation. We suggest specific challenges and opportunities due to cross-cultural diversity dimensions in GVTs for each level. At the *dyadic* level, the cross-cultural dimensions can offer unique attributes concerning problem-solving, communication, language, gender, and other heterogeneous issues. At the *team* level, role definition, differences in perspectives and leadership will have a characteristic interplay. Lastly, at the *organizational* level, Time perspective, training, organizational development, and company-wide value sensitization are expected to play a key influence.

In the subsequent sections of this paper, we first present a brief literature review on GVTs, emphasizing the dearth of research in a cross-cultural context. The second section discusses the framework to discuss the dimensions of diversity across different levels of implementation in GVTs. Then, a discussion will be followed by a conclusion with practical and theoretical implications.

Literature Review

Jarvenpaa and Leidner (1999) define GVTs as a "temporary, culturally diverse, geographically dispersed, and electronically communicating workgroup" (p. 792). In simple terms, the teams comprising of geographically dispersed members to interact and work using electronic media are termed as global virtual teams or GVTs (Anawati & Craig, 2006; Griffin, 2012; Robinson, 2013). It is an intricate arrangement of members from different nations, cultures, and linguistic characteristics separated by time and space but functioning towards a common goal using computer-mediated technologies (Zakaria, 2009). Culture is a key ingredient in global virtual teams (Johnston & Rosin, 2011; Scott & Wildman, 2015). The diversity in GVTs manifests in the influence of a wide variety of cultural factors, for instance, ethnicity, organization, and the national culture (Duarte & Snyder, 2011).

Researchers often rely on the Hofstede (1984) cultural dimensions of individualistic versus collectivistic culture to understand culture-specific behavior and value orientations. Individuals from collectivist orientations are relationship-oriented and are inclined to seek and adhere to team goals, while individualistic cultures are task-oriented (Gómez et al., 2000), which becomes more evident in GVTs. Teams are ubiquitous in organizations nowadays in all their dynamism and forms. As teams are aggregated units composed of individuals, teamwork is also sourced from member behavior. Teamwork and behavior related to the culture have been studied by scholars at different levels – such as nationality, group, and societal level at which culture is observed (e.g., Calabuig et al., 2018; Chiou & Mercado, 2016; Salk & Brannen, 2000; Schroeder, 2010). Behaviors such as trust and communication are indispensable to effective teamwork in this regard (Congden et al., 2009; Kimble, 2011).

Implications of cross-cultural diversity in teams are therefore sourced from patterns in behavioral interactions within the team that take place as a response to both cross-cultural factors and diversity. Virtual teams, and GVTs, are no exceptions to the influences of cross-cultural settings and diversity (Clark et al., 2017; Nouri et al., 2013; Oertig & Buergi, 2006). The depth of effects of different kinds of diversity on teamwork and virtual teamwork is as far-reaching as that of culture. Moreover, diversity stems from a culture in distinctive ways, and understanding of the mechanisms through which they impact teams and organizational work has been evolving in the literature (Ahmed & Swan, 2006; Chuang et al., 2004; Pless & Maak, 2004). Given that GVTs are global by definition, diversity is a natural presence in them, whether explicitly acknowledged or not. In this regard, the global element in virtual teams is well represented by cultural diversity.

The links between culture and behavior have a long history of exploration across many disciplines of study. As we have seen, culture can be difficult to define and quantify (Huggins & Thompson, 2015; Soares et al., 2007). Only components of culture can be used to operationalize it in terms of the situation being studied. The effects of culture on behavior can also be varied and multifarious since there is a multitude of ways in which the smallest of cultural cues take shape to result in or shape behavior (Arensberg, 1972; Yamagishi et al., 2008). Predicting human behavior falls under the domain of Anthropology, and the predictions are still suggestive at best, even after decades of research. In the modern workplace, especially when a significant part of work takes place virtually or the workflow has sizeable components of online interventions, behavior is key to ensuring productivity (Alexander et al., 2020; Mercado et al., 2016).

Though there have been strong research efforts at cross-cultural context building among teams outside of virtual work too (Tian et al., 2015), the place of cultural diversity in GVTs and their continuously changing modes of working has not been explored. Our review of GVTs revealed interesting findings in the context of communication within teams (Berry, 2011; Jarvenpaa & Leidner, 1999; Maznevski & Chudoba, 2000); conflicts (Montoya-Weiss et al., 2001); team collaboration (Majchrzak et al., 2000a) and, trust (Jarvenpaa, & Leidner, 1999). Other scholars in GVTs studied leadership (Kayworth & Leidner, 2002; Ziek & Smulowitz, 2014); creativity (Nemiro, 2000, 2016); group identification (Anttonen et al., 2018), and technology adaptation (Majchrzak et al., 2000b). It is important to note that limited attention has been paid to understanding the implications of cross-cultural diversity and its implications, for instance, behavioral adaptation (Anawati & Craig, 2006), subgroup dynamics (Hinds et al., 2014), and social categorization process (Klitmøller et al., 2015) to name a few.

Focusing on the influences of cultural diversity in the working of GVTs is difficult since diversity is the distillation of multiple interactions, dynamics, and cognitive processes, which are not precisely observable and are context-dependent in most cases (Picherit-Duthler, 2014). However, a consolidation of cultural diversity-related processes and characteristics is the need of the hour to enable the exposition of integrative insights into global teamwork and the opportunities or challenges that arise from it. Technological aids are indispensable to organizational functioning in the modern world (Bailey et al., 2019). Finding dimensions along which they can be arranged from the perspective of virtual teamwork in a global context, such that effectiveness remains intact and universality in implications can be introduced, is an important step in the direction of consolidation of this important field of research and practice. In this manner, multicultural and cross-cultural contexts can be distinguished in teamwork and appropriation of efforts made more streamlined (Congden et al., 2009; Connaughton & Shuffler, 2007). It is also important to note that a distinctive sub-culture within the team could be established during teamwork (Schroeder, 2010). However, our concern here is with a particular type of diversity that occurs through team membership. As the theory directs, interactions are the basis of cultural diversity, and we carry out an explication of knowledge about the levels of virtual work, which enable us to provide suitable implications in the modern team context through our proposed framework.

Integrative Framework

GVTs have become a persistent presence in organizational work, even becoming indispensable to certain kinds of organizations in some situations. According to scholars, there are many directions to the study of virtual teams and diversity, which have developed concurrently and strongly (Taras et al., 2019). Though the study of GVTs is situated majorly at the team level within the organizations, the study of cultural diversity is not so restricted and, therefore, wider in scope and applications. Both empirical and qualitative evidence regarding GVTs and cultural diversity is abundant when considered in isolation (Adler & Aycan, 2018; Scott & Wildman, 2015). However, there is value in considering the evidence together holistically – such that the critical elements are decluttered/integrated, and explorations into implications are enabled. Additionally, relatively common elements of diversity are different from traditional representations of cross-cultural dynamics in modern teams. Therefore, interventions targeted at smooth and continuous handling of diversity in workplaces (especially of the cultural kind) can be tricky without the introduction of a holistically integrative framework. It is worth mentioning here that virtual teams do not entirely assimilate into traditional team management techniques but require more effort from the leader/ manager (Ābeltiņa & Rizhamadze, 2021; Hertel et al., 2005; Nydegger & Nydegger, 2010; Serrat, 2017). Therefore, diversity is only one of the departures from face-to-face teams that need to be mitigated in GVTs, and that too in conjunction with other differences and/or developing external issues. Modern modes of remaining connected do make it easier and difficult to build synergies in the context of modern volatilities in the environment (e.g., Bulmer & Buchanan-Oliver, 2004). Hence, to lend hues of adaptability, flexibility, and practicability to implications of cultural diversity in GVTs, we first provide a framework that relates to basic functions of management as relates to teamwork in virtual settings. Figure 11.1 presents this framework for organizing the extensive empirical and theoretical evidence which is available in the scholarly literature about cultural diversity and GVTs.

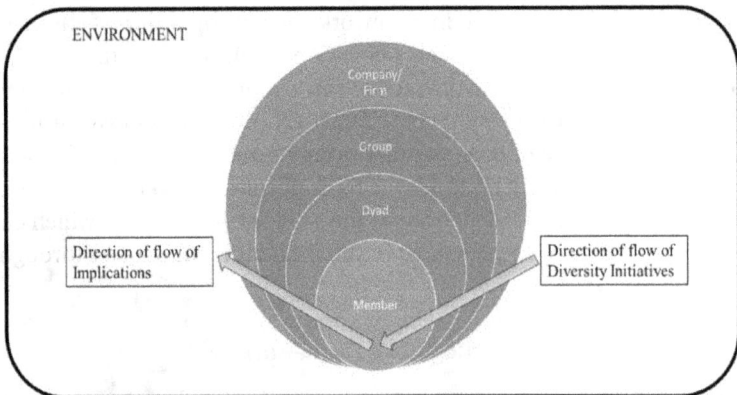

Figure 11.1: Integrative Framework on Cross-Cultural Diversity and Global Virtual Teams

The framework presented in *figure 11.1* is a tool to organize the existing knowledge to ascertain how the features/ dimensions of cross-cultural diversity and GVTs may be considered together for arriving at the implications of cultural diversity in GVTs. To be able to put the implications of the various challenges and opportunities that arise in the modern workplace (as is the remit of this article), a clarification of levels is necessary to clarify who within the organization is impacted and how. The initiatives or interventions to be taken in this regard are depicted as flowing down from the corporate or the firm level, as shown in the figure. This is because taking actions related to diversity always involves institutionalization and propagation of company-wide values as an intended or extended objective. Similarly, for leaders and managers, being attentive to the implications of having cross-cultural diversity within the organization should be clear so that the issues arising from them may be controlled as and when required. The levels can be seen as indicators of the presence of cross-cultural diversity within the organization. We have explained briefly the trends of observing behavior arising from and propagating through cultural differences. We have shown levels other than teams in our organizing framework since interactions are the source of implications of diversity, and interactions at the team level affect other levels. Therefore, we find in the literature implications of cross-cultural diversity sometimes a combination of influences over several levels. For instance, consider the following:

- At the firm level, cross-functional teams are present which make decisions for the whole organization (Knein et al., 2020; Webber, 2002).

- The dyad level is the most important in cross-cultural interactions and is embedded within the team level. The dyad level is, in fact, where most of the leadership literature in teams is located (Kim et al., 2020).

The individual and individual-oriented factors are not considered in the framework since the focus here is on a discussion of diversity in groups. For the group itself, the establishment of within-group norms is an important part of working as a single entity. The objective of finding implications within GVTs is to work out how seeing virtual work beyond the two dimensions of the computer screen can help in achieving on-the-ground results. There are hybrid modes of working being experimented with by organizations as well (de Guinea et al., 2012), and the implications of cross-cultural diversity apply in those situations. Anyhow, GVTs are a reality and are here to stay with their associated challenges and opportunities. Some pros and cons, which are summed up as implications of cross-cultural diversity in GVTs, are summarized in Table 11.1.

Table 11.1: Implications of Cross-Cultural Diversity, with associated challenges and opportunities, for interventions aimed at promoting Global Virtual Team effectiveness

Diversity characteristics	Challenges	Opportunities	Level of Implementation
Company-wide value sensitization	Creating properly worded and toned instruments for the propagation of diverse cultural values.	A more aware and more involved workforce able to identify with its own and others' unconscious behaviors	Company/ Firm
Training	Finding the right set of people and teaching aids for conveying CCD-related complexities at work to a possibly uninterested audience.	Creating organizationally transmitted 'stories' that turn unique experiences into protocols.	
Time-limitations	Creating the infrastructure and other facilitating tools to build connections among people with different time-related constraints/ zones/ preferences.	Tapping into a pool of talent not available locally or without virtual connections.	M E
Difference in perspectives	Building synergy required by the team or for the task at hand in the face of strongly held biases.	Increase in speed and efficiency of handling tasks as the team compatibility grows.	Group M
Conflict Management	Merging the different styles of conflict management which may be carried over from respective cultural norms or learning.	Building of an ecosystem of health within and between competitions for the group, which may be conducive to performance.	B E
Leadership and Role Definition	Handling teams and teamwork when an embedded sense of hierarchy and roles may be present.	More hands-on and people-oriented role-keeping among employees. Flexibility in the discharge of responsibilities in the face of unprecedented situations.	R
Gender and other heteronormative issues	Ignoring the most visible form of diversity may be difficult for people with strong biases based on their respective cultures.	Having a good environment where talent can thrive.	Dyad

Communications and Language	Integrating technology with non-verbal or interpreted cues while communicating virtually.	More connected and expressive employees over any medium.
Problem-Solving	Cultural biases may force even constructive suggestions as criticism or a difference of stance	Problem-solving through unexplored or undocumented ways emerging from cultural wisdom.

The challenges and opportunities detailed in the table are the implications of cross-cultural diversity in GVTs presented in the form of actionable information for the benefit of managers. Applicable interventions can be designed and implemented by the managers/ leaders in any organization based on these insights. Since the interventions are related to cultural diversity, they must touch upon every level of teamwork. However, the levels from which major concerns or work may likely be located are presented here for managers/ leaders seeking to apply the framework. The direction of the flow of affecting factors also guides the direction of implementation/ initiatives flow, as the framework suggests. In the sense that the implications of any intervention are never instantly visible, the flow of implications is indicated as the reverse. Therefore, the implications of cross-cultural diversity are apparent through sustained and concerted efforts within the organization. The actual behavioral change occurs at the member level (which is the most embedded) and is a result of the interventions or possible advantage. The effects at this level are guided by the team dynamics, which are built and sustained during teamwork. Still, it must be kept in mind that the impact is spread organization-wide with flows as indicated in *figure 11.1* and multiple stakeholder involvement.

Discussion

To delineate the implications of cross-cultural diversity in GVTs, we first take into account the existing evidence on both constructs to show where and how those implications might flow through modern work organizations. We next increase the employability of those implications by showing at what levels the implications are visible under different heads – an approach that increases the value of those implications in the design of strong interventions with associated challenges and opportunities. The relative importance of cross-cultural diversity and GVTs is evident in the wide scope of instances in organizational life where they exist. However, the ground implications of both, especially in the interactive sense, have been brought out in fragmented terms as part of both streams of literature, which makes it difficult to distill critical insights. Thus, the value of the implications developed here is mainly integrative.

The characteristics of diversity that form the basis of the implications of cross-cultural diversity are labels around which implementation or interventions can be centered in terms of opportunities and challenges provided. These dimensions have sometimes been found as shared characteristics among GVTs, and as distinctive or differentiating from others. These dimensions are included here, given their continued value in the global context and the modern workplace, especially where diversity may come into play. For instance, though GVTs with cross-functionality require at least some value sensitization and training in all instances, some additional limitations may be faced owing to time limitations, conflicts, role definitions, or communication specifically as a result of cross-cultural diversity. These dimensions are by no means exhaustive, but it is expected that they lend some completeness to commonly observed directions of effects found in GVTs through cross-cultural diversity.

Another part of the framework showing the flow of implications among levels within the organization and the implications themselves is the member level. Any manager or practitioner is well aware that the requirements of and concerns of different individuals diverge more often than not, especially within the ambit of remote or virtual work. Our implications show that all the implications straddle the member level. Thus, the member level of analysis is of implicit importance as far as further actions based on the implications are concerned. Additionally, the framework seeks to help those members of any organization who are relatively new to different modes of virtual work or teamwork in the presence of diversity and does not assume prior knowledge outside of the details furnished through this article. Also, the levels within the organization are evolving continuously, and adaptability is a significant issue, even for seasoned managers or practitioners. It is because of this evolving nature of GVTs and cross-cultural diversity that some challenges and opportunities presented here may not seem to be geared only towards the GVTs; since they are based on interactions among levels and also arise from interactions between work and diversity in general.

Conclusion

The discovery of implications of working with Cross-Cultural Diversity in entities of growing importance, such as Global Virtual Teams, leads to valuable recommendations for leaders and managers at all levels of the organization toward the building and sustaining of effectiveness centered on a diverse workforce. An integration of research findings on GVTs brings about the possibility of creating widespread organizational interventions to alter the working styles of employees and reduce the disruptive impact of unprecedented or unforeseen events. This has immense applications for building synergies which continue to prevail even when the membership of the team or any other of its defining attributes is altered. Also, connectedness is the basic differentiating factor for work in GVTs, since they must rely heavily on the availability and applications of technological media (Cherry, 2010; Raghuram et al., 2019). Synergies, when present, bring about connectedness within any work unit. Culture and cross-cultural diversity have the potential to turn advantageous as well as disastrous, depending on the control exercised by the manager or leader. However, as technology advances at an accelerating pace, so does connectedness among individuals. It is only prudent to be able to bring this connectedness in social interactions to connect in work situations. In the face of disruptions like the COVID-19 pandemic and subsequent restrictions, virtual work and GVTs have proved increasingly dependable for ensuring the continuity of work. The growing emphasis on virtuality in organizational work shows how the interactive effects of virtual work spill over to other domains (Bhargava, 2020; Handke et al., 2020). Hence, our framework and recommendations hold additional weight in the current world order.

The dimensions of cross-cultural diversity, using which we detail the implications of cross-cultural diversity in GVTs, take further the theoretical links between culture and diversity. The implications are discussed in the form of influences arising from the dimensions of cross-cultural diversity available in the literature on the topic. The literature is extensive, and the insights are drawn using a framework for organizing the evidence-based practical requirements. That said, online modes present their unique constraints and facilitation, more so when the advancements are rapid and the applications limitless. In the present scenario, access to technological infrastructure has been steadily increasing and easing across the globe. Therefore, connecting to work online is set to become a norm shortly, making diversity a vital stake playing out in organizational work. Guiding courses of action are also immediately discoverable for leveraging cross-cultural diversity in GVTs. Still, they must be attuned to the specific needs of any organization and must balance individual preferences and styles with the interests of the team and the organization.

On a final note, having cross-cultural diversity as a primary consideration in organizational and virtual work opens avenues for the unification of globally diverse work perspectives in different situations. Teams are based on synergies, and having global values for carrying out collaborative efforts can bring about those synergies. Hence, it is prudent to evaluate and be inclusive of the implications of cross-cultural diversity while designing work in organizations and ensuring that this work is as people-centric as possible while also being respectful of their diverse origins and identity.

References

Ābeltiņa, A., & Rizhamadze, K. (2021). Challenges to Managing Virtual Teams in Georgian SMEs. *SHS Web of Conferences, 119,* 03003. https://doi.org/10.1 051/shsconf/202111903003

Adamovic, M. (2018). An employee-focused human resource management perspective for the management of global virtual teams. *The International Journal of Human Resource Management, 29*(14), 2159-2187. https://doi.org /10.1080/09585192.2017.1323227

Adler, N. J., & Aycan, Z. (2018). Cross-cultural interaction: What we know and what we need to know. *Annual Review of Organizational Psychology and Organizational Behavior, 5,* 307-333.

Ahmed, S., & Swan, E. (2006). Doing Diversity. *Policy Futures in Education, 4*(2), 96–100. doi: 10.2304/pfie.2006.4.2.96

Alexander, A., Smet, A. De, & Mysore, M. (2020). Reimagining the postpandemic workforce. *McKinsey Quarterly.* Retrieved from https://www.mckinsey.com/ business-functions/organization/our-insights/reimagining-the-postpandemic-workforce

Anawati, D., & Craig, A. (2006). Behavioral adaptation within cross-cultural virtual teams. *IEEE transactions on professional communication, 49*(1), 44-56.

Anttonen, M., Stenberg, P. D. E., & Karhu, M. S. A. (2018). Group Identification in the Context of Global Virtual Teams.

Arensberg, C. M. (1972). Culture as Behavior: Structure and Emergence. *Annual Review of Anthropology, 1*(1), 1–27. https://doi.org/10.1146/annurev .an.01.100172.000245

Bailey, D., Faraj, S., Hinds, P., von Krogh, G., & Leonardi, P. (2019). Special Issue of Organization Science: Emerging Technologies and Organizing. *Organization Science, 30*(3), 642–646. https://doi.org/10.1287/orsc.2019.1299

Barsade, S. G., Ward, A. J., Turner, J. D., & Sonnenfeld, J. A. (2000). To your heart's content: A model of affective diversity in top management teams. *Administrative science quarterly, 45*(4), 802-836.

Berry, G. R. (2011). Enhancing effectiveness on virtual teams: Understanding why traditional team skills are insufficient. *The Journal of Business Communication, 48*(2), 186-206.

Bhargava, S. (2020). Virtuality and teams: Dealing with crises and catastrophes. *Human Systems Management, 39*(4), 537–547. https://doi.org/10.3233/HSM-201050

Bulmer, S., & Buchanan-Oliver, M. (2004). Meaningless or meaningful? Interpretation and intentionality in post-modern communication. *Journal of Marketing Communications, 10*(1), 1-15.

Calabuig, V., Olcina, G., & Panebianco, F. (2018). Culture and team production. *Journal of Economic Behavior & Organization, 149,* 32–45. https://doi.org/1 0.1016/j.jebo.2018.03.004

Chamakiotis, P., Panteli, N., & Davison, R. M. (2021). Reimagining e-leadership for reconfigured virtual teams due to Covid-19. *International Journal of Information Management*, 60, 102381.

Cherry, M. A. (2010). A Taxonomy of Virtual Work. *Georgia Law Review, 45*(4), 951.

Chin, J. L. (2013). Diversity leadership: Influence of ethnicity, gender, and minority status. *Open Journal of Leadership, 2*(01), 1.

Chiou, A. Y., & Mercado, B. K. (2016). Flexible Loyalties: How Malleable Are Bicultural Loyalties? *Frontiers in Psychology, 7*(DEC), 1-8. https://doi.org/10.3389/fpsyg.2016.01985

Chuang, Y., Church, R., & Zikic, J. (2004). Organizational culture, group diversity and intra-group conflict. *Team Performance Management: An International Journal, 10*(1/2), 26–34. https://doi.org/10.1108/13527590410527568

Clark, L., Birkhead, A. S., Fernandez, C., & Egger, M. J. (2017). A Transcription and Translation Protocol for Sensitive Cross-Cultural Team Research. *Qualitative Health Research, 27*(12), 1751–1764. https://doi.org/10.1177/1049732317726761

Congden, S. W., Matveev, A. V., & Desplaces, D. E. (2009). Cross-cultural Communication and Multicultural Team Performance: A German and American Comparison. *Journal of Comparative International Management, 12*(2), 73–89.

Connaughton, S. L., & Shuffler, M. (2007). Multinational and Multicultural Distributed Teams: A Review and Future Agenda. *Small Group Research, 38*(3), 387–412. https://doi.org/10.1177/1046496407301970

Cordery, J., Soo, C., Kirkman, B., Rosen, B., & Mathieu, J. (2009). Leading Parallel Global Virtual Teams: Lessons from Alcoa. *Organizational Dynamics, 38*(3), 204-216.

de Guinea, A. O., Webster, J., & Staples, D. S. (2012). A meta-analysis of the consequences of virtualness on team functioning. *Information & Management, 49*(6), 301–308. https://doi.org/10.1016/j.im.2012.08.003

Dondanville, C., & Stafford, T. (2006). Benefiting from Open Source Development Methodologies in Global Information Systems Organizations. *AMCIS 2006 Proceedings*, 106. Duarte, D. L., & Snyder, N. T. (2011). *Mastering virtual teams: Strategies, tools, and techniques that succeed.* John Wiley & Sons.

Duarte, D. L., & Snyder, N. T. (2011). *Mastering virtual teams: Strategies, tools, and techniques that succeed.* John Wiley & Sons.

Dwivedi, Y. K., Hughes, D. L., Coombs, C., Constantiou, I., Duan, Y., Edwards, J. S., ... & Upadhyay, N. (2020). Impact of COVID-19 pandemic on information management research and practice: Transforming education, work and life. *International journal of information management*, 55, 102211.

Fleury, M.T.L. (1999). The management of culture diversity: lessons from Brazilian companies. *Industrial Management & Data Systems*, 99(3), 109-114.

Goettsch, K. L. (2014). Understanding intercultural communication on global virtual teams: exploring challenges of language, culture, technology, and collaboration. *Doctoral Dissertation.* University of Minnesota.

Gómez, C., Kirkman, B. L., & Shapiro, D. L. (2000). The impact of collectivism and in-group/out-group membership on the evaluation generosity of team members. *Academy of management Journal, 43*(6), 1097-1106.

Griffin, K. S. (2012). Leadership effectiveness in virtual teams: A quantitative analysis of the impact of perception. *Order,* (3517090).

Handke, L., Klonek, F. E., Parker, S. K., & Kauffeld, S. (2020). Interactive Effects of Team Virtuality and Work Design on Team Functioning. *Small Group Research, 51*(1), 3–47. https://doi.org/10.1177/1046496419863490

Harrison, D. A., & Klein, K. J. (2007). What's the difference? Diversity constructs as separation, variety, or disparity in organizations. *Academy of management review,* 32(4), 1199-1228.

Harrison, D. A., Price, K. H., & Bell, M. P. (1998). Beyond relational demography: Time and the effects of surface-and deep-level diversity on work group cohesion. *Academy of Management Journal, 41*(1), 96-107.

Hertel, G., Geister, S., & Konradt, U. (2005). Managing virtual teams: A review of current empirical research. *Human Resource Management Review, 15*(1), 69–95. https://doi.org/10.1016/j.hrmr.2005.01.002

Hinds, P. J., Neeley, T. B., & Cramton, C. D. (2014). Language as a lightning rod: Power contests, emotion regulation, and subgroup dynamics in global teams. *Journal of International Business Studies, 45*(5), 536-561.

Huggins, R., & Thompson, P. (2015). Culture and Place-Based Development: A Socio-Economic Analysis. *Regional Studies, 49*(1), 130–159. https://doi.org/10.1080/00343404.2014.889817

Jarvenpaa, S. L., & Leidner, D. E. (1999). Communication and trust in global virtual teams. *Organization science, 10*(6), 791-815.

Jimenez, A., Boehe, D. M., Taras, V., & Caprar, D. V. (2017). Working across boundaries: Current and future perspectives on global virtual teams. *Journal of International Management, 23*(4), 341-349.

Johnston, K. A., & Rosin, K. (2011, May). Global virtual teams: How to manage them. In *2011 International Conference on Computer and Management (CAMAN)* (pp. 1-4). IEEE.

Kankanhalli, A., Tan, B. C., & Wei, K. K. (2006). Conflict and performance in global virtual teams. *Journal of management information systems, 23*(3), 237-274.

Kayworth, T. R., & Leidner, D. E. (2002). Leadership effectiveness in global virtual teams. *Journal of management information systems, 18*(3), 7-40.

Kim, J., Yammarino, F. J., Dionne, S. D., Eckardt, R., Cheong, M., Tsai, C. Y., ... & Park, J. W. (2020). State-of-the-science review of leader-follower dyads research. *The Leadership Quarterly, 31*(1), 101306.

Kimble, C. (2011). Building effective virtual teams: How to overcome the problems of trust and identity in virtual teams. *Global Business and Organizational Excellence, 30*(2), 6–15. https://doi.org/10.1002/joe.20364

Klitmøller, A., & Lauring, J. (2013). When global virtual teams share knowledge: Media richness, cultural difference and language commonality. *Journal of world Business, 48*(3), 398-406.

Klitmøller, A., Schneider, S. C., & Jonsen, K. (2015). Speaking of global virtual teams: Language differences, social categorization and media choice. *Personnel Review.*

Knein, E., Greven, A., Bendig, D., & Brettel, M. (2020). Culture and cross-functional coopetition: The interplay of organizational and national culture. *Journal of International Management, 26*(2), 100731. https://doi.org/10.101 6/j.intman.2019.100731

Lauring, J. (2008). Rethinking social identity theory in international encounters: Language use as a negotiated object for identity making. *International Journal of Cross Cultural Management, 8*(3), 343-361.

Majchrzak, A., Rice, R. E., King, N., Malhotra, A., & Ba, S. (2000a). Computer-mediated inter-organizational knowledge-sharing: Insights from a virtual team innovating using a collaborative tool. *Information Resources Management Journal (IRMJ), 13*(1), 44-53.

Majchrzak, A., Rice, R. E., Malhotra, A., King, N., & Ba, S. (2000b). Technology adaptation: The case of a computer-supported inter-organizational virtual team. *MIS quarterly,* 569-600.

Maznevski, M. L., & Chudoba, K. M. (2000). Bridging space over time: Global virtual team dynamics and effectiveness. *Organization science, 11*(5), 473-492.

Mercado, B. K., Dilchert, S., Giordano, C., & Ones, D. S. (2016). Counterproductive Work Behaviors. In *The SAGE Handbook of Industrial, Work and Organizational Psychology: Personnel Psychology and Employee Performance* (pp. 109–210). London: SAGE Publications. https://doi.org/10. 4135/9781473914940.n7

Montoya-Weiss, M. M., Massey, A. P., & Song, M. (2001). Getting it together: Temporal coordination and conflict management in global virtual teams. *Academy of management Journal, 44*(6), 1251-1262.

Nemiro, J. E. (2000). The glue that binds creative virtual teams. In *Knowledge management and virtual organizations* (pp. 101-123). IGI Global.

Nemiro, J. E. (2016). Connection in creative virtual teams. *Journal of Behavioral and Applied Management, 2*(2), 814.

Nouri, R., Erez, M., Rockstuhl, T., Ang, S., Leshem-Calif, L., & Rafaeli, A. (2013). Taking the bite out of culture: The impact of task structure and task type on overcoming impediments to cross-cultural team performance. *Journal of Organizational Behavior, 34*(6), 739–763. https://doi.org/10.1002/job.1871

Nydegger, R., & Nydegger, L. (2010). Challenges In Managing Virtual Teams. *Journal of Business & Economics Research (JBER), 8*(3), 69–82. https://doi.org /10.19030/jber.v8i3.690

Oertig, M., & Buergi, T. (2006). The challenges of managing cross-cultural virtual project teams. *Team Performance Management, 12*(1–2), 23–30. https://doi.org /10.1108/13527590610652774

Pauleen, D. J., & Yoong, P. (2001). Relationship building and the use of ICT in boundary-crossing virtual teams: a facilitator's perspective. *Journal of Information Technology, 16*(4), 205-220.

Picherit-Duthler, G. (2014). How Similar or Different are We? In I. R. Management Association (USA) (Ed.), *Cross-Cultural Interaction* (pp. 80–92). IGI Global. https://doi.org/10.4018/978-1-4666-4979-8.ch006

Pless, N., & Maak, T. (2004). Building an Inclusive Diversity Culture: Principles, Processes and Practice. *Journal of Business Ethics, 54*(2), 129–147. https://doi.org/10.1007/s10551-004-9465-8

Portes, A., & Vickstrom, E. (2015). Diversity, social capital, and cohesion. *SERIES «ETUDESEUROPEENNES, 41.*

Presbitero, A. (2021). Communication accommodation within global virtual team: The influence of cultural intelligence and the impact on interpersonal process effectiveness. *Journal of International Management, 27*(1), 100809.

Raghuram, S., Hill, N. S., Gibbs, J. L., & Maruping, L. M. (2019). Virtual Work: Bridging Research Clusters. *Academy of Management Annals, 13*(1), 308–341. https://doi.org/10.5465/annals.2017.0020

Rice, R. E., & Leonardi, P. M. (2014). Information and communication technologies in organizations. The SAGE handbook of organizational communication: advances in theory, research, and methods, 425-448.

Robinson, K. J. (2013). An examination of virtual teams: Exploring the relationship among emotional intelligence, collective team leadership, and team effectiveness. *Doctoral Dissertation.* Capella University.

Salk, J. E., & Brannen, M. Y. (2000). National Culture, Networks, and Individual Influence in a Multinational Management Team. *Academy of Management Journal, 43*(2), 191–202. https://doi.org/10.2307/1556376

Schroeder, P. J. (2010). Changing team culture: The perspectives of ten successful head coaches. *Journal of Sport Behavior, 33*(1), 63–88.

Scott, C. P., & Wildman, J. L. (2015). Culture, communication, and conflict: A review of the global virtual team literature. *Leading global teams,* 13-32.

Serrat, O. (2017). Managing Virtual Teams. In *Knowledge Solutions* (pp. 619–625). Singapore: Springer Singapore. https://doi.org/10.1007/978-981-10-0983-9_68

Shachaf, P. (2008). Cultural diversity and information and communication technology impacts on global virtual teams: An exploratory study. *Information & Management, 45*(2), 131-142.

Soares, A. M., Farhangmehr, M., & Shoham, A. (2007). Hofstede's dimensions of culture in international marketing studies. *Journal of Business Research, 60*(3), 277–284. https://doi.org/10.1016/j.jbusres.2006.10.018

Stahl, G. K., & Maznevski, M. L. (2021). Unraveling the effects of cultural diversity in teams: A retrospective of research on multicultural work groups and an agenda for future research. *Journal of International Business Studies, 52*(1), 4-22.

Stahl, G. K., Maznevski, M. L., Voigt, A., & Jonsen, K. (2010). Unraveling the effects of cultural diversity in teams: A meta-analysis of research on multicultural work groups. *Journal of international business studies, 41*(4), 690-709.

Taras, V., Baack, D., Caprar, D., Dow, D., Froese, F., Jimenez, A., & Magnusson, P. (2019). Diverse effects of diversity: Disaggregating effects of diversity in global virtual teams. *Journal of International Management, 25*(4), 100689.

Tian, L., Li, Y., Li, P. P., & Bodla, A. A. (2015). Leader–member skill distance, team cooperation, and team performance: A cross-culture study in a context of sport teams. *International Journal of Intercultural Relations, 49*, 183–197. https://doi.org/10.1016/j.ijintrel.2015.10.005

Townsend, A. M., DeMarie, S. M., & Hendrickson, A. R. (1998). Virtual teams: Technology and the workplace of the future. *Academy of Management Perspectives, 12*(3), 17-29.

Webber, S. (2002). Leadership and trust facilitating cross-functional team success. *Journal of Management Development, 21*(3), 201–214. https://doi.org/10.1108/02621710210420273

Wright, P.M. and Noe, R.A. (1996), Management of Organizations, Irwin McGraw-Hill

Yamagishi, T., Hashimoto, H., & Schug, J. (2008). Preferences Versus Strategies as Explanations for Culture-Specific Behavior. *Psychological Science, 19*(6), 579–584. https://doi.org/10.1111/j.1467-9280.2008.02126.x

Zakaria, N. (2000). The effects of cross-cultural training on the acculturation process of the global workforce. *International Journal of Manpower.*

Zakaria, N. (2009). Using computer mediated communication as a tool to facilitate intercultural collaboration of global virtual teams. In Encyclopedia of Multimedia Technology and Networking, Second Edition (pp. 1499-1505). IGI Global.

Ziek, P., & Smulowitz, S. (2014). The impact of emergent virtual leadership competencies on team effectiveness. *Leadership & Organization Development Journal.*

Zivick, J. (2012). Mapping global virtual team leadership actions to organizational roles. *The Business Review, 19*(2), 18-25.

Chapter 12

Implications of Cross-Cultural Business Communication in the Digital Environment

Chandra Sekhar Patro

Gayatri Vidya Parishad College of Engineering (A),
Visakhapatnam, India

Abstract: In the digitally globalized world, cross-cultural communication in the social and business environment has become more widespread than ever before. Many organizations have widespread their business units overseas not only to strengthen their financial status but also to establish a strong business network worldwide. Cultural awareness shapes how business firms behave in cross-culturally reflected international markets. Therefore, understanding cultural differences is one of the most important skills for firms to develop to have a competitive advantage in international business. Digital technologies and digital media are changing the environment through which business organizations interact with their clients. The marketing relationship is becoming increasingly imperative as a means to meet the marketing needs of organizations. The chapter articulates changing business environment and the need for cross-cultural communication in the digital environment. The influences of globalization on cross-cultural communication, adoption of various communicative strategies, cultural impacts, issues faced by global managers, and overcoming barriers to cultural adaptations are assessed.

Keywords: Business organizations, Communication, Cross-culture, Digital technologies, Environment, Globalization

***

Introduction

Cross-cultural management describes the behaviour of individuals in enterprises around the world. It expresses the working conditions of employees and clients from different cultures. Organizational culture refers to norms, shared values, and expectations that regulate an enterprise. It states how individuals interact and approach work processes (Lewis, 2014). It is deceptive that culture contributes significantly to organizational effectiveness; if it does not, this may signal the need for internal or external changes to the enterprise. The internal sources may include a change in managers, employees or technology, while the external sources may be political, technological or economic (Onyusheva et al., 2020).

With the increased importance of international business and the growing number of multinational companies, the issue of cross-cultural communication has become critical as it impacts many managerial processes, including planning and organizing activities, decision-making, and public relations (Kesari et al., 2014). Within the global business environment, the ability to communicate effectively can be a challenge. Even when both parties speak the same language, there can still be misunderstandings due to ethnic and cultural differences. Understanding the impact of globalization on cross-culture communication is imperative for organizations seeking to create a competitive advantage in the global market. As society becomes more globally connected, the ability to communicate across cultural boundaries has gained increasing prominence. Global businesses must understand how to communicate with employees and customers from different cultures to fulfill the organization's mission and build value for stakeholders (Okoro, 2013).

New technologies, globalization, and changing organizational cultures affect cross-cultural communication. Communication is one of the most important functions to master for any business to succeed in today's increasingly competitive markets, particularly for international organizations. Cross-cultural communication significantly contributes to the success of business operations (Bauman & Shcherbina, 2018). The use of technology has a profound impact on how businesses communicate globally and market their products and services across the globe. Cultural factors have long been known to influence the communication and success potential of competition. Cultural awareness shapes how business firms behave in cross-culturally reflected international markets. It is broadly recognized that cultural factors act as invisible barriers in international business communications (Guang & Trotter, 2012).

Digital technologies and media are changing the environments through which business organizations interact with their clients. The evolution of digital organizational forms, customer technology use, and the nature of customer journeys differ significantly across global markets. The explosive growth of innovative digital technologies over the past two decades has revolutionized how customers browse for information, compare products and services, make purchases, and engage with enterprises and other customers.

Customers today interact with enterprises and other customers through multiple online touchpoints in multiple channels and media. Although the basic technologies underlying digital innovations are much the same worldwide, the nature of customers' interactions with different touchpoints in a digital environment differs significantly across global markets (Nam & Kannan, 2020).

Cross-cultural business communication demands that enterprises be aware of and sensitive to cultural differences. To respect the right to culture by consumers in various cultures and marketplaces, marketers should understand that their customers have a right to their cultures. If marketers want success in cross-cultural marketing, they must work to respect the consumer's values and the right to their culture. Therefore, marketers benefit from understanding the market's cultural environment to match marketing with consumer preferences, purchasing behavior, and product-use patterns. Enterprises should not focus on cultural differences only to adjust business communication programs to make them acceptable to consumers. It requires that firms discover if markets are viable by including the study of the culture in which the company will do business in its business and marketing planning. To do this, the firms should identify cultural factors that can be employed to support business communication in proposed markets.

The chapter articulates changing business environment and the need for cross-cultural communication in the digital environment. The chapter assesses the influence of globalization on cross-cultural communication, the adoption of various communicative strategies in cross-cultural business communication, framing cross-cultural communication, and cross-cultural negotiation. Further, the chapter examines the cultural impacts and issues faced by global managers in cross-cultural business communication and overcoming barriers to cultural adaptations.

Theoretical Background

Recent political changes in countries around the world, economic cooperation and interdependencies, and information and communication technologies increased the degree of globalization as well as changed both labor markets and work environments (Thompson et al., 2013). Many organizations have transformed from domestic into multicultural as they operate in the international, multinational, global or transnational environment (Anand, 2014). These changes increase the role of communication in the overall success of the business and emphasize the need for employees with cross-cultural communication skills (Safina & Valeev, 2015). Hofstede et al. (2010) provide an in-depth analysis of national cultures' dimensions, which represent independent preferences for one state of affairs over another that distinguish countries from each other. The Hofstede model of national culture consists of six dimensions, including power distance, individualism/collectivism, masculinity/femininity, uncertainty avoidance, long-term/short-term orientation, and indulgence/restraint (Minkov, 2018). Colbert et al. (2016) emphasize that digitalization reduces authenticity in terms of less face-to-face communication and interactions characterized by less fully present participants. Lifintsev and Wellbrock (2019) identified that new generations (Millennials and Generation Z) are highly interested in cross-cultural communication and believe that digitalization significantly simplifies cross-cultural communication processes, including facilitating language barrier problems.

According to Barker et al. (2017), sensitivity to diversity now demands a strategic understanding of the importance of cross-cultural communication competence in every action in organizations, communities, and nations throughout the world. Glover and Friedman (2015) stated that functioning successfully within different cultures can be a struggle for many professionals. As the world changes, it becomes clear that dealing with other cultures, both domestic and international, requires competence in both identifying and transcending cultural boundaries. Language barriers, differences in values and standards of behaviour, lack of experience, lack of trust, and inadequate knowledge about other cultures or stereotypical thinking are among the most widespread obstacles to cross-cultural communication (Lifintsev & Canavilhas, 2017). Willyarto et al. (2021) stated that cross-cultural communication supported MSMEs in using social media to improve more if they were willing to open their mind and learn from others. Informants were using all means of communication, such as social media, messaging apps and old fashion verbal or written communication. Accordingly, the characteristics of successful businessmen/women with high enthusiasm could be seen in their ability to innovate and tolerate diversity.

Global business communication is a process that crosses national boundaries for business purposes. Communication among individuals from the same culture is often difficult. Therefore, communication between individuals from different cultures from the point of view of language, values, beliefs, customers and ways of thinking will be far more difficult, with a degree of miscommunication being almost inevitable (Ferraro, 2021). Cross-cultural communication is the interaction between culturally diverse people with different value orientations and varied communication codes within a community of work and socialization (Abugre, 2018). Successful cross-cultural interaction between multinational staff has now been accepted as the most critical management issue in international business both at the individual and group levels of analysis (Barner-Rasmussen et al., 2014), as it can impact positively on expatriates' work outcomes in Multinational Corporations

(MNCs). Cross-cultural business communication demands that organizations be aware of and sensitive to cultural differences. To respect the right to culture by consumers in various cultures and marketplaces, marketers should understand that their customers have a right to their cultures. If marketers want success in cross-cultural marketing, they must work in a way that respects the consumer's values and the right to their culture. Business communication is not independent but related to all other business or market behaviors (Guang & Trotter, 2012).

Tung (2008) proposes a need to balance cross-national and cross-cultural investigations to understand the globalization of cultural phenomena truly. The differences in cultures and multicultural team members working together in MNCs vary in their communicative behaviors, which can pose a challenge to effectively understanding each other. Thus, prescriptions for effective communication in cross-cultural encounters often suggest adapting one's behaviour to that of the other culture by learning to understand the value systems and communicative behaviours of the local or indigenous people (Abugre & Debrah, 2019). It is why communicating parties normally attribute cultural meanings to their experiences and actions shaped by the social and political relationships in which they are embedded (Lauring & Klitmøller, 2015). Harzing and Feely (2008) argue that failure to communicate effectively leads to uncertainty, anxiety, and mistrust, which produces misattribution, conflict and cognitive distortion of expatriates in subsidiary locations. Thus, an important role of expatriates or global managers is to effectively communicate across cultures to produce a well-managed team comprising expatriates and local or indigenous staff. Fraccastoro et al. (2021) stated that social media is usually preferred for generating new business opportunities, and digital sales communication tools are particularly useful for developing their scope of business by enabling the reaching and closing of deals with more geographically distant international customers and traditional sales communication tools are most employed to manage strategic customer relationships and the relationships with those clients in need of technological assistance.

Influence of Globalization on Cross-Cultural Communication

In today's world of globalization and the internationalization of businesses, the marketing relationship is becoming increasingly important as a means to meet the marketing needs of sales firms. However, when it comes to establishing specific business relationships in a particular culture, business people can resort to their cultural values and communication strategies, which may go beyond the area of marketing to include broader social dimensions (Zhu et al., 2006).

Because of globalization and the rapid development of economics, multinational firms are more and more prevalent. Companies that extend their business abroad have to face the challenge of cross-cultural communication. Communication is the only approach by which group members can cooperate toward the goal of the organization. Especially for multi-culture firms with some subsidiaries in other countries, managers must have frequent communication and a sufficient understanding of the organizational goal. Technical developments have removed most of the physical barriers to communication. However, managers still encounter some cultural barriers. To achieve success, managers working in global environments must be proficient in cross-cultural communication (Erez, 1992). By contrast, the differences in management style, staff behaviors and communication systems between different cultures and the barriers to cross-cultural communication in multi-nation firms can be found (He & Liu, 2010).

Globalization of markets or the flow of products, resources, and culture requires professionals to find ways to communicate effectively and efficiently. As companies become global and outsource manufacturing, assembly, and delivery of products to international partners, they rely on communication technologies that allow cross-cultural teams to work together across time zones and geographical distances (Holtbrügge et al., 2013). Although communication devices such as phones and fax have existed for decades, the Internet, especially the introduction of Web 2.0 in 2004, made a breakthrough with interactive tools. Web 2.0 describes a set of technologies allowing people to create content on the Internet rather than on their desktops (O'Reilly, 2005). The most significant changes in the workplace are caused by technological tools, such as blogging and, wikis, video and audio conferencing, which employees use to virtually work together either synchronously (at the same time) or asynchronously (with the delay in response time) as their schedules allow (Deal et al., 2010). This transformation of communication was noted as one of the most significant changes in the work environment.

The organization's profitability is largely determined by its business communication strategies and skills. However, top managers in organizations working globally sometimes neglect the significance of the invisible barriers that create cultural differences in business communication. Cultural factors play an important role in functioning as invisible barriers. Even as the world is becoming globalized, many economies have increasingly voiced their claim to a right to culture in international businesses. It is predicted that national culture will be a critical factor affecting economic development, demographic behaviour, and general business policies worldwide. Such claims at the macro level will be important for making trade policy, protecting intellectual property rights, and creating resources for national benefits. At the micro-level, these claims could be invisible barriers for firms working in or wanting to enter international markets (Lillis & Tian, 2010).

If globalization is an inevitable process, then cross-culture will also be inevitable. On the one hand, the world is becoming more homogeneous, and distinctions between national markets are fading and, for some products, disappearing altogether. This means that business communication is now a world-encompassing discipline (Guang & Trotter, 2012). Consequently, the cultural differences between nations, regions and ethnic groups, far from being extinguished, are becoming stronger (Lillis & Tian, 2010). This means that global business communication, a cross-cultural process, requires managers to be well-informed about cultural differences nationally, locally, and ethnically to win in global markets. Therefore, cross-cultural solutions to international business are increasingly being suggested as a valid and necessary method for enhancing communication and interaction in and between business partners, organizations and customers, and coworkers.

Types of Communicative Strategies

In cross-cultural business environments, communication plays an imperative role. Every reasonable business person in the international professional community understands and values communication. However, a proper understanding of its significance cannot stand for successful business and closed business deals. This is where communication strategies come in handy and take the lead. Communication strategies forge and help maintain connections, and communication strategies, when properly applied, help build up international teams and develop cross-border business effectively. Communication strategies stand at attention to translate the message smoothly to reach the desired communicative goal. Thus, the frequently used communicative strategies in the global business environment include (Chaika, 2020).

1. **Nomination:** Nomination refers to a communicative strategy employing which the speaker/sender of the information wants to open a topic with some people an individual is talking to or demonstrating an object. This strategy allows for collaboration and productivity at the same time. When an individual employs nomination, the speaker/ encoder presents a particular topic clearly, distinctly and truthfully. The key aspect of nomination is to say only what is relevant. It is also important to mention that the encoder may use nomination not only for introducing an idea or object but also during their interaction. In such a situation, nomination deliverables are associated with ways of continuing communication. Thus, with the nomination as a communicative strategy, an individual can consider certain criteria attributable to the interaction. These criteria include the introduction

of an idea, object, etc., as well as the continuance of communication, presentation of the information clearly and understandably to the recipient/decoder, and relevance of the topic presented.

2. **Restriction:** Restriction refers to a communicative strategy employed with limitations of any kind, which may arise with the speaker/sender of the relevant information. In certain contexts, the speaker/sender of the information faces several constraints. Such constraints may include constrained response/reaction within a set of categories and restricted response (fully or partially) of the other communicant/decoder involved in the communication act. The decoder, i.e. the listener/observer, has to respond only within that set of categories, which is made by the encoder/speaker.

3. **Turn-Taking:** Turn-taking as a communicative strategy pertains to the process by which speakers, both the encoder and the decoder, decide who takes the conversational floor. It is worth mentioning that across cultures, people may keep to some accepted behaviors that may envelop into social attributes and thought patterns. However, the underlying part is to establish and move along a productive conversation, and the key to success is the idea of giving all communicators a chance to speak and share their understanding, agree or disagree on the mentioned information. Yet, it is not the only criterion to establish the strategy. The two others inter alia are *timing and ways of communication* and *stepping in at the appropriate moment.* The former relates to recognizing the proper moment to speak in a certain environment as well as how to speak or start speaking when their turn comes. The latter requires that everyone among the speakers – encoders and decoders, respects all the communicants and attributes the encoding role, a role of the speaker, only when it is their turn in the course of interaction.

4. **Topic Control:** Topic control is another communicative strategy employed to cover the ways of procedural formality and informality influencing the development of the topic once the speaker/encoder of the message introduces it and takes it further into a conversation. As the matter concerns, it is important to develop the topic collectively once it is initiated. This helps the communicants avoid interruptions, untimely questions, and topic shifts. Topic control rests on the question and answers formula that helps to move the discussion forward and keeps the interaction live and ongoing using asking questions and listening to replies. Altogether, the strategy enables the communicants to take turns, share their ideas or argue points, and develop the discussion.

5. **Topic Shifting:** Topic shifting is another communicative strategy that involves a change in the topic, i.e. gradual or unexpected movement from one topic to another. The strategy anticipates two stages. Stage one foresees the end of one topic in a conversation or part of the conversation. Stage two envelopes the introduction of the new topic to be followed by its continuation among the communicants or introduction of another adjacent topic. Topic shifting as a strategy in communication works best with a follow-through. It means that it is critical for strategy employment that the newly introduced topic develops into further discussion. There are a lot of introductory phrases and parentheses, which open the message, among the other signs, in the beginning, middle or end of the message.

6. **Repair:** Repair is a communicative strategy that refers to how the speaker/the encoder of the message addresses some difficulties or lack of experience in speaking, listening, and understanding the message, which the speaker/encoder/decoder may encounter in a conversation. Repair aims to overcome interaction breakdown to send more understandable messages that the recipient/the decoder may find easier to decode and translate.

7. **Termination:** Termination as a communicative strategy anticipates closing/winding up a conversation. Thus, termination can be described via the following means attributable to this communicative strategy.

   ▪ Close-initiating phrases, expressions, set clusters that end the topic in a conversation,

   ▪ Use of verbal and non-verbal signs to mean the end of the interaction,

   ▪ The speaker/encoder of the message and the listener/decoder of the message to each other sends verbal and non-verbal messages that end communication.

Termination may be quick and short, or it may last longer to make room for clarifications, further questions and answers. Sometimes the topic may continue into further discussion; however, the language, including body language, speaks of approaching the end, and this is an interaction point just about to end the communication.

Framing in Cross-Cultural Communication

The field of business communication is a specific division of social intercourse, where the constant pressure of framing is further enhanced by such stakes as professional prestige and position in the organization hierarchy. Here, the role acting is even stricter than in regular social interaction since the rules are proportionately more rigid, and the people involved are more aware and hunting for weak spots to exploit to their organization's benefit. Transferred to the level of international communication, this issue gains new dimensions not only in terms of extension but also due to the wide range of systems of values involved. In the age of globalization, where geographic borders have gradually lost their traditional separating rigidity, gaining an integrative rather than a separating meaning, cross-cultural communication abilities have become crucial for the survival and development of any company.

Therefore, communicating across cultures involves a good command of a complex network of cultural frames that yields a heterogeneous business environment, where people bring along their individual culturally and ethnically determining values, beliefs, and perceptions. Under these circumstances, awareness of different framing systems endows the business person with the flexibility of thinking and behaviour, as well as with the ability to adjust and react efficiently when in contact with other cultural backgrounds. According to Goman (1994), cultural differences go as deep as the medium of communication, whose variations delineate three basic oppositions: high-context/low-context, sequential/synchronic, and affective/neutral cultures.

1. **High-context and Low-context Cultures:** In high-context cultures, communication relies more on the context, extracting meaning from such non-verbal cues as body language, silence, and pauses rather than from the spoken or written message. In such cultures, personal relations and informal agreements are more bindings than any formal contract. Low-context cultures value explicit and specific messages, the precision of the spoken or written words underlying interpersonal relations being considered of utmost importance. The major business challenge for people in a low-context culture is to realize the importance of building and maintaining personal relationships when dealing with high-context cultures.

2. **Sequential and Synchronic Cultures:** These culture types display different ways of perceiving time and the associated concepts of timing, dealing with deadlines and scheduling. Sequential cultures appropriate temporality as a sequence, according to which time becomes a linear commodity to spend, save or waste. Synchronic cultures perceive temporality as a constant, circular flow that can be experienced only fragmentarily. This divergent perception has a determining impact on building business relations, as it establishes the meaning of being on time and implicitly the approach to such concepts as deadlines, strategic thinking, investments, and long-term

planning. These elements can cause misunderstandings between people from a sequential culture, who view being late as a sign of bad planning or disrespect, and people from a synchronic culture, who consider the insistence on timeliness as a sign of immature impatience. In sequential cultures, business people give full attention to one agenda item after another, whereas professionals in other parts of the world regularly do several things at the same time.

3. **Effective and Neutral Cultures:** This distinction is established according to the proportion of reason and emotion involved in business interactions and delineates two categories of cultural framing. The effective type, in which people show their feelings plainly, and the neutral type, is characterized by carefully controlled and subdued emotions. Cultural framing is a matter of actively using our cultural background, determining our way of thinking and acting and, more importantly, providing the criteria by which an individual perceives and appreciates others. That is why experts in intercultural communication recommend that productive business relations should be built on the awareness that cultures are not right or wrong, better or worse; they are just different. Therefore, in the contemporary global business community, what is proper in one culture may be ineffective or even offensive in another, and therefore, the key to cross-cultural success is the understanding of and respect for diversity.

Cross-Cultural Negotiation

Cross-cultural negotiation is a specialized area within the field of cross-cultural communication that provides a theoretical framework for the training of negotiators and sales personnel so that they should have a solid knowledge of the culture, values, beliefs, etiquette and approaches to business, meetings and negotiations in the target countries to maximize the potential of a positive outcome (Storti, 2011a). Training in cross-cultural negotiation involves a series of factors that can influence the proceedings of a business interaction (Dumbravă, 2010). These include:

1. **Eye Contact:** In certain organizations, strong direct eye contact conveys confidence, sincerity, and trustworthiness, whereas prolonged eye contact is considered rude and is generally avoided in other organizations.

2. **Personal Space and Touch:** In business, people usually leave a certain amount of distance between themselves when interacting, as touching is permitted only between friends and family members. However, in some business organizations, people are tactile; therefore, personal space shrinks significantly. These non-verbal cues require special attention

since they have a much greater impact and higher reliability than the spoken word due to an individual's capacity to interpret symbols and cues recognizable on the level of collective memory (Dumbravă & Koronka, 2009).

3. **Time:** In some businesses, people are clock-conscious, and punctuality is crucial as being late is taken as an insult, whereas in certain organizations, being on time for a meeting does not carry the same sense of urgency.

4. **Meeting and Greeting:** Although most international business people meet with a handshake, this is not appropriate for genders in some countries. At the same time, some cultures view a weak handshake as a sign of weakness, whereas others perceive a firm handshake as aggressive. Other useful details are related to addressing people by first name, surname or title and the suitability of small talk.

5. **Gift Giving:** Some organizations have the protocol of gift-giving as an integral part of the business protocol; in some organizations, it has negative connotations. The major details to be considered are where gifts should be exchanged, colors that should be avoided, and whether they should be lavish, wrapped or reciprocated (Storti, 2011b).

Cross-cultural negotiation training starts from the premise that cultural blunders can have disastrous consequences in business and relies on understanding etiquette and approaches to business abroad before focusing on cross-cultural negotiation styles and techniques. Therefore, specialists in this field have detected three interconnected aspects that need to be considered before entering into cross-cultural negotiation:

- **Basis of Relationship:** The basis of the relationship has to do with the affective-neutral divergence in terms of cultural framing. For instance, where personal relationships are seen as unhealthy and dangerous to objectivity, business is mostly contractual. On the contrary, for some organizations, business is personal, and partnerships will be made only between people who know, trust and feel comfortable with one another. Therefore, in this type of culture, it is necessary to invest in relationship-building before conducting business.

- **Information:** Some business cultures emphasize presented and rationally argued business proposals using statistics and facts, while others are more visual and oral, preferring information presented through speech or using maps, graphs and charts.

- **Negotiation:** Negotiation styles also differ significantly across cultures. The organizations approach in different manners. Organizations can make decisions using various approaches like talking simultaneously rather than sequentially, negotiating and making decisions as a team, by the senior figure, making detailed analyses, and deals are closed under the pressure of deadlines.

These are the main factors that must be considered when approaching cross-cultural negotiation to prepare effective presentations and adjust our behaviour following a particular global business environment.

Cultural Challenges Faced by Global Managers

Global managers are often met with many challenges in managing the global workforce. This is because employees across borders have their own cultures that may affect the business operation and performance. According to Jain & Pareek (2019), the cultural challenges faced by global managers are:

1. **Narrow-mindedness:** Individuals might think that organizations from the country where they originate operate with the same scope of responsibilities and processes as the global businesses that they are newly engaging with. However, the reality is that global business activities have wider scope and responsibilities than domestic organizations, and the social system differs from the former organization. So, the employees tend to be narrow-minded, and they fail to realize the differences between their own culture and other cultures and remain to behave with their own culture over the new culture brought by internationalization. They also perceive the triviality of their culture and the new culture resulting in non-recognition.

2. **Uniqueness:** Several employees become distinctive rather than collective. So, the idea of teamwork seems difficult to attain because the employees do not aspire to be team builders, but the attitude is more inclined to self-interest and self-gratification. Hence, they are steered by the motto of 'self-first before others'.

3. **Ethnocentrism:** Another barrier to cultural acceptance is the idea of ethnocentrism. This holds that employees from their homeland tend to smear their own culture in the global environment and workplace. They always believed that their country's culture, conditions, and working environment were far better than the new environment, which hindered them from adopting the new culture. Moreover, their judgment and perception are based on self-criterion that eventually negatively affects their productivity and performance. So, there is a need to understand other cultures and temporarily forget the native homeland's culture.

4. **Cultural Detachment:** Cultural detachment plays an imperative part in assessing the quantity of cultural adaptation that employees can

achieve in moving from one's homeland to another country. Cultural distance impacts the feedback and responses of employees in the business. The difficulty of employees distinguishing the homeland's culture from the new culture signifies the higher degree of cultural distance that might result in being ethnocentric. So, managing this problem is important to remove cultural barriers.

5. **Culture Shock:** Culture shock can be described as a condition that employee experience by having difficulty to adapt the new culture because of insecurities and disorientations facing different cultures. Employees might not know how to react or respond to the conditions. They lose self-confidence and may be emotionally upset. Although it is a universal condition, many people are struggling much that it may result in others isolating themselves or even planning to go back home because they have not overcome their fears and insecurities. Some reasons for cultural shock are different management philosophies, language, food, dresses, driving patterns, attitude towards work and productivity, and separation from friends and colleagues.

Overcoming Challenges to Cultural Adaptations

There are several steps that the organization can undertake to prevent cultural shock and reduce the impact of the other challenges listed above. Some of them include the following:

1. **Vigilant Selection:** Employees can be selected based on the attitude of low ethnocentrism and other possibly troublesome features. The desire to experience other cultures and live in another nation and learning the attitude of employee's spouses towards the assignment may also be an important prerequisite attitude worth assessing.

2. **Like-minded Preps:** The adjustment to a new country becomes easy for the employees, especially on their first international assignment if they are sent to countries similar to their homeland.

3. **Pre-departure Training:** Many organizations try to accelerate fine-tuning to a host nation by encouraging employees to learn the local language. They offer training before giving the assignments. It often includes orientation to the geography, customs, culture and political environment in which the employees live.

4. **Orientation and Support:** In the new country, adjustment is further encouraged after arrival if there is a special effort made to help the employee and family get settled. This may include assistance with housing, transportation and shopping. It is especially helpful if a mentor can be assigned to ease the transition.

5. **Incentives and Assurances:** Another problem that can arise when employees transfer to another culture is that their need satisfaction is not as great as those of comparable employees who remain at home. Although moving to another nation may be an exciting opportunity that provides new challenges, responsibilities, and recognition, an international job assignment may bring about financial difficulties, inconveniences, insecurities, and separation from relatives and friends. To motivate such employees to accept such assignments in other nations, organizations should frequently give them extra pay and fringe benefits to compensate for the problems they may experience. They should also be assured of a better position in the organization upon their return to their home country, which could help them to relieve their job insecurities.

6. **Preparation for Reentry:** Employees returning to their home country after a foreign assignment tends to suffer some cultural shock in their own country. This is sometimes called cross-cultural reentry and may cause reverse cultural shock. After adjusting to the culture of another nation and enjoying its uniqueness, it is difficult for employees to readjust to the surroundings of their home country. This situation is made more difficult by the multitude of changes that have occurred since they departed.

Managerial Implications

Although every culture is unique, certain basic guidelines are appropriate for consistent cross-cultural success. Successful managers acquire a base of knowledge about the values, attitudes, and lifestyles of the cultures with which they interact. Managers need to be aware of the political and economic background of target countries, their history, current national affairs, and perceptions about other cultures. Such knowledge facilitates understanding of the partner's mindset, organization, and objectives. Decisions and events become substantially easier to interpret. Higher levels of language proficiency pave the way for acquiring competitive advantages. In the long run, managers knowing multiple languages are more likely to negotiate successfully and have positive business interactions than managers who speak only one language.

Conceivably the principal cause of culture-related problems is the ethnocentric assumptions managers may unconsciously hold. Problems arise when managers assume that foreigners think and behave just like the people back home. They misrepresent communications with foreigners. They may perceive the other's behavior as odd and possibly inappropriate. Such situations may affect the manager's ability to interact effectively with the foreigner, even leading to communication interruption. In this way, cultural bias can be a significant barrier to successful interpersonal communication. Most people view their own culture as the norm, and everything else may seem eccentric. Understanding the self-reference criterion is a critical first step to avoiding cultural bias and ethnocentric reactions. Working effectively with counterparts from other cultures requires an investment in professional development. Each culture has its ways of carrying out business transactions, negotiations, and dispute resolution.

Conclusion

The organizations notice that current business trends of globalization, diverse workforce, team-based organizations, advances in technology, and flatter organizational structure impact communication trends in the workplace. Moreover, technology is brought down to the level of the individual, and the physical location of an employee often does not matter as employees become a part of the global network. Between globalization and technology, 'modern business communication' has become a diverse, dynamic field that has increased its relevance and significance more than ever before.

Organizations' ability to attract, retain, and motivate people from diverse cultural backgrounds may lead to competitive advantages in cost structures and through maintaining the highest quality human resources. Further capitalizing on the potential benefits of cultural diversity in workgroups, organizations may gain a competitive advantage in creativity, problem-solving, and flexible adaptation to change. A multicultural workforce is becoming the custom. To achieve organizational goals and avoid potential risks, managers should be culturally sensitive and promote creativity and motivation through flexible leadership.

References

Abugre, J. B., & Debrah, Y. A. (2019). Assessing the impact of cross-cultural communication competence on expatriate business operations in multinational corporations of a Sub-Saharan African context. *International Journal of Cross Cultural Management, 19*(1), 85-104.

Abugre, J. B. (2018). Cross-cultural communication imperatives: critical lessons for western expatriates in multinational companies (MNCs) in Sub-Saharan Africa. *Critical Perspectives on International Business, 14*(2/3), 170–187.

Anand, P. K. K. (2014). Cross cultural diversity in today's globalized era. *Journal of Human Resource Management, 2*(6-1), 12-16.

Barker, K., Day, C. R., Day, D. L., Kujava, E. R., Otwori, J., Ruscitto, R. A., Smith, A., & Xu, T. (2017). Global Communication and Cross-Cultural Competence: Twenty-First Century Micro-Case Studies. *Global Advances in Business Communication, 6*(1), 5.

Barner-Rasmussen, W., Ehrnrooth, M., Koveshnikov, A., & Mäkelä, K. (2014). Cultural and language skills as resources for boundary spanning within the MNC. *Journal of International Business Studies, 45*(7), 886-905.

Bauman, A. A., & Shcherbina, N. V. (2018). Millennials, technology, and cross-cultural communication. *Journal of Higher Education Theory and Practice, 18*(3), 75-85.

Colbert, A., Yee, N., & George, G. (20160. The digital workforce and the workplace of the future. *Academy of management journal, 59*(3), 731-739.

Deal, J. J., Altman, D. G., & Rogelberg, S. G. (2010). Millennials at work: What we know and what we need to do (if anything). *Journal of Business and Psychology, 25*(2), 191-199.

Dumbravă, G., & Koronka, A. (2009). "Actions Speak Louder than Words" – Body Language in Business Communication. *Annals of the University of Petroşani. Economics, 9*(3), 249-254.

Dumbravă, G. (2010). The concept of framing in cross-cultural business communication. *Annals of the University of Petroşani-Economics, 10*(Part I), 83-90.

Erez, M. (1992). Interpersonal communication systems in organizations, and their relationships to cultural values, productivity and innovation: The case of Japanese corporations. *Applied Psychology: An International Review, 41*(1), 43-64.

Ferraro, G. P. (2021). *The cultural dimension of international business.* Prentice-Hall.

Fraccastoro, S., Gabrielsson, M., & Pullins, E. B. (2021). The integrated use of social media, digital, and traditional communication tools in the B2B sales process of international SMEs. *International Business Review, 30*(4), 1-15.

Glover, J., & Friedman, H. L. (2015). *Transcultural competence: Navigating cultural differences in the global community.* American Psychological Association.

Goman, C. K. (1994). *Managing in a global organization: Keys to success in a changing world.* Thomson Crisp Learning.

Guang, T., & Trotter, D. (2012). Key issues in cross-cultural business communication: Anthropological approaches to international business. *African Journal of Business Management, 6*(22), 6456-6464.

Harzing, A. W., & Feely, A. J. (2008). The language barrier and its implications for HQ-subsidiary relationships. *Cross Cultural Management: An International Journal, 15*(1), 49-61.

He, R., & Liu, J. (2010). Barriers of cross cultural communication in multinational firms: A case study of Swedish company and its subsidiary in China. *Halmstad School of Business and Engineering,* 1-32.

Hofstede, G., Hofstede G. J., & Minkov, M. (2010). *Cultures and organizations: Software of the mind. Revised and Expanded* (3rd Edition). New York: McGraw-Hill.

Holtbrügge, D., Weldon, A., & Rogers, H. (2013). Cultural determinants of email communication styles. *International Journal of Cross Cultural Management, 13*(1), 89-110.

Jain, T., & Pareek, C. (2019). Managing Cross-Cultural Diversity: issues and Challenges. *Global Management Review*, *13*(2), 23-32.

Kesari, B., Soni, R., & Khanuja, R. S. (2014). A review on the need of cross cultural management in multinational corporations. *International Journal of Advanced Research in Management and Social Sciences*, *3*(8), 120-127.

Lauring, J., & Klitmøller, A. (2015). Corporate language-based communication avoidance in MNCs: A multi-sited ethnography approach. *Journal of World Business*, *50*(1), 46-55.

Lewis, R. (2014). How different cultures understand time. *Business Insider*, *1*.

Lifintsev, D., & Wellbrock, W. (2019). Cross-cultural communication in the digital age. *Estudos em Comunicação*, *1*(28), 93-104.

Lifintsev, D. S., & Canhavilhas, J. (2017). Cross-cultural management: obstacles to effective cooperation in a multicultural environment. *Scientific Bulletin of Polissya*, *2* (2 (10)), 195-202.

Lillis, M., & Tian, R. (2010). Cultural issues in the business world: An anthropological perspective. *Journal of Social Sciences*, *6*(1), 99-112.

Minkov, M. (2018). A revision of Hofstede's model of national culture: old evidence and new data from 56 countries. *Cross Cultural and Strategic Management*, *25*(2), 231-256.

Nam, H., & Kannan, P. K. (2020). Digital environment in global markets: cross-cultural implications for evolving customer journeys. *Journal of International Marketing*, *28*(1), 28-47.

O'Reilly, T. (2005). What is Web 2.0: Design patterns and business models for the next generation of software. Retrieved from http://www.oreillynet. com/pub/a/oreilly/tim/news/2005/09/3 0/what-is-web-20. html

Okoro, E. (2013). International Organizations and Operations: An Analysis of Cross-Cultural Communication Effectiveness and Management Orientation. *Journal of Business & Management*, *1*(1), 1-13.

Onyusheva, I., Thammashote, L., & Thongaim, J. (2020). Urban Business Environment: Managing Cross-Cultural Problems. *The EUrASEANs: Journal on Global Socio-Economic Dynamics*, *1*(20), 30-43.

Safina, M. S., & Valeev, A. A. (2015). Study of humanitarian high school students' readiness for intercultural communication formation. *Review of European Studies*, *7*(5), 52-60.

Storti, C. (2011a). *Figuring foreigners out: A practical guide*. Hachette UK.

Storti, C. (2011b). *The Art of Crossing Cultures*. Hachette UK.

Thompson, A., Peteraf, M., Gamble, J., Strickland III, A. J., & Jain, A. K. (2013). *Crafting & executing strategy 19/e: The quest for competitive advantage: Concepts and cases*. McGraw-Hill Education.

Tung, R. L. (2008). The cross-cultural research imperative: The need to balance cross-national and intra-national diversity. *Journal of International Business Studies*, *39*(1), 41-46.

Willyarto, M. N., Wahyuningtyas, B. P., Yunus, U., & Heriyati, P. (2021, August). Cross-Cultural Communication in Micro/Small/Medium Enterprises Business by Using Social Media. In *2021 International Conference on Information Management and Technology (ICIMTech)* (Vol. 1, pp. 88-92). IEEE.

Zhu, Y., Nel, P., & Bhat, R. (2006). A cross cultural study of communication strategies for building business relationships. *International Journal of Cross Cultural Management, 6*(3), 319-341.

Chapter 13

'We Can't Go Back to Normal': Global Value Chain Approach to Diversity Management in Multinational Enterprises

Rifat Kamasak
Yeditepe University, Istanbul, Turkey

Mustafa F. Ozbilgin
Brunel University, London, UK

Kurt April
University of Cape Town, South Africa

Meltem Yavuz Sercekman
Brunel University, London, UK

Joana Vassilopoulou
Brunel University, London, UK

Abstract: The current coronavirus crisis demonstrated the need for transnational coordination to combat the pandemic. The crisis may be viewed as an opportunity to reconfigure our global economy for a better future that fosters equality and opportunity beyond national regulation and throughout the global value chains (GVCs). Taking the preservation of the common good as our philosophical approach, the paper moves the diversity management theory with the introduction of the GVC perspective as both a method of analysis and a theoretical lens from which to regulate the management of diversity in global organizations. The paper explicates the utility of moving from diversity management driven by shareholder and stakeholder value at the national and international levels towards a global value chain approach that accounts for how organizations use their resources and capabilities transnationally across the value chain.

Keywords: Diversity Management, Global Diversity Management, Global Value Chain, International Management, Qualitative Analysis, The Common Good

***

Introduction

'We can't go back to normal' is a sentence often heard since the start of the corona crisis. Times of crisis usually induce societal change, and some believe that the current pandemic can be seen as an opportunity to build a better future and a better society, locally as well as globally (Palalar et al., 2022). There are several countervailing arguments about globalization and diversity. On the one hand, global corporations that are the most lucrative products of globalization are hailed to play significant roles in the development efforts of nations; on the other hand, they serve as "important mediators of the impact of business on poverty and inequality" (Wadhwani, 2018, p. 548). If the advice from international trade and finance organizations and supporters of globalization are followed, global organizations could help national development efforts and combat different forms of inequality among diverse populations (Wadhwani, 2018; April & Dharani, 2021; Palalar et al., 2022), particularly in the aftermath of the current global corona crisis, since early evidence suggests that women, migrants, BME communities, disabled, etc. are disproportionately affected by the corona crisis. For instance, in the USA, female unemployment has reached double digits for the first time since 1948. "The economic crisis brought on by the coronavirus is hitting women, particularly women of color, the hardest. Women accounted for 55% of the 20.5 million jobs lost in America" (Ewing-Nelson, 2020, p. 3). Kaplinsky (2013) demonstrates a direct link between globalization and global poverty as globalization suppresses wages, entrenches inequality and increases poverty.

The weakness of the current globalised economic model has become particularly visible during the current pandemic. One such example is how the coronavirus is influencing garment workers' rights in supply chains around the world, particularly in Bangladesh, where thousands of workers have not received any wages since the crisis began due to global organizations cancelling or simply not paying for orders (Clean Clothes Campaign, 2020). Such practice does not surprise considering the detrimental role global organizations have played in creating wage inequalities (Cobb, 2016; Kamasak et al., 2022). Hamann and Bertels (2018) present how international corporations lead to severe diversity and social degradation problems by adopting a "migrant labor system and single-sex compounds" in the mining industry in South Africa, which mirrors similar issues in the global oil and gas industry around the world. Other well-known cases of labor abuses include the West African cocoa industry, the Uzbek cotton industry and agriculture in Spain (Crane, 2013). Crane (2013) suggests that global organizations use slavery-like practices and consider labor exploitation part of their routine business. Due to the duality of positive and negative discourses on the consequences of globalization, there has been little progress on effective regulation of global organizations regarding their detrimental impact on diversity.

Such regulation is now of utmost importance for mitigating the consequences of the pandemic. More recent international corporate scandals, which involve mismanagement of diversity, have also demonstrated how difficult it is to regulate global organizations and encourage them to manage diversity effectively. Sexual harassment cases in Uber, anti-diversity responses in Google and Nike's failure to change its male and white-dominated corporate culture are only three corporate scandals among many that show the problematic nature of diversity issues in global organizations. To date, global organizations have not been subjected to any strenuous efforts and measures to keep their exploitative practices under control.

This chapter discusses the problematic lack of effective regulation of diversity in global organizations. It proposes the global value chain (GVC) approach, which is defined as the measurement and management of diversity interventions from the inception of a product or service idea to its consumption in terms of impact on society, economy and environment to ensure effective and equitable management of diversity, as an innovative way to measure and manage variety in global organizations. The chapter proposes the GVC approach as both a method of analysis and a suggested way to regulate global organizations. Society, indeed, can't go back to normal after the pandemic. The proposed GVC approach may offer an effective way to ensure effective and equitable global management of diversity in the future.

Managing Diversity In Global Organizations: Bringing In The Global Value Chain

The foundation for contemporary diversity management was laid during the US civil rights movement, which resulted in the introduction of different HR practices in the 1980s and 90s that aimed at increasing the inclusion of underrepresented groups, such as women and ethnic minorities, in organizations (Kamasak et al., 2020a; Shore et al., 2018; Nkomo & Hoobler, 2014). With the introduction of diversity management, the focus shifted from underrepresented groups to individual employees. Diversity management was thought of as a measure that could help deal with social and cultural differences of individuals in terms of equality of opportunity, valuing diversity and fostering inclusion for all (Baykut et al., 2021; Song, 2022) while at the same time benefiting organizations from the diversity of its employees (Hoang et al., 2022). Diversity management is at a significant crossroads between progress and setbacks: there has been considerable progress in legal protections offered to gender diversity, thanks to the push that the CEDAW (Convention on Elimination of Discrimination Against Women) by the UN (United Nations) has provided since 1995 (Ozbilgin, 2018) and expansion of national and international legal and social protections afforded to other dimensions of diversity such as ethnicity, disability, sexual orientation, age, migration and displacement to be protected (Ozbilgin & Tatli, 2008; Syed & Ozbilgin, 2009; Kamasak et al., 2020c).

As a support to the efforts of CEDAW, another framework, "Protect, Respect and Remedy" by the UNGP (United Nations Guiding Principles for Business and Human Rights), was endorsed in 2011 (UN, 2011). The soft law framework of the UNGP received broad support from the global business community because it required "little meaningful action by business" and did not include coercive measures "to protect human rights with the private law, transnational, and social norm-based responsibility of enterprises to respect human rights" (Backer, 2016, p. 419), thus it seemed ineffective to prevent corporate abuse. This has become particularly apparent in the aftermath of the global economic crisis in 2008 and during the current global pandemic. Soft and voluntary laws have not proven to answer the challenges to equality and diversity in organizations during and after the global crisis. Accordingly, moving to a more comprehensive treaty in global business activity becomes indispensable.

A recent attempt, the establishment of the IGWG (Intergovernmental Working Group) by the UN Human Rights Council in July 2014, accelerated the process of "internationalizing the legal regulation of corporate social, economic and cultural responsibilities" (Backer, 2016, p. 419) of transnational and global corporations. IGWG has aimed to offer a better functioning and legally binding instrument to regulate the actions of global corporations concerning human rights violations and promoting diversity. Yet, these developments have not been without their backlash and setbacks, which overshadow the feeling of international progress and achievement (Dobbin & Kalev, 2006; Ozbilgin, 2018).

First, despite the availability of international bodies, conventions and agreements on better regulation of human rights and diversity, these remain voluntary in nature and limited in scope and impact in the absence of coercive measures, which prove to be more effective in terms of management of diversity (Kamasak et al., 2020d; Jonsen et al., 2013; Klarsfeld, 2009). Therefore, the current arrangements to regulate global firms to curb malpractice and mistreatment of diversity remain ineffective. Second, diversity management is theorized in national settings in the main (Álvarez-Figueroa et al., 2022; Tatli et al., 2012), and most of the legal protections on diversity are nationally embedded due to variations in historical, cultural and legal nuances and idiosyncratic differences between national contexts (Hamann & Bertels, 2018; Clarke & Boersma, 2017; Vassilopoulou, 2017). The nationally embedded nature of diversity management efforts offers only patchy and meagre protection against global capitalist interests that continue to exploit vulnerabilities of labor in countries with limited legal and social regulation (Yamahaki & Frynas, 2016). Third, the current political climate is growing hostile to diversity with severe attacks (Ozbilgin et al., 2022; April 2021; Kamasak et al., 2020a; Kováts, 2018) on women's rights, the rise of nationalism and racism, increased incidents of violence against LGBTI+ individuals and the resurgence of protectionism in the world economic order. One must wait and see how this will develop further after the current global pandemic.

Because of these three distinct setbacks, management of diversity in global organizations lacks innovative solutions, and it is often left to global organizations' voluntary and soft measures. The explanation of how such soft and voluntary approaches to managing diversity in global firms fail is below.

Voluntary Approaches to Managing Diversity in Global Firms

In regulating and managing diversity, global organizations draw on two voluntary drivers. First, global organizations legitimate diversity management activities if those attitudes deliver shareholder value (Zheng et al., 2020; Luanglath et al., 2019). Second, some global organizations listen to their stakeholders and activate diversity management interventions that capture the needs and expectations of their stakeholders (Kimani et al., 2021; Rao & Tilt, 2016). While the shareholder approach already relegates the management of diversity secondary to the financial strategies of the organization (Lauring, 2013; Nishii & Ozbilgin, 2007), the broad-based stakeholder approach to diversity management is complicated in terms of stakeholder voice and noise, which are shaped by the often conflicting nature of stakeholder interests and the power imbalances between stakeholder groups (Abdelzaher et al., 2019; Ozbilgin et al., 2016). Both rationales and drivers for the management of diversity fail to deliver desired outcomes such as equality of opportunity, valuing of diversity and inclusion for all (Hoang et al., 2022; Jonsen et al., 2013). As a way forward, the GVC approach is proposed for diversity management, which allows for examining the structures and dynamics of different actors involved in managing diversity in global organizations (Crane et al., 2019; Gereffi & Fernandez-Stark, 2011).

Implementing multidimensional perspectives to explore diversity management is not new (Syed & Ozbilgin, 2009; Sippola & Smale, 2007). Healy and Oikelome (2011) adopt a multi-layered approach to illustrate the complex interplay of migration, gender, ethnicity, and work in the health services sector to regulate the global health industry. Although shareholder and stakeholder approaches are widely studied in understanding how global organizations account for and handle diversity (e.g. Semenova & Hassel, 2019; Cobb, 2016), the GVC approach remains underexplored in the field of diversity management (Ozbilgin et al., 2016; Lakhani et al., 2013). This manuscript presents GVC as a theoretical expansion to the effective regulation of global organizations in terms of their diversity management efforts.

The GVC approach to diversity management has the potential to open up possibilities for global organizations to be held accountable across all nodes of the value chain from design to delivery and consumption of products or services (Gibbon et al., 2008; Van Tulder et al., 2009; Matos & Silvestre, 2013). For diversity, this means that from the inception of an idea to the consumption of a product or service that a global organization delivers, there should be the accountability of diversity impact across all operations. Global value chain approaches promise to expose the imbalances and inadequacies in the international transfer of diversity practices and policies, challenging due to contextual differences (Fritz & Silva, 2018; Lakhani et al., 2013; Syed & Ozbilgin, 2009). The challenge of international transfer of diversity management approaches has, on the one hand, allowed global organizations to localize their diversity efforts, and on the other, scrutiny of such practices has been made near impossible. For example, Ferner et al. (2005) identify challenges of transfer of US diversity management policies to other countries. They note the resistance of UK workers to the direct adoption of US diversity policies and highlight how contextual differences between the US and the UK render the adoption of US policies meaningless in the UK in certain regards. In contrast, Crane and Matten (2016) show that some global organizations conduct political, corporate social responsibility activities. They transfer some activities with positive social impact even when those practices are more sophisticated than local practices. Thus, the cross-border transfer of diversity interventions may be possible but complicated by power relations. Therefore, applying the GVC approach does not eliminate the challenge that the transfer of diversity activities may face. Instead, it holds global organizations accountable for parity and balance in the impact of their diversity management efforts across national operations, between functional areas and product and service lines.

Diversity management theory has shown considerable attention to the management of diversity in global organizations. Yet the focus of global diversity management literature has been predominantly on organizations' local and national concerns. Whether nongovernmental, non-profit or profit-seeking, all organizations have focused on leading or instructing business operations towards congruity among their staff and managing their international teams (Kamasak et al., 2019; Jonsen et al., 2013; Syed & Ozbilgin, 2009). Soni (2000) suggests that internal and external pressures direct organizations implement diversity management. However, there has not been any attention to the consistency of diversity efforts across national borders or in an organization's value chain (Acquier et al., 2017; Ozbilgin et al., 2016). According to Jackson et al. (2013), global diversity management frameworks have "centered on individual actors embedded in distinct national institutional contexts, and the impacts of these national contexts on firm strategies" (p. 427). Global organizations achieve partial success in diversity management in specific national settings, often at the expense of diversity failures in other local operations.

It is yet to be discovered effective means by which the power of global capitalism could be curbed to ensure equality and diversity in global organizations. To date, this aim remains a utopian vision because there is a lack of global regulations to control and monitor the diversity management activities of global organizations in their value chains (Backer, 2016; Jackson et al., 2013). Many global organizations profess to internationalize in pursuit of cheap labor, weak regulatory contexts, tax advantages, access to specific skills, and unexploited markets. Most of these moves clash with the idea of managing diversity with the intention of equality, fairness and inclusion (Li & Cui, 2018). As outlined above, the regulatory power that international organizations such as the UN and ILO have is limited in motivating global organizations to adopt better diversity practices. In such a regulatory vacuum, we explore further how a GVC approach may operate in this paper.

To activate accountability for a GVC approach, there are several regulatory pressures that a global organization may experience. First, there is the power of social movements (Davis et al., 2005; Lorbiecki, 2001). Second, several international organizations regulate labor market conditions, such as the ILO and the United Nations (Baccaro & Mele, 2012; Crane et al., 2019). Third, there are seemingly helpful international and supranational agreements and conventions such as CEDAW and IGWG (Backer, 2016; Risse-Kappen et al., 1999). Fourth, global organizations demonstrate self-governance and self-regulation (May 2015), e.g., transfer certain ideas such as diversity and equality across their operations. Fifth, there is the soft power of customers.

As will be discussed later, broader considerations related to regulation and GVC are crucial to understanding and accounting for the impact of workforce diversity. Some of these approaches, such as stakeholder and shareholder value, have been traditionally more popular among participating organizations. In contrast, others, such as the regulatory context and GVC, emerged as novel approaches that address the potential future pressures that face diversity management practices (Aguilera & Jackson, 2003; Marginson et al., 2010). With the inclusion of diversity impact into the accounting field, discussions have not yet made an easy, smooth and substantial transition of diversity regulations into practical business practices. Nonetheless, national regulation efforts eliminate minor unjust procedures in labor markets, partly because of their locality (Louche et al., 2020). The institutions are still not practitioners of the GVC system, even though it has advanced (Ozbilgin et al., 2016). Also, practical asymmetries occur with many decisions locally different in accounting for diversity impact, which jeopardizes the relations with employees, families and firms with some infamies and injuries. To prevent adverse consequences, the working conditions, salary scale, unionized or other legal rights, and contractual liabilities for the laborers should be considered in accounting for diversity (Felix et al., 2021; Lakhani et al., 2013).

The regulatory framework is built upon such social pillars as integrity, dignity, decency, and solidarity that may be invisible or immaterial but indispensable for an economic system (Foster et al., 2021; Weil & Mallo, 2007). According to one attendant, diversity accounting is not supposed to be so influential in stimulating actions without a compelling legal system. Even though legal enforcement is likely to be a deterrent, it will be constrained within the national borders and, unfortunately, could be neglected for the sake of foreign investments, particularly by developing countries (Doh et al., 2015; Bair & Palpacuer, 2012) having nothing to fear but oriented to attract them.

Methodology

This study draws on a qualitative research methodology from an abductive perspective (Özbilgin & Erbil, 2019). The abductive perspective starts with identifying patterns in the data, and then researchers may move between the data and the literature to make sense of the identified patterns. In this study, the participants' experiences that point to multilevel influences on the diversity practices were discussed. Interviews with 12 senior executive officers of global companies were conducted in different national contexts. They were either global diversity directors/board members or senior board members who had to engage diversity in their portfolios to understand diversity management's complex phenomenon and practice. The participants present a difficult-to-reach demography as they are senior executives whose contact details are not publicly available. Using the academic and professional networks of one of the authors, access was sought, and data were garnered.

The privacy and anonymity of respondents were ensured by excluding any information that could disclose their identities. Demographic information about the participants is provided in *Table 13.1*.

Table 13.1: Demographic information about the participants

	Gender	Ethnicity	Country	Industry	Role
1.	Female	Indian	USA	Hospitality	Chief Diversity & Sustainability Officer
2.	Male	Mixed Race (Colored)	South Africa	Telecommunications	Group Chief Human Resources & Corporate Affairs Officer
3.	Male	White	USA	FMCG	Chief Diversity Officer
4.	Male	Mixed Race (British-Zimbabwean)	South Africa	Financial Services	Chief Human Resources Officer
5.	Female	Latino	USA	Gender Non-Profit	Chief Executive Officer
6.	Male	Mixed Race (Swedish-American)	USA	Management Consulting	Chief Executive Officer
7.	Female	Mixed Race (Colored)	South Africa	Chemicals	Group Human Capital Executive
8.	Male	Malay	Malaysia	Oil & Gas	Senior Manager, HR Strategy & Planning
9.	Female	White	USA	Management Consulting	Chief Executive Officer
10.	Female	Black	South Africa	FMCG	Group Human Resources Director
11.	Female	Indian	South Africa	Human Performance Consulting	Chief Executive Officer
12.	Male	White	USA	Higher Education	Professor of Entrepreneurship

A survey method was impractical due to the elite status of participants and the availability of limited numbers of executives with this particular focus on global organizations. Therefore, a qualitative case study methodology, in which the organization was our unit of analysis, employing a written, constructivist self-report approach from each senior executive, was used (Searle, 1995; Yin, 2003). This approach required each respondent to answer the "how" and "why" questions related to regional and international diversity management and describe their own organizational experiences and stories in their own words (Crabtree & Miller, 1999; Yin, 2003). We have incorporated their insights throughout our theoretical treatment of the global value chain approach. Four co-authors independently coded and analyzed the data thematically to investigate the participants' diversity management experiences. The procedure continued by encoding the qualitative data through explicit codes that led to emerging patterns. The emerging patterns were discussed among the authors. When researchers could not reach a consensus on specific themes, the theme was either omitted or reconstructed until the researchers reached a common ground. Due to the exploratory nature of the data gathered, the main limitation of our study is that it is merely indicative of the global diversity management context.

Global Value Chain Approach

Many rules and resources play significant roles in explaining the relationship between workforce diversity and organizational outcomes (Ozbilgin et al., 2016; Singh et al., 2013; Gong et al., 2011). Most of the literature on diversity management is locked in dichotomous or exclusive discussions of voluntary, social, market-based and coercive regulation of diversity and the varied impacts on the effectiveness of diversity practices. Klarsfeld et al. (2012) illustrate that the false dichotomy between social and voluntary regulation can be overcome since voluntary measures include social regulation, which has a voluntaristic characteristic. Self-regulation of diversity and ideologically driven diversity practices mutually reinforce each other. Therefore, it is essential to acknowledge the interconnected nature of different forms of regulation in affecting change toward equality and diversity in organizations. The categories of diversity regulation presented in this paper should not be taken as mutually exclusive categories. Instead, it is essential to note that organizations use a wide range of repertoires, including shareholder, stakeholder and value chain approaches, at the same time to regulate and account for their diversity practices.

Although voluntary and coercive measures are used by the shareholder and stakeholder approaches for accounting diversity, the effectiveness of voluntary measures is criticised by theorists and practitioners where they are employed in isolation (Ozbilgin et al., 2016; Ozbilgin & Tatli, 2011). In this regulatory setting, the GVC approach is important. It falls outside the imagination of diversity management as it is theorized and practised today. Yet in the field of corporate governance and development studies (Elms &

Low, 2013), value chains are used to examine the impact and sustainability of organizational practices, i.e., technology, knowledge and innovation transfer (Kawai & Chung, 2019; Di Pietro et al., 2018; Mueller et al., 2009) and human resource efficiency on various communities. This theorization of the field of diversity is extended in this paper. If the GVC approach is applied to diversity, global organizations can measure their diversity practices across countries and other operational divisions (Kano, 2018; Verbeke & Kano, 2016). Such an accounting practice helps the organization see any disparities across parts of the organization in regulating diversity. The most prominent of these differences is the cross-national difference in managing diversity (Tatli et al., 2012). The GVC approach, once used for data collection purposes (Kaplinsky, 2000), can inform the bases for international and global regulation of diversity practices. Such internal law does not currently exist, despite some early signs of UN work regulating human rights issues for international businesses (Wettstein et al., 2019). Instead, soft measures such as their bylaws and voluntary initiatives (Crane & Matten, 2016; Park et al., 2014) are used by organizations to balance their social responsibility practices internationally. Yet, such soft measures often remain ineffectual as organizations do not perceive such balancing acts as imperative for effective diversity management and that non-compliance is neither monitored nor penalized.

The Common Good

Behind the notion of GVC, an essential assumption is that the world is a common good and that there should be equal access and share of that common good (Arjoon et al., 2018; Argandoña, 1998; Kano, 2018). The current global coronavirus crisis has highlighted this assumption. Thus, this paper examines how understanding the common good can help redefine the organizational purpose and serve to regulate them in sustainable, equitable, and fair ways. The common good is defined as "a set of conditions which enables the members of a community to attain for themselves reasonable objectives, or to realize for themselves the value(s) for the sake of which they have reason to collaborate with each other (positively and/or negatively) in a community" (Finnis, 1999, p. 155). At the firm level, the common good refers to an exchange relationship between the firm and its social context (Sison & Fontrodona, 2013; Houtart, 2012). The common good of the firm is the work that "allows human beings not only to produce goods and services, but more importantly, to develop technical or artistic skills, and intellectual and moral virtues, as a result of the workings of the firm" (Sison & Fontrodona, 2012, p. 212). The political community's common good consists in the flourishing (eudaimonia) that each of its citizens or members can achieve, only to the extent that all the other citizens or members achieve.

The firm's fundamental purpose is traditionally assumed to maximize value for investments of firm owners (Sison, 2007). In contrast with this generalization, Sison (2007) has developed an alternative theory/perspective to argue that the firm's primary purpose should be to contribute to the common good, a flourishing life in society for all of society's members. According to him, firms produce not only material wealth, goods and services but also habits, skills, and virtues. Therefore, firms have to consider the material consequences and a lot more than their member's full flourishing. The common good can also motivate organizational leaders to commit to managing diversity in organizations. While leaders are predominantly motivated by the prospect of increasing profits, "... a moral obligation or a personal desire to be associated with a program of social importance and/or to leave a positive legacy" (Ng & Wyrick, 2011, p. 368) may increase their commitment to diversity and inclusive leadership (Kurland & McCaffrey, 2016).

Business–society relations are generally examined by the stakeholder theory (Freeman et al., 2004; Donaldson & Preston, 1995) and the Aristotelian-Thomistic tradition (Sison & Fontrodona, 2012; Whelton, 1996) and the common good (Argandoña, 1998; Arjoon et al., 2018) to corporate citizenship (Moon et al., 2005), global citizenship (Waddock & Smith, 2000), human rights (Boele et al., 2001), and most commonly corporate social responsibility (Campbell, 2007) and corporate governance (Lazonick & O'Sullivan, 2000). Steurer (2006) has remapped these perspectives by developing the triple-perspective typology to examine the business–stakeholder interface. In this paper, taking the common good as the fundamental assumption, the diversity management theory is moved with the introduction of the GVC approach as both a method of analysis and a proposed way to regulate global organizations, particularly in the aftermath of the coronavirus crisis and the economic crisis that is to follow.

The universal principles include the best values for humanity at any time, even in the presence of local individualistic requests or aspirations. Localities are not the primary source to determine our beliefs and attitudes towards diversity, and for instance, one organization adopted universalities on top of its local approach, maybe, in the thought that unity and solidarity can be achieved to have a solid and sustainable organization in the only way of the uniform regulations derived from universal guidelines. On a value chain basis, the recent global scandals demonstrate that organizations have to foster and promote diversity concerns at the utmost level, not just locally but internationally. High diplomacy and active partnership across nations are required in international accounting diversity to achieve this. Raising interaction and communication among countries or multinational entities has potential benefits in aligning with supra-national labor standards and global governance principles.

Introducing Global Value Chain Precepts to the Management of Diversity in Global Organizations

Although there is considerable regulatory and normative pressure on organizations to practice diversity management for shareholder value and stakeholder value reasons, there has been scant attention to the disparate, partial and often imbalanced nature of diversity management efforts of global organizations across national borders. A leading Chief Diversity Officer in the hospitality industry in the USA, but who has worked at several other large-scale global FTSE and S&P companies around the globe, shared a number of her observations with us about the challenges encountered in implementing D&I strategies:

> Many companies develop and design their D&I strategy from a headquarters and national-domiciled base. Key stakeholders typically include the Board, Chairperson, CEO, President, members of Executive Management, and others who are typically based, work or lead operations from the home base. This often results in command and control, top-down cascading of D&I priorities and goals and failure to take into consideration regional aspects or nuances and can lead to a lack of trust and buy-in in local markets.

> When deploying a global D&I strategy, it is critical to account for regional and national regulations, laws, and cultural norms. It is not a case of 'one size fits all'. Companies often fail or neglect to consider how offices or staff in local markets can actually deploy or apply global goals or priorities at a country level. It is vital to empower local leaders and staff to understand, interpret and apply global goals in the context of local market considerations and to have the ability to adapt as needed or to create local goals.

> Measurement methodology for D&I should be designed at global, national and regional levels. For example, metrics for hiring women in the workplace or representation in the company can be done globally, at a regional, country, and local office level. However, metrics for the USA, UK or South Africa by race or ethnicity vary dramatically due to legal classifications/descriptions and other considerations. Questionnaires need to be customized, taking into account the correct legally defined terms and racial/ethnic population categories. I have seen instances

where lists with all racial/ethnic categories have been distributed at companies internally, creating employee backlash in markets where descriptions are viewed as offensive or are not in common use.

Table 13.2: Antecedents, correlates and consequences of global value chain approach for diversity management in global organizations

Drivers	Challenges	Activities	Outcomes
Social-political context demanding better regulation of diversity in the value chain	Voluntarism and individualism in diversity management	Global accounting of value chain for diversity management	Consistent management of diversity across the value chain
International and supranational organizations that promote a value chain approach to diversity management	Lack of coercive measures for diversity management	Global regulation of value chain for diversity management	Building corporate reputation because of principled diversity management strategy
International agreements and conventions that demand consistency for cross-national diversity management practices	Locally embedded policy and regulation of diversity management	Transversal policy on diversity management.	Less risk of exposure to political and international scrutiny because of diversity management in the value chain
Self-governance and self-regulation of organizations to future proof their diversity management efforts in the value chain.	Backlash against diversity management.		Accruing of diversity management dividends such as increases in employee engagement, innovative potential, psychological contract and decreases in turnover intention and backlash against diversity.

Companies should also set up mechanisms to allow for the sharing and communication of practices at local to regional to global levels and, conversely, from global to regional to local levels, encouraging two-way information flows across an enterprise. This presents tremendous opportunities to listen, learn, observe and share winning practices, ideas, and models. However, the global value chain approach to diversity management offers the potential to address the global imbalances that remain unaddressed in the local pursuit of diversity management practices in global organizations (Table 13.2).

Yet, the GVC approach remains challenging because global organizations have no coercive regulatory pressure to ensure consistency across their diversity interventions across national borders. There are a number of structural and cultural reasons that impede the standardization of diversity practices. First, the priorities of diversity management are often locally specific. In many countries, gender is a big focus, simply because there is no equity yet for women in management, senior management and executive roles – as witnessed in the engagement with a leading global pharmaceutical company. Additionally, in the entrepreneurship space, one of the research respondents (Elizabeth Vazquez, President and CEO of WEConnect International – an organization specializing in women's economic empowerment and global supplier diversity and inclusion) reiterated the fact that globally women-owned businesses earn less than 1% of the money spent on products and services by large corporations and governments – hence, suffering discrimination both inside and outside of the corporate world. This continues even after a McKinsey survey (NWBC, 2012) found that 34% said working with women-owned suppliers had increased profits. As a result, some national contexts currently prioritize gender diversity over other categories. In others, categories such as ethnicity, class, age, and disability status may be particularly important for organizations depending on varied pressures on organizations due to the perceived appeal of certain categories in that national setting.

Second, dealing with certain categories such as ethnic diversity, i.e., collecting ethnic data, could face legal challenges in some countries, e.g., France and Germany. Similarly, sexual orientation diversity is protected in only a few countries internationally, and it is legally challenged in others. Third, even when similar categories are covered by legislation, the implementation and definition of these categories may be differentiated by history, culture, leadership intent and commitment, institutions and laws in each country (Kamasak et al., 2020b; Kartolo & Kwantes, 2019; Alfarran et al., 2018). A Global HR Director of a Finance company operating exclusively in the wealth sector in Columbia, China and across the continent of Africa shared the following with us relating to its South African operation:

Locally in South Africa, for instance, this particular company has been fairly effective in articulating its diversity policy, practices and procedures as prescribed by the country's employment equity act and associated broad-based black economic empowerment (BBB-EE) policies, put in place to redress the economic marginalization of the majority population of the country. However, the company still found it difficult to fully implement these diversity initiatives in meaningful, practical ways – mostly because it has not effectively held senior leaders accountable – i.e., not appropriately incorporating and translating the required diversity achievement levels across its entire value chain, as prescribed by and communicated to the Department of Labor, into KPA's / KPI's of the senior and executive leaders.

Being a designated employer, the company is required by national law to conduct an analysis of employment policies, practices, procedures, and working environment to identify employment barriers that adversely affect members of designated- and previously marginalized groups.

The company has been hugely challenged in dealing with/addressing employment barriers via an affirmative action (related to either policy, procedure, or practice) in achieving the required diversity levels (the information relating to the employment barriers has been garnered via surveys conducted regularly with staff across the company – in South Africa, but not in the other countries in which the company operates). This challenge has been attributable to the complexity of appropriately aligning affirmative action across staff diversity committees (as prescribed by the employment equity act in South Africa), managers / senior leaders, and staff in general. Therefore, this complexity creates constraints in the company's ability to realize inclusivity.

Even 26 years after the end of formal Apartheid, the organization has only recently instituted a company. The value associated with diversity and inclusion is in the process of defining what inclusion means for the organization. The challenges it faces are that, without defining and aligning staff to what inclusion means, it will face challenges in meeting another of its values linked to innovation. Without inclusion to unlock diversity of thought and perspectives, innovation will be limited. There is no personal conscious drive or intent to be inclusive, hence the need to formalize it.

The national BBB-EE policies require companies to have majority ownership by black people and females in order to gain favorable trading levels/status to deal with public institutions and other private companies. Also, from a BBB-EE perspective, which includes diversity measures and accounting, the company is being pressured in meeting the procurement requirements across its entire value chain, set by state-owned enterprises who want to physically see the diversity of staff (i.e. economically active populations from previously disadvantaged groups) that make up the ecosystem of the company. Additionally, these designated/under-represented groups are appropriately represented across the categories of top leadership / senior management / middle management / junior management. The organization is still articulating its procurement requirements from preferred suppliers regarding their D&I policies, procedures and practices.

Due to these complexities, there are many barriers to the effective implementation of the global value chain approach. In the absence of legal support for the GVC approach, and due to the three challenges above, the development of the GVC approach has remained relatively stunted. Yet, there are several reasons which render GVC a future-proofing imperative for organizations.

First, there is the support or hostility of the socio-political context that shapes the diversity management practices of global organizations. Social and political mores are shaped by both public opinion and mass public protest. Women's protest marches, the MeToo campaign, BlackLivesMatter and Global Decolonization movements have inculcated considerable international interest. These movements have galvanized interest and attention to equality from an intersectional approach highlighting growing demands for social justice. Ozbilgin (2018) suggests that the global practice of intersectional solidarity can encourage organizations to address imbalances across the practices of global organizations. Yet, the author cautions that while gender inequality appears as an umbrella category with a degree of international and intersectional solidarity, struggles towards other equality categories remain local. Therefore, other social movements need to learn from the women's movement if they are to bring their demands to the level of international and global regulation. International organizations which serve to regulate labor market conditions, such as the International Labor Organization and the United Nations, and international and supranational agreements and conventions, such as the Convention on Elimination of All Kind Discrimination against Women (CEDAW) and Global Compact, help internationalize the value systems that underpin equality and diversity at work. As such, these international institutions and agreements influence global organizations to consider diversity management practices and their consistency across their value chain.

Second, leadership and resources are essential antecedents for organizations to consider the consistency of their practices across international operations. For instance, the diversity leadership concept is underpinned by an organization's desire to accrue the benefits of diversity with the principles of social responsibility (Orij et al., 2021; Williams, 2013). Diversity leadership focuses on the benefits of diversity and reducing transactional costs, such as avoiding administrative fines issued by regulatory bodies in cases of non-compliance. Leaders play a vital role in leveraging diversity and HR diversity practices' potential in organizations (Buengeler et al., 2018; Li, 2016). An organization's investment in diversity management is an indicator of its willingness to invest in diversity. Global organizations transfer certain ideas, such as diversity and equality across their operations, and the expansion of the diversity discourse owes much to the efforts of global organizations to disseminate diversity management practices internationally.

Global organizations are urged to transpose diversity management across borders due to several pressures, such as the pressure to have consistency across international operations, to capture the spirit of globalization, garner the benefits of a talented workforce that is becoming more diverse internationally, and to manage talent throughout their career lifecycles effectively. Megan Stowe, Greater European Region Strategic Sourcing Director and International Supplier Diversity Manager at Intel, made the point that five years ago, global supplier diversity efforts were driven from the very top, with the CEO setting a public target of reaching $1 billion in annual global spend with underutilized suppliers by the end of 2020 (Vazquez & Frankel, 2017).

Yet, the implementation of diversity management has yielded patchy success. Kalev et al. (2006) show that diversity training had only a limited effect on the recruitment of diverse talent. Whereas efforts to combat social isolation have been moderately successful, and the delegation of diversity across the organization as an individual responsibility was successful in promoting management diversity in the case of the USA. Diversity interventions that are resourced well succeed, and poorly resourced diversity initiatives would not be similarly successful (Dahanayake, 2018; Pitts, 2007). Pitts (2007) also notes that the more specific, targeted and supported the diversity intervention is, the more effective it will be in practice. One of our respondents, a global HR Director of a Chemicals company and previous Board member of a global FMCG, explained the challenges between global and local knowledge:

... the lack of understanding of local imperatives about overall global D&I goals often frustrated the outcomes and intent of our transformation programs. Further, the development of global D&I training content lost its local relevance, as most of the managerial teams might never have travelled internationally or engaged with people from various nationalities in the normal course of developing their careers. Therefore, using content that refers to how D&I is impacting counterparts, for instance, in Europe or Asia, bears low relevance in an African context, whilst Africans need to understand how to engage with other Africans on the continent since we have seen the rise of xenophobia on the continent in recent years.

Similarly, another Executive Director of an FMCG company shared the following with us:

... I have seen the desire to have control of overseas entities wherein the prevailing culture will be that of the headquarters. If D&I is a priority back home, then such strategies may be applied in local operations overseas. Having said that, I have seen two issues: (1) the implementation of D&I strategies as mere compliance rather than value creation strategies across the value chains of the company, and (2) local organizations being led by foreign heads, who always carry a bit of their 'home culture' and meaning of diversity with them, which ultimately means that you do not get full localization-fit of D&I efforts.

Drawing on a case study with boxing professionals, Dortants and Knoppers (2013) show in their study that embodied practice of discipline can be an effective method for the practice of diversity. Their work highlights the possibility of global organizations engaging with diversity at the level of lived experience rather than as policy alone. Third, the maturity and legitimacy of the organization's diversity management effort can help the organizations to move from surface-level treatment of diversity to deeper level engagement with diversity concerns, e.g., the GVC approach. In shaping the maturity and legitimacy of organizational efforts, the soft power of customers, employees and communities can help global organizations invest in diversity. Many organizations try to build strong corporate reputations.

Strong corporate reputations and brand identities help organizations secure sustainable customer loyalty. Customers and communities that engage with global organizations also tend to avoid associating with, and consuming, brands that have tarnished reputations through practices of discrimination, inequality and exploitation (Villadsen & Wulff, 2018).

Global organizations manage diversity by drawing on three significant rationales (Figure 13.1). First, global organizations can use shareholder value inherent in the effective management of diversity as a rationale. Shareholder value incorporates regulation of diversity for profitability as the single bottom line in the corporate sectors or value for money reasons in state and third sectors. The business case for diversity in organizations often presents the economic, social, legal and political rationale for organizations to consider the regulation of diversity. In most organizations, the stakeholder value approach does not exist in pure form as organizations have to consider the legal, social and environmental contexts and rationales for effective management and ultimate shareholder value maximization reasons. Therefore, the shareholder and stakeholder value approaches are not mutually exclusive.

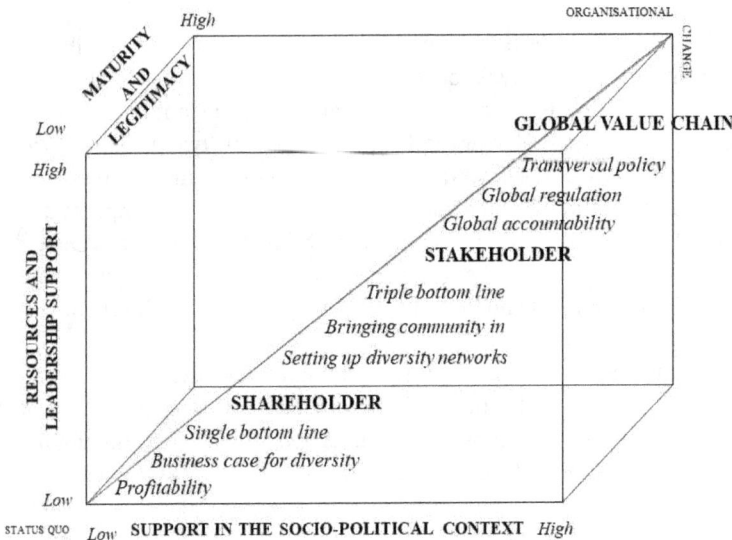

Figure 13.1: Locating the GVC Approach in the Management of Diversity in Global Organizations

Second, global organizations may reflect on the contribution of effective diversity management on the triple bottom line, i.e., social, economic and environmental concerns. In order to bring social, economic and environmental considerations into the design and delivery of diversity management interventions, organizations can bring in diversity networks and communities outside the organization within. This can allow voice behavior to be activated in organizations. Both shareholder and stakeholder approaches engage organizations in the effective regulation of diversity. Nevertheless, these two approaches focus on local and community demands with a single nation-state with some engagement across international operations. Organizations with higher maturity levels for diversity, resources, and leadership support for such efforts can move to the global value chain approach.

The GVC approach to diversity management has at least three distinct manifestations. First, the measurement of diversity in the GVC approach is not limited to listing diversity interventions but engages in the accounting of the impact of diversity practices across the value chain. One of the research respondents, a former Global Chief Diversity Office for a beverages multinational operating in 200 countries, shared with us how metrics were used in a diversity strategy to drive business performance:

> In terms of diversity linked to innovation across the value chain, the company put together an extremely diverse team to seek out and assess innovative new ideas for products/brands/categories and/or acquisitions. The team was measured on their performance at delivering new products/brands/categories and their impact on sales, revenue and financial performance. This same company put together another extremely diverse team with the goal of disrupting the marketplace on a product delivery system. Their performance was to be based on the impact their work would have on sales, revenue, financial performance and customer satisfaction. Their end product not only disrupted the marketplace but also disrupted the industry. Their innovation launched several years ago, and the technology is unique in that industry and has led to double-digit sales growth on a year-over-year basis.
>
> The company launched a global women's empowerment program designed to create 5,000,000 jobs for women across its value chain and the globe. This company also launched a comprehensive D&I strategy that encompassed workplace, marketplace, community (this included philanthropic giving, media relations, and corporate social responsibility) and partners (this included suppliers, as well as D&I consulting the company, did for its customers). In the marketplace, metrics were put in place to measure sales and revenue growth across all brands and all demographics as a result of the diversity strategy driven through all marketing plans. There was an extensive set of metrics in the workplace regarding the diverse workforce and all of the strategies, programs, practices, and processes that touched employees. In the community, metrics were in place regarding dollars provided to

diverse constituencies through the company's philanthropic giving, media stories about the company's D&I work, and the value that D&I held with various D&I-related CSR stakeholders. Regarding partners, metrics were put in place regarding supplier spending with diverse ownership groups (women-owned, minority-owned), as well as contributions to customers through the consulting practice that was established.

Second, global regulation of the value chain approach means that the organization engages in global and sectoral voluntary agreements and initiatives to better regulate its value chain (Partiti, 2022; Locke et al., 2009). Third, organizations need to design and implement policies that recognize local differences and yet act on global principles across the value chain (Bos et al., 2017). Such efforts are called transversal policy in global organizations (Bennett, 2001; Ney, 2006). Transversal diversity policy is an outcome of engagement among members of the diversity council drawn from different functional and geographic areas of the organization (Jonsen & Ozbilgin, 2013). Karabacakoglu and Ozbilgin (2010) explain that, in Ericsson, transversal policy-making was used to mediate between local demands and global policy. Transversal policy emerges as local priorities are collated to identify cross-cutting priorities and imbalances in resourcing and the impact of diversity interventions. The transverse policy addresses the shortcomings of localization by transcending the entrenched priorities of local branches and overcomes the ill-fitting global principles by exposing them to local logic. Therefore, the transversal policy mediates the organization's need for localization and standardization in the value chain.

The Group Chief Human Resources and Corporate Affairs Officer of a global telecommunications multinational, a company that operates in over 20 countries in the Middle East and Africa, explained to us the challenges and considerations they have to make:

> Diversity and Inclusion tends to be viewed as an HR or CSR imperative as opposed to being embedded into the organization's DNA. This is perhaps the first barrier we experience within the company. Driving D&I as a deliberate effort across the business value chain is pivotal to progress in D&I truly. It needs to show up in the way we design products and services, deliver services to customers, hire and retain talent, equitably develop our people, make strategic leadership decisions, contribute to our communities and stakeholders, and most of all, in the way our company and people treat each other. Every single part of the organizational value chain needs to overlay the lens

of diversity and inclusion. We have worked in this direction within our company and continue to make strides in:

Employee policies, processes and infrastructure – From our pay and benefits models to gender-friendly policies, unbiased hiring practices, employee engagements to specific facility infrastructure(s) designed to be inclusive to our diverse population. **Customer priorities** – Some of our markets have made conscious efforts to build products/services and customer service infrastructures to cater to and reach our diverse customers across the continents in which we operate (targeted at gender, differently-abled, and religious backgrounds, amongst others). This type of 'empathic' thinking in the business creates transformational shifts in the company and our markets. **Partner ecosystems** – We have a naturally diverse partnering ecosystem that gets us to integrate and work with people and companies from almost every continent. In [our home regional] context, we do have certain preferences of suppliers we work with based on their employment equity contributions; at a global scale, we generally only form partnerships with organizations that are active contributors to society, people and the common good. **Community commitments** – In addition to traditional sustainability initiatives, we do believe in 'standing true' to critical social causes. Be it in the case of our activism pledge towards gender-based violence or xenophobic causes or our commitments to developing women/children, working with and developing differently-abled communities. What works to our advantage of being in 22 different markets in Africa and the Middle East is that we have the ability to target social causes and commitments that matter most in the context of that specific market.

The second challenge in D&I is that it is multidimensional. Very often, diversity is traditionally referenced to gender and color and therefore tends to be narrow and limited in its focal point for actions. Expanding this thinking to consider various aspects, including ethnicity, language, culture, religion, physical and mental abilities, sexual orientations, personalities, and preferences, gives D&I a richer and more holistic perspective of how we need to show up as an organization. In our company, we built our entire D&I philosophy, approach and strategy to act, respect and celebrate 'everything' that is diverse. This guides the interventions and actions we take to uplift D&I in the organization. We also make it a point to ensure that we educate our people on diversity and inclusion in the same way – this is specifically to overcome, as far as possible, the challenge of 'unconscious biases, which tends to inform our thinking, action and priorities. For this reason, we formulated Inclusion Forums in almost every market to make this meaningful to their context and yet consistent in approach globally.

The third challenge is that in vast geography like ours, the interpretation and acceptance of diversity is informed and (at times) enforced by local laws and regulations of social structures. This does create a level of complexity to our D&I strategy, which is designed to be broad-based. Our view of approaching this challenge is to work closely with the constitution-makers and regulators to drive social activism that can help transform society and the marketplace. While this is often a lengthy process, we believe there is merit if we truly want to operate a diverse company catering to diverse customers.

Global diversity management based on the value chain approach is not an end in itself. Nishii and Ozbilgin (2007) identify a number of dividends associated with the effective management of diversity in global organizations. These include an increase in staff engagement, knowledge-sharing practices and innovation. They also show that turnover intentions and the risk of backlash against diversity interventions may drop if diversity is managed effectively. To date, there are no published empirical studies exploring the use of value chain thinking in the field of global diversity management. The only exception is the Ozbilgin et al. (2016) study which shows that there is increased awareness among corporate leaders to manage diversity in their value chains in more effective ways. As such, organizations are increasingly using transversal diversity councils as a way to increase communication between sections of the organization across their value chains with the distinct purpose of tackling inconsistencies in managing diversity across international, national and functional divisions.

Conclusion

The current global coronavirus crisis is impacting countries around the world. The real extent of damage done to economies around the world and what this might mean for already disadvantaged groups in different societies around the world should be seen. In such a dire situation, the management of diversity in global organizations cannot be trusted to single measures, such as the voluntarism of global organizations or their collective initiatives in the global context. In fact, research demonstrates that such single measures have not been effective in managing diversity in global organizations to date (Lauring, 2013), and it's unlikely that they will be effective in the aftermath of this global pandemic. Management of diversity in global organizations has garnered inconsistent outcomes across international and national networks of global organizations (Golgeci et al., 2021; Sippola & Smale, 2007). In order to address this inconstancy, a concept from corporate governance and development studies literature is borrowed, the GVC theory, to explicate the utility of value chains for better management of diversity in global organizations.

The GVC theory is now a well-established topic of study (Gibbon & Ponte, 2008). Furthermore, its potential has been highlighted for developing theory and practice in the field of diversity management (Ozbilgin et al., 2016). The current situation with diversity management is akin to a Polanyian nightmare (Faulconbridge & Muzio, 2018), which denotes the domination of the market logic in the intricate relationship between the market, the state and society as actors of embedded strategy. The GVC approach for managing diversity would require transnational monitoring and accountability for all the actors beyond the heavily emphasized demands of the market as studied in the mainstream diversity literature. The current political climate, which rests mainly on global organizations' desires to self-regulate based on market needs without the pressure of international law or social movements, is leaving broad scope for inequalities and exploitation in the global economic system. The GVC perspective on diversity management brings about the transnational accountability that is missing in current formulations of diversity management.

Times are changing. The human rights agenda is setting roots in the field of international business, and the expectations from global organizations are formalized by the UN (Wettstein et al., 2019). There is growing recognition of the challenges of achieving consistency in diversity management practices across countries. The current coronavirus crisis only strengthens this call by highlighting vast fault lines and inequalities by class, gender, ethnicity, age, disability, and other social divisions. Furthermore, global organizations continue to benefit from imbalances in human rights laws and customs and labor protections in different countries. This has been problematized in the field of development studies.

The GVC perspective on diversity management offers to reveal, through a collection of transnational data, knowledge on the impact of diversity across different national settings in which global organizations operate and the potential to set up structures to address transnational inequalities induced by nationally and globally based diversity management efforts. Such data can then be used to inform management and HR practitioner interventions to combat such imbalances (Kaplinsky, 2000). The utility of value chain analyses for addressing poverty is discussed extensively by Hall and Matos (2010). Once GVC data is made available, as Scherer and Palazzo (2011) identify, one of the realistic ways that GVC approaches could be managed rests with the redefinition and legitimation of global organizations as public and social actors. Only through such a process may it be possible to expect global organizations to acknowledge and accept duty and responsibility towards fair, balanced, consistent, effective and responsible management of global diversity.

However, the current political climate and organizational trends suggest that diversity consistently suffers setbacks in global organizations (OECD, 2018). The progress towards better regulation of diversity is, at best, slow. In the absence of coercive regulatory pressures, despite early signs of globalization of regulation (Drahos & Braithwaite, 2001), the notion of the common good should be highlighted, arguing that the common good of the firm ought to be embedded within a broader common good at the transnational plane, encompassing inclusion of all parties involved in the creation of value and consumption of goods and services in global organizations.

In terms of effective management of cross-cultural issues, the GVC approach promises to attend to one of the significant challenges that multinational enterprises experience, i.e. the uneven nature of power relations and resource allocations across national borders. The GVC approach to diversity management offers to address these imbalances, offering remedial interventions to some of the challenges, such as neocolonial relations between the global north and global south (Yalkin & Ozbilgin, 2022). Many multinational enterprises come under the scrutiny of social movements such as the BlackLivesMatter and MeToo, which have gained global character (Ozbilgin & Erbil, 2021). The uneven treatment of gender issues and the neocolonial organization of international business could be tackled by the GVC approach to diversity management, which examines diversity issues across national borders and cross-cultural lenses. Of particular import in decolonizing global organizations and cross-national management is understanding differences in how diversity is defined, framed and regulated differently in the regulated contexts of the global north and the unregulated contexts of the global south (Küskü et al., 2021). These differences often serve to entrench and sustain the power imbalances and injustice in the neocolonial order between the colonizing countries and the colonized territories. The GVC theory is traditionally used to explore and problematize such imbalances of power in the global operations of multinational enterprises. Therefore, the GVC approach to diversity management offers to unpack, reveal and address such cross-national concerns over where inequalities reside and how they could be solved internationally.

References

Acquier, A., Valiorgue, B., & Daudigeos, T. (2017). Sharing the shared value: A transaction cost perspective on strategic CSR policies in global value chains. *Journal of Business Ethics, 144*(1), 139-152.

Aguilera, R. V., & Jackson, G. (2003). The cross-national diversity of corporate governance: Dimensions and determinants. *Academy of Management Review, 28*(3), 447-465.

Alfarran, A., Pyke, J., & Stanton, P. (2018). Institutional barriers to women's employment in Saudi Arabia. *Equality, Diversity and Inclusion, 37*(7), 713-727.

Álvarez-Figueroa, F., Queupil, J. P., & Díaz, D. A. (2022). The discovery of diversity in Chile: a review of legislation and research concerning equality, inclusion and diversity management. *Research Handbook on New Frontiers of Equality and Diversity at Work.*

April, K. & Dharani, B. (2021). Diversity and entrepreneurship in South Africa: Intersections and purposive collaboration. In K. April, & B. Zolfaghari (Eds.), *Values-driven entrepreneurship and societal impact: Setting the agenda for entrepreneuring across (Southern) Africa* (pp. 241-254). KR Publishing.

April, K. (2021). The narratives of racism in South Africa. In P. Daya., & K. April (Eds.), *12 lenses into diversity in South Africa* (pp. 11-31). KR Publishing.

Argandoña, A. (1998). The stakeholder theory and the common good. *Journal of Business Ethics, 17*(9-10), 1093-1102.

Arjoon, S., Turriago-Hoyos, A., & Thoene, U. (2018). Virtuousness and the Common Good as a Conceptual Framework for Harmonizing the Goals of the Individual, Organizations, and the Economy. *Journal of Business Ethics, 147*(1), 143-163.

Baccaro, L., & Mele, V. (2012). Pathology of path dependency? The ILO and the challenge of new governance. *ILR Review, 65*(2), 195-224.

Backer, L. C. (2016). Shaping a global law for business enterprises: Framing principles and the promise of a comprehensive treaty on business and human rights. *North Carolina Journal of International Law & Commercial Regulation, 42*(2), 417-504.

Bair, J., & Palpacuer, F. (2012). From varieties of capitalism to varieties of activism: The antisweatshop movement in comparative perspective. *Social Problems, 59*(4), 522-543.

Baykut, S., Özbilgin, M. F., Erbil, C., Kamasak, R., & Baglama, S. (2021). The impact of hidden curriculum on international students in the context of a toxic triangle of diversity. *The Curriculum Journal, 33*(2), 156-177. https://doi.org/1 0.1002/curj.135

Bennett, T. (2001). Differing Diversities: Transversal Study on the Theme of Cultural Policy and Cultural Diversity. Strasbourg: Council of Europe.

Boele, R., Fabig, H., & Wheeler, D. (2001). Shell, Nigeria and the Ogoni. A study in unsustainable development: II. Corporate social responsibility and 'stakeholder management' versus a rights-based approach to sustainable development. *Sustainable Development, 9*(3), 121-135. https://doi.org/10.10 02/sd.168

Bos, B., Faems, D., & Noseleit, F. (2017). Alliance concentration in multinational companies: Examining alliance portfolios, firm structure, and firm performance. *Strategic Management Journal, 38*(11), 2298-2309. https://doi.org/10.1002/smj.2 652

Buengeler, C., Leroy, H., & De Stobbeleir, K. (2018). How leaders shape the impact of HR's diversity practices on employee inclusion. *Human Resource Management Review, 28*(3), 289-303. https://doi.org/10.1016/j.hrmr.2018.02 .005

Campbell, J. L. (2007). Why would corporations behave in socially responsible ways? An institutional theory of corporate social responsibility. *Academy of Management Review, 32*(3), 946-967.

Clarke, T., & Boersma, M. (2017). The governance of global value chains: Unresolved human rights, environmental and ethical dilemmas in the Apple supply chain. *Journal of Business Ethics, 143*(1), 111–131.

Clean Clothes Campaign (2020). Live-blog: How the Coronavirus affects garment workers in supply chains. Available at: https://cleanclothes.org/news /2020/live-blog-on-how-the-coronavirus-influences-workers-in-supply-chains (May 2020).

Cobb, J. A. (2016). How firms shape income inequality: Stakeholder power, executive decision making, and the structuring of employment relationships. *Academy of Management Review, 41*(2), 324-348.

Crabtree, B. F., & Miller, W. L. (1999). *Doing qualitative research (2nd edition)*. New York: SAGE Publications.

Crane, A. (2013). Modern slavery as a management practice: exploring the conditions and capabilities for human exploitation. *Academy of Management Review, 38*(1), 49–69.

Crane, A., & Matten, D. (2016). *Business Ethics: Managing Corporate Citizenship and Sustainability in the Age of Globalization*. Oxford University Press.

Crane, A., LeBaron, G., Allain, J., & Behbahani, L. (2019) Governance gaps in eradicating forced labor: From global to domestic supply chains. *Regulation & Governance, 13*(1), 86-106.

Dahanayake, P., Rajendran, D., Selvarajah, C. & Ballantyne, G. (2018). Justice and fairness in the workplace: a trajectory for managing diversity. *Equality, Diversity and Inclusion, 37*(5), 470-490.

Davis, G. F., McAdam, D., Scott, W. R. & Zald, M. N. (eds.) (2005). *Social Movements and Organization Theory*. Cambridge: Cambridge University Press.

Di Pietro, F., Prencipe, A., & Majchrzak, A. (2018). Crowd Equity Investors: An Underutilized Asset for Open Innovation in Startups. *California Management Review, 60*(2), 43-70.

Dobbin, F., & Kalev, A. (2016). Why diversity programs fail. *Harvard Business Review, 94*(7-8), 3-10.

Doh, J., McGuire, S., & Ozaki, T. (2015). The Journal of World Business Special Issue: Global governance and international nonmarket strategies: Introduction to the special issue. *Journal of World Business, 50*(2), 256-261.

Donaldson, T., & Preston, L. E. (1995). The stakeholder theory of the corporation: Concepts, evidence, and implications. *Academy of Management Review, 20*(1), 65-91.

Dortants, M., & Knoppers, A. (2013). Regulation of diversity through discipline: Practices of inclusion and exclusion in boxing. *International Review for the Sociology of Sport, 48*(5), 535-549. https://doi.org/10.1177/10 12690212445279

Drahos, P., & Braithwaite, J. (2001). The globalization of regulation. *Journal of Political Philosophy, 9*(1), 103-128.

Elms, D. K., & Low, P. (Eds.). (2013). Global Value Chains in a Changing World. Geneva: World Trade Organization.

Ewing-Nelson, C. (2020). After a Full Month of Business Closures, Women Were Hit Hardest By April's Job Losses. National Women's Law Center. May 2020. Fact Sheet.

Faulconbridge, J. R., & Muzio, D. (2018). Karl Polanyi on strategy: the effects of culture, morality and double-movements on embedded strategy. *Critical Perspectives on Accounting, 73*. https://doi.org/10.1016/j.cpa.2020.102171

Felix, R., Pevzner, M., & Zhao, M. (2021). Cultural Diversity of Audit Committees and Firms' Financial Reporting Quality. *Accounting Horizons, 35*(3), 143-159.

Ferner, A., Almond, P., & Colling, T. (2005). Institutional theory and the cross-national transfer of employment policy: The case of 'workforce diversity' in US multinationals. *Journal of International Business Studies, 36*(3), 304-321.

Finnis, J. (1999). *Natural law and natural rights.* Oxford: Clarendon Press.

Foster, B. P., Manikas, A., Preece, D., & Kroes, J. R. (2021). Noteworthy diversity efforts and financial performance: Evidence from DiversityInc's top 50. *Advances in Accounting, 53*, 100528.

Freeman, R. E., Wicks, A. C., & Parmar, B. (2004). Stakeholder theory and "the corporate objective revisited". *Organization Science, 15*(3), 364-369.

Fritz, M. M. C., & Silva, M. E. (2018). Exploring supply chain sustainability research in Latin America. *International Journal of Physical Distribution & Logistics Management. 48*(8), 818-841.

Gereffi, G., & Fernandez-Stark, K. (2011). Global value chain analysis: a primer. Center on Globalization, Governance & Competitiveness (CGGC), Duke University, North Carolina, USA.

Gibbon, P. & Ponte, S. (2008). Global value chains: From governance to governmentality? *Economy and Society, 37*(3), 365–392.

Gibbon, P., Bair, J., & Ponte, S. (2008). Governing global value chains: An introduction. *Economy and Society, 37*(3), 315–338.

Golgeci, I., Makhmadshoev, D., & Demirbag, M. (2021). Global value chains and the environmental sustainability of emerging market firms: A systematic review of literature and research agenda. *International Business Review, 30*(5), 101857.

Hall, J., & Matos, S. (2010). Incorporating impoverished communities in sustainable supply chains. *International Journal of Physical Distribution & Logistics Management, 40*(1/), 124-147.

Hamann, R., & Bertels, S. (2018). The institutional work of exploitation: Employers' work to create and perpetuate inequality. *Journal of Management Studies, 55*(3), 394-423.

Healy, G., & Oikelome, F. (2011). Diversity, Ethnicity, Migration and Work: UK and US Perspectives. In Diversity, Ethnicity, Migration and Work (pp. 36-66). Palgrave Macmillan, London.

Hoang, T., Suh, J., & Sabharwal, M. (2022). Beyond a Numbers Game? Impact of Diversity and Inclusion on the Perception of Organizational Justice. *Public Administration Review, 82*(3), 537-555. https://doi.org/10.1111/puar.13463

Houtart, F. (2012). From the 'Common Goods' to the 'Common Good of Humanity', B. Daiber & Houtart (Eds.). In A Postcapitalist Paradigm: The Common Good of Humanity (pp. 1–16). Brussels: Rosa-Luxemburg Foundation.

Jackson, G., Kuruvilla, S., & Frege, C. (2013). Across boundaries: The global challenges facing workers and Rmployment research. *British Journal of Industrial Relations, 51*(3), 425-439.

Jonsen, K., & Ozbilgin, M. (2013). Models of global diversity management. In Ferdman, B. M. & Deane, B. R. (Eds.), *Diversity at Work: The Practice of Inclusion* (pp. 364-390). John Wiley & Sons. https://doi.org/10.1002/9781118 764282.ch12

Jonsen, K., Tatli, A., Ozbilgin, M. F., & Bell, M. P. (2013). The tragedy of the uncommons: Reframing workforce diversity. *Human Relations, 66*(2), 271-294.

Kalev, A., Dobbin, F., & Kelly, E. (2006). Best practices or best guesses? Assessing the efficacy of corporate affirmative action and diversity policies. *American Sociological Review, 71*(4), 589-617.

Kamasak, R., James, S. R., & Yavuz, M. (2019). The interplay of corporate social responsibility and corporate political activity in emerging markets: The role of strategic flexibility in nonmarket strategies. *Business Ethics: A European Review, 28*(3): 305–320.

Kamasak, R., Özbilgin, M. F., Baykut, S., & Yavuz, M. (2020a). Moving from individual intersections to institutional intersections: Insights from LGBTQ individuals in Turkey. *Journal of Organizational Change Management, 33*(3): 456–476.

Kamasak, R., Özbilgin, M. F., Küçükaltan, B., & Yavuz, M. (2020d). Regendering of dynamic managerial capabilities in the context of binary perspectives on gender diversity. *Gender in Management: An International Journal, 35*(1), 19–36.

Kamasak, R., Özbilgin, M.F., & Yavuz, M. (2020c). Understanding intersectional analyses. In: King, E., Roberson, Q. and Hebl, M. (eds.), *Research on Social Issues in Management on Pushing Understanding of Diversity in Organizations* (pp. 93–115). Charlotte, USA: Information Age Publishing.

Kamasak, R., Ozbilgin, M.F., Yavuz, M., & Akalin, C. (2020b). Race discrimination at work in the UK. In: Vassilopoulou, J., Brabet, J., Kyriakidou, O., & Shovunmi, V. (eds.), *Race Discrimination and the Management of Ethnic Diversity at Work: European Countries Perspective.* Bingley, UK: Emerald Publishing.

Kamasak, R., Palalar, A. D., Yesildal, E., & Vassilopoulou, J. (2022). Ethnicity and precarity relationship: The refugee case in Turkey. In: Meliou, M., Vassilopoulou J. and Ozbilgin, M. (eds.), *Diversity and Precarious Work During Socio-economic Upheaval: The Missing Link.* Cambridge, UK: Cambridge University Press.

Kano, L. (2018). Global value chain governance: A relational perspective. *Journal of International Business Studies, 49*(6), 1-22, 684–705.

Kaplinsky, R. (2000). Globalization and unequalisation: What can be learned from value chain analysis? *Journal of Development Studies, 37*(2), 117-146.

Kaplinsky, R. (2013). *Globalization, Poverty and Inequality: Between a Rock and a Hard Place.* John Wiley & Sons.

Karabacakoglu, F., & Ozbilgin, M. (2010). Global Diversity Management at Ericsson: The Business Case, In Cases in Strategic Management (pp.79-91). London: McGraw-Hill.

Kartolo, A., & Kwantes, C. (2019). Organizational culture, perceived societal and organizational discrimination. *Equality, Diversity and Inclusion, 38*(6), 602-618.

Kawai, N., & Chung, C. (2019). Expatriate utilization, subsidiary knowledge creation and performance: the moderating role of subsidiary strategic context. *Journal of World Business, 54*(1), 24-36.

Kimani, D., Ullah, S., Kodwani, D., & Akhtar, P. (2021). Analysing corporate governance and accountability practices from an African neo-patrimonialism perspective: Insights from Kenya. *Critical Perspectives on Accounting, 78*, 102260.

Klarsfeld, A. (2009). Managing diversity: The virtue of coercion. In Ozbilgin, MF (ed.), *Equality, Diversity and Inclusion at Work* (pp. 322–331). Edward Elgar.

Klarsfeld, A., Ng, E., & Tatli, A. (2012). Social regulation and diversity management: A comparative study of France, Canada and the UK. *European Journal of Industrial Relations, 18*(4), 309-327.

Kováts, E. (2018). Questioning consensuses: Right-wing populism, anti-populism, and the threat of 'gender ideology'. *Sociological Research Online*, 1360780418764735.

Kurland, N. B., & McCaffrey, S. J. (2016). Social Movement Organization Leaders and the Creation of Markets for "Local" Goods. *Business & Society, 55*(7), 1017–1058.

Küskü, F., Aracı, Ö., & Özbilgin, M. F. (2021). What happens to diversity at work in the context of a toxic triangle? Accounting for the gap between discourses and practices of diversity management. *Human Resource Management Journal, 31*(2), 553-574.

Lakhani, T., Kuruvilla, S., & Avgar, A. (2013). From the firm to the network: Global value chains and employment relations theory. *British Journal of Industrial Relations, 51*(3), 440-472.

Lauring, J. (2013). International diversity management: Global ideals and local responses. *British Journal of Management, 24*(2), 211-224.

Lazonick, W., & O'sullivan, M. (2000). Maximizing shareholder value: a new ideology for corporate governance. *Economy and Society, 29*(1), 13-35.

Li, C. (2016). The Role of Top-team Diversity and Perspective Taking in Mastering Organizational Ambidexterity. *Management and Organization Review, 12*(4), 769-794.

Li, Y., & Cui, L. (2018). The Influence of Top Management Team on Chinese Firms' FDI Ambidexterity. *Management and Organization Review, 14*(3), 513-542.

Locke, R., Amengual, M., & Mangla, A. (2009). Virtue out of necessity? Compliance, commitment, and the improvement of labor conditions in global supply chains. *Politics & Society, 37*(3), 319-351.

Lorbiecki, A. (2001). Changing views on diversity management: The rise of the learning perspective and the need to recognize social and political contradictions. *Management Learning, 32*(3), 345-361.

Louche, C., Staelens, L. & D'Haese, M. (2020). When workplace unionism in global value chains does not function well: Exploring the impediments. *Journal of Business Ethics, 162*(2), 379–398.

Luanglath, N., Ali, M., & Mohannak, K. (2019). Top management team gender diversity and productivity: the role of board gender diversity. *Equality, Diversity and Inclusion, 38*(1), 71-86.

Marginson, P., Edwards, P., Edwards, T., Ferner, A., & Tregaskis, O. (2010). Employee representation and consultative voice in multinational companies operating in Britain. *British Journal of Industrial Relations, 48*(1), 151-180.

Matos, S., & Silvestre, B.S. (2013). Managing stakeholder relations when developing sustainable business models: the case of the Brazilian energy sector. *Journal of Cleaner Production, 45*, 61-73.

May, C. (2015). Who's in charge? Corporations as institutions of global governance. *Palgrave Communications*, 1, 1-10.

Moon, J., Crane, A., & Matten, D. (2005). Can corporations be citizens? Corporate citizenship as a metaphor for business participation in society. *Business Ethics Quarterly, 15*(3), 429-453.

Mueller, M., dos Santos, V. G., & Seuring, S. (2009). The contribution of environmental and social standards towards ensuring legitimacy in supply chain governance. *Journal of Business Ethics, 89*(4), 509–523.

Ney, S. (2006). Messy issues, policy conflict and the differentiated polity: Analysing contemporary policy responses to complex, uncertain and transversal policy problems. Unpublished doctoral dissertation, LOS Center for Bergen, Vienna, Austria.

Ng, E. S., & Wyrick, C. R. (2011). Motivational bases for managing diversity: A model of leadership commitment. *Human Resource Management Review, 21*(4), 368-376.

Nishii, L. H., & Ozbilgin, M. F. (2007). Global diversity management: towards a conceptual framework. *The International Journal of Human Resource Management, 18*(11), 1883-1894.

Nkomo, S., & Hoobler, J. M. (2014). A historical perspective on diversity ideologies in the United States: Reflections on human resource management research and practice. *Human Resource Management Review, 24*(3), 245-257.

NWBC (National Women's Business Council) (2012). What is supplier diversity? Retrieved from URL: https://cdn.www.nwbc.gov/wp-content/uploads/2012/01/05065029/fact-sheet-supplier-diversity.png.

OECD (2018) Diversity Survey Report. https://survey.oecd.org/Survey.aspx?s=f0363306250a408a9ae40c139e88215c

Orij, R. P., Rehman, S., Khan, H., & Khan, F. (2021). Is CSR the new competitive environment for CEOs? The association between CEO turnover, corporate social responsibility and board gender diversity: Asian evidence. *Corporate Social Responsibility and Environmental Management, 28*(2), 731-747.

Ozbilgin, M. (2018). What the racial equality movement can learn from the global fight for women's right. http://theconversation.com/what-the-racial-equality-movement-can-learn-from-the-global-fight-for-womens-rights-10 5616

Ozbilgin, M. F., & Erbil, C. (2021). Social movements and wellbeing in organizations from multilevel and intersectional perspectives: The case of the #blacklivesmatter movement. *The SAGE Handbook of Organizational Wellbeing,* 119-138.

Ozbilgin, M., & Erbil, C. (2019). Yönetim çalışmaları alanındaki kısır yöntem ikilemlerini dışaçekimsel ve geçmişsel yaklaşım ve eleştirel gerçekçilikle yöntem yelpazesine dönüştürmek. *Yönetim ve Çalışma Dergisi, 3*(1), 1–24

Ozbilgin, M., & Tatli, A. (2008). *Global Diversity Management: An Evidence Based Approach.* London: Palgrave MacMillan.

Ozbilgin, M., Tatli, A., Ipek, G., & Sameer, M. (2016). Four approaches to accounting for diversity in global organizations. *Critical Perspectives on Accounting, 35,* 88-99.

Palalar, A. D., Ozbilgin, M. F., & Kamasak, R. (2022). Social innovation in managing diversity: Covid-19 as a catalyst for change. *Equality, Diversity & Inclusion, 41*(5), 709-725. https://doi.org/10.1108/EDI-07-2021-0171

Park, B., Chidlow, A., & Choi, J. (2014). Corporate social responsibility: Stakeholders influence on MNEs' activities. *International Business Review, 23,* 966–980.

Partiti, E. (2022). The place of voluntary standards in managing social and environmental risks in global value chains. *European Journal of Risk Regulation, 13*(1), 114-137.

Pitts, D. W. (2007). Implementation of diversity management programs in public organizations: Lessons from policy implementation research. *International Journal of Public Administration, 30*(12-14), 1573-1590.

Rao, K., & Tilt, C. (2016). Board composition and corporate social responsibility: The role of diversity, gender, strategy and decision making. Journal of Business Ethics, 138(2), 327-347.

Risse-Kappen, T., Risse, T., Ropp, S. C., & Sikkink, K. (Eds.). (1999). *The power of human rights: International norms and domestic change* (Vol. 66). Cambridge University Press.

Scherer, A. G., & Palazzo, G. (2011). The new political role of business in a globalized world: A review of a new perspective on CSR and its implications for the firm, governance, and democracy. *Journal of Management Studies, 48*(4), 899-931.

Searle, J. R. (1995). *The construction of social reality.* New York: The Free Press.

Semenova, N., & Hassel, L. G. (2019). Private engagement by Nordic institutional investors on environmental, social, and governance risks in global companies. *Corporate Governance: An International Review, 27*(2), 144-161.

Shore, L. M., Cleveland, J. N., & Sanchez, D. (2018). Inclusive workplaces: A review and model. *Human Resource Management Review, 28*(2), 176-189.

Sippola, A., & Smale, A. (2007). The global integration of diversity management: A longitudinal case study. *The International Journal of Human Resource Management, 18*(11), 1895-1916.

Sison, A. J. G. (2007). Toward a common good theory of the firm: The Tasubinsa case. *Journal of Business Ethics, 74*(4), 471-480.

Sison, A. J. G., & Fontrodona, J. (2012). The common good of the firm in the Aristotelian-Thomistic tradition. *Business Ethics Quarterly, 22*(2), 211-246.

Sison, A. J. G., & Fontrodona, J. (2013). Participating in the common good of the firm. *Journal of Business Ethics, 113*(4), 611-625.

Song, S. (2022). Cultural diversification, human resource-based coordination, and downside risks of multinationality. *Journal of Business Research, 142*, 562-571.

Soni, V. (2000). A twenty-first-century reception for diversity in the public sector: a case study. *Public Administration Review, 60*(5), 395-408.

Steurer, R. (2006). Mapping stakeholder theory anew: from the 'stakeholder theory of the firm' to three perspectives on business–society relations. *Business Strategy and the Environment, 15*(1), 55-69.

Syed, J., & Ozbilgin, M. (2009). A relational framework for international transfer of diversity management practices. *The International Journal of Human Resource Management, 20*(12), 2435-2453.

Tatli, A., Vassilopoulou, J., Ariss, A. A., & Ozbilgin, M. (2012). The role of regulatory and temporal context in the construction of diversity discourses: The case of the UK, France and Germany. *European Journal of Industrial Relations, 18*(4), 293-308.

UN (2011). *Guiding Principles on Business and Human Rights: Implementing the UN "Protect, Respect and Remedy" Framework.* https://www.ohchr.org/sites/default/files/Documents/Publications/GuidingPrinciplesBusinessHR_EN.pdf

Van Tulder, R., Van Wijk, J., & Kolk, A. (2009). From chain liability to chain responsibility. *Journal of Business Ethics, 85*(2), 399–412.

Vasquez, E. A., & Frankel, B. (2017). The business case for global supplier diversity and inclusion: The critical contributions of women and other underutilized suppliers to corporate value chains. WeConnect International, Retrieved from https://weconnectinternational.org/images/Report.pdf

Vassilopoulou, J. (2017). Diversity management as window dressing? A company case study of a Diversity Charta member in Germany. In Management and Diversity: Perspectives from Different National Contexts (pp. 281-306). Emerald Publishing.

Verbeke, A., & Kano, L. (2016). An internalization theory perspective on the global and regional strategies of multinational enterprises. *Journal of World Business, 51*(1), 83-92.

Villadsen, A. R., & Wulff, J. N. (2018). Is the public sector a fairer employer? Ethnic Employment Discrimination in the public and private sectors. *Academy of Management Discoveries, 4*(4). https://doi.org/10.5465/amd.2016.0029

Waddock, S., & Smith, N. (2000). Relationships: The real challenge of corporate global citizenship. *Business and Society Review, 105*(1), 47-62.

Wadhwani, R. D. (2018). Poverty's monument: Social problems and organizational field emergence in historical perspective. *Journal of Management Studies, 55*(3), 545-577.

Weil, D., & Mallo, C. (2007). Regulating labour standards via supply chains: Combining public/private interventions to improve workplace compliance. *British Journal of Industrial Relations, 45*(4), 791-814.

Wettstein, F., Giuliani, E., Santangelo, G. D., & Stahl, G. K. (2019). International business and human rights: A research agenda. *Journal of World Business, 54*(1), 54-65,

Whelton, B. (1996). A philosophy of nursing practice: An application of the Thomistic Aristotelian concepts of nature to the science of nursing. Unpublished doctoral dissertation, The Catholic University of America, Washington, DC.

Williams, D. A. (2013). *Strategic Diversity Leadership: Activating Change and Transformation in Higher Education.* Stylus Publishing, LLC.

Yalkin, C., & Ozbilgin, M. F. (2022). Neo-colonial hierarchies of knowledge in marketing: Toxic field and illusio. *Marketing Theory, 22*(2), 191–209. https://doi.org/10.1177/14705931221075369

Yamahaki, C., & Frynas, J. G. (2016). Institutional determinants of private shareholder engagement in Brazil and South Africa: The role of regulation. *Corporate Governance: An International Review, 24*(5), 509–527.

Yin, R. K. (2003). Case study research: Design and methods (3e). Sage.

Zheng, W., Shen, R., Zhong, W., & Lu, J. (2020). CEO Values, Firm Long-Term Orientation, and Firm Innovation: Evidence from Chinese Manufacturing Firms. *Management and Organization Review, 16*(1), 69-106.

Chapter 14

Entrepreneurial Socio-Interculturality in Higher Education: A Case on a Postgraduate Program in Economics and International Business of an Indigenous University

José G. Vargas-Hernández

Instituto Tecnológico José Mario Molina Pasquel y Henríquez, Unidad Zapopan, Jalisco

Ernesto Guerra García

Autonomous Indigenous University of Mexico, México

Abstract: This chapter aims to elaborate on a critical assessment of socio-intercultural entrepreneurship. The study is supported by the assumption that culture and social entrepreneurship are limited and that it is necessary to have a framework analysis that helps improve the understanding of the socio-economic realities. The main elements of socio-intercultural entrepreneurship were found through a micro-ethnographic study in the 2017-2021 generation of an indigenous university's postgraduate program in economics. It is concluded that socio-intercultural entrepreneurship presents a methodological frame that allows entrepreneurs to perceive global and local realities significantly.

Keywords: Entrepreneurship, Socio-interculturalism, Interculturality

***

Introduction

In economic globalization, these socio-intercultural entrepreneurial interactions become inevitable in any business transaction and analysis. The study of international entrepreneurship is current in emerging economies (Kiss et al., 2012) and is a holistic organizational process that integrates the organization immersed in several cultures to explore opportunities in the international market and generate value (Dimitratos & Plakoyiannaki, 2003). However, socio-interculturalism in international entrepreneurship is a neglected issue not even explored, as it has been in social and intercultural entrepreneurship. In developing countries, social entrepreneurship activities are supported by those who promote social changes in politics and the media to solve social inequality, poverty, and environmental sustainability (Dey, 2006; Dacin et al., 2011).

The countries with the most excellent socio-intercultural entrepreneurial exchanges tend to have economic, trade and financial liberalization and integration policies. Various organizations and social networks support the contribution of social entrepreneurs to society, although the issue of intercultural social entrepreneurship is still neglected. Socio-intercultural entrepreneurship is a complex issue to study and analyze; however, it brings a framework for negotiation in global and international business, trade, and commerce.

This observation allows the transformation of the social and cultural entrepreneur into a new type of socio-intercultural entrepreneur whose main difference is having high visibility of the business in diversity context. In the first place, the study begins with the socio-intercultural concept to continue with the analysis of the relationship between social and cultural entrepreneurship to centre on socio-interculturalism entrepreneurship. From this point, a creative socio-intercultural entrepreneurship integration policy model is proposed. It is briefly exemplified by the case of the postgraduate program in the economy and international business of an indigenous university in Mexico, and finally, the analysis presents some concluding remarks.

The Socio-Intercultural Concept

In order to specify the socio-intercultural concept is necessary to start with Bourdieu (2007), who conceives that society is structured with two types of relationships: socials, the ones of *strength*, referring to the value of uses and changes and that encompasses entwined, other types of relationships such as the ones of *sense*, which are responsible for the organization of the relationships of meaning in social life; these last ones, in his perspective, are the ones that constitute culture. Society "is conceived as the ensemble of structures somewhat objectives that organize the distribution of the production media and power between individuals and social groups, and that determine social, economic and political practices" (García-Canclini, 2004, p. 32).

On the other hand, culture is the result of the interactions between society and nature through social processes of material and spiritual production. Culture manifests itself in the behavior of human beings that belong to the same culture. The cultural, intra-cultural, and intercultural processes are phenomena that the dynamics of societies cannot control; In other words, the cultural relationship between peoples as an equitable, congruent, responsible, and tolerant act is a noble intention and an elusive purpose. Furthermore, interculturalism and multiculturalism are polysemic concepts that have acquired different meanings and connotations depending on the context and policies of the welfare state (Vargas-Hernández et al., 2017). On this basis, it is understood that society and culture are two interrelated concepts. In an allusion that culture also refers to a collective, in a society, some cultures relate with each other (interculturality), but none of them is static and is modified within time (intracultural); even so, there are forces that affect all cultures (intra-social) and that impress that strength that Bordieau mentions.

The socio-interculturality concept goes beyond culturalistic postures that leave aside social power and economy-centered postures, where culture and its relationships are minimized. It refers to processes involving many variables in the continuous interrelation between societies that occur in violent opposition situations (Guerra-García, 2005, 2004a, 2004b). Socio-interculturalism is also a process that notices the intimate relationship between nature, society, and culture (Ochoa-Zazueta, 2006), which allows identifying the relationship of meanings as a fundamental component of other cultures, such as the indigenous worldview with understanding, explanation and where appropriate, the possession of assets that are required for the interaction of natural forces and that explain cultural practices.

Socio-interculturalism is the dynamic relationship that overcomes the history of modern politics in which the fight for equality was developed, but adding the consideration of differences, in other words, in this posture is considered what Touraine (2000) proposes, conjugating equality and difference in human coexistence. That brings together and interrelates several societies with their respective cultures in an indivisible socio-intercultural process (Figueroa-Rivera, 2016). This perspective connects social, cultural, genetic, psychological, and anthropological elements, with a focus on gender, ethnicity, culture and social class, inclusiveness of masculinity and femininity values and their power relations, in its search for symmetrical egalitarian interaction and in favor of the integration of the socio-cultures that coexist and cohabit in the same territorial space.

As Vargas-Hernández et al. (2017) have argued, the notion of intercultural citizenship is critical to interculturalism because it considers the differentiated rights of small groups and minorities in such a way that they are oriented to create the social cohesion that liberalism rejects. This notion of differentiated intercultural citizenship based on the individual and collective rights of native cultures is resumed in socio-interculturality. However, interculturality is just an aspect of socio-interculturality; studying reality comprehensively through culturalistic postures focusing only on interculturality and minimizing socio-economic aspects can bring naïve concepts about what is happening.

The socio-interculturalism implicit in welfare regimes should not be an institutionalized process of structural inter-social violence exercised by mono-cultural, hegemonic, colonialist, asymmetric and acculturating nationalist structures, but on the contrary, that favors the integration and assimilation of all minority cultures of society through the recognition of their rights and the development of a multicultural and poly-ethnic citizenship agenda that fosters social cohesion (Vargas-Hernández et al., 2017).

Socio-Intercultural Dynamics and Entrepreneurship

Entrepreneurship opportunities are perceived differently in diverse cultures, but this also depends on the economic opportunities that social forces present. The intercultural dynamic can be an interpretive framework relevant to any dimension of entrepreneurship that makes sense of the individuals' and groups' behavior and determines their attitudes. A specific culture supporting entrepreneurship can develop more potential and activities. However, more extensively, the socio-intercultural dynamic indicates the level of entrepreneurial behavior, opportunities and exploitation in the specific society. In any specific society, the socio-intra-cultural dynamic indicates how it is considered entrepreneurial behaviors such as innovativeness, risk-taking, opportunity recognition, growth orientation and exploitation.

If talking about a single national culture were possible, this could be defined in terms of shared values and practices in one country (House et al., 2004). Culture is related to entrepreneurial behavior at the individual level as a manifestation of belonging to a culture, but the intra-cultural, intercultural and intra-social dynamics influence, positively or negatively, the individual's behavior (Hayton et al., 2002). Some factors encourage or discourage entrepreneurial activity subject to the different countries, regions, and cultures, requiring further recognition of differences and their causes. Entrepreneurial activities are the action of individuals' collectivities innovating and taking risks. Harmful activities attached to entrepreneurship sometimes are inevitable transitional development that may not be well accepted and may foster anti-entrepreneurial values.

According to the current economic structure, social forces have oriented the individuals to generate an entrepreneurial attitude, but there are examples of collectivities that have taken their risks and generated ventures in a regional matter; for example, El Pochotal in El Fuerte, Sinaloa, a yoreme-mayo community whose women decided to elaborate an artisanal bread in the face of their husband's lack of work; this community have sold this product for over 50 years. Another example is the entrepreneurship of the Mennonites in Mexico, who produce cheese and other products and have successfully maintained themselves over hundreds of years.

The entrepreneurial culture can be driven by individuals and collectivities that exhibit entrepreneurial behaviors such as making decisions and having initiatives and actions to create new opportunities. Driving a culture of empowerment and entrepreneurship requires organizational commitment and encouraging individuals to become confident.

Culture influences the personal values and behaviors of individuals and groups related to people's practices in terms of intra-cultural dimensions relevant to entrepreneurship. The authors conclude that some cultural dimensions influence the creation of social entrepreneurial activities and are more involved in the social economy. The cultural dimensions proposed by anthropologists are related to cultural characteristics, an intercultural vision, and actions of social enterprises (Urbano et al., 2010; Dacin et al., 2011; Dey, 2006). But, more broadly, socio-intercultural elements, such as cultural values, entrepreneurial activity and the economic level of a country, can explain entrepreneurial activity (Jaén et al., 2013).

The intra-cultural and intercultural dynamics have a significant effect on entrepreneurial behavior and values. Comparing cultural values and entrepreneurial behavior can partially explain why some cultures are more sensitive, conducive, and supportive of entrepreneurship. On several occasions, a clash of cultural values between population and entrepreneur groups may drive self-employed into actual self-employment (Baum et al., 2007). In the broader sense, entrepreneurial behavior is incentivized in specific socio-intercultural dynamics in societies where a combination of individualism and collectivism promotes the creation of ideas and innovations of major social benefit.

Until today, capitalism has promoted individualism as the only entrepreneurial form. But, benefits to society have not been maximized, while collectivism, characteristic of cultures and ethnic groups in the current social structure, has not shown entrepreneurial effect but represents an option that could provide to society.

There is a difference between socio-intercultural entrepreneurship and cultural or social entrepreneurship. Social entrepreneurs can be cultural entrepreneurs and vice versa (Dacin et al., 2011). The social entrepreneur is committed to society, guided by innovative practices to solve social problems in diverse ways beyond the established margins (Dacin et al., 2011, Mitchell et al., 2007, Tracey et al., 2011; Gaglio, 2004). The emergence and development of the cultural entrepreneur have a purpose for their action, the creation of healthy habits with the creation of social value that, unlike social entrepreneurs, have a more excellent economic orientation in the market (Lounsbury & Glynn, 2001). Cultural entrepreneurs are oriented to change behaviors, mentalities, and attitudes using persuasive communication.

Recent research highlights social and cultural entrepreneurship differentiated by the purpose of their actions (Lounsbury & Glynn, 2001). While social entrepreneurs are oriented to systems and the market, cultural entrepreneurs are oriented to the creation of healthy habits and the promotion of values using persuasive communication to change attitudes, beliefs, and behaviors in the change of mentalities toward a better world. The cultural entrepreneur uses persuasive communication to influence each other to change behaviors, attitudes, and beliefs. Of course, these entrepreneurs can indistinctly assume social or cultural roles (Dacin et al., 2011), conforming to the circumstances and conditions that require it.

Social entrepreneurship creates value in society (Austin et al., 2003; Mair & Martí, 2006). The objective of social entrepreneurship is the creation of value through social innovation processes to solve problems in society (Urbano et al., 2010, Zadek & Thake, 1997; Austin et al., 2003; Harding, 2006). Social entrepreneurship solves social problems by developing innovative entrepreneurial activities that are directed to create a positive social impact with the reasonable obtaining of a financial profit. Social entrepreneurship works in its habitat without having geographical limits for its global growth in solving social problems. It goes beyond the social and cultural entrepreneurs and provides opportunities and resources across cultures.

Social entrepreneurs are characterized by the ability to recognize social value, create opportunities, and make decisions based on finding innovative solutions to social problems (Gaglio, 2004) through proactive actions that go beyond margins and assumption risk (Tracey et al., 2011; Sullivan et al., 2003). Social entrepreneurs focus on markets and systems, and the culture is oriented to change the mentalities of individuals.

Socio-intercultural entrepreneurs can understand intra-cultural, intercultural and intra-social dynamics to make decisions to benefit individually, culturally, and socially. They establish a relationship of respect and dialogue with the diversity of cultures that it recognizes as a complex enrichment process by collaborating in promoting values related to social plurality and diversity of gender, race, ethnicity, etc. Socio-intercultural and ethnic diversity, multiculturalism and interculturalism are a phenomenon and a constant historical fact in the development processes of human societies and cultures with differentiated specifications and conceptualizations in different contexts.

Socio-intercultural entrepreneurship is a notion beyond professional relationships in individuals from diverse cultures in which intercultural group relationships and contacts are relevant in plural societies and intercultural businesses and companies. The models that explain the socio-intercultural relations focus on the efficacy of the results (Kim 1989), centered on socio-intercultural communication and the complexity of adaptive processes of socio-intercultural relations between individuals, collectivities, and contexts. From a micro-social perspective, the content of the determinants of socio-intercultural relationships is structured around the reception of intra- and intergroup and interpersonal relationships.

An entrepreneur has the function of understanding socio-intercultural dynamics to reinforce and revolutionize the creation and production patterns by innovating, inventing, or proving a technical possibility to design, develop and produce a new product or an old one in a new process to provide new sources of materials and inputs, new organizational forms, etc. (Duarte & Ruiz, 2009). The entrepreneur develops the skills of visualization, conceptualization and implementation based on a leading foundation of emerging activities; and maintains communication and empathy with society to determine the skills required by the markets. The entrepreneurs must perform socio-intercultural entrepreneurial activities as a career option to achieve personal goals during socio-intercultural diversity.

Additionally, to play their role, entrepreneurs need social acceptance to legitimate their activities and access and control financial, material, and human resources to initiate new ventures (Backes–Gellner & Werner, 2007). The traditional role the entrepreneurs perform finds reasons to put their resources at risk and expose them to failure. The outcome of entrepreneurial activities depends on personal effort (Mueller & Thomas, 2001).

From a socio-intercultural perspective, entrepreneurs anticipate the problems by taking into account all the possible foreseeable pros and cons, the (private and social) costs involved in the activities, determining the equilibrium points of all the operations of the company, making decisions based on vital information and data analysis for strategic planning, the business plan with the initial investment required, finds financing sources, convince potential investors and take measures on the best time on cost control, price of products and services, sales planning, profits, etc.

The role of an entrepreneur is central to any new emergent business. They determine the worth of going into business and explain step by step the work process in manufacturing and production, the materials needed to be used, the machinery and equipment used, the time used and the responsible person to accomplish it.

Entrepreneurship is the attitude that an individual takes on objectives to advance new projects, innovating or adding value to existing businesses, products, and services. It is assumed as a tool of social technologies to achieve innovation and competitiveness, which fosters productive socio-organizational environments and consolidates the creation of companies that promote job creation in national, regional, and local contexts. Entrepreneurship is a tool that strengthens the social capital of citizens based on the satisfaction of their needs and the improvement of their quality of life (Peredo & McLean, 2006).

Due to the influence of socio-intercultural diversity, the entrepreneurial orientation is divided into risk-taking, innovation and positivity (Lumpkin & Dess, 1996). Its relationship with performance is influenced by contingent variables such as the organizational structure (Slevin & Covin, 1990), resources of the organization (Ostgaard & Birley, 1994), characteristics of the industry (Eisenhardt & Schoonhoven, 1990), culture (Stuart & Abetti, 1987), environment (Covin & Slevin, 1989) and strategy (Venkatraman, 1989). Performance orientation is the society encouraging and rewarding individuals for improvement based on the achievement and high quality of entrepreneurship (Hayton et al., 2002).

Cross-national socio-intercultural differences in entrepreneurial activities related to socio-economic, cultural, and psychological motives and values, the diversity of relationships, practices and activities are beyond the cultural economy, produced and embedded in small social groups and collectives, communities, ethnic and Aboriginal groups, minorities and social organizations, urban cultures, and subcultures making relevant contributions to socio-intercultural entrepreneurship.

A relevant factor that classifies the profile of the entrepreneurs is socio-intercultural sensitivity. Socio-interculturally sensitive people are based on accepting cultural differences and have the will to understand, appreciate and accept cultural differences (Vásquez et al., 2014). This sensitivity is enriched by the traditions, customs, beliefs, conceptions, values, and norms of each society in its place where it is interacting and is directly connected to the human abilities of each different inhabitant. However, it also generates an understanding of the cultural differences in the broader society where economic forces are ineludible.

Individually, emotional development is a vital capacity of entrepreneurs to strengthen their self-esteem and moral autonomy to make the best decisions from among several options that require evaluation processes regarding social responsibility and commitment to global sustainability (Del Solar,

2010). Socio-intercultural relationships and interactions between individuals from diverse cultures are factors that ramp up innovation, creativity, entrepreneurial activities and success at solving problems.

The diversity initiatives are related to the inclusion of different and divergent cultural subgroups and small groups not represented by the majority culture, which are not necessarily involved in achieving competitive advantages and more favorable results. One of these initiatives is that practicing socio-intercultural communication in international business is part of achieving success in your projects. It requires an open mind, without prejudice or paradigms, the ability to adapt to different environments and contexts, and the ability to integrate differentiated groups diversity in plural communities and with inclusive identities.

Organizational socio-intercultural diversity breeds entrepreneurship and innovation leveraged from diverse cultures, genders, ethnic backgrounds, and perspectives. Corporate socio-intercultural entrepreneurial diversity policies and programs at the workplace already emphasize ethical socio-intercultural values such as tolerance, loyalty, and solidarity. However, it is required more than that, an innovative approach to make innovative and creative solutions to create new business projects and ventures. In the management of social entrepreneurship, the valuations of the specificities of each culture and their diversity are considered to achieve the socio-intercultural objectives of multinational organizations.

Any entrepreneurial action, like starting a venture or establishing a business, is considered a means for generating self-employment and income and has critical socio-intercultural dimensions in entrepreneurship (Lounsbury & Glynn, 2001). The socio-intercultural vision of entrepreneurship is based on the analysis of the mentioned intra-cultural, intercultural and intra-social dynamics, which explain the intensity of the social practices of diverse cultures (Shane & Venkataraman, 2000; Schwartz, 1999). Cultural features favor the development of an area with Hofstede's cultural dimensions for social entrepreneurship with the performance of social economy activities (Hofstede, 2007). From a socio-intercultural perspective, they should be considered beyond the borders of their own culture, with a more global vision, considering social and environmental values and the satisfaction of needs that the economy cannot satisfy by itself. Socio-intercultural entrepreneurial management is beyond awareness, using different approaches, an understanding, and interactions of respect to differences in adjusting behaviors and attitudes within diverse socio-cultures in the global and international contexts. The analysis of social entrepreneurship can be done from a socio-intercultural management perspective based on the cultural characteristics of entrepreneurs that can be explained from cultural dimensions; that is, social entrepreneurship actions are examined from a socio-intercultural perspective, considering that culture explains human behavior (Hofstede, 2001).

Socio-intercultural entrepreneurship is a perspective that recognizes socio-intercultural features such as the cultural dimension of the distance of power between the entrepreneur and his followers and measures the interpersonal relationship to promote innovation (Hofstede, 2001). It influences patterns of thought and mindset as a response to solving problems at any level, space, activity, or process; it refers to the design, creation and development of business involving interactions and interrelationships between people from diverse cultures but considering social forces. It allows one to become self-aware and to step outside of the comfortable and usual cultural reference framework, gaining more perspective about the issues and avoiding internal struggles and external conflicts. Its development requires self-awareness for a frame-shifting of references and routines in thinking outside the box based on creativity and innovation.

The Socio-intercultural entrepreneur is oriented to solve social problems in his environment and add value to society in the cultural dimension of individualism-collectivism (Hofstede, 2001). Countries with high social entrepreneurship activity have a partially proven relationship showing a level of inclination to find innovative solutions (Sullivan et al., 2003; Tracey et al., 2011) but not thoroughly evaluating their social entrepreneurship activities and the socio-intercultural dimension.

The Socio-intercultural entrepreneur develops the capacities to recognize social value, make innovative decisions to create opportunities, be proactive, take risks (Sullivan, 2003) and conduct activities of social and cultural entrepreneurs and vice versa. It refers to competent entrepreneurs with a greater sense of self-efficacy who are more willing to engage in new experiences with goal setting in novel cross-cultural settings. The competencies configuration model allows for identifying and analyzing the socio-intercultural requirements of competent entrepreneurship in terms of the individuals, functions and activities that make up the socio-intercultural organizational system, the coordination of the components of the socio-technical system and the interdependence with the environment (Álvarez & Asunción, 2005).

Socio-Intercultural Entrepreneurship

The socio-intercultural entrepreneurship approach examines the variables of the social and cultural environments influencing the entrepreneur's behavior and personality, including the thinking and emotional processes in the interrelationships, contacts and connections with other people and social groups. These variables are gender, ethnicity, religion, and social class. According to the contact hypothesis elaborated by Allport (1955) and Pettigrew (1971), it is the nature of the socio-intercultural contact that generates favorable attitudes in intergroup behaviors to participate and cooperate in common goals in a climate of acceptance and support (Cook & Reichardt, 1986).

The operationalization of the socio-intercultural concept registers the relations of the encounter of societies and their cultures in the context of the reality of the interaction of society, culture, and nature. The dynamic interaction of socio-interculturalism manifests itself at the macro level in the economic, social, political, and cultural spheres and at the micro level in the interrelationships of gender, class, and ethnicity. However, the socio-intercultural approach is a multidimensional approach to the diversity of social classes, popular culture, technological tools, poverty, and problems of humanity, according to Guerra-García (2004b).

Socio-interculturalism for Guerra-García (2004b) is the source to derive principles that combine the social, technological, and economic in the face of diversity through the will and performance of each actor, individual or collective. The sense of individual and collective action that social actors construct based on socio-intercultural attributes delimits individual and community identities (Vargas-Hernández, 2005). An example of an analysis of socio-interculturalism is found in Guerra-García et al. (2020), who examined socio-intercultural dynamics of the Topolobampo colony, Sinaloa, Mexico, described the intercultural relations were the aspects of feminism, racism, discrimination, and the ideas of limited and utopian socialism, as well as the political intention and economy for the urban and agricultural development of the region.

Socio-intercultural dimensions of entrepreneurship refer to how diverse cultures are interrelated in societal organizations enhancing the various levels of entrepreneurial activities and contributing to competitiveness, economic growth, and job creation. It produces positive interactions between community members, whether at the diplomatic, academic, business or administration levels (Maldonado, 2007). Socio-socio-intercultural entrepreneurship facilitates individuals to consider multiple points of view and challenges to learning through communicative interactions about other cultures and avoiding the obstacles of an ethnocentric perspective. It is a two-way of sharing the burden of communication and responsibility of cultural awareness (Ferraro, 1994) to accommodate themselves to cultural practices.

Socio-intercultural entrepreneurship communication is supported by understanding the cultural elements that influence the socio-cultural interactions between individuals with diverse cultural backgrounds that impact the global business environment. According to Maheshkar & Sharma (2018, 2021), socio-cultural interaction involves a combination of social and cultural factors. The socio-interculturalism of entrepreneurs involves other people with diverse cultures that help to achieve the objectives of undertaking business in other countries, motivated to learn from other cultures beyond those with which language is shared that facilitate communication.

The socio-cultural theory explains individual mental functioning focusing on participation in social interactions and activities in social, cultural, historical, and institutional contexts. This theory stresses the interactions between people and culture in a socio-ecosystem environment. Sandoval et al. (2008) explain a case in which the socio-intercultural context creates tensions. Aboriginal students are forced to be absent intermittently from their studies at Mexico's Autonomous Indigenous University, requiring them to change its policies to adjust to the reality of its Aboriginal target population. He concludes that all exogenous causes come from intra-social, intercultural and socio-cultural dynamics in which the institution cannot have a decisive impact in the face of these social and cultural macro dynamics where the search for the culprits becomes idle.

The awareness of the socio-intercultural entrepreneurial process facilitates the communication and understanding processes between people from diverse cultural backgrounds in the context of effective interactions. Startup and pre-accelerator programs are based on facilitating socio-intercultural entrepreneurial relationships to create business and social outcomes from the facilitators' socio-cultural background experiences, innovation, and creativity.

Socio-interculturalism makes it possible to compare western and eastern cultural perspectives to conclude that at the level of societies, socio-interculturalism raises the existence of internal cultural relations and produces identities that after each unit that enters a coalition with the others becomes part of something more significant than the previous cultural configuration (Maheshkar & Sharma, 2021, 2018). The activities across borders of nations and regions are linked to differences in values and beliefs among diverse population groups and entrepreneurs. In this way, socio-interculturalism manifests itself as the reciprocal learning of the various ethnic groups and other human groups.

Materials and Methods

Through ethnographic work, we briefly describe the group of professors and students of the 2017-2021 generation of the postgraduate economics and international business postgraduate program of the indigenous university mentioned. The importance of these results aims to explain the socio-intercultural entrepreneurship proposed because of their interaction. From the methodological point of view, it is important to place ourselves at a specific level of observation; to get discursive elements oriented to explain socio-interculturality in practice. The study considers the historical space-time context in which this group developed to understand their positions better.

The method consisted of two fundamental aspects: 1) the ethnographic practice centered on fieldwork, and 2) anthropological reflection, centered on desk work. As it is mentioned by Restrepo (2016), ethnography emphasizes the description of and situated interpretations. It offers a description of several aspects of social life, taking into consideration the meanings associated with the specific actors.

More specifically, we performed a microehtnography, which is centered on the analysis of patterns with which the members of the community interact; from there, we focused our attention on the identification and characterization of the group of professors and the students' group, without aspiring to have the scope of the ethnography, given that, instead of trying to analyze the phenomenon from a holistic standpoint, we studied the interactional situations according to the object of study.

Program in Economics and International Business

At the Autonomous Indigenous University of Mexico (UAIM, in Spanish), a postgraduate program in the economy and international business was created. As a social institution, it is sensitive to students from different ethnic groups and young people with limited economic resources in the country, so the program creation may seem strange.

UAIM was born in 2001 in the yoreme-mayo ethnoregion (one of the autochthonous ethnic groups of the country), but it brings attention to yaqui, raramuri, ch'ol, tzotzil and tzeltal students to name some of the over twenty-five Indigenous groups where the students come from. It is part of the intercultural universities of the country. Because of its nature, culturalistic postures have tried to orient the curricula to attend only cultural aspects such as languages and indigenous tourism, but UAIM's socio-intercultural posture is that there exist social aspects that go beyond the cultures, international understanding, international business, information technologies and communication; they are matters of a wider society where the cultures are immersed. That is why the economy and international business program and other academic programs such as accounting and computational systems engineering are offered.

The program offers the advantage of positioning in a local and international intercultural context in a way that intercultural competencies are acquired during daily coexistence; furthermore, entrepreneurship's problems, which are themes of the academic program, are discussed in relation to the participating cultures and the difficulties of the Mexican and global society.

The Professor's Perspective

The professors who are mestizos have studied in different national institutions and are concerned with two things: 1) the critical analysis of management theories in terms of their adaptation to the intercultural contexts of companies in Mexico and 2) the acquisition of tools and technologies so that students can compete in the international arena, either as researchers or entrepreneurs in transnational companies.

In the courses, the cultural change of Mexicans is promoted as a background, not only in the sense of having more excellent order and a better structure in their activities, aspects such as teamwork, leadership, empowerment, and organizational climate have become cultural repertoires that try to adapt and adopt from the mono-cultural proposals that promote them to a kind of methodological syncretism. Also, the idea shared is to generate entrepreneurs in the locality who see for themselves and promote employment and socio-economic growth.

By having the profile of an indigenous university, ethnicity acquires greater relevance, and each topic seen in class is problematized since interculturality in Mexico has reached a constitutional category.

The Student Perspective

Mestizo and Indigenous students, who are university professors and businesspeople, are there to improve their economic situation through social mobility that weakly allows doctoral credentialing. Micro-entrepreneurs seek training in management methodologies that allow them to grow their companies. The idea of the students is to open opportunities in the international arena but at the same time improve the conditions of their current context; for this reason, they develop projects with a nuance of social benefit.

Some differences between mestizo and Indigenous students are reflected in their inter-relationships. The formers have a better academic language and a more fabulous vocation for social and community work. Most do not have English proficiency, so it represents a more significant challenge despite their intention to internationalize. On the other hand, some of the mestizos are micro-entrepreneurs and have had the opportunity to practice the knowledge they have acquired.

Socio-Interculturality is a concept that allows observing the dynamics in this educational program – 1) the intra-social aspects that go beyond culture, the macro-economy, the international institutions, and TICS; 2) generate adaptive changes in students who come from other cultures, in other words, intra-cultural changes are provoked to generate adaptation to emergent environments; likewise, interchanges are generated between students that come from different cultures, in other words, intercultural relations favor educational dynamics.

Also, the understanding that the place, which is part of international negotiation, requires understanding the intra-cultural dynamics is reinforced. In other words, what happens inside each culture, the intercultural, the relationship between them and the intra-socials, and the economic forces that go beyond cultures. Therefore, economic aspects must be considered, and the present cultural forces should be explained to fulfill the established objectives.

There is an intra-cultural dynamic in the Indigenous students of this program that comes from their interest in learning management and negotiating online with an international reach; that is why it is a mistake to see these groups as static. Most Indigenous communities in Mexico have not economically developed because indigenous politics have tried to maintain their population in poverty despite all the political speeches. The intercultural interchange in the program has been between Indigenous and non-Indigenous people, and between entrepreneurs and non-entrepreneurs, who have enriched the themes and thesis addressed.

The program tries to incorporate students from the lowest economic levels, so they can understand the global economy and manage ventures with international business in the International Labor Market. Socio-intercultural sensibility is a strength since each of them belongs to cultures and communities and can understand local and global dynamics.

Conclusion

The value of socio-intercultural entrepreneurial interactions results in new businesses, ventures, projects, products, and markets meeting the needs of people. Entrepreneurial activities require support programs designed and implemented based on the specific intra-cultural, intercultural and intra-social dynamics of the environment, as confirmed.

The increasing global business transactions require developing new forms of socio-socio-intercultural entrepreneurship, such as multinational strategic alliances and joint ventures. The entrepreneur needs to understand and practice socio-interculturalism in internationalization processes to develop the ability to break down the barriers that exist between the various cultures of the world.

The relationship between innovation and social entrepreneurship has been partially proven from a socio-intercultural perspective, as confirmed by Sullivan et al. (2003) and Tracey et al. (2011). However, the relationship between the cultural dimension and social economy activities has not been proven. Nevertheless, it can be concluded that economies with social activities show a high degree of innovation.

The relationship between the cultural dimension and the activity of the social economy is not proven. The cultural dimensions have relationships with the entrepreneurship orientation and its behaviors, although the entrepreneurial practices may vary in diverse cultures in such a way that the same entrepreneurial practices may be successful in one culture but dysfunctional in other.

An academic program in the economy and international business is an excellent example of socio-interculturality. Intra-social forces are found explicit in the intention of looking into economic knowledge and international business; in the program, students from very diverse Latin-American ethnic groups where relationships between their cultures are promoted (the interculturality) can participate, but at the same time, this dynamic provokes changes, not only from the individuals who participate in the program but in the communities where they come.

The intra-cultural, intercultural and intra-social dynamics allow understanding of what happens in a determined business context and help the socio-intra-cultural entrepreneur be more assertive at making decisions. Socio-intercultural entrepreneurship presents a methodological frame to understand the society in which the enterprise is immersed and to take more proactive decisions, not only for the enterprise's benefit but also to maximize social benefits and minimize environmental damage.

References

Allport, G.W. (1955). Becoming: Basic Consideration for a Psychology of Personality. New Haven, Yale University Press.

Álvarez, A., & Asunción. A. (2005) Competencias interculturales transversales en la empresa: un modelo para la detección de necesidades formativas. https://www.tdx.cat/handle/10803/2343#page=1

Austin, J., Stevenson, H. & Wei-skillern, J. (2003). Social Entrepreneurship and Commercial Entrepreneurship: Same, Different, or Both? Working Paper Series, No. 04-029, Harvard Business School.

Backes–Gellner U., & Werner A. (2007). Entrepreneurial Signaling via education: success factor in innovative start-ups. Small Business Economics, 29(2), 173–190. https://doi.org/10.1007/s11187-006-0016-9

Baum, J. R., Frese, M., Baron, R. A., & Katz, J. A. (2007). Entrepreneurship as an area of psychology study: an introduction. In The Psychology of Entrepreneurship, 1-18.

Bourdieu, P. (2007). El Sentido Práctico. Siglo XXI.

Cook, T. D., & Reichardt, C. S. (1986). Métodos cualitativos y cuantitativos en la investigación educativa. Morata.

Covin, J. G., & Slevin, D. P. (1989). Strategic management of small firms in hostile and benign environments. Strategic Management Journal, 10(1), 75-87. https://doi.org/10.1002/smj.4250100107

Dacin, M.T., Dacin, D.A., & Tracey, P. (2011). Social Entrepreneurship: A Critique and Future Directions, Organization Science, 22(5), 1203-1213.

Del Solar, S. (2010). Emprendedores en el aula. Guía para la formación en valores y habilidades sociales de docentes y jóvenes emprendedores. Fondo Multilateral de Inversiones del Banco Interamericano de Desarrollo.

Dey, P. (2006). The rhetoric of social entrepreneurship: Paralogy and new language games in academic discourse. In Steyaert, C. & Hjorth, D. (eds.), Entrepreneurship as Social Change. Edward Elgar. https://doi.org/10.4337/9781847204424.00015

Dimitratos, P. & Plakoyiannaki, E. (2003). Theoretical foundations of an international entrepreneurial culture. *Journal of International Entrepreneurship*, 1(2), 187-215. https://doi.org/10.1023/A:1023804318244

Duarte, T. & Ruiz, M. (2009). Emprendimiento, una opción para el desarrollo. Scienta Et Technica, 15(43), 326-331.

Eisenhardt, K. M., & Schoonhoven, C. B. (1990). Organizational growth: linking founding team, strategy, environment, and growth among us semiconductor ventures, 1978-1988. Administrative Science Quarterly, 35(3), 504-529.

Ferraro, G. P. (1994). The cultural dimension of international business. Prentice Hall.

Figueroa-Rivera, A. N. (2016). Antología de antropología social. Unideal Universidad Matías Romero de Avendaño, Oaxaca.

Gaglio, C. M. (2004). The role of mental simulations and counterfactual thinking in the opportunity identification process. Entrepreneurship Theory Practice, 28(6), 533–552. https://doi.org/10.1111/j.1540-6520.2004.00063.x

García-Canclini, N. (2004). Diferentes, desiguales y desconectados: mapas de la interculturalidad. Gedisa.

Guerra-García, E. (2004). La sociointerculturalidad y la educación indígena, en Eduardo Andrés Sandoval Forero y Manuel Antonio Baeza (coords.). Cuestión étnica, culturas, construcción de identidades, México: Universidad Autónoma Indígena de México, Asociación Latinoamericana de Sociología y ediciones el Caracol.

Guerra-García, E. (2005). La Anerogogía de la Voluntad, propuesta educativa sociointercultural de la Universidad Autónoma Indígena de México. Ra Ximhai, 1(1), 15-38.

Guerra-García, E., Caro-Dueñas, M. A., Corrales-Baldenebro A. L., (2020). Dinámica sociointercultural del surgimiento del puerto de Topolobampo en México. Revista CoPaLa, Construyendo Paz Latinoamericana, 10(5), 102-125. https://doi.org/10.35600.25008870.2020.10.0174

Harding, R. (2006). Social Entrepreneurship Monitor, London Global Entrepreneurship Monitor. Google Scholar. https://scholar.google.com/citations?user=IKAsBdIAAAAJ&hl=en

Hayton, J.C., George, G., & Zahra, S.A. (2002). National culture and entrepreneurship: A review of behavioral Research. Entrepreneurship Theory and Practice, 26(4), 33–52.

Hofstede, G. (2001). Cultures and Organizations. Software of the Mind. McGraw-Hill.

Hofstede, G. (2007). Geert Hofstede Cultural Dimensions. www.geert-hofstede.com

House R., Hanges P., Javidan M., & Dorfman P. (2004). Culture, Leadership and Organizations: the GLOBE Study of 62 Societies. Sage.

Jaén I., Fernandez-Serrano J., & Liñan, F. (2013). Valores culturales, nivel de ingresos y actividad emprendedora. Revista de Economía Mundial, 35, 35-52.

Kim, Y. (1989). Intercultural Adaptation. In Asante, M. K. & Gudykunst, W. (Eds.), Handbook of International and Intercultural Communication (pp. 275-294). Sage.

Kiss, A. N., Danis, W. N, & Cavusgil, S. T. (2012). International entrepreneurship research in emerging economies: A critical review and research agenda. Journal of Business Venturing, 27(2), 266-290. https://doi.org/10.1016/j.jbusvent.2011.09.004

Lounsbury, M., & Glynn, M.A. (2001). Cultural entrepreneurship: Stories, legitimacy, and the acquisition of resources. Strategic management journal, 22(6-7), 545-564. https://doi.org/10.1002/smj.188

Lumpkin, G.T. & Dess, G.G. (1996). Clarifying the entrepreneurial orientation construct and linking it to performance. Academy of Management Review, 21(1), 135–172. https://doi.org/10.2307/258632

Maheshkar, C., & Sharma, V. (2018) (Eds.). Cross-cultural Business Education: Leading Businesses around the Cultures. In Handbook of Research on Cross-Cultural Business Education (pp. 1-35). IGI Global. https://doi.org/10.4018/978-1-5225-3776-2.ch001

Maheshkar, C., & Sharma, V. (2021) (Eds.). Cross-cultural Business Education: Leading Businesses around the Cultures. In Research Anthology on Business and Technical Education in the Information Era (pp. 677-711). Business Science Reference. https://doi.org/10.4018/978-1-7998-5345-9.ch038

Mair, J. & Martí, I. (2006). Social entrepreneurship research: A source of explanations, prediction, and delight. Journal of World Business, 41(1), 36-44. https://doi.org/10.1016/j.jwb.2005.09.002

Maldonado, K. (2007). La interculturalidad de los negocios internacionales. Universidad Empresa Bogotá (Colombia), 6(12), 261-291.

Mitchell, R.K., Busenitz, L.W., Bird, B., Marie Gaglio, C., Mcmullen, J.S., Morse, E.A., & Smith, J.B. (2007). The central question in entrepreneurial cognition research 2007, Entrepreneurship Theory and Practice, 31(1), 1-27. https://doi.org/10.1111/j.1540-6520.2007.00161.x

Mueller, S. L., & Thomas, A. S., (2001). Culture and entrepreneurial potential: A nine country study of locus of control and innovativeness, Journal of Business Venturing, 16(1), 51-75. https://doi.org/10.1016/S0883-9026(99)00039-7

Ochoa-Zazueta, J. Á. (2006) *Entrevista personal.* Los Mochis, Sinaloa, mayo marzo 16.

Ostgaard, T. A., & Birley, S. (1994). Personal networks and firm competitive strategy: a strategic or coincidental match? Journal of Business Venturing, 9(4), 281-305. https://doi.org/10.1016/0883-9026(94)90009-4

Peredo, A. M., & Mclean, M. (2006). Social entrepreneurship: A critical review of the concept. Journal of World Business, 41(1), 56-65. https://doi.org/10.1016/j.jwb.2005.10.007

Pettigrew, T.F. (1971). Racial separate or together? McGraw-Hill.

Restrepo, E. (2016). El proceso de investigación etnográfica: consideraciones éticas. Etnografías contemporáneas, 1(1). http://revistasacademicas.unsam.edu.ar/index.php/etnocontemp/article/view/395

Sandoval-Forero, E. A., Guerra-García, E., & Delgado-Buelna, R. A. (2008). Una visión sociointercultural del ausentismo intermitente de yoremes y mestizos en la UAIM. Tiempo de Educar, 9 (17), 9-34.

Schwartz, S.H. (1999). A Theory of Cultural Values and Some Implications for Work. Applied Psychology: An International Review, 48(1), 23-47.

Shane S. and Venkataraman S. (2000). The promise of entrepreneurship as a field of research. The Academy Management Review, 25(1), 217–226. https://doi.org/10.2307/25927

Slevin, D. P., & Covin, J. G. (1990). New venture strategic posture, structure, and performance: an industry life cycle analysis. Journal of Business Venturing, 5(2), 123-135. https://doi.org/10.1016/0883-9026(90)90004-D

Stuart, R., & Abetti, P. A. (1987). Start-up ventures: towards the prediction of initial success. Journal of Business Venturing, 2(3), 215-230. https://doi.org/10.1016/0883-9026(87)90010-3

Sullivan, G., Weerawardena, J., & Carnegie, K. (2003). Social entrepreneurship: Towards conceptualization. International Journal of Nonprofit and Voluntary Sector Marketing, 8(1), 76-88. https://doi.org/10.1002/nvsm.202

Thompson, J. L. (2002). The world of the social entrepreneur. International Journal of Public Sector Management, 15(5), 412-431. https://doi.org/10.1108/09513550210435746

Touraine, A. (2000). Igualdad y diversidad: las nuevas tareas de la democracia. Fondo de Cultura Económica.

Tracey, P., Phillips, N., & Jarvis, O. (2011). Bridging institutional entrepreneurship and the creation of new organizational forms: a multilevel model. Organization Science, 22(1), 60-80.

Urbano, D., Toledano, N., & Soriano, D. R. (2010). Analyzing social entrepreneurship from an institutional perspective: evidence from Spain. Journal of social entrepreneurship, 1 (1), 54-69. https://doi.org/10.1080/19420670903442061

Vargas-Hernández, J. G. (2005). Emergencia de la nueva cultura institucional: impacto en la transformación del escenario de la globalización económica. Economía, Sociedad y Territorio, 5(17), 27-61.

Vargas-Hernández, J. G., Guerra García, E., & Valdez Zepeda (2017). La nueva gobernanza instrumental del estado de bienestar: transformaciones y retos. Editorial Universitaria: Universidad de Guadalajara, Centro Universitario de Ciencias Económico Administrativas, Guadalajara, Jalisco.

Vásquez, O., Fernández, M., & Álvarez, P. (2014). La aportación de los grados al desarrollo de la sensibilidad y competencia intercultural. Perspectiva comparada entre Trabajo Social y Psicología Revista: Cuadernos de Trabajo Social, 27(2), 307-317.

Venkatraman, N. (1989). The concept of fit in strategy research: toward verbal and statistical correspondence. The Academy of Management Review, 1(3), 423-444. https://doi.org/10.2307/258177

Zadek, S. & Thake, S. (1997): Practical people, noble causes. How to support community-based social entrepreneurs. New Economics Foundation, London.

Bibliography

Abdelkafi, N. & Täuscher, K. (2016). Business models for sustainability from a system dynamics perspective. Organization & Environment, 29, 74-96. https://doi.org/10.1177/1086026615592930

Abdelzaher, D., Fernandez, W. D., & Schneper, W. D. (2019). Legal rights, national culture and social networks: Exploring the uneven adoption of United Nations Global Compact. International Business Review, 28(1), 12-24.

Ābeltiņa, A., & Rizhamadze, K. (2021). Challenges to Managing Virtual Teams in Georgian SMEs. SHS Web of Conferences, 119, 03003. https://doi.org/10.1051/shsconf/202111903003

Abrar, P. (2021, July 8). E-commerce firm DealShare's valuation crosses $455 mn after raising $144 mn. Businessstandard.Com. Retrieved March 2, 2022, from https://www.business-standard.com/article/companies/e-commerce-firm-dealshare-s-valuation-crosses-455-mn-after-raising-144-mn-121070800679_1.html

Abugre, J. B. (2018). Cross-cultural communication imperatives: critical lessons for western expatriates in multinational companies (MNCs) in Sub-Saharan Africa. Critical Perspectives on International Business, 14(2/3), 170–187.

Abugre, J. B., & Debrah, Y. A. (2019). Assessing the impact of cross-cultural communication competence on expatriate business operations in multinational corporations of a Sub-Saharan African context. International Journal of Cross Cultural Management, 19(1), 85-104.

Acosta, O., & Gonzalez, J. I. (2010). A Themodynamic Approach for the Emergence of Globalization. In Deng, K. G. (Ed.), Globalization - Today, Tomorrow. IntechOpen. https://doi.org/10.5772/10223

Acquier, A., Valiorgue, B., & Daudigeos, T. (2017). Sharing the shared value: A transaction cost perspective on strategic CSR policies in global value chains. Journal of Business Ethics, 144(1), 139-152.

Acs, Z.J., Estrin, S., Mickiewicz, T. & Szerb, L. (2018). Entrepreneurship, institutional economics, and economic growth: an ecosystem perspective. Small Business Economics, 51, 501–514. https://doi.org/10.1007/s11187-018-0013-9

Adamovic, M. (2018). An employee-focused human resource management perspective for the management of global virtual teams. The International Journal of Human Resource Management, 29(14), 2159-2187. https://doi.org/10.1080/09585192.2017.1323227

Adeoye, B. & Tomei, L. (2014). Effects of information capitalism and globalization on teaching and learning. IGI Global. https://doi.org/10.4018/978-1-4666-6162-2

Adler, N. J., & Aycan, Z. (2018). Cross-cultural interaction: What we know and what we need to know. Annual Review of Organizational Psychology and Organizational Behavior, 5, 307-333.

Admin-Demo. (2021). Social Commerce – the virtual shopping stroll with friends. Just Style. Retrieved October 12, 2021, from https://www.just-style.com/comment/social-commerce-the-virtual-shopping-stroll-with-friends.

Aguilera, R. V., & Jackson, G. (2003). The cross-national diversity of corporate governance: Dimensions and determinants. Academy of Management Review, 28(3), 447-465.

Ahmed, S., & Swan, E. (2006). Doing Diversity. Policy Futures in Education, 4(2), 96–100. doi: 10.2304/pfie.2006.4.2.96

Alchon, G. (1992). Mary Van Kleeck and Scientific Management. In Nelson, D. (Ed.), A mental revolution: scientific management since Taylor (pp. 102-129). Ohio State University Press.

Alexander, A., Smet, A. De, & Mysore, M. (2020). Reimagining the postpandemic workforce. McKinsey Quarterly. Retrieved from https://www.mckinsey.com/business-functions/organization/our-insights/reimagining-the-postpandemic-workforce

Alfarran, A., Pyke, J. and Stanton, P. (2018). Institutional barriers to women's employment in Saudi Arabia. Equality, Diversity and Inclusion, 37(7), 713-727.

Allport, G.W. (1955). Becoming: Basic Consideration for a Psychology of Personality. New Haven, Yale University Press.

Al-Mashari, M. (2002). Electronic commerce: A comparative study of organizational experiences. Benchmarking: An International Journal.

Alon, I., Boulanger, M., Elston, J. A., Galanaki, E., Martínez de Ibarreta, C., Meyers, J., Muñiz-Ferrer, M., Vélez-Calle, A. (2018). Business cultural intelligence quotient: A five-country study. Thunderbird International Business Review, 60(3), 237–250. https://doi.org/10.1002/tie.21826

Alon, I., Boulanger, M., Meyers, J., Taras, V., Tung, R., & Ralston, D. (2016). The development and validation of the business Cultural Intelligence Quotient. Cross Cultural and Strategic Management, 23(1), 78–100. https://doi.org/10.1108/CCSM-10-2015-0138

Álvarez, A., & Asunción. A. (2005) Competencias interculturales transversales en la empresa: un modelo para la detección de necesidades formativas. https://www.tdx.cat/handle/10803/2343#page=1

Álvarez-Figueroa, F., Queupil, J. P., & Díaz, D. A. (2022). The discovery of diversity in Chile: a review of legislation and research concerning equality, inclusion and diversity management. Research Handbook on New Frontiers of Equality and Diversity at Work.

American Speech-Language-Hearing Association. (2010). Cultural competence checklist: Personal reflection. http://www.asha.org/uploadedFiles/Cultural-Competence-Checklist-Personal-Reflection.pdf

Amichai-Hamburger, Yair, Galit Wainapel, and Shaul Fox. "On the Internet no one knows I'm an introvert": Extroversion, neuroticism, and Internet interaction." Cyberpsychology & behavior 5, no. 2 (2002): 125-128.

Amit, R. & Zott, C. (2015). Crafting business architecture: The antecedents of business model design. Strategic Entrepreneurship Journal, 9, 331-350. https://doi.org/10.1002/sej.1200

Anand, P. K. K. (2014). Cross cultural diversity in today's globalized era. Journal of Human Resource Management, 2(6-1), 12-16.

Anawati, D., & Craig, A. (2006). Behavioral adaptation within cross-cultural virtual teams. IEEE transactions on professional communication, 49(1), 44-56.

Ang, S., & Van Dyne, L. (2008). Conceptualization of cultural intelligence: Definition, distinctiveness, and nomological network. In S. Ang, & L. Van Dyne (Eds.), Handbook of cultural intelligence: Theory, measurement, and applications (pp. 3–15). Sharpe.

Ang, S., & Van Dyne, L. (2008). Handbook of cultural intelligence. M.E. Sharpe.

Ang, S., Van Dyne, L., & Koh, C. (2006). Personality Correlates of the Four-Factor Model of Cultural Intelligence. Group & Organization Management, 31(1), 100–123. https://doi.org/10.1177/1059601105275267

Ang, S., Van Dyne, L., & Rockstuhl, T. (2015). Cultural intelligence: Origins, conceptualizations, evolution, and methodological diversity. In M. J. Gelfand, C. Chiu, & Y. Hong (Eds.), The handbook of advances in culture and psychology (pp. 273–323). Oxford University Press.

Ang, S., Van Dyne, L., & Tan, M. L. (2011). Cultural intelligence. In R. J. Sternberg & S. B. Kaufman (Eds.), The Cambridge handbook of intelligence (pp. 582–602). Cambridge University Press.

Ang, S., Van Dyne, L., Koh, C., Ng, K. Y., Templer, K. J., Tay, C., & Chandrasekar, N. A. (2007). Cultural intelligence: Its measurement and effects on cultural judgment and decision making, cultural adaptation and task performance. Management and Organization Review, 3(3), 335–371. https://doi.org/10.111 1/j.1740-8784.2007.00082.x

Anttonen, M., Stenberg, P. D. E., & Karhu, M. S. A. (2018). Group Identification in the Context of Global Virtual Teams.

Appadurai, A. (1996). Modernity at Large: Cultural Dimensions of Globalization. University of Minnesota Press.

April, K. (2021). The narratives of racism in South Africa. In P. Daya., & K. April (Eds.), 12 lenses into diversity in South Africa (pp. 11-31). Randburg: KR Publishing.

April, K. & Dharani, B. (2021). Diversity and entrepreneurship in South Africa: Intersections and purposive collaboration. In K. April, & B. Zolfaghari (Eds.), Values-driven entrepreneurship and societal impact: Setting the agenda for entrepreneuring across (Southern) Africa (pp. 241-254). Randburg: KR Publishing.

Arend, R. J. (2013). The business model: Present and future—beyond a skeumorph. Strategic Organization, 11(4), 390–402. https://doi.org/10.1177/ 1476127013499636

Arensberg, C. M. (1972). Culture as Behavior: Structure and Emergence. Annual Review of Anthropology, 1(1), 1–27. https://doi.org/10.1146/annurev.an.01.10 0172.000245

Argandoña, A. (1998). The stakeholder theory and the common good. Journal of Business Ethics, 17(9-10), 1093-1102.

Arjoon, S., Turriago-Hoyos, A. and Thoene, U. (2018). Virtuousness and the Common Good as a Conceptual Framework for Harmonizing the Goals of the Individual, Organizations, and the Economy. Journal of Business Ethics, 147(1), 143-163.

Aupperle, K. E., & Karimalis, G.N. (2001). Using metaphors to facilitate cooperation and resolve conflict: Examining the case of Disneyland Paris. Journal of Change Management 2(1), 23-32. https://doi.org/10.1080/714042489

Austin, J., Stevenson, H. & Wei-skillern, J. (2003). Social Entrepreneurship and Commercial Entrepreneurship: Same, Different, or Both? Working Paper Series, No. 04-029, Harvard Business School.

Aycan, Z., Schyns, B., Sun, J., Felfe, J., & Saher, N. (2013). Convergence and divergence of paternalistic leadership: A cross-cultural investigation of prototypes. Journal of International Business Studies, 44, 962-969.

Aydin, O. T. (2012). The Impact of Theory X, Theory Y and Theory Z on Research Performance: An Empirical Study from A Turkish University. International Journal of Advances in Management and Economics,1(5), 24-31.

Baccaro, L., & Mele, V. (2012). Pathology of path dependency? The ILO and the challenge of new governance. ILR Review, 65(2), 195-224.

Backer, L. C. (2016). Shaping a global law for business enterprises: Framing principles and the promise of a comprehensive treaty on business and human rights. North Carolina Journal of International Law & Commercial Regulation, 42(2), 417-504.

Backes–Gellner U., & Werner A. (2007). Entrepreneurial Signaling via education: success factor in innovative start-ups. Small Business Economics, 29(2), 173–190. https://doi.org/10.1007/s11187-006-0016-9

Bailey, D., Faraj, S., Hinds, P., von Krogh, G., & Leonardi, P. (2019). Special Issue of Organization Science: Emerging Technologies and Organizing. Organization Science, 30(3), 642–646. https://doi.org/10.1287/orsc.2019.1299

Bair, J., & Palpacuer, F. (2012). From varieties of capitalism to varieties of activism: The antisweatshop movement in comparative perspective. Social Problems, 59(4), 522-543.

Baker, L. (2010). Metacognition, In, P. Peterson, E. Baker, & B. McGaw (Eds), International Encyclopedia of Education (3rd Ed) (pp. 204-210). Elsevier. https://doi.org/10.1016/B978-0-08-044894-7.00484-X.

Banaji, M. R., & Greenwald, A. G. (2013). Blind spot: Hidden biases of good people. Delacorte Press.

Barber, W., & Badre, A. (1998). Culturability: The merging of culture and usability. Proceedings of the 4th Conference on Human Factors and the Web, 7(4), 1-10. https://www.usj.edu.lb/moodle/stephane.bazan/obs_interculturelle/Barber%20and%20Badre.pdf

Bardhan, P. (1989). The new institutional economics and development theory: A brief critical assessment. World development, 1389-1395.

Barker, K., Day, C. R., Day, D. L., Kujava, E. R., Otwori, J., Ruscitto, R. A., Smith, A., & Xu, T. (2017). Global Communication and Cross-Cultural Competence: Twenty-First Century Micro-Case Studies. Global Advances in Business Communication, 6(1), 5.

Barner-Rasmussen, W., Ehrnrooth, M., Koveshnikov, A., & Mäkelä, K. (2014). Cultural and language skills as resources for boundary spanning within the MNC. Journal of International Business Studies, 45(7), 886-905.

Barsade, S. G., Ward, A. J., Turner, J. D., & Sonnenfeld, J. A. (2000). To your heart's content: A model of affective diversity in top management teams. Administrative science quarterly, 45(4), 802-836.

Barzel, Y. (1997). Economic Analysis of Property Rights. Cambridge: Cambridge University Press. https://doi.org/10.1017/CBO9780511609398

Basabe, N., & Ros, M. (2005). Cultural dimensions and social behavior correlates: Individualism-collectivism and power distance. International Review Social Psychology, 18(1), 189-225.

Baum, J. R., Frese, M., Baron, R. A., & Katz, J. A. (2007). Entrepreneurship as an area of psychology study: an introduction. In The Psychology of Entrepreneurship, 1-18.

Bauman, A. A., & Shcherbina, N. V. (2018). Millennials, technology, and cross-cultural communication. Journal of Higher Education Theory and Practice, 18(3), 75-85.

Baykut, S., Özbilgin, M. F., Erbil, C., Kamasak, R., & Baglama, S. (2021). The impact of hidden curriculum on international students in the context of a toxic triangle of diversity. The Curriculum Journal. https://doi.org/10.1002/curj.135

Bean, R. (2008). Cross-cultural training and workplace performance. National Centre for Vocational Education Research. https://files.eric.ed.gov/fulltext/ED503402.pdf.

Becerra, E. P., & Korgaonkar, P. K. (2009). Hispanics' information Search and Patronage Intentions Online. Journal of Electronic Commerce Research, 10(2).

Bennett, T. (2001). Differing Diversities: Transversal Study on the Theme of Cultural Policy and Cultural Diversity. Strasbourg: Council of Europe.

Bergh, R. V. D. & Plessis, Y. D. (2016). The Role of Cognitive and Meta-Cognitive Cultural Intelligence in The Adjustment Experiences of SIE Women. European Academy of Management, Paris.

Bernardo, A. B. I., & Presbitero, A. (2018). Cognitive flexibility and cultural intelligence: Exploring the cognitive aspects of effective functioning in culturally diverse contexts. International Journal of Intercultural Relations, 66, 12–21. https://doi.org/10.1016/j.ijintrel.2018.06.001

Berry, G. R. (2011). Enhancing effectiveness on virtual teams: Understanding why traditional team skills are insufficient. The Journal of Business Communication, 48(2), 186-206.

Bhargava, S. (2020). Virtuality and teams: Dealing with crises and catastrophes. Human Systems Management, 39(4), 537–547. https://doi.org/10.3233/HSM-201050

Bian, Y. & Shuai, M. (2020). Elective affinity between guanxi favouritism and market rationality: Guanxi circles as governance structure in China's private firms. Asia Pacific Business Review, 26(2), 149-168.

Bird, A.W., & Stevens, M.J. (2003). Toward an emergent global culture and the effects of globalization on obsolescing national cultures. Journal of International Management, 9(4), 395-407. https://doi.org/10.1016/j.intman.2003.08.003

Blanco-González, A., Del-Castillo-Feito, C., & Miotto, G. (2021). The influence of business ethics and community outreach on faculty engagement: the mediating effect of legitimacy in higher education. European Journal of Management and Business Economics, 30(3), 281-298. https://doi.org/10.11 08/EJMBE-07-2020-0182

Bocken, N. M. P., Rana, P., & Short, S. (2015). Value mapping for sustainable business thinking. Journal of Industrial and Production Engineering, 32, 67-81. https://doi.org/10.1080/21681015.2014.1000399

Boden, J. (2008). The Wall Behind China's Open Door: Towards Efficient Intercultural Management in China. ASP Editions.

Boele, R., Fabig, H., & Wheeler, D. (2001). Shell, Nigeria and the Ogoni. A study in unsustainable development: II. Corporate social responsibility and 'stakeholder management' versus a rights-based approach to sustainable development. Sustainable Development, 9(3), 121-135.

Boretti, A. (2020). Covid 19 impact on atmospheric CO_2 concentration. International Journal of Global Warming, 21(3), 317-323.

Bos, B., Faems, D., & Noseleit, F. (2017). Alliance concentration in multinational companies: Examining alliance portfolios, firm structure, and firm performance. Strategic Management Journal, 38(11), 2298-2309.

Bosnjak, M., Galesic, M., &Tuten, T. (2007). Personality determinants of online shopping: Explaining online purchase intentions using a hi- erarchical approach. Journal of Business Research, 60(6), 597–605.

Bourdieu, P. (2007). El Sentido Práctico. Siglo XXI.

Boykin, G. (2017, November 21). What Impact Does Culture Have on Market Strategy and Segmentation? Your Business. https://yourbusiness.azcentral. com/impact-culture-market-strategy-segmentation-26371.html

Broussard, M. (2018, January 30). Indian iPhone Users Discuss Apple's Poor Services Performance: 'Apple Maps is a Joke'. MacRumors. https://www.mac rumors.com/2018/01/30/indian-iphone-users-apple-maps

Bryman, A. (2003). McDonald's as a Disneyized Institution: Global Implications. American Behavioral Scientist, 47(2), 154–167. https://doi.org /10.1177/0002764203256181

Bryman, A. (2006). Global implications of McDonaldization and Disneyization. In G. Ritzer (Ed.), McDonaldization: The reader (pp. 319-325). Pine Forge Press.

Bucher, R. D. (2008). Building cultural intelligence (CQ): Nine megaskills. Pearson.

Buda, R., & Elsayed-Elkhouly, S. M. (1998). Cultural Differences between Arabs and Americans: Individualism-Collectivism Revisited. Journal of Cross-Cultural Psychology, 29(3), 487–492. https://doi.org/10.1177/002202219829 3006

Buengeler, C., Leroy, H., & De Stobbeleir, K. (2018). How leaders shape the impact of HR's diversity practices on employee inclusion. Human Resource Management Review, 28(3), 289-303.

Bulmer, S., & Buchanan-Oliver, M. (2004). Meaningless or meaningful? Interpretation and intentionality in post-modern communication. Journal of Marketing Communications, 10(1), 1-15.

Cai, S., & Xu, Y. (2008). Designing product lists for e-commerce: The effects of sorting on consumer decision making. Intl. Journal of Human–Computer Interaction, 24(7), 700-721.

Calabuig, V., Olcina, G., & Panebianco, F. (2018). Culture and team production. Journal of Economic Behavior & Organization, 149, 32–45. https://doi.org/10.1016/j.jebo.2018.03.004

Campbell, J. L. (2007). Why would corporations behave in socially responsible ways? An institutional theory of corporate social responsibility. Academy of Management Review, 32(3), 946-967.

Cao, J. & Huang, Q. (2004). System transition, management upgrade, and growth of private enterprises: Huafeng group corporation sample of Zhejiang Province. The Chinese Economy, 37(6), 7-27.

Cashmore, P. (2010, April 15). Group buying: A Billion-dollar web trend? CNN. Retrieved October 15, 2021, from http://www.cnn.com/2010/TECH/04/15/cashmore.group.buying/index.html.

Cavalcante, S., Kesting, P., & Ulhøi, J. (2011). Business model dynamics and innovation: (re)establishing the missing linkages. Management Decision, 49, 1327-1342. https://doi.org/10.1108/00251741111163142

CBS News (2003, September 11). Saudis Bust Barbie's 'Dangers'. CBS News. https://www.cbsnews.com/news/saudis-bust-barbies-dangers/

Central Vancouver Island Multicultural Society. (n.d.). Cultural competence self-assessment checklist. http://rapworkers.com/wp-content/uploads/2017/08/cultural-competence-selfassessment-checklist-1.pdf

Chakraborty, J. (2013). Cross Cultural Design Considerations in HealthCare. In: Kurosu, M. (eds.) Human-Computer Interaction. Applications and Services (pp. 13-19). Springer. https://doi.org/10.1007/978-3-642-39262-7_2

Chamakiotis, P., Panteli, N., & Davison, R. M. (2021). Reimagining e-leadership for reconfigured virtual teams due to Covid-19. International Journal of Information Management, 60, 102381.

Chen, A. S. (2015). International Journal of Intercultural Relations CQ at work and the impact of intercultural training: An empirical test among foreign laborers. International Journal of Intercultural Relations, 47, 101–112. https://doi.org/10.1016/j.ijintrel.2015.03.029

Chen, C., Li, Z., Su, X., & Sun, Z. (2011). Rent-seeking incentives, corporate political connections, and the control structure of private firms: Chinese evidence. Journal of Corporate Finance, 17, 229-243.

Chen, M. (Ed.). (1995). Asian management systems. Routledge.

Cheng, B., Chou, L., Wu, T., Huang, M. & Farh, J. (2004). Paternalistic leadership and subordinate responses: Establishing a leadership model in Chinese organizations. Asian Journal of Social Psychology, 7(1), 89-117.

Cheng, H. H., & Huang, S. W. (2013). Exploring antecedents and consequence of online group-buying intention: An extended perspective on theory of planned behavior. International Journal of Information Management, 33(1), 185-198.

Cherry, M. A. (2010). A Taxonomy of Virtual Work. Georgia Law Review, 45(4), 951.

Chikere, H. & Jude, N. (2015). The Systems Theory of Management in Modern Day Organizations - A Study of Aldgate Congress Resort Limited Port. International Journal of Scientific and Research Publications, 5(9).

Chin, J. L. (2013). Diversity leadership: Influence of ethnicity, gender, and minority status. Open Journal of Leadership, 2(01), 1.

Chiou, A. Y., & Mercado, B. K. (2016). Flexible Loyalties: How Malleable Are Bicultural Loyalties? Frontiers in Psychology, 7(DEC), 1–8. https://doi.org/10.3389/fpsyg.2016.01985

Chua, R. Y. J., Morris, M. W., & Mor, S. (2012). Collaborating across cultures: Cultural metacognition and affect-based trust in creative collaboration. Organizational Behavior and Human Decision Processes, 118(2), 179–188. https://doi.org/10.1016/j.obhdp.2012.03.005

Chuang, Y., Church, R., & Zikic, J. (2004). Organizational culture, group diversity and intra-group conflict. Team Performance Management: An International Journal, 10(1/2), 26–34. https://doi.org/10.1108/13527590410527568

Clark, L., Birkhead, A. S., Fernandez, C., & Egger, M. J. (2017). A Transcription and Translation Protocol for Sensitive Cross-Cultural Team Research. Qualitative Health Research, 27(12), 1751–1764. https://doi.org/10.1177/1049732317726761

Clarke, T., & Boersma, M. (2017). The governance of global value chains: Unresolved human rights, environmental and ethical dilemmas in the Apple supply chain. Journal of Business Ethics, 143(1), 111–131.

Clayton, J. (2020). Multiculturalism. In Kobayashi, A. (Ed.), International Encyclopedia of Human Geography (2e) (pp. 211-219). Elsevier. https://doi.org/10.1016/B978-0-08-102295-5.10296-3

Clean Clothes Campaign (2020). Live-blog: How the Coronavirus affects garment workers in supply chains. Available at: https://cleanclothes.org/news/2020/live-blog-on-how-the-coronavirus-influences-workers-in-supply-chains (May 2020).

CNNIC. (n.d.). Retrieved October 15, 2021, from http://www.cnnic.cn/hlwfzyj/hlwxzbg/dzswbg/201208/P020120827473850053431.pdf.

Coase, R., & Wang, N. (2012). How China become Capitalist. Palgrave Macmillan.

Cobb, J. A. (2016). How firms shape income inequality: Stakeholder power, executive decision making, and the structuring of employment relationships. Academy of Management Review, 41(2), 324-348.

Colbert, A., Yee, N., & George, G. (20160. The digital workforce and the workplace of the future. Academy of management journal, 59(3), 731-739.

Conerly, T. R., Holmes, K., & Tamang, A. L. (2021). Introduction to Sociology (3e). OpenStax.

Congden, S. W., Matveev, A. V., & Desplaces, D. E. (2009). Cross-cultural Communication and Multicultural Team Performance: A German and American Comparison. Journal of Comparative International Management, 12(2), 73–89.

Connaughton, S. L., & Shuffler, M. (2007). Multinational and Multicultural Distributed Teams: A Review and Future Agenda. Small Group Research, 38(3), 387–412. https://doi.org/10.1177/1046496407301970

Cook, T. D., & Reichardt, C. S. (1986). Métodos cualitativos y cuantitativos en la investigación educativa. Morata.

Cooke, B. (2003). The denial of slavery in management studies. Journal of Management Studies, 40(8), 1895-1918. https://doi.org/10.1046/j.1467-6486.2 003.00405.x

Cooke, F. L. & Kim, S. (2018). Human Resource Management in Asia in the Global Context. Routledge Handbook of Human Resource Management in Asia, 3-20, Chicago.

Cordery, J., Soo, C., Kirkman, B., Rosen, B., & Mathieu, J. (2009). Leading Parallel Global Virtual Teams: Lessons from Alcoa. Organizational Dynamics, 38(3), 204-216.

Covin, J. G., & Slevin, D. P. (1989). Strategic management of small firms in hostile and benign environments. Strategic Management Journal, 10(1), 75-87. https://doi.org/10.1002/smj.4250100107

Cowen, T. (2002). Creative Destruction: How Globalization is Changing the World's Cultures, Princeton. Princeton University Press.

Cox, T. H., & Blake, S. (1991). Managing cultural diversity: Implications for organizational competitiveness. Academy of Management Perspectives, 5(3), 45-56.

Crabtree, B. F., & Miller, W. L. (1999). Doing qualitative research (2nd edition). New York: SAGE Publications.

Crane, A. (2013). Modern slavery as a management practice: exploring the conditions and capabilities for human exploitation. Academy of Management Review, 38(1), 49–69.

Crane, A., & Matten, D. (2016). Business Ethics: Managing Corporate Citizenship and Sustainability in the Age of Globalization. Oxford University Press.

Crane, A., LeBaron, G., Allain, J., & Behbahani, L. (2019) Governance gaps in eradicating forced labor: From global to domestic supply chains. Regulation & Governance, 13(1), 86-106.

Cristopher, E. (2015). International Management and Intercultural Communication: A collection of case studies (Volume 1). Palgrave Macmillan.

Crowne, K. A. (2012). The relationships among social intelligence, emotional intelligence and cultural intelligence. Organization Management Journal, 6(3), 37–41. https://doi.org/10.1057/omj.2009.20

Cucculelli, M. & Bettinelli, C. (2015). Business models, intangibles and firm performance: Evidence on corporate entrepreneurship from Italian manufacturing SMEs. Small Business Economics, 45, 329-350. https://doi.org/ 10.1007/s11187-015-9631-7

Cultural Intelligence Center. (n.d.). Cultural intelligence self-assessments. https://culturalq.com/products-services/assessments/cqselfassessments/

Czaja, J., Boot, W., Charness, N., & Rogers, W. (2019). Designing for Older Adults: Principles and Creative Human Factors Approaches. CRC Press. https://doi.org/10.1201/b22189

Dacin, M.T., Dacin, D.A., & Tracey, P. (2011). Social Entrepreneurship: A Critique and Future Directions, Organization Science, 22(5), 1203-1213.

Dahan, N. M., Doh, J. P., Oetzel, J., & Yaziji, M. (2010). Corporate-NGO collaboration: Co-creating new business models for developing markets. Long Range Planning, 43, 326-342. https://doi.org/10.1016/j.lrp.2009.11.003

Dahanayake, P., Rajendran, D., Selvarajah, C. & Ballantyne, G. (2018). Justice and fairness in the workplace: a trajectory for managing diversity. Equality, Diversity and Inclusion, 37(5), 470-490.

Dahles, H. (2004). Venturing across Borders: Investment Strategies of Singapore—Chinese Entrepreneurs in Mainland China. Asian Journal of Social Science, 32(1), 19-41.

DaSilva, C. M., & Trkman, P. (2014). Business model: What it is and what it is not. Long Range Planning, 47, 379-389. https://doi.org/10.1016/j.lrp.2013.08.004

Dass, M., &Vinnakota, S. (2019). Cross-Cultural Mistakes by Renowned Brands – Evaluating the Success and Failures of Brands in Host Nations. International Journal of Trend in Scientific Research and Development, 3(2), 38-42.

Davis, G. F., McAdam, D., Scott, W. R. & Zald, M. N. (eds.) (2005). Social Movements and Organization Theory. Cambridge: Cambridge University Press.

Dawer, N., & Frost, T. (1999). Competing with Giants: Survival Strategies for Local Companies in Emerging Markets. Harvard Business Review. https://hbr.org/1999/03/competing-with-giants-survival-strategies-for-local-companies-in-emerging-markets

de Guinea, A. O., Webster, J., & Staples, D. S. (2012). A meta-analysis of the consequences of virtualness on team functioning. Information & Management, 49(6), 301–308. https://doi.org/10.1016/j.im.2012.08.003

De Mooij, M. (2019). Consumer behavior and culture: Consequences for global marketing and advertising. Sage.

Deal, J. J., Altman, D. G., & Rogelberg, S. G. (2010). Millennials at work: What we know and what we need to do (if anything). Journal of Business and Psychology, 25(2), 191-199.

Deekay (2020). What is the Scope of Management in Today's Business? DailyOjo Articles. http://dailyojo.com/articles/what-is-the-scope-of-management-in-todays-business.html

Del Solar, S. (2010). Emprendedores en el aula. Guía para la formación en valores y habilidades sociales de docentes y jóvenes emprendedores. Fondo Multilateral de Inversiones del Banco Interamericano de Desarrollo.

Demil, B., & Lecocq, X. (2010). Business model evolution: In search of dynamic consistency. Long Range Planning, 43(2-3), 227-246. https://doi.org/10.1016/j.lrp.2010.02.004

Derr, C.B. and Laurent, A. (1989) The Internal and External Career: A Theoretical and Crosscultural Perspective. In Arthur, M.B., Hall, D.T., & Lawrence, B.S. (Eds.), Handbook of Career Theory (454-471). Cambridge University Press.

Dey, P. (2006). The rhetoric of social entrepreneurship: Paralogy and new language games in academic discourse. In Steyaert, C. & Hjorth, D. (eds.), Entrepreneurship as Social Change. Edward Elgar. https://doi.org/10.4337/9781847204424.00015

Di Pietro, F., Prencipe, A., & Majchrzak, A. (2018). Crowd Equity Investors: An Underutilized Asset for Open Innovation in Startups. California Management Review, 60(2), 43-70.

Dimitratos, P. & Plakoyiannaki, E. (2003). Theoretical foundations of an international entrepreneurial culture. Journal of International Entrepreneurship, 1(2), 187-215. https://doi.org/10.1023/A:1023804318244

Dirkes, M. A. (1985). Metacognition: Students in charge of their thinking. Roeper Review, 8(2), 96–100. https://doi.org/10.1080/02783198509552944

Djamen, R., Georges, L., & Pernin, J. L. (2020). Understanding the cultural values at the individual level in central Africa: A test of the cvscale in Cameroon. International Journal of Marketing and Social Policy (IJMSP).

Djankov, S. (2016). The Doing Business Project. Journal of Economic Perspectives, 247–248.

Dobbin, F., & Kalev, A. (2016). Why diversity programs fail. Harvard Business Review, 94(7-8), 3-10.

Doda, B., Gennaioli, C., Gouldson, A., Grover, D., & Sullivan, R. (2016). Are corporate carbon management practices reducing corporate carbon emissions?. Corporate Social Responsibility and Environmental Management, 23(5), 257-270.

Doh, J., McGuire, S., & Ozaki, T. (2015). The Journal of World Business Special Issue: Global governance and international nonmarket strategies: Introduction to the special issue. Journal of World Business, 50(2), 256-261.

Dolan, S. L., & Kawamura, K. M. (2015). Cross cultural competence: A field guide for developing global leaders and managers. Emerald.

Donaldson, J., & Fafaliou, I. (2003). Business ethics, corporate social responsibility and corporate governance: a review and summary critique. European Research Studies Journal, 0(1-2), 97-118.

Donaldson, T., & Preston, L. E. (1995). The stakeholder theory of the corporation: Concepts, evidence, and implications. Academy of Management Review, 20(1), 65-91.

Dondanville, C., & Stafford, T. (2006). Benefiting from Open Source Development Methodologies in Global Information Systems Organizations. AMCIS 2006 Proceedings, 106. Duarte, D. L., & Snyder, N. T. (2011). Mastering virtual teams: Strategies, tools, and techniques that succeed. John Wiley & Sons.

Dong, B., Peng, W., & Zhou, Y. (2012, June). The credit evaluation system for marketers of online group buying. In 2012 Fifth International Joint Conference on Computational Sciences and Optimization (pp. 85-88). IEEE.

Dortants, M., & Knoppers, A. (2013). Regulation of diversity through discipline: Practices of inclusion and exclusion in boxing. International Review for the Sociology of Sport, 48(5), 535-549.

Drahos, P., & Braithwaite, J. (2001). The globalization of regulation. Journal of Political Philosophy, 9(1), 103-128.

Duarte, D. L., & Snyder, N. T. (2011). Mastering virtual teams: Strategies, tools, and techniques that succeed. John Wiley & Sons.

Duarte, T. & Ruiz, M. (2009). Emprendimiento, una opción para el desarrollo. Scienta Et Technica, 15(43), 326-331.

Dumbravă, G. (2010). The concept of framing in cross-cultural business communication. Annals of the University of Petroşani-Economics, 10(Part I), 83-90.

Dumbravă, G., & Koronka, A. (2009). "Actions Speak Louder than Words" – Body Language in Business Communication. Annals of the University of Petroşani. Economics, 9(3), 249-254.

Durupinar, F., Pelechano, N., Allbeck, J. M., Gudukbay, U., & Badler, N. I. (2011). How the Ocean personality model affects the perception of crowds. IEEE computer graphics and applications, 31(3), 22–31. https://doi.org/10.1109/MCG.2009.105

Dwivedi, Y. K., Hughes, D. L., Coombs, C., Constantiou, I., Duan, Y., Edwards, J. S., ... & Upadhyay, N. (2020). Impact of COVID-19 pandemic on information management research and practice: Transforming education, work and life. International journal of information management, 55, 102211.

Earley, P. C. (1987). Intercultural Training for Managers: A Comparison of Documentary and Interpersonal Methods. Academy of Management Journal, 30(4), 685–698. https://doi.org/10.5465/256155

Earley, P. C. (2002). Redefining interactions across cultures and organizations: Moving forward with cultural intelligence. Research in Organizational Behavior, 24, 271–299. https://doi.org/10.1016/S0191-3085(02)24008-3.

Earley, P. C., & Ang, S. (2003). Cultural intelligence: Individual interactions across cultures. Stanford University Press.

Earley, P. C., & Mosakowski, E. (2004). Cultural Intelligence. Retrieved from https://hbr.org/2004/10/cultural-intelligence

Earley, P. C., & Mosakowski, E. (2004, October). Cultural intelligence. Harvard Business Review, 82(10), 139–46. https://hbr.org/2004/10/cultural-intelligence

Earley, P. C., & Peterson, R. S. (2004). The elusive Cultural Chameleon: Cultural Intelligence as a new approach to intercultural training for the global manager. Academy of Management Learning and Education, 3(1), 100–115. https://doi.org/10.5465/AMLE.2004.12436826

E-commerce lessons from China: How group buying pays off. SmartBrief. (2019, April 4). Retrieved October 12, 2021, from https://www.smartbrief.com/original/2019/04/e-commerce-lessons-china-how-group-buying-pays-0.

Ehrenberg, A., Juckes, S., White, K.M., &Walsh, S. P. (2008). Personality and self-esteem as predictors of young people's technol- ogy use. Cyberpsychology & Behavior, 11(6), 739–741.

Eisenhardt, K. M., & Schoonhoven, C. B. (1990). Organizational growth: linking founding team, strategy, environment, and growth among us semiconductor ventures, 1978-1988. Administrative Science Quarterly, 35(3), 504-529.

Ellickson, R. C. (1991). Order without Law: How Neighbors Settle Disputes. Harvard University Press. https://doi.org/10.2307/j.ctvk12rdz

Elms, D. K., & Low, P. (Eds.). (2013). Global Value Chains in a Changing World. Geneva: World Trade Organization.

Emamjomehzadeh, S. J., Damirchi, Q. V., Zamanzadeh, D. & Sharifi, S. (2012). The cross-cultural adaptability among university facilities. Interdisciplinary Journal of Contemporary Research in Business, 3 (19), 205-212.

Ember, C. R. (2007). Using the HRAF Collection of Ethnography in Conjunction With the Standard Cross-Cultural Sample and the Ethnographic Atlas. Cross-Cultural Research, 41(4), 396–427. https://doi.org/10.1177/1069397107306593

Engle, R. L. & Crowne, K. A. (2014). The impact of international experience on cultural intelligence: an application of contact theory in a structured short-term programme. Human Resource Development International, 17(1), 30-46. https://doi.org/10.1080/13678868.2013.856206

Erdoğmuş, I. E., & Čiçek, M. (2011). Online Group Buying: What Is There for The Consumers? Procedia - Social and Behavioral Sciences, 24, 308–316. https://doi.org/10.1016/J.SBSPRO.2011.09.138

Erez, M. (1992). Interpersonal communication systems in organizations, and their relationships to cultural values, productivity and innovation: The case of Japanese corporations. Applied Psychology: An International Review, 41(1), 43-64.

Ewing-Nelson, C. (2020). After a Full Month of Business Closures, Women Were Hit Hardest By April's Job Losses. National Women's Law Center. May 2020. Fact Sheet.

Fang, F., Schei, V., & Selart, M. (2018). International Journal of Intercultural Relations Hype or hope ? A new look at the research on cultural intelligence. International Journal of Intercultural Relations, 66. https://doi.org/10.1016/j.ijintrel.2018.04.002

Farh, J. & Cheng, B. (2000). A cultural analysis of paternalistic leadership in Chinese organizations. In J. T. Li, A. S. Tsui & E. Weldon (eds.), Management and organizations in the Chinese context (pp. 84-130). MacMillan Press.

Farh, J., Cheng, B., Chou, L., & Chu, X. (2006). Authority and benevolence: employees' response to paternalistic leadership in China. In Tsui, A. S., Bian, Y. & Cheng, L. (eds.), China's domestic private firms: Multidisciplinary perspectives on management and performance (pp. 230-260). M.E. Sharpe.

Faulconbridge, J. R., & Muzio, D. (2018). Karl Polanyi on strategy: the effects of culture, morality and double-movements on embedded strategy. Critical Perspectives on Accounting.

Featherstone, M. (1995). Undoing Culture: Globalization, Postmodernism and Identity. Sage.

Feeny, D., Berkes, F., McCay, B.J. Acheson, J. M. (1990). The Tragedy of the Commons: Twenty-two years later. Human Ecology, 18, 1–19. https://doi.org/10.1007/BF00889070

Feldman, A., & Msibi, S. (2014). Influence of cross-cultural leadership on organizational culture: Arcelormittal, Newcastle, a South African perspective. African Journal of Hospitality, Tourism and Leisure, 3(1), 1-9.

Felix, R., Pevzner, M., & Zhao, M. (2021). Cultural Diversity of Audit Committees and Firms' Financial Reporting Quality. Accounting Horizons, 35(3), 143-159.

Fernandes, T. (1994). Global interface design. Proceedings of Conference Companion on Human Factors in Computing Systems (pp. 373-374). https://doi.org/10.1145/259963.260509

Ferner, A., Almond, P., & Colling, T. (2005). Institutional theory and the cross-national transfer of employment policy: The case of 'workforce diversity' in US multinationals. Journal of International Business Studies, 36(3), 304-321.

Ferraro, G. P. (1994). The cultural dimension of international business. Prentice Hall.

Ferraro, G. P. (2021). The cultural dimension of international business. Prentice-Hall.

Figueroa-Rivera, A. N. (2016). Antología de antropología social. Unideal Universidad Matías Romero de Avendaño, Oaxaca.

Finnis, J. (1999). Natural law and natural rights. Oxford: Clarendon Press.

Fischer, R. (2011). Cross-cultural training effects on cultural essentialism beliefs and cultural intelligence. International Journal of Intercultural Relations, 35(6), 767–775. https://doi.org/10.1016/j.ijintrel.2011.08.005

Fleury, M.T.L. (1999). The management of culture diversity: lessons from Brazilian companies. Industrial Management & Data Systems, 99(3), 109-114.

Foster, B. P., Manikas, A., Preece, D., & Kroes, J. R. (2021). Noteworthy diversity efforts and financial performance: Evidence from DiversityInc's top 50. Advances in Accounting, 53, 100528.

Fraccastoro, S., Gabrielsson, M., & Pullins, E. B. (2021). The integrated use of social media, digital, and traditional communication tools in the B2B sales process of international SMEs. International Business Review, 30(4), 1-15.

Freeman, R. E., Wicks, A. C., & Parmar, B. (2004). Stakeholder theory and "the corporate objective revisited". Organization Science, 15(3), 364-369.

Fritz, M. M. C., & Silva, M. E. (2018). Exploring supply chain sustainability research in Latin America. International Journal of Physical Distribution & Logistics Management. 48(8), 818-841.

Gaglio, C. M. (2004). The role of mental simulations and counterfactual thinking in the opportunity identification process. Entrepreneurship Theory Practice, 28(6), 533–552. https://doi.org/10.1111/j.1540-6520.2004.00063.x

Gao, L. (2014). Customers' online group buying decision-making in emerging market: A Quantitative Study of Chinese online group buying (thesis).

García-Canclini, N. (2004). Diferentes, desiguales y desconectados: mapas de la interculturalidad. Gedisa.

George, G. & Bock, A. J. (2011). The business model in practice and its implications for entrepreneurship research. Entrepreneurship Theory and Practice, 35, 83-111. https://doi.org/10.2139/ssrn.1490251

Gereffi, G., & Fernandez-Stark, K. (2011). Global value chain analysis: a primer. Center on Globalization, Governance & Competitiveness (CGGC), Duke University, North Carolina, USA.

Gertsen, M. C., & Søderberg, A. (2011). Intercultural collaboration stories: On narrative inquiry and analysis as tools for research in international business. Journal of International Business Studies, 42(6), 787–804. https://doi.org/10.1057/jibs.2011.15

Gibbon, P. & Ponte, S. (2008). Global value chains: From governance to governmentality? Economy and Society, 37(3), 365–392.

Gibbon, P., Bair, J. & Ponte, S. (2008). Governing global value chains: An introduction. Economy and Society, 37(3), 315–338.

Gilmore, A. (2014, November 12). Raising our quality of life. Centre for Labour and Social Studies. http://classonline.org.uk/pubs/item/raising-our-quality-of-life

Glover, J., & Friedman, H. L. (2015). Transcultural competence: Navigating cultural differences in the global community. American Psychological Association.

Gobo, G. (2008). Doing ethnography. Sage. https://dx.doi.org/10.4135/978085 7028976

Goettsch, K. L. (2014). Understanding intercultural communication on global virtual teams: exploring challenges of language, culture, technology, and collaboration. Doctoral Dissertation. University of Minnesota.

Golgeci, I., Makhmadshoev, D., & Demirbag, M. (2021). Global value chains and the environmental sustainability of emerging market firms: A systematic review of literature and research agenda. International Business Review, 30(5), 101857.

Goman, C. K. (1994). Managing in a global organization: Keys to success in a changing world. Thomson Crisp Learning.

Gómez, C., Kirkman, B. L., & Shapiro, D. L. (2000). The impact of collectivism and in-group/out-group membership on the evaluation generosity of team members. Academy of management Journal, 43(6), 1097-1106.

Gould, E. W., Honold, P., Kurosu, M., Melican, J., Marcus, A., & Yu, L. A. (2003). Culture issues and mobile UI design. Proceedings of CHI'03: Extended Abstracts on Human Factors in Computing Systems (pp. 702-703).

Graham, N. (n.d.). The why behind DEI: How diversity, equity, and inclusion initiatives benefit business. Workhuman. https://www.workhuman.com/resources/globoforce-blog/the-why-behind-d-i-how-diversity-and-inclusion-initiatives-benefit-business

Gray, H. (2016). Access orders and the 'new'new institutional economics of development. Development and Change, 51-75.

Greenwald, A. G., McGhee, D. E., & Schwartz, J. L. K. (1998). Measuring individual differences in implicit cognition: The implicit association test. Journal of Personality and Social Psychology, 74(6), 1464–1480. https://doi.org/10.1037//0022-3514.74.6.1464

Griffin, K. S. (2012). Leadership effectiveness in virtual teams: A quantitative analysis of the impact of perception. Order, (3517090).

Guang, T., & Trotter, D. (2012). Key issues in cross-cultural business communication: Anthropological approaches to international business. African Journal of Business Management, 6(22), 6456-6464.

Guðmundsdóttir, S. (2015). Nordic expatriates in the US: The relationship between cultural intelligence and adjustment. International Journal of Intercultural Relations, 47, 175–186. https://doi.org/10.1016/j.ijintrel.2015.0 5.001

Guerra-García, E. (2004). La sociointerculturalidad y la educación indígena, en Eduardo Andrés Sandoval Forero y Manuel Antonio Baeza (coords.). Cuestión étnica, culturas, construcción de identidades, México: Universidad Autónoma Indígena de México, Asociación Latinoamericana de Sociología y ediciones el Caracol.

Guerra-García, E. (2005). La Anerogogía de la Voluntad, propuesta educativa sociointercultural de la Universidad Autónoma Indígena de México. Ra Ximhai, 1(1), 15-38.

Guerra-García, E., Caro-Dueñas, M. A., Corrales-Baldenebro A. L., (2020). Dinámica sociointercultural del surgimiento del puerto de Topolobampo en México. Revista CoPaLa, Construyendo Paz Latinoamericana, 10(5), 102-125. https://doi.org/10.35600.25008870.2020.10.0174

Gustavson, R. (2011). Business ethics as field of teaching, training and research in Oceania. Journal of business ethics, 104(1), 63-72.

Hall, E. T., & Hall, M., R. (1990). Understanding Cultural Differences, Germans, French and Americans. Intercultural Press.

Hall, J., & Matos, S. (2010). Incorporating impoverished communities in sustainable supply chains. International Journal of Physical Distribution & Logistics Management, 40(1/), 124-147.

Hamann, R., & Bertels, S. (2018). The institutional work of exploitation: Employers' work to create and perpetuate inequality. Journal of Management Studies, 55(3), 394-423.

Handke, L., Klonek, F. E., Parker, S. K., & Kauffeld, S. (2020). Interactive Effects of Team Virtuality and Work Design on Team Functioning. Small Group Research, 51(1), 3–47. https://doi.org/10.1177/1046496419863490

Hanley, J. (1999). Beyond the tip of the iceberg. Reaching Today's Youth, 3(2), 9-12.

Hardin, G. (1968). The tragedy of the common. Science, 1243-1248.

Harding, R. (2006). Social Entrepreneurship Monitor, London Global Entrepreneurship Monitor. Google Scholar. https://scholar.google.com/citations?user=IKAsBdIAAAAJ&hl=en

Harris, P. R., Moran, R. T. & Moran, S. V. (1999). Managing cultural differences. Global leadership strategies for the 21st century (6e). Elsevier/Butterworth-Heinemann

Harrison, D. A., & Klein, K. J. (2007). What's the difference? Diversity constructs as separation, variety, or disparity in organizations. Academy of management review, 32(4), 1199-1228.

Harrison, D. A., Price, K. H., & Bell, M. P. (1998). Beyond relational demography: Time and the effects of surface-and deep-level diversity on work group cohesion. Academy of Management Journal, 41(1), 96-107.

Harzing, A. W., & Feely, A. J. (2008). The language barrier and its implications for HQ-subsidiary relationships. Cross Cultural Management: An International Journal, 15(1), 49-61.

Hayes, A. (2022). Glocalization: What It Means, Advantages, and Examples. Investopedia. https://www.investopedia.com/terms/g/glocalization.asp

Hayton, J.C., George, G., & Zahra, S.A. (2002). National culture and entrepreneurship: A review of behavioral Research. Entrepreneurship Theory and Practice, 26(4), 33–52.

He, R., & Liu, J. (2010). Barriers of cross cultural communication in multinational firms: A case study of Swedish company and its subsidiary in China. Halmstad School of Business and Engineering, 1-32.

Healy, G., & Oikelome, F. (2011). Diversity, Ethnicity, Migration and Work: UK and US Perspectives. In Diversity, Ethnicity, Migration and Work (pp. 36-66). Palgrave Macmillan, London.

Helen, D. (2013). International Management: Managing across Borders and Cultures. Upper Prentice Hall.

Hertel, G., Geister, S., & Konradt, U. (2005). Managing virtual teams: A review of current empirical research. Human Resource Management Review, 15(1), 69–95. https://doi.org/10.1016/j.hrmr.2005.01.002

Hill, C. (2000). International Business: Competing in the Global Marketplace. McGraw Hill.

Hill, C.W.L. (2007). International Business Competing in the Global marketplace (6e). McGraw-Hill/Irwin.

Hinds, P. J., Neeley, T. B., & Cramton, C. D. (2014). Language as a lightning rod: Power contests, emotion regulation, and subgroup dynamics in global teams. Journal of International Business Studies, 45(5), 536-561.

Hoang, T., Suh, J., and Sabharwal, M. (2022). Beyond a Numbers Game? Impact of Diversity and Inclusion on the Perception of Organizational Justice. Public Administration Review.

Hodgson, A. (2017). Reperceiving the Future. World Futures Review, 9(4), 208-224. https://doi.org/10.1177/1946756717729511

Hoffman, W. M. (1991). Business and environmental ethics. Business Ethics Quarterly, 1(2), 169-184.

Hofstede Insights. (2022). Hofstede Insights: Organizational, Culture, Consulting. Hofstede-insights. https://www.hofstede-insights.com/

Hofstede, G. (1984a). National cultures and corporate cultures. In L.A. Samovar & R.E. Porter (Eds.), Communication Between Cultures. Wadsworth.

Hofstede, G. (2001). Cultures and Organizations. Software of the Mind. McGraw-Hill.

Hofstede, G. (2007). Geert Hofstede Cultural Dimensions. www.geert-hofstede.com

Hofstede, G. (2010). Cultures and Organizations: Software of the Mind (3e). McGraw-Hill Education.

Hofstede, G. (2011). Dimensionalizing cultures: The Hofstede model in context. Online readings in psychology and culture, 2(1), 2307-0919.

Hofstede, G. (1984). Culture's Consequences: International Differences in Work-Related Values (2e). Beverly Hills CA: SAGE Publications.

Hofstede, G., Hofstede G. J., & Minkov, M. (2010). Cultures and organizations: Software of the mind. Revised and Expanded (3rd Edition). New York: McGraw-Hill.

Holcombe, C. (2017). A History of East Asia. Cambridge University Press.

Holden, N. (2002). Cross-cultural management: A knowledge management perspective. Pearson.

Hollensen, S. (2004). Global Marketing. England.

Hollenson, S. (2007). Global Marketing (6e). Pearson.

Holtbrügge, D., Weldon, A., & Rogers, H. (2013). Cultural determinants of email communication styles. International Journal of Cross Cultural Management, 13(1), 89-110.

Hopkins, C. D., Ferrell, O. C., Ferrell, L., & Hopkins, K. H. (2021). Changing Perceptions of Marketing Ethics and Social Responsibility in Principles of Marketing. Journal of Marketing Education, 43(2), 244–259. https://doi.org/10.1177/0273475321995553

Hossain, M. A., & Rahman, S. (2021). Investigating the Success of OGB in China: The Influence of Personality Traits. Information Systems Frontiers, 23(3), 543–559. https://doi.org/10.1007/s10796-019-09968-0

House R., Hanges P., Javidan M., & Dorfman P. (2004). Culture, Leadership and Organizations: the GLOBE Study of 62 Societies. Sage.

Houtart, F. (2012). From the 'Common Goods' to the 'Common Good of Humanity', B. Daiber & Houtart (Eds.). In A Postcapitalist Paradigm: The Common Good of Humanity (pp. 1–16). Brussels: Rosa-Luxemburg Foundation.

Howard, B. C., McGee, S., Shin, N., & Shia, R. (2001). The triarchic theory of intelligence and computer-based inquiry learning. Educational Technology Research and Development, 49(4), 49–69. https://doi.org/10.1007/BF02504947

Hsu, C. L., & Lin, J. C. C. (2008). Acceptance of blog usage: The roles of technology acceptance, social influence and knowledge sharing motivation. Information & management, 45(1), 65-74.

Hu, E. (2005). The core of the global warming problem: energy. International Journal of Global Energy Issues, 23(4), 354-359.

Hu, N., Wu, J., & Gu, J. (2019). Cultural intelligence and employees' creative performance: The moderating role of team conflict in interorganizational teams. Journal of Management & Organization, 25(1), 96–116. https://doi.org/10.1017/jmo.2016.64

Huggins, R., & Thompson, P. (2015). Culture and Place-Based Development: A Socio-Economic Analysis. Regional Studies, 49(1), 130–159. https://doi.org/10.1080/00343404.2014.889817

Hülsheger, U. R., Alberts, H. J. E. M., Feinholdt, A., & Lang, J. W. B. (2013). Benefits of mindfulness at work: The role of mindfulness in emotion regulation, emotional exhaustion, and job satisfaction. Journal of Applied Psychology, 98(2), 310–325. https://doi.org/10.1037/a0031313

Hunt, V., Yee, L., Prince, S., & Dixon-Fyle, S. (2018). Delivering through Diversity. McKinsey & Company. https://www.mckinsey.com/capabilities/people-and-organizational-performance/our-insights/delivering-through-diversity

India Education Diary (2021, September 15). Gyandhan launches Gyandhan Allied – India's first group buying plan for Abroad Education Loans. India Education | Latest Education News | Global Educational News | Recent Educational News. Retrieved March 2, 2022, from https://indiaeducationdiary.

in/gyandhan-launches-gyandhan-allied-indias-first-group-buying-plan-for-abroad-education-loans/

International Hydropower Association (2022). Country profile: Cameroon. IHA https://www.hydropower.org/country-profiles/cameroon

Islam, M. S., & Eva, S. A. (2017). Application of Mcgregor's Theory X and Theory Y: Perception of Management toward the Employees in the Banking Industry of Bangladesh. The International Journal of Business & Management, 5(11), 135-145.

Jackson, G., & Deeg, R. (2008). Comparing capitalisms: Understanding institutional diversity and its implications for international business. Journal of International Business Studies, 39(4), 540-561.

Jackson, G., Kuruvilla, S., & Frege, C. (2013). Across boundaries: The global challenges facing workers and employment research. British Journal of Industrial Relations, 51(3), 425-439.

Jacob, N. (2004). Intercultural Management. Kogan Page.

Jaén I., Fernandez-Serrano J., & Liñan, F. (2013). Valores culturales, nivel de ingresos y actividad emprendedora. Revista de Economía Mundial, 35, 35-52.

Jain, T., & Pareek, C. (2019). Managing Cross-Cultural Diversity: issues and Challenges. Global Management Review, 13(2), 23-32.

Jarvenpaa, S. L., & Leidner, D. E. (1999). Communication and trust in global virtual teams. Organization science, 10(6), 791-815.

Jaworska, S. (2018) Change but no climate change: discourses of climate change in corporate social responsibility reporting in the oil industry. International Journal of Business Communication, 55(2), 194-219.

Jenab, K., & Staub, S. (2012). Analyzing Management Style and Successful Implementation of Six Sigma. International Journal of Strategic Decision Sciences, 3(3), 13-23, https://doi.org/10.4018/jsds.2012070102

Jensen, M. C. (2010). Value maximization, stakeholder theory, and the corporate objective function. Journal of Applied Corporate Finance, 22(1), 32-42.

Jiang, X., & Deng, S. (2014). Optimal strategy for selling on group-buying website. Journal of Industrial Engineering and Management, 7(4), 769-784. https://doi.org/10.3926/jiem.1153

Jimenez, A., Boehe, D. M., Taras, V., & Caprar, D. V. (2017). Working across boundaries: Current and future perspectives on global virtual teams. Journal of International Management, 23(4), 341-349.

Johnston, K. A., & Rosin, K. (2011, May). Global virtual teams: How to manage them. In 2011 International Conference on Computer and Management (CAMAN) (pp. 1-4). IEEE.

Jones, C., Parker, M., & ten Bos, R. (2005). For Business Ethics. Routledge. https://doi.org/10.4324/9780203458457

Jonscher, C. & Summerfield, A. (1994). Prospects for Western Food Companies in Central and Eastern Europe. British Food Journal, 96(1), 4-9. https://doi.org/10.1108/00070709410061041

Jonsen, K., & Ozbilgin, M. (2013). Models of global diversity management. Diversity at Work: The Practice of Inclusion, San Francisco: John Wiley & Sons, Inc, 364-390.

Jonsen, K., Tatli, A., Ozbilgin, M. F., & Bell, M. P. (2013). The tragedy of the uncommons: Reframing workforce diversity. Human Relations, 66(2), 271-294.

Kahn, R.L. (1979). Aging and Social Support. In: Riley, M.W. (Ed.), Aging from Birth to Death: Interdisciplinary Perspectives (pp.77-91), Westview Press.

Kai, C., Xiaofan, W., Qiuying, Z., & Huanhuan, L. (2013). An Exploratory Study of Influence Factors about Consumers Online Group Buying Intention. Journal of Applied Sciences, 13(8), 1370-1375.

Kaikati, J.G., & Kaikati, A.M. (2003). A rose by any other name: Rebranding campaigns that work. Journal of Business Strategy, 24(6), 17-23. https://doi.org/10.1108/02756660310509451

Kalev, A. (2014). How you downsize is who you downsize: Biased formalization, accountability, and managerial diversity. American Sociological Review, 79(1), 109-135.

Kalev, A., Dobbin, F., & Kelly, E. (2006). Best practices or best guesses? Assessing the efficacy of corporate affirmative action and diversity policies. American Sociological Review, 71(4), 589-617.

Kamasak, R., James, S. R., & Yavuz, M. (2019). The interplay of corporate social responsibility and corporate political activity in emerging markets: The role of strategic flexibility in nonmarket strategies. Business Ethics: A European Review, 28(3): 305–320.

Kamasak, R., Özbilgin, M. F., Baykut, S., & Yavuz, M. (2020a). Moving from individual intersections to institutional intersections: Insights from LGBTQ individuals in Turkey. Journal of Organizational Change Management, 33(3): 456–476.

Kamasak, R., Özbilgin, M. F., Küçükaltan, B., & Yavuz, M. (2020d). Regendering of dynamic managerial capabilities in the context of binary perspectives on gender diversity. Gender in Management: An International Journal, 35(1): 19–36.

Kamasak, R., Özbilgin, M.F., & Yavuz, M. (2020c). Understanding intersectional analyses. In: King, E., Roberson, Q. and Hebl, M. (eds.), Research on Social Issues in Management on Pushing Understanding of Diversity in Organizations (pp. 93–115). Charlotte, USA: Information Age Publishing.

Kamasak, R., Ozbilgin, M.F., Yavuz, M., & Akalin, C. (2020b). Race discrimination at work in the UK. In: Vassilopoulou, J., Brabet, J., Kyriakidou, O., & Shovunmi, V. (eds.), Race Discrimination and the Management of Ethnic Diversity at Work: European Countries Perspective. Bingley, UK: Emerald Publishing.

Kamasak, R., Palalar, A. D., Yesildal, E., & Vassilopoulou, J. (2022). Ethnicity and precarity relationship: The refugee case in Turkey. In: Meliou, M., Vassilopoulou J. and Ozbilgin, M. (eds.), Diversity and Precarious Work During Socio-economic Upheaval: The Missing Link. Cambridge, UK: Cambridge University Press.

Kanigel, R. (1997). Taylor-made. The Sciences, 37(3), 18-23.

Kankanhalli, A., Tan, B. C., & Wei, K. K. (2006). Conflict and performance in global virtual teams. Journal of management information systems, 23(3), 237-274.

Kano, L. (2018). Global value chain governance: A relational perspective. Journal of International Business Studies, 49(6), 1-22, 684–705

Kaplinsky, R. (2000). Globalization and unequalisation: What can be learned from value chain analysis? Journal of Development Studies, 37(2), 117-146.

Kaplinsky, R. (2013). Globalization, Poverty and Inequality: Between a Rock and a Hard Place. John Wiley & Sons.

Kappagomtula, C. L. (2017). Overcoming challenges in leadership roles – managing large projects with multi or cross culture teams. European Business Review, 29(5), 572-583. https://doi.org/10.1108/EBR-12-2015-0177

Karabacakoglu, F., & Ozbilgin, M. (2010). Global Diversity Management at Ericsson: The Business Case, In Cases in Strategic Management (pp.79-91). London: McGraw-Hill.

Kartolo, A. and Kwantes, C. (2019). Organizational culture, perceived societal and organizational discrimination. Equality, Diversity and Inclusion, 38(6), 602-618.

Kauffman, R. J., & Wang, B. (2001). New buyers' arrival under dynamic pricing market microstructure: The case of group-buying discounts on the internet. Journal of Management Information Systems, 18(2), 157-188.

Kaufman, S. R., U, P., & Hwang, A. (n.d.). The Role of Mindfulness in Cultural Intelligence (CQ). Pace Pacing And Clinical Electrophysiology, 2003, 87601–87619.

Kawai, N., & Chung, C. (2019). Expatriate utilization, subsidiary knowledge creation and performance: the moderating role of subsidiary strategic context. Journal of World Business, 54(1), 24-36.

Kayworth, T. R., & Leidner, D. E. (2002). Leadership effectiveness in global virtual teams. Journal of management information systems, 18(3), 7-40.

Kelley, C. & Meyers, J. E. (1993). Cross-Cultural Adaptability Inventory manual. National Computer Systems.

Kesari, B., Soni, R., & Khanuja, R. S. (2014). A review on the need of cross cultural management in multinational corporations. International Journal of Advanced Research in Management and Social Sciences, 3(8), 120-127.

Kim, J., Yammarino, F. J., Dionne, S. D., Eckardt, R., Cheong, M., Tsai, C. Y., ... & Park, J. W. (2020). State-of-the-science review of leader-follower dyads research. The Leadership Quarterly, 31(1), 101306.

Kim, U. (2000). Indigenous, cultural, and cross-cultural psychology: A theoretical, conceptual, and epistemological analysis. Asian Journal of Social Psychology, 3(3), 265–287. https://doi.org/10.1111/1467-839X.00068

Kim, Y. (1989). Intercultural Adaptation. In Asante, M. K. & Gudykunst, W. (Eds.), Handbook of International and Intercultural Communication (pp. 275-294). Sage.

Kimani, D., Ullah, S., Kodwani, D., & Akhtar, P. (2021). Analysing corporate governance and accountability practices from an African neo-patrimonialism perspective: Insights from Kenya. Critical Perspectives on Accounting, 78, 102260.

Kimble, C. (2011). Building effective virtual teams: How to overcome the problems of trust and identity in virtual teams. Global Business and Organizational Excellence, 30(2), 6–15. https://doi.org/10.1002/joe.20364

Kinne, A. (2020, July 22). Back to basics: What are career milestones? Workhuman. https://www.workhuman.com/resources/globoforce-blog/back-to-basics-what-are-career-milestones

Kiss, A. N., Danis, W. N, & Cavusgil, S. T. (2012). International entrepreneurship research in emerging economies: A critical review and research agenda. Journal of Business Venturing, 27(2), 266-290. https://doi.org/10.1016/j.jbusvent.2011.09.004

Klarsfeld, A (2009). Managing diversity: The virtue of coercion. In: Ozbilgin, MF (ed.) Equality, Diversity and Inclusion at Work. Cheltenham: Edward Elgar, 322–331.

Klarsfeld, A., Ng, E., & Tatli, A. (2012). Social regulation and diversity management: A comparative study of France, Canada and the UK. European Journal of Industrial Relations, 18(4), 309-327.

Klitmøller, A., & Lauring, J. (2013). When global virtual teams share knowledge: Media richness, cultural difference and language commonality. Journal of world Business, 48(3), 398-406.

Klitmøller, A., Schneider, S. C., & Jonsen, K. (2015). Speaking of global virtual teams: Language differences, social categorization and media choice. Personnel Review.

Knein, E., Greven, A., Bendig, D., & Brettel, M. (2020). Culture and cross-functional coopetition: The interplay of organizational and national culture. Journal of International Management, 26(2), 100731. https://doi.org/10.1016/j.intman.2019.100731

Knights, D., & Roberts, J. (1982). The power of organization or the organization of power?. Organization Studies, 3(1), 47-63.

Kolovou, T. (2020, February 21). Developing cross-cultural intelligence: Working across cultures: A path of discovery. LinkedIn Learning.

Kopp, C. M. (2021). Cross Culture. Investopedia Business Essentials. https://www.investopedia.com/terms/c/cross-culture.

Kováts, E. (2018). Questioning consensuses: Right-wing populism, anti-populism, and the threat of 'gender ideology'. Sociological Research Online, 1360780418764735.

Koveshnikov, A., & Ehrnrooth, M. (2018). The Cross-Cultural Variation of the Effects of Transformational Leadership Behaviors on Followers' Organizational Identification: The Case of Idealized Influence and Individualized Consideration in Finland and Russia. Management and Organization Review, 14(4), 747-779.

Krecl, P., Targino, A. C., Oukawa, G. Y., & Junior, R. P. C. (2020). Drop in urban air pollution from COVID-19 pandemic: Policy implications for the megacity of São Paulo. Environmental Pollution, 265(B), 114883. https://doi.org/10.1016/j.envpol.2020.114883

Kumar, N., Rose, R. C., & Ramalu, S. (2008). The Effects of Personality and Cultural Intelligence on International Assignment Effectiveness: A Review. Journal of Social Sciences, 4(4), 320–328. https://doi.org/10.3844/jssp.2008.320.328

Kurland, N. B., & McCaffrey, S. J. (2016). Social Movement Organization Leaders and the Creation of Markets for "Local" Goods. Business & Society, 55(7), 1017–1058.

Küskü, F., Aracı, Ö., & Özbilgin, M. F. (2021). What happens to diversity at work in the context of a toxic triangle? Accounting for the gap between discourses and practices of diversity management. Human Resource Management Journal, 31(2), 553-574.

Lakhani, T., Kuruvilla, S., & Avgar, A. (2013). From the firm to the network: Global value chains and employment relations theory. British Journal of Industrial Relations, 51(3), 440-472.

Latouche, S. (1996). The Westernization of the World. Polity Press.

Lau, K. & Young, A. (2013). Why China shall not completely transit from a relation based to a rule based governance regime: A Chinese perspective. Corporate Governance: An International Review, 21 (6), 577-585.

Lauring, J. (2008). Rethinking social identity theory in international encounters: Language use as a negotiated object for identity making. International Journal of Cross Cultural Management, 8(3), 343-361.

Lauring, J. (2013). International diversity management: Global ideals and local responses. British Journal of Management, 24(2), 211-224.

Lauring, J., & Klitmøller, A. (2015). Corporate language-based communication avoidance in MNCs: A multi-sited ethnography approach. Journal of World Business, 50(1), 46-55.

LawyersTech (2021). 9 reasons why iPhone is not successful in India. https://www.lawyerstech.com/why-is-apple-iphone-not-so-successful-in-india/

Lazonick, W., & O'sullivan, M. (2000). Maximizing shareholder value: a new ideology for corporate governance. Economy and Society, 29(1), 13-35.

Leading Online Group buying brands. Verified Market Research. (2021, July 26). Retrieved October 13, 2021, from https://www.verifiedmarketresearch.com/blog/leading-online-group-buying-brands/

Lebron, A., & Mendez, A. (2013). What is culture? Merit Research Journal of Education and Review, 1(6), 126-132.

Lee, J., Jang, S. & Lee, S. (2018). Knowledge sharing with outsiders in emerging economies: Based on social exchange relations within the China context. Personnel Review, 47(5), 1094-1115.

Lee, S., & Klassen, R. D. (2016). Firms' Response to Climate Change: The Interplay of Business Uncertainty and Organizational Capabilities. Business Strategy and the Environment, 25(8), 577-592. https://doi.org/10.1002/bse.1890

Lewis, P. V. (1985). Defining 'business ethics': Like Nailing Jello to a Wall. Journal of Business ethics, 4(5), 377-383.

Lewis, R. (2014). How different cultures understand time. Business Insider, 1.

Li, C. (2016). The Role of Top-team Diversity and Perspective Taking in Mastering Organizational Ambidexterity. Management and Organization Review, 12(4), 769-794.

Li, C., Sycara, K., & Scheller-Wolf, A. (2010). Combinatorial coalition formation for multi-item group-buying with heterogeneous customers. Decision Support Systems, 49(1), 1-13.

Li, Y., & Cui, L. (2018). The Influence of Top Management Team on Chinese Firms' FDI Ambidexterity. Management and Organization Review, 14(3), 513-542.

Liao, C. (2009). The governance structures of Chinese firms: Innovation, competitiveness, and growth in a dual economy. Springer.

Liao, C., Palvia, P., & Lin, H. N. (2006). The roles of habit and web site quality in e-commerce. International Journal of Information Management, 26(6), 469-483.

Lifintsev, D. S., & Canhavilhas, J. (2017). Cross-cultural management: obstacles to effective cooperation in a multicultural environment. Scientific Bulletin of Polissya, 2 (2 (10)), 195-202.

Lifintsev, D., & Wellbrock, W. (2019). Cross-cultural communication in the digital age. Estudos em Comunicação, 1(28), 93-104.

Lillis, M., & Tian, R. (2010). Cultural issues in the business world: An anthropological perspective. Journal of Social Sciences, 6(1), 99-112.

Lin, Y. (2006). The sweatshop and beyond. In Tsui, A. S., Bian, Y. & Cheng, L. (eds.), China's domestic private firms: Multidisciplinary perspectives on management and performance (pp. 82-96). M.E. Sharpe.

Liu, Y., Ruiz-Menjivar, J., Zhang, L., Zhang, J., & Swisher, M. E. (2019). Technical training and rice farmers' adoption of low-carbon management practices: the case of soil testing and formulated fertilization technologies in Hubei, China. Journal of Cleaner Production, 226, 454-462. https://doi.org/10.1016/j.jclepro.2019.04.026

Locke, R. M., Qin, F., & Brause, A. (2007). Does monitoring improve labor standards? Lessons from Nike. ILR Review, 61(1), 3-31.

Locke, R., Amengual, M., & Mangla, A. (2009). Virtue out of necessity? Compliance, commitment, and the improvement of labor conditions in global supply chains. Politics & Society, 37(3), 319-351.

Lorbiecki, A. (2001). Changing views on diversity management: The rise of the learning perspective and the need to recognize social and political contradictions. Management Learning, 32(3), 345-361.

Louche, C., Staelens, L. & D'Haese, M. (2020). When workplace unionism in global value chains does not function well: Exploring the impediments. Journal of Business Ethics, 162(2), 379–398.

Lounsbury, M., & Glynn, M.A. (2001). Cultural entrepreneurship: Stories, legitimacy, and the acquisition of resources. Strategic management journal, 22(6-7), 545-564. https://doi.org/10.1002/smj.188

Lovelace, D. (n.d.). Communication within teams. LinkedIn Learning. https://www.linkedin.com/learning/communication-within-teams/how-high-performing-teams-communicate?u=70115025

Luanglath, N., Ali, M. & Mohannak, K. (2019). Top management team gender diversity and productivity: the role of board gender diversity. Equality, Diversity and Inclusion, 38(1), 71-86.

Lumpkin, G.T. & Dess, G.G. (1996). Clarifying the entrepreneurial orientation construct and linking it to performance. Academy of Management Review, 21(1), 135–172. https://doi.org/10.2307/258632

Luthans, F. (2005). Organization Behavior. McGraw Hill.

Madhavan, S. (2012). Cross-Cultural Management. Oxford University Press.

Madhavan, S. (2016). Cross Cultural Management- Concepts and Cases (2e). Oxford University Press.

Maheshkar, C. (2016). HRD Scholar-Practitioner: An Approach to Filling Research, Theory and Practice Gaps. In Hughes, C. & Gosney, M. W. (Eds.), Bridging the Scholar-Practitioner Gap in Human Resource Development (pp 20-46). USA: IGI Global. https://doi.org/10.4018/978-1-4666-9998-4.ch002

Maheshkar, C., & Sharma, V. (2018) (Eds.). Cross-cultural Business Education: Leading Businesses around the Cultures. In Handbook of Research on Cross-Cultural Business Education (pp. 1-35). IGI Global. https://doi.org/10.4018/978-1-5225-3776-2.ch001

Maheshkar, C., & Sharma, V. (2021) (Eds.). Cross-cultural Business Education: Leading Businesses around the Cultures. In Research Anthology on Business and Technical Education in the Information Era (pp. 677-711). Business Science Reference. https://doi.org/10.4018/978-1-7998-5345-9.ch038

Mair, J. & Martí, I. (2006). Social entrepreneurship research: A source of explanations, prediction, and delight. Journal of World Business, 41(1), 36-44. https://doi.org/10.1016/j.jwb.2005.09.002

Majchrzak, A., Rice, R. E., King, N., Malhotra, A., & Ba, S. (2000a). Computer-mediated inter-organizational knowledge-sharing: Insights from a virtual team innovating using a collaborative tool. Information Resources Management Journal (IRMJ), 13(1), 44-53.

Majchrzak, A., Rice, R. E., Malhotra, A., King, N., & Ba, S. (2000b). Technology adaptation: The case of a computer-supported inter-organizational virtual team. MIS quarterly, 569-600.

Maldonado, K. (2007). La interculturalidad de los negocios internacionales. Universidad Empresa Bogotá (Colombia), 6(12), 261-291.

Mamman, A., Kamoche, K., & Bakuwa, R. (2012). Diversity, organizational commitment and organizational citizenship behavior: An organizing framework. Human Resource Management Review, 22(4), 285-302.

Marcus, A. (2005). User interface design and culture. Usability and internationalization of information technology, 3, 51-78.

Marcus, A. (2013). Cross-cultural user-experience design. Proceedings of SIGGRAPH Asia 2013 Courses, 8, 1-31. https://doi.org/10.1145/2542266.254 2274

Marginson, P., Edwards, P., Edwards, T., Ferner, A., & Tregaskis, O. (2010). Employee representation and consultative voice in multinational companies operating in Britain. British Journal of Industrial Relations, 48(1), 151-180.

Marmer, R. L., Ridgeway, D. A., Sherman, C. E., Bass, H., & Epps, J. (n.d.). Implicit bias task force toolkit PowerPoint instruction manual ABA section of litigation. Academic Press.

Matos, S., & Silvestre, B.S. (2013). Managing stakeholder relations when developing sustainable business models: the case of the Brazilian energy sector. Journal of Cleaner Production, 45, 61-73.

Matsumoto, D., LeRoux, J. A., Robles, Y., & Campos, G. (2007). The Intercultural Adjustment Potential Scale (ICAPS) predicts adjustment above and beyond personality and general intelligence. International Journal of Intercultural Relations, 31(6), 747–759. https://doi.org/10.1016/j.ijintrel.2007.08.002

Matusitz, J. (2010). Disneyland Paris: a case analysis demonstrating how glocalization works. Journal of Strategic Marketing, 18(3), 223-237. https://doi.org/10.1080/09652540903537014

May, C. (2015). Who's in charge? Corporations as institutions of global governance. Palgrave Communications, 1, 1-10.

Maznevski, M. L., & Chudoba, K. M. (2000). Bridging space over time: Global virtual team dynamics and effectiveness. Organization science, 11(5), 473-492.

Mele, C., Pels, J., & Polese, F. (2010). A Brief Review of Systems Theories and Their Managerial Applications. Service Science, 2, 126-135. https://doi.org/10.1287/serv.2.1_2.126

Ménard, C., & Shirley, M. (2005). Handbook of new institutional economics. Dordrecht: Springer.

Mercado, B. K., Dilchert, S., Giordano, C., & Ones, D. S. (2016). Counterproductive Work Behaviors. In The SAGE Handbook of Industrial, Work and Organizational Psychology: Personnel Psychology and Employee Performance (pp. 109–210). London: SAGE Publications. https://doi.org/10.4135/9781473914940.n7

Merk, V. (2003). Communication across Cultures: from cultural awareness to reconciliation of the dilemmas. SSRN Electronic Journal. http://dx.doi.org/10.2139/ssrn.464720

Metzgar, C. R. (2004). The principles of scientific management/The one best way: Frederick Winslow Taylor & the Enigma of Efficiency. Professional Safety, 49(2), 49.

Minkov, M. (2018). A revision of Hofstede's model of national culture: old evidence and new data from 56 countries. Cross Cultural and Strategic Management, 25(2), 231-256.

Mintzer, I. (1987). A matter of degrees. The potential for limiting the greenhouse effect. Bulletin of Science, Technology & Society, 8(3), 344–344. https://doi.org/10.1177/027046768800800375

Mitchell, R.K., Busenitz, L.W., Bird, B., Marie Gaglio, C., Mcmullen, J.S., Morse, E.A., & Smith, J.B. (2007). The central question in entrepreneurial cognition research 2007, Entrepreneurship Theory and Practice, 31(1), 1-27. https://doi.org/10.1111/j.1540-6520.2007.00161.x

Molinsky, A. (2018). Boost your cultural intelligence [Video file]. https://valo.skillport.com/skillportfe/main.action?assetid=141695

Montoya-Weiss, M. M., Massey, A. P., & Song, M. (2001). Getting it together: Temporal coordination and conflict management in global virtual teams. Academy of management Journal, 44(6), 1251-1262.

Moon, J. (2007). The contribution of corporate social responsibility to sustainable development. Sustainable development, 15(5), 296-306. https://doi.org/10.1002/sd.346

Moon, J., Crane, A., & Matten, D. (2005). Can corporations be citizens? Corporate citizenship as a metaphor for business participation in society. Business Ethics Quarterly, 15(3), 429-453.

Mor, S., Morris, M. W., & Joh, J. (2013). Identifying and training adaptive cross-cultural management skills: The crucial role of cultural metacognition. Academy of Management Learning and Education, 12(3), 453–475. https://doi.org/10.5465/amle.2012.0202

Mueller, M., dos Santos, V. G., & Seuring, S. (2009). The contribution of environmental and social standards towards ensuring legitimacy in supply chain governance. Journal of Business Ethics, 89(4), 509–523.

Mueller, S. L., & Thomas, A. S., (2001). Culture and entrepreneurial potential: A nine country study of locus of control and innovativeness, Journal of Business Venturing, 16(1), 51-75. https://doi.org/10.1016/S0883-9026(99)00039-7

Muller, J. E., & Nathan, D. G. (2020). COVID-19, nuclear war, and global warming: lessons for our vulnerable world. The Lancet, 395(10242), 1967-1968. https://doi.org/10.1016/S0140-6736(20)31379-9

Mullin, L. J. (2005). Management and organizational behavior (7e). Prentice Hall.

Nabli, M. K., & Nugent, J. B. (1989). The new institutional economics and its applicability to development. World Development, 1333-1347.

Nam, H., & Kannan, P. K. (2020). Digital environment in global markets: cross-cultural implications for evolving customer journeys. Journal of International Marketing, 28(1), 28-47.

Nan, R. (2013). Chinese private enterprises' management innovation. Asian Social Science, 9 (4). https://doi.org/10.5539/ass.v9n4p51

Nemiro, J. E. (2000). The glue that binds creative virtual teams. In Knowledge management and virtual organizations (pp. 101-123). IGI Global.

Nemiro, J. E. (2016). Connection in creative virtual teams. Journal of Behavioral and Applied Management, 2(2), 814.

Neuliep, J. (2014). Intercultural Communication: A Contextual Approach (6e). Sage.

Ney, S. (2006). Messy issues, policy conflict and the differentiated polity: Analysing contemporary policy responses to complex, uncertain and transversal policy problems. Unpublished doctoral dissertation, LOS Center for Bergen, Vienna, Austria.

Ng, E. S., & Wyrick, C. R. (2011). Motivational bases for managing diversity: A model of leadership commitment. Human Resource Management Review, 21(4), 368-376.

Ng, K.-Y., Van Dyne, L., & Ang, S. (2012). Cultural intelligence: A review, reflections, and recommendations for future research. In A. M. Ryan, F. T. L.

Leong, & F. L. Oswald (Eds.), Conducting multinational research: Applying organizational psychology in the workplace (pp. 29–58). American Psychological Association.

Niehans, J. (2008). Transaction Costs. In The new Palgrave dictionary of economics (p. 13782). Palgrave Macmillan.

Nisbett, R. E., & Miyamoto, Y. (2005). The influence of culture: Holistic versus analytic perception. Trends in Cognitive Sciences, 9(10), 467-473.

Nishii, L. H., & Ozbilgin, M. F. (2007). Global diversity management: towards a conceptual framework. The International Journal of Human Resource Management, 18(11), 1883-1894.

Nkomo, S., & Hoobler, J. M. (2014). A historical perspective on diversity ideologies in the United States: Reflections on human resource management research and practice. Human Resource Management Review, 24(3), 245-257.

North, D. C. (1990). Institutions, institutional change and economic performance. Cambridge University Press. https://doi.org/10.1017/CBO978 0511808678

North, D. C. (1993). The new institutional economics and development. Economic History, 1-8.

Nouri, R., Erez, M., Rockstuhl, T., Ang, S., Leshem-Calif, L., & Rafaeli, A. (2013). Taking the bite out of culture: The impact of task structure and task type on overcoming impediments to cross-cultural team performance. Journal of Organizational Behavior, 34(6), 739–763. https://doi.org/10.1002/job.1871

NWBC (National Women's Business Council) (2012). What is supplier diversity? Retrieved from URL: https://cdn.www.nwbc.gov/wp-content/uploads/2012/01/05065029/fact-sheet-supplier-diversity.png.

Nydegger, R., & Nydegger, L. (2010). Challenges In Managing Virtual Teams. Journal of Business & Economics Research (JBER), 8(3), 69–82. https://doi.org/10.19030/jber.v8i3.690

O'Reilly, C.A., & Chatman, J.A. (1996). Culture as social control: corporations, cult and commitment. Research in Organizational behaviour, 18, 157-200.

O'Reilly, T. (2005). What is Web 2.0: Design patterns and business models for the next generation of software. Retrieved from http://www. oreillynet.com/pub/a/oreilly/tim/news/2005/09/3 0/what-is-web-20. html.

Ochieng, E.G., Price, A.D.F., Ruan, X., Egbu, C.O., & Moore, D. (2013). The effect of cross-cultural uncertainty and complexity within multicultural construction teams. Engineering, Construction and Architectural Management, 20(3), 307-324. https://doi.org/10.1108/09699981311324023

Ochoa-Zazueta, J. Á. (2006) Entrevista personal. Los Mochis, Sinaloa, mayo marzo 16.

OECD (2018) Diversity Survey Report. .https://survey.oecd.org/Survey.aspx?s=f0363306250a408a9ae40c139e88215c

Oertig, M., & Buergi, T. (2006). The challenges of managing cross-cultural virtual project teams. Team Performance Management, 12(1–2), 23–30. https://doi.org/10.1108/13527590610652774

Oh, J. M., & Moon, N. (2013). Towards a cultural user interface generation principles. Multimedia tools and applications, 63(1), 195-216.

Ohmae, K. (1990/1999). The borderless world. Harper Business.

Okoro, E. (2013). International Organizations and Operations: An Analysis of Cross-Cultural Communication Effectiveness and Management Orientation. Journal of Business & Management, 1(1), 1-13.

Olsen, S. O., Tudoran, A. A., Honkanen, P., & Verplanken, B. (2016). Differences and similarities between impulse buying and variety seeking: A personality-based perspective. Psychology & Marketing, 33(1), 36-47.

Onyusheva, I., Thammashote, L., & Thongaim, J. (2020). Urban Business Environment: Managing Cross-Cultural Problems. The EUrASEANs: Journal on Global Socio-Economic Dynamics, 1(20), 30-43.

Oppenheim, C., & Ward, L. (2006). Evaluation of web sites for B2C e-commerce. Aslib Proceedings, 58(3), 237–260. https://doi.TsauTsaiorg/10.1108/00012530610701022

Ordorica, S. (2020, November 23). Getting Lost In Translation: Three Critical Ways Businesses Fail in Global Markets. Forbes https://www.forbes.com/sites/forbesbusinesscouncil/2020/11/23/getting-lost-in-translation-three-critical-ways-businesses-fail-in-global-markets/?sh=48050d946c4a

Orij, R. P., Rehman, S., Khan, H., & Khan, F. (2021). Is CSR the new competitive environment for CEOs? The association between CEO turnover, corporate social responsibility and board gender diversity: Asian evidence. Corporate Social Responsibility and Environmental Management, 28(2), 731-747.

Ostgaard, T. A., & Birley, S. (1994). Personal networks and firm competitive strategy: a strategic or coincidental match? Journal of Business Venturing, 9(4), 281-305. https://doi.org/10.1016/0883-9026(94)90009-4

Oyserman, D., & Lee, S. W. (2008). Does culture influence what and how we think? Effects of priming individualism and collectivism. Psychological Bulletin, 134(2), 311-342.

Ozbilgin, M. (2018). What the racial equality movement can learn from the global fight for women's right. http://theconversation.com/what-the-racial-equality-movement-can-learn-from-the-global-fight-for-womens-rights-105616

Özbilgin, M. F., & Erbil, C. (2021). Social movements and wellbeing in organizations from multilevel and intersectional perspectives: The case of the# blacklivesmatter movement. The SAGE Handbook of Organizational Wellbeing, 119-138.

Ozbilgin, M., & Erbil, C. (2019). Yönetim çalışmaları alanındaki kısır yöntem ikilemlerini dışaçekimsel ve geçmişsel yaklaşım ve eleştirel gerçekçilikle yöntem yelpazesine dönüştürmek. Yönetim ve Çalışma Dergisi, 3(1), 1–24

Ozbilgin, M., & Tatli, A. (2008). Global Diversity Management: An Evidence Based Approach. London: Palgrave MacMillan.

Ozbilgin, M., Tatli, A., Ipek, G., & Sameer, M. (2016). Four approaches to accounting for diversity in global organizations. Critical Perspectives on Accounting, 35, 88-99.

Palalar, A. D., Özbilgin, M. F., & Kamasak, R. (2022). Covid-19: A catalyst for social innovation in managing diversity. Equality, Diversity & Inclusion.

Park, B., Chidlow, A., & Choi, J. (2014). Corporate social responsibility: Stakeholders influence on MNEs' activities. International Business Review, 23, 966–980.

Partiti, E. (2022). The place of voluntary standards in managing social and environmental risks in global value chains. European Journal of Risk Regulation, 13(1), 114-137.

Pauleen, D. J., & Yoong, P. (2001). Relationship building and the use of ICT in boundary-crossing virtual teams: a facilitator's perspective. Journal of Information Technology, 16(4), 205-220.

Payne, G., & Payne, J. (2004). Key concepts in social research. Sage.

Peng, A. C., Van Dyne, L., & Oh, K. (2015). The Influence of Motivational Cultural Intelligence on Cultural Effectiveness Based on Study Abroad: The Moderating Role of Participant's Cultural Identity. Journal of Management Education, 39(5), 572–596. https://doi.org/10.1177/1052562914555717

Peredo, A. M., & Mclean, M. (2006). Social entrepreneurship: A critical review of the concept. Journal of World Business, 41(1), 56-65. https://doi.org/10.1016/j.jwb.2005.10.007

Peric, M., Durkin, J. & Vitezic, V. (2017). The Constructs of a Business Model Redefined: A Half-Century Journey. Sage Open, 7(3). https://doi.org/10.1177/2158244017733516

Pettigrew, T.F. (1971). Racial separate or together? McGraw-Hill.

Phelan, J. E. (2018). Research, theories, and pedagogical practices of cultural metacognition in cross-cultural business education. In Maheshkar, C. & Sharma, V. (Eds.), Handbook of research in cross-cultural business education (pp. 115–139). IGI Global. https://doi.org/10.4018/978-1-5225-3776-2.ch006.

Pi, S. M., Liao, H. L., Liu, S. H., & Lee, I. S. (2011). Factors influencing the behavior of online group-buying in Taiwan. African Journal of Business Management, 5(16), 7120-7129.

Picherit-Duthler, G. (2014). How Similar or Different are We? In I. R. Management Association (USA) (Ed.), Cross-Cultural Interaction (pp. 80–92). IGI Global. https://doi.org/10.4018/978-1-4666-4979-8.ch006

Pitts, D. W. (2007). Implementation of diversity management programs in public organizations: Lessons from policy implementation research. International Journal of Public Administration, 30(12-14), 1573-1590.

Pless, N., & Maak, T. (2004). Building an Inclusive Diversity Culture: Principles, Processes and Practice. Journal of Business Ethics, 54(2), 129–147. https://doi.org/10.1007/s10551-004-9465-8

Porter, M.(1990). Competitive Advantage of Nations. Harvard Business Review.

Portes, A., & Vickstrom, E. (2015). Diversity, social capital, and cohesion. SERIES «ETUDESEUROPEENNES, 41.

Powell, W. & DiMaggio, P. (Ed.). (1991). The new institutionalism in organizational analysis. University Chicago Press.

Prasetyo, P. E., & Kistanti, N. R. (2020a). Human Capital, Institutional Economics and Entrepreneurship as a Driver for Quality & Sustainable Economic Growth. Entrepreneurship and Sustainability Issues, 7, 2575-2589. https://doi.org/10.9770/jesi.2020.7.4(1)

Presbitero, A. (2021). Communication accommodation within global virtual team: The influence of cultural intelligence and the impact on interpersonal process effectiveness. Journal of International Management, 27(1), 100809.

Pye, L. W. (1985). Asian power and politics. Belknap Press of Harvard University Press.

Raghuram, S., Hill, N. S., Gibbs, J. L., & Maruping, L. M. (2019). Virtual Work: Bridging Research Clusters. Academy of Management Annals, 13(1), 308–341. https://doi.org/10.5465/annals.2017.0020

Rana, M. (2018). Cultural Variations in Organizations of India and United States: A Comparative Study. International Journal of Arts and Commerce, 7(1), 16-28.

Rao, K., & Tilt, C. (2016). Board composition and corporate social responsibility: The role of diversity, gender, strategy and decision making. Journal of Business Ethics, 138(2), 327-347.

Reeves, M., Wesselink, E., & Whitaker, K. (2020, July 1). The end of bureaucracy, again? BCG Henderson Institute. https://bcghendersoninstitute.com/the-end-of-bureaucracy-again/

Reinecke, K., & Bernstein, A. (2013). Knowing What a User Likes: A Design Science Approach to Interfaces that Automatically Adapt to Culture. MIS Quarterly, 37(2), 427–453. http://www.jstor.org/stable/43825917

Restrepo, E. (2016). El proceso de investigación etnográfica: consideraciones éticas. Etnografías contemporáneas, 1(1). http://revistasacademicas.unsam.edu.ar/index.php/etnocontemp/article/view/395

Reynolds, C. R. & Fletcher-Janzen, E. (Eds.) (2008). Pluralism, Cultural. Encyclopedia of Special Education. https://doi.org/10.1002/9780470373699.speced1627

Reynolds, K. (2018). 13 benefits and challenges of cultural diversity in the workplace. HULT International Business School Blog. https://www.hult.edu/blog/benefits-challenges-cultural-diversity-workplace/

Rice, R. E., & Leonardi, P. M. (2014). Information and communication technologies in organizations. The SAGE handbook of organizational communication: advances in theory, research, and methods, 425-448.

Riding, A. (2006, December 26). American culture's French connection. The New York Times. https://www.nytimes.com/2006/12/26/books/26martel.html

Rinne, T., Steel, G. D., & Fairweather, J. (2012). Hofstede and Shane Revisited: The Role of Power Distance and Individualism in National-Level Innovation Success. Cross-Cultural Research, 46(2), 91–108. https://doi.org/10.1177/1069397111423898

Risse-Kappen, T., Risse, T., Ropp, S. C., & Sikkink, K. (Eds.). (1999). The power of human rights: International norms and domestic change (Vol. 66). Cambridge University Press.

Ritzer, G. & Malone, E. (2001). Globalization theory: Lessons from the exportation of McDonaldization and the new means of consumption. In G. Ritzer (Ed.), Explorations in the sociology of consumption. Sage.

Ritzer, G. (2003). Rethinking Globalization: Glocalization/Grobalization and Something/Nothing. Sociological Theory, 21(3), 193-209.

Ritzer, G. (2010). Globalization: A Basic Text. Wiley.

Robertson, R. (2001). Globalization Theory 2000+: Major Problematics. In G. Ritzer & B. Smart (Eds.), Handbook of Social Theory. Sage.

Robinson, K. J. (2013). An examination of virtual teams: Exploring the relationship among emotional intelligence, collective team leadership, and team effectiveness. Doctoral Dissertation. Capella University.

Rohm Jr., F. W. (2010). American and Arab Cultural Lenses. Inner Resources for Leaders, 3(2).

Roland, G. (2016). Development economics. Routledge.

Romani, I., & Claes, M. T. (2014). Why critical intercultural communication studies are to be taken seriously in cross-cultural management research? International Journal of Cross Cultural Management, 14(1), 127-132. https://doi.org/10.1177/1470595813507156

Ross, C., Orr, E. S., Sisic, M., Arseneault, J. M., Simmering, M. G., & Orr, R. R. (2009). Personality and motivations associated with Facebook use. Computers in human behavior, 25(2), 578-586.

Rowe, M. (2008). Micro-affirmations and micro-inequities. Journal of the International Ombudsman Association, 1(1), 1–9.

Roy, D. (2019). The adaptation of cross-cultural competence. Training Industry, 13(1). https://www.nxtbook.com/nxtbooks/trainingindustry/tiq_2 0191112/index.php#/p/52

Ruggie, J., & Des Nations, P. (2011). Guiding Principles on Business and Human Rights: Implementing the UN "Protect, Respect and Remedy" Framework. Report of the Special Representative of the Secretary General on the issue of human rights and transnational corporations and other business enterprises.

Rusko, R. (2014). Mapping the perspectives of coopetition and technology-based strategic networks: A case of smartphones. Industrial Marketing Management, 43(5), 801-812. https://doi.org/10.1016/j.indmarman.2014.04 .013

Russ, T. L. (2011). 'Theory X/Y assumptions as predictors of managers' propensity for participative decision making. Management Decision, 49 (5), 823-883.

Ryan, T., & Xenos, S. (2011). Who uses Facebook? An investigation into the relationship between the Big Five, shyness, narcissism, loneliness, and Facebook usage. Computers in human behavior, 27(5), 1658-1664.

Safina, M. S., & Valeev, A. A. (2015). Study of humanitarian high school students' readiness for intercultural communication formation. Review of European Studies, 7(5), 52-60.

Sager, K. L. (2008). An Exploratory Study of the Relationships between Theory X/Y Assumptions and Superior Communicator Style. Management Communication Quarterly, 22(2), 288–312. https://doi.org/10.1177/0893318 908323148

Salas, E., Burke, C.S., Fowlkes, J.E., & Wilson, K.A. (2004). Challenges and Approaches to Understanding Leadership Efficacy in Multi-Cultural Teams. In Kaplan, M. (Ed.), Cultural Ergonomics (Advances in Human Performance and Cognitive Engineering Research, Vol. 4) (pp. 341-384). Emerald Group Publishing. https://doi.org/10.1016/S1479-3601(03)04012-8

Salk, J. E., & Brannen, M. Y. (2000). National Culture, Networks, and Individual Influence in a Multinational Management Team. Academy of Management Journal, 43(2), 191–202. https://doi.org/10.2307/1556376

Salkar, R. (2021). The Importance and Future Scope of Management & Strategy in Today's Market. https://www.consultantsreview.com/cxoinsights/the-importance-and-future-scope-of-management--strategy-in-today-s-market-vid-490.html

Sandoval-Forero, E. A., Guerra-García, E., & Delgado-Buelna, R. A. (2008). Una visión sociointercultural del ausentismo intermitente de yoremes y mestizos en la UAIM. Tiempo de Educar, 9 (17), 9-34.

Santoso, H.B., & Schrepp, M. (2019). The impact of culture and product on the subjective importance of user experience aspects. Heliyon, 5(9), e02434. https://doi.org/10.1016/j.heliyon.2019.e02434

Sarkar, S. (2021, July 16). DealShare, a social commerce startup, is using the community group-buying model to cater to the online shopping interests of consumers belonging to smaller Indian towns and cities. Dutch Uncles. https://dutchuncles.in/discover/dealshare-promoting-the-community-group-buying-model/

Saudi police outlaw Barbie (2003, September 10). The Sydney Morning Herald. https://www.smh.com.au/world/saudi-police-outlaw-barbie-20030 910-gdhd5i.html

Scheibel, S. (2012). Against all odds: Evidence for the 'true' cosmopolitan consumer. [Masters Dissertation, London School of Economics and Political Science]. MEDIA@LSE. https://www.lse.ac.uk/media-and-communications /assets/documents/research/msc-dissertations/2011/63.pdf

Schein, E. H. (1990). Organizational culture. American Psychologist, 45(2), 109–119. https://doi.org/10.1037/0003-066X.45.2.109

Scherer, A. G., & Palazzo, G. (2008). Globalization and corporate social responsibility. Globalization and Corporate Social Responsibility. In Crane, A., Matten, D., McWilliams, A., Moon, J. & Siegel, D.S. (Eds.), The Oxford Handbook of Corporate Social Responsibility (pp. 413-431). Oxford University Press.

Scherer, A. G., & Palazzo, G. (2011). The new political role of business in a globalized world: A review of a new perspective on CSR and its implications for the firm, governance, and democracy. Journal of Management Studies, 48(4), 899-931.

Schiffman, L. G. & Kanuk, L. L. (2010). Consumer Behaviour (10e). Pearson.

Schiffman, L., Wisenblit, J., & Kumar, S. R. (2016). Consumer Behavior (11e). Pearson India.

Schlevogt, K. (2002). The art of Chinese management: Theory, evidence, and applications. Oxford University Press.

Schmitz, A. (2012). Leading with cultural intelligence. Saylor Academy. Retrieved from https://saylordotorg.github.io/text_leading-with-cultural-intelligence/index.html

Schroeder, P. J. (2010). Changing team culture: The perspectives of ten successful head coaches. Journal of Sport Behavior, 33(1), 63–88.

Schulz, K. (2019, December 23). Shopping in a collective – Social commerce is evolving into social group buying. Dmexo.Com. Retrieved March 7, 2022, from https://dmexco.com/stories/shopping-in-a-collective-social-commerce-is-evolving-into-social-group-buying

Schwartz, S.H. (1999). A Theory of Cultural Values and Some Implications for Work. Applied Psychology: an international review, 48(1), 23-47.

Scott, C. P., & Wildman, J. L. (2015). Culture, communication, and conflict: A review of the global virtual team literature. Leading global teams, 13-32.

Scott, R. (2002). The changing world of Chinese enterprise: An institutional perspective. In Tsui, A. S. & Lau, C. (eds.), The management of enterprises in the People's Republic of China (pp. 59-78). Kluwer Academic Publishers.

Scroggins, W. A., Mackie, D. M., Allen, T. J., & Sherman, J. W. (2016). Reducing prejudice with labels: Shared group memberships attenuate implicit bias and expand implicit group boundaries. Personality and Social Psychology Bulletin, 42(2), 219–229. https://doi.org/10.1177/0146167215621048

Seah, L. (2021). The importance of cultural awareness in international business. International Business Blog. https://www.airswift.com/blog/importance-of-cultural-awareness

Searle, J. R. (1995). The construction of social reality. New York: The Free Press.

Seitz, V., Razzouk, N., & Nakayama, C. (2007). Leading the Fight Against Global Warming: Hybrid Cars in Emerging Markets. Proceedings of International Research Conference Change Leadership in Romania's New Economy (p. 89). California State University of San Bernardino, USA.

Semenova, N., & Hassel, L. G. (2019). Private engagement by Nordic institutional investors on environmental, social, and governance risks in global companies. Corporate Governance: An International Review, 27(2), 144-161.

Serrat, O. (2017). Managing Virtual Teams. In Knowledge Solutions (pp. 619–625). Singapore: Springer Singapore. https://doi.org/10.1007/978-981-10-0983-9_68

Shachaf, P. (2008). Cultural diversity and information and communication technology impacts on global virtual teams: An exploratory study. Information & Management, 45(2), 131-142.

Shala, B., Prebreza, A. & Ramosaj, B. (2021). The Contingency Theory of Management as a Factor of Acknowledging the Leaders-Managers of Our Time Study Case: The Practice of the Contingency Theory in the Company Avrios. Open Access Library Journal, 8, 1-20. https://doi.org/10.4236/oalib.1107850

Shane S. and Venkataraman S. (2000). The promise of entrepreneurship as a field of research. The Academy Management Review, 25(1), 217–226. https://doi.org/10.2307/25927

Sharma, S. (2010, August 27). Group buying ventures are here to stay in India? entrepreneurs and investors talk on the current opportunities and challenges in this space. YourStory.com. Retrieved October 12, 2021, from https://yourstory.com/2010/08/group-buying-ventures-are-here-to-stay-in-india-entrepreneurs-and-investors-talk-on-the-current-opportunities-and-challenges-in-this-space/amp.

Shiau, W. L., & Luo, M. M. (2012). Factors affecting online group buying intention and satisfaction: A social exchange theory perspective. Computers in Human Behavior, 28(6), 2431-2444.

Shiraev, E. B. & Leavy, D. A. (2010). Cross-Cultural Psychology: Critical Thinking and Contemporary Applications (4e). Allyn & Bacon.

Shneiderman, B. (1998). Designing the User Interface. Addison-Wesley.

Shore, L. M., Cleveland, J. N., & Sanchez, D. (2018). Inclusive workplaces: A review and model. Human Resource Management Review, 28(2), 176-189.

Silin, R. (1976). Leadership and values. Harvard University Press.

Sippola, A., & Smale, A. (2007). The global integration of diversity management: A longitudinal case study. The International Journal of Human Resource Management, 18(11), 1895-1916.

Sison, A. J. G. (2007). Toward a common good theory of the firm: The Tasubinsa case. Journal of Business Ethics, 74(4), 471-480.

Sison, A. J. G., & Fontrodona, J. (2012). The common good of the firm in the Aristotelian-Thomistic tradition. Business Ethics Quarterly, 22(2), 211-246.

Sison, A. J. G., & Fontrodona, J. (2013). Participating in the common good of the firm. Journal of Business Ethics, 113(4), 611-625.

Slevin, D. P., & Covin, J. G. (1990). New venture strategic posture, structure, and performance: an industry life cycle analysis. Journal of Business Venturing, 5(2), 123-135. https://doi.org/10.1016/0883-9026(90)90004-D

Soares, A. M., Farhangmehr, M., & Shoham, A. (2007). Hofstede's dimensions of culture in international marketing studies. Journal of Business Research, 60(3), 277–284. https://doi.org/10.1016/j.jbusres.2006.10.018

Social commerce – The virtual shopping stroll with friends. (2021, March 2). Just-Style.Com. Retrieved March 7, 2022, from https://www.just-style.com/comment/social-commerce-the-virtual-shopping-stroll-with-friends/

Society for Human resource Management (SHRM). (2015). Cultural intelligence: The essential intelligence for the 21st century. SHRM Foundation. Retrieved from https://www.shrm.org/hr-today/trends-and-forecasting/special-reports-and-expert-views/Documents/Cultural-Intelligence.pdf

Søderberg, A.-M., & Holden, N. (2002). Rethinking Cross Cultural Management in a Globalizing Business World. International Journal of Cross-Cultural Management, 2(1), 103–121. https://doi.org/10.1177/147059580221007

Søderberg, A.-M., & Holden, N. (2002). Rethinking Cross Cultural Management in a Globalizing Business World. International Journal of Cross Cultural Management, 2(1), 103–121. https://doi.org/10.1177/147059580221007

Song, S. (2022). Cultural diversification, human resource-based coordination, and downside risks of multinationality. Journal of Business Research, 142, 562-571.

Soni, V. (2000). A twenty-first-century reception for diversity in the public sector: a case study. Public Administration Review, 60(5), 395-408.

Staats, C., Capatosto, K., Tenney, L., & Mamo, S. (2017). Implicit bias review. https://kirwaninstitute.osu.edu/

Stahl, G. K., & Maznevski, M. L. (2021). Unraveling the effects of cultural diversity in teams: A retrospective of research on multicultural work groups and an agenda for future research. Journal of International Business Studies, 52(1), 4-22.

Stahl, G. K., Maznevski, M. L., Voigt, A., & Jonsen, K. (2010). Unraveling the effects of cultural diversity in teams: A meta-analysis of research on multicultural work groups. Journal of international business studies, 41(4), 690-709.

Stallard, M. L., Pankau, J., & Stallard, K. P. (2015). Connection culture. ATD Press.

Stefan, G. (2010). Carbon Management in Tourism: Mitigating the Impacts on Climate Change (1st ed.). Routledge. https://doi.org/10.4324/9780203861523

Steinberg, S. R., & Kincheloe, J. L. (2009). Smoke and Mirrors: More than one way to be diverse and multicultural. In S. R. Steinberg (Ed.), Diversity and Multiculturalism: a Reader (pp. 3–22). New York: Peter Lang.

Sternberg, R. J. (1984). Toward a triarchic theory of human intelligence. Behavioral and Brain Sciences, 7(2), 269–287. https://doi.org/10.1017/S014052 5X00044629

Sternberg, R. J. (1988). The triarchic mind: A new theory of human intelligence. Viking Press.

Steurer, R. (2006). Mapping stakeholder theory anew: from the 'stakeholder theory of the firm' to three perspectives on business–society relations. Business Strategy and the Environment, 15(1), 55-69.

Storti, C. (2011a). Figuring foreigners out: A practical guide. Hachette UK.

Storti, C. (2011b). The Art of Crossing Cultures. Hachette UK.

Stuart, R., & Abetti, P. A. (1987). Start-up ventures: towards the prediction of initial success. Journal of Business Venturing, 2(3), 215-230. https://doi.org/ 10.1016/0883-9026(87)90010-3

Stulec, Ivana, and Kristina Petljak. (2010). Moc grupne kupovine. Suvremena trgovina 35 (6): 22–25.

Sue, D. W., Capodilupo, C. M., Torino, G. C., Bucceri, J. M., Holder, A. M., Nadal, K. L., & Esquilin, M. (2007). Racial microaggressions in everyday life: Implications for clinical practice. American Psychologist, 62(4), 271–286. https://doi.org/10.1037/0003-066X.62.4.271

Sullivan, G., Weerawardena, J., & Carnegie, K. (2003). Social entrepreneurship: Towards conceptualization. International Journal of Nonprofit and Voluntary Sector Marketing, 8(1), 76-88. https://doi.org/10.1002/nvsm.202

Syed, J., & Ozbilgin, M. (2009). A relational framework for international transfer of diversity management practices. The International Journal of Human Resource Management, 20(12), 2435-2453.

Tamanaha, B. (2015). The knowledge and policy limits of new institutional economics on development. Journal of Economic Issues, 49(1), 89-109. https://doi.org/10.1080/00213624.2015.1013881

Tandon, S. (2021, May 4). Social Commerce gets closer to being 'formal'. mint. Retrieved October 12, 2021, from https://www.livemint.com/industry/retail/ social-commerce-gets-closer-to-being-formal-11620156344574.html.

Tang, J. & Ward, A. (2002). The changing face of Chinese management. Routledge.

Taras, V., Baack, D., Caprar, D., Dow, D., Froese, F., Jimenez, A., & Magnusson, P. (2019). Diverse effects of diversity: Disaggregating effects of diversity in global virtual teams. Journal of International Management, 25(4), 100689.

Tatli, A., Vassilopoulou, J., Ariss, A. A., & Ozbilgin, M. (2012). The role of regulatory and temporal context in the construction of diversity discourses: The case of the UK, France and Germany. European Journal of Industrial Relations, 18(4), 293-308.

Taylor, E. (1871). Primitive Culture. Putnam's Son.

Taylor, W. F. (2008). The Principles of Scientific Management. Digireads Publishing.

The Economic Times. (2021, June 13). Amway plans to invest Rs 170 crore over the next two to three years in India. Retrieved from https://economictimes. indiatimes.com//news/company/corporate-trends/amway-plans-to-invest -rs-170-crore-over-the-next-two-to-three-years-in-india/articleshow/83480 060.cms?utm_source=contentofinterest&utm_medium=text&utm_campaig n=cppst

The World Bank. (2022). International Comparison Program, World Bank. The World Bank. https://data.worldbank.org/indicator/NY.GNP.MKTP.PP.KD

Thomas, D. C. (2006). Domain and development of cultural intelligence: The importance of mindfulness. Gr. Organ. Manag., 31(1), 78–99. https://doi.org /10.1177/1059601105275266

Thomas, D. C., Elron, E., Stahl, G., Ekelund, B. Z., Ravlin, E. C., Cerdin, J. L., & Maznevski, M. (2008). Cultural intelligence: Domain and assessment. International Journal of Cross Cultural Management, 8(2), 123–143. https:// doi.org/10.1177/1470595808091787

Thompson, A., Peteraf, M., Gamble, J., Strickland III, A. J., & Jain, A. K. (2013). Crafting & executing strategy 19/e: The quest for competitive advantage: Concepts and cases. McGraw-Hill Education.

Thompson, J. L. (2002). The world of the social entrepreneur. International Journal of Public Sector Management, 15(5), 412-431. https://doi.org/10.110 8/09513550210435746

Thompson, P., & Mchugh, D. (2002). Management and Control. Work organizations (2e), Palgrave.

Tian, L., Li, Y., Li, P. P., & Bodla, A. A. (2015). Leader–member skill distance, team cooperation, and team performance: A cross-culture study in a context of sport teams. International Journal of Intercultural Relations, 49, 183–197. https://doi.org/10.1016/j.ijintrel.2015.10.005

Tomar, B. (2019). The Importance of Cross-Cultural Management. Forbes. https://www.forbes.com/sites/forbeslacouncil/2019/04/23/the-importance-of-cross-cultural-management/?sh=4021b971b5c3

Tong, C.K. &Yong, P.K. (2014). Guanxi Bases, Xinyong and Chinese Business Networks. In Tong, CK. (Ed.), Chinese Business. Springer. https://doi.org/10. 1007/978-981-4451-85-7_3

Tong, C.K. (2014). The Rise of China and Its Implications. In: Tong, CK. (Ed.), Chinese Business. Springer. https://doi.org/10.1007/978-981-4451-85-7_8

Top Group Buying Startups. (2022, January 14). Tracxn.Com. Retrieved March 7, 2022, from https://tracxn.com/d/trending-themes/Startups-in-Group-Buying

Touraine, A. (2000). Igualdad y diversidad: las nuevas tareas de la democracia. Fondo de Cultura Económica.

Townsend, A. M., DeMarie, S. M., & Hendrickson, A. R. (1998). Virtual teams: Technology and the workplace of the future. Academy of Management Perspectives, 12(3), 17-29.

Tracey, P., Phillips, N., & Jarvis, O. (2011). Bridging institutional entrepreneurship and the creation of new organizational forms: a multilevel model. Organization Science, 22(1), 60-80.

Trevino, L. K., & Weaver, G. R. (1994). Business ETHICS/BUSINESS ethics: One Field or Two?. Business Ethics Quarterly, 4(2), 113-128. https://doi.org/10.23 07/3857484

Tsai, K. S. (2007). Capitalism without democracy: The private sector in contemporary China. Cornell University Press.

Tsai, W. H. S., & Zhang, J. (2016). Understanding the Global Phenomenon of Online Group Buying: Perspective from China and the United States. Journal of Global Marketing, 29(4), 188–202. https://doi.org/10.1080/08911762.2016 .1138565

Tsui, A. S. & Lau, C. (Ed.). (2002). The management of enterprises in the People's Republic of China. Kluwer Academic Publishers.

Tsui, A. S., Bian, Y. & Cheng, L. (Ed.). (2006). China's domestic private firms: Multidisciplinary perspectives on management and performance. M.E. Sharpe. Walder, A. (1986). Communist neo-traditionalism: Work and authority in Chinese industry. University of California Press.

Tung, R. L. (2008). The cross-cultural research imperative: The need to balance cross-national and intra-national diversity. Journal of International Business Studies, 39(1), 41-46.

Turan, H. (2015). Taylor's "Scientific Management Principles": Contemporary Issues in Personnel Selection Period. Journal of Economics, Business and Management, 3(11), 1102-1105.

Turban, E., King, D., Lee, J. K., & Viehland, D. (2006). Electronic Commerce: A Managerial Approach.

Tzu-Ping, Y. & Wei-Wen, C. (2017). The Relationship between Cultural Intelligence and Psychological Well-being with the Moderating Effects of Mindfulness: A Study of International Students in Taiwan. European Journal of Multidisciplinary Studies, 5(1), 384. https://doi.org/10.26417/ejms.v5i1.p384-391

Urbano, D., Toledano, N., & Soriano, D. R. (2010). Analyzing social entrepreneurship from an institutional perspective: evidence from Spain. Journal of social entrepreneurship, 1 (1), 54-69. https://doi.org/10.1080/19420 670903442061

Van der Zee, K.I., & Van Oudenhoven, J.P. (2000). The Multicultural Personality Questionnaire: A multidimensional instrument of multicultural effectiveness. European Journal of Personality, 14(4), 291–309.

Van Dyne, L., Ang, S., & Koh, C. (2008). Development and validation of the CQS: The cultural intelligence scale. In S. Ang & L. Van Dyne (Eds.), Handbook of cultural intelligence: Theory, measurement, and application (pp. 16–38). M.E. Sharpe.

Van Dyne, L., Ang, S., Ng, K. Y., Rockstuhl, T., Tan, M. L., & Koh, C. (2012). Sub-Dimensions of the Four Factor Model of Cultural Intelligence: Expanding the conceptualization and measurement of cultural intelligence. Social and Personality Psychology Compass, 6(4), 295–313. https://doi.org/10.1111/j.1751-9004.2012.00429.x

Van Tulder, R., Van Wijk, J., & Kolk, A. (2009). From chain liability to chain responsibility. Journal of Business Ethics, 85(2), 399–412.

Vargas-Hernández, J. G. (2005). Emergencia de la nueva cultura institucional: impacto en la transformación del escenario de la globalización económica. Economía, Sociedad y Territorio, 5(17), 27-61.

Vargas-Hernández, J. G., Guerra García, E., & Valdez Zepeda (2017). La nueva gobernanza instrumental del estado de bienestar: transformaciones y retos. Editorial Universitaria: Universidad de Guadalajara, Centro Universitario de Ciencias Económico Administrativas, Guadalajara, Jalisco.

Vasquez, E. A., & Frankel, B. (2017). The business case for global supplier diversity and inclusion: The critical contributions of women and other underutilized suppliers to corporate value chains. WeConnect International, Retrieved from URL: https://weconnectinternational.org/images/Report.pdf

Vásquez, O., Fernández, M., & Álvarez, P. (2014). La aportación de los grados al desarrollo de la sensibilidad y competencia intercultural. Perspectiva comparada entre Trabajo Social y Psicología Revista: Cuadernos de Trabajo Social, 27(2), 307-317.

Vassilopoulou, J. (2017). Diversity management as window dressing? A company case study of a Diversity Charta member in Germany. In Management and Diversity: Perspectives from Different National Contexts (pp. 281-306). Emerald Publishing Limited.

Venkatesh, V., Sykes, T. A., & Venkatraman, S. (2014). Understanding e-government portal use in rural India: Role of demographic and personality characteristics. Information Systems Journal, 24(3), 249–269.

Venkatraman, N. (1989). The concept of fit in strategy research: toward verbal and statistical correspondence. The Academy of Management Review, 1(3), 423-444. https://doi.org/10.2307/258177

Verbeke, A., & Kano, L. (2016). An internalization theory perspective on the global and regional strategies of multinational enterprises. Journal of World Business, 51(1), 83-92.

Vich, M. (2015). The emerging role of mindfulness research in the workplace and its challenges. Central European Business Review, 4(3), 35–47. https://doi.org/10.18267/j.cebr.131

Victor, D. A. (1992). International business communication. HarperCollins.

Waddell, D., Jones, G.R., & George, J. (2013). Contemporary Management (3e). McGraw-Hill Education.

Waddock, S., & Smith, N. (2000). Relationships: The real challenge of corporate global citizenship. Business and Society Review, 105(1), 47-62.

Wadhwani, R. D. (2018). Poverty's monument: Social problems and organizational field emergence in historical perspective. Journal of Management Studies, 55(3), 545-577.

Walder, A. (1989). Factory and manager in an era of reform. China Quarterly, 118, 242-264.

Wallis, A. (2020). How to create a personal growth and development plan. Southern New Hampshire University. Retrieved July 21, 2021 from https://www.snhu.edu /about-us/newsroom/2018/07/personal-development-plan

Wang, C., Tee, D. & Ahmed, P. (2012). Entrepreneurial leadership and context in Chinese firms: A tale of two Chinese private enterprises. Asian Pacific Business Review, 18(4), 505-530.

Wang, X., Bruning, N. & Peng, S. (2007). Western high-performance HR practices in China: A comparison among public-owned, private and foreign-invested enterprises. International Journal of Human Resource Management, 18 (4), 684-701.

Wang, Y. (2015). Globalization and Territorial Identification: A Multilevel Analysis Across 50 Countries. International Journal of Public Opinion Research, 28(3), 401-414. https://doi.org/10.1093/ijpor/edv022

Wang, Y. (2018). Trust, job security and subordinate-supervisor guanxi: Chinese employees in joint ventures and state-owned enterprises. Asia Pacific Business Review, 24(5), 638-655.

Wank, D. (1999). Commodifying communism: Business, trust, and politics in Chinese society. Cambridge University Press.

Ward, C., Bochner, S., & Furnham, A. (2001). The psychology of culture shock. Routledge.

Ward, P. R., Mamerow, L., & Meyer, S. B. (2014). Interpersonal trust across six Asia-Pacific countries: testing and extending the 'high trust society' and 'low trust society' theory. PloS one, 9(4), e95555.

Webber, S. (2002). Leadership and trust facilitating cross-functional team success. Journal of Management Development, 21(3), 201–214. https://doi.org /10.1108/02621710210420273

Weil, D., & Mallo, C. (2007). Regulating labour standards via supply chains: Combining public/private interventions to improve workplace compliance. British Journal of Industrial Relations, 45(4), 791-814.

Wettstein, F., Giuliani, E., Santangelo, G. D., & Stahl, G. K. (2019). International business and human rights: A research agenda. Journal of World Business, 54(1), 54-65,

Whelton, B. (1996). A philosophy of nursing practice: An application of the Thomistic Aristotelian concepts of nature to the science of nursing. Unpublished doctoral dissertation, The Catholic University of America, Washington, DC.

White, N. (2014). Mechanisms of Mindfulness: Evaluating Theories and Proposing a Model (Unpublished master's thesis). Victoria University of Wellington, New Zealand. https://researcharchive.vuw.ac.nz/xmlui/bitstream /handle/10063/3377/thesis.pdf?sequence=2

Wigley, T. M. L. (1991). Could reducing fossil-fuel emissions cause global warming?. Nature, 349(6309), 503-506. https://doi.org/10.1038/349503a0

Wikipedia (2020). BaFa' BaFa'. In Wikipedia, The Free Encyclopedia. Retrieved on Apr. 7, 2021 from https://en.wikipedia.org/wiki/BaFa%27_BaFa%27

Wilkinson, B., Gamble, J., Humphrey, J., Morris, J., & Anthony, D. (2001). The new international division of labour in Asian electronics: Work organization and human resources in Japan and Malaysia. Journal of Management Studies, 38(5), 675-695.

Williams, D. A. (2013). Strategic Diversity Leadership: Activating Change and Transformation in Higher Education. Stylus Publishing, LLC.

Williams, G. A. (2020, September 2). What can luxury learn from group buying? Jing Daily. Retrieved October 13, 2021, from https://jingdaily.com/what-can-luxury-learn-from-group-buying/.

Willyarto, M. N., Wahyuningtyas, B. P., Yunus, U., & Heriyati, P. (2021, August). Cross-Cultural Communication in Micro/Small/Medium Enterprises Business by Using Social Media. In 2021 International Conference on Information Management and Technology (ICIMTech) (Vol. 1, pp. 88-92). IEEE.

Wong, G., Derthick, A. O., David, E. J. R., Saw, A., & Okazaki, S. (2014). The what, the why, and the how: A review of racial microaggressions research in psychology. Race and Social Problems, 6(2), 181–200. https://doi.org/10.1007/s12552-013-9107-9

Wood, A. E., & Mattson, C. A. (2019). Quantifying the effects of various factors on the utility of design ethnography in the developing world. Research in Engineering Design, 30(3), 317-338.

Wright, P.M. & Noe, R.A. (1996), Management of Organizations, Irwin McGraw-Hill.

Wright, T. (2010). Accepting authoritarianism: State-society Relations in China's reform era. Stanford University Press. Xia, F. & Walker, G. (2015). How much does owner type matter for firm performance? Manufacturing firms in China. Strategic Management Journal, 36, 576-585.

Xiong, M., Wang, C., Cui, N. & Wang, T. (2021). The influence of clan culture on business performance in Asian private-owned enterprises: The case of China. Industrial marketing management, 99, 97-110.

Xu, F. (2011, August). A comparative study of online group-coupon sale in USA and China. In 2011 2nd International Conference on Artificial Intelligence, Management Science and Electronic Commerce (AIMSEC) (pp. 1806-1809). IEEE.

Yalkin, Cagri, and Mustafa F. Özbilgin. (2022). Neo-colonial hierarchies of knowledge in marketing: Toxic field and illusio. Marketing Theory: 14705931221075369.

Yamagishi, T., Hashimoto, H., & Schug, J. (2008). Preferences Versus Strategies as Explanations for Culture-Specific Behavior. Psychological Science, 19(6), 579–584. https://doi.org/10.1111/j.1467-9280.2008.02126.x

Yamahaki, C., & Frynas, J. G. (2016). Institutional determinants of private shareholder engagement in Brazil and South Africa: The role of regulation. Corporate Governance: An International Review, 24(5), 509–527.

Yang, B., & Lester, D. (2005). Gender differences in e-commerce. Applied Economics, 37(18), 2077-2089.

Yang, L., Wang, N., Chen, Y., Yang, W., Tian, D., Zhang, C., Zhao, X., Wang, J., & Niu, S. (2020). Carbon management practices regulate soil bacterial communities in response to nitrogen addition in a pine forest. Plant and Soil, 452, 137-151.

Yang, Y., Ren, L., Li, H., Wang, H., Wang, P., Chen, L., Yue, X., & Liao, H. (2020). Fast climate responses to aerosol emission reductions during the COVID-19 pandemic. Geophysical Research Letters, 47(19), e2020GL089788. https://doi.org/10.1029/2020GL089788

Yin, R. K. (2003). Case study research: Design and methods (3rd ed.). Thousand Oaks, CA: Sage.

Yong, C. T. (2014). Guanxi Bases, Xinyong and Chinese Business Networks. In C. Tong, Chinese Business - Rethinking Guanxi and Trust in Chinese Business Networks. Singapore: Springer.

Zadek, S. & Thake, S. (1997): Practical people, noble causes. How to support community-based social entrepreneurs. New Economics Foundation, London.

Zakaria, N. (2000). The effects of cross-cultural training on the acculturation process of the global workforce. International Journal of Manpower.

Zakaria, N. (2009). Using computer mediated communication as a tool to facilitate intercultural collaboration of global virtual teams. In Encyclopedia of Multimedia Technology and Networking, Second Edition (pp. 1499-1505). IGI Global.

Zhang, H., Ding, D., & Ke, L. (2019). The effect of R&D input and financial agglomeration on the growth private enterprises: Evidence from Chinese manufacturing industry. Emerging Markets Finance & Trade, 55, 2298-2313.

Zhang, J. J., & Tsai, W. H. S. (2015). United We Shop! Chinese Consumers' Online Group Buying. Journal of International Consumer Marketing, 27(1), 54–68. https://doi.org/10.1080/08961530.2014.967902

Zhang, J., & Tsai, W. S. (2017). What Promotes Online Group-Buying? A Cross-Cultural Comparison Study between China and the United States. Journal of Promotion Management, 23(5), 748–768. https://doi.org/10.1080/10496491.2017.1297986

Zhang, X. (2009). Trade unions under the modernization of paternalist rule in China. Working USA: the Journal of Labor and Society, 12, 193-218. Zhong, Q. (2011). Models of trust-sharing in Chinese private enterprises. Economic Modelling, 28, 1017-1029.

Zheng, W., Shen, R., Zhong, W., & Lu, J. (2020). CEO Values, Firm Long-Term Orientation, and Firm Innovation: Evidence from Chinese Manufacturing Firms. Management and Organization Review, 16(1), 69-106.

Zhou, Q. (2020). Property Rights and Changes in China. Springer. https://doi.org/10.1007/978-981-15-9885-2

Zhou, X., Cai, H & Li, Q. (2006). Property rights regimes and firm behavior: Theory versus evidence. In Tsui, A. S., Bian, Y. & Cheng, L., China's domestic private firms: Multidisciplinary perspectives on management and Performance (pp. 97-119). M.E. Sharpe.

Zhu, J. & Delbridge, R. (2021). The management of second-generation migrant workers in China: A case study of centrifugal paternalism. Human Relations, 1872672110329. https://doi.org/10.1177/00187267211032948.

Zhu, Y., Nel, P., & Bhat, R. (2006). A cross cultural study of communication strategies for building business relationships. International Journal of Cross Cultural Management, 6(3), 319-341.

Zhu, Y., Webber, M. & Benson, J. (2010). The everyday impact of economic reform in China: management change, enterprise performance and daily life. Routledge.

Ziek, P., & Smulowitz, S. (2014). The impact of emergent virtual leadership competencies on team effectiveness. Leadership & Organization Development Journal.

Zivick, J. (2012). Mapping global virtual team leadership actions to organizational roles. The Business Review, 19(2), 18-25.

About the Contributors

Arti Sharma is a Fellow of the Indian Institute of Management, Indore (India) and is currently working as Assistant Professor at Jindal Global Business School, O.P. Jindal Global University, Sonipat, Haryana (India). She studied the impact and implications of affective group composition in her dissertation. She is a recipient of the Junior Research Fellowship (JRF) awarded by the University Grants Commission (UGC), India. She has also qualified for the National Eligibility Test for Lecturership conducted by UGC, India. She has presented her work at national and international conferences, such as the European Group of Organisation Studies, the British Academy of Management, the Australia & New Zealand Academy of Management, the Indian Academy of Management, and the PAN IIM conference. She has published papers, case studies, and book chapters in national and international peer-reviewed avenues. Her research interests lie in emotions, affective compositions and diversity.

Chandan Maheshkar is one of the founders of the East Nimar Society for Education (2019) dedicated to quality improvement in higher education and the development of educator competencies. As a Senior Consultant, he has served the Centre for Internal Quality Assurance (CIQA), Madhya Pradesh Bhoj (Open) University, Bhopal, India. He is associated with several management institutes in central India, including the University of Indore, India, in various academic roles. Dr. Maheshkar earned his MBA and Ph.D. from the University of Indore, India. In 2014, the University of Indore awarded him *Golden Jubilee Research Scholarship* on the occasion of completion of its successful 50 years. Business education, HRD, Cross-Culture Business, and organizational behavior are his core areas of research interests. His research papers and book chapters have been published in journals of international repute and edited collections by Sage, Emerald, Taylor & Francis, IGI Global and others, respectively.

Vinod Sharma is working as an Associate Professor at Symbiosis Centre for Management and Human Resource Development (SCMHRD), Symbiosis International (Deemed University), Pune, India. He has around 22 years of experience in both academia and industry, at different levels of management, which has prepared him to be an effective researcher and instructor. His areas of expertise include Marketing Research & Analytics, Marketing Strategy, and

Consumer Behaviour. He has authored over 75 papers in national and international journals of repute and completed three international projects on climate change and business strategy. He has been involved in various consultation research projects, conducted various research workshops, and also conducted training programs in association with MSME and FIEO on various subjects of management. He holds a Doctorate in Management from DAVV, Indore, India, and an MBA from the University of Wales in the United Kingdom.

Sushant Bhargava finished his Ph.D. in Organizational Behavior and Human Resource Management in 2022 with a concentration in Team Studies from the Indian Institute of Management Lucknow (India). He pursues rigorous research and teaching in various areas of management scholarship, such as sustainability, experimental methods, innovation, organizational change, and post-COVID work experiences. Dr. Bhargava has previous work experience in the Indian public sector banking sector. Currently, he is working as an Assistant Professor at the Indian Institute of Management Jammu (India) and pursues language learning and cultural studies as a hobby.

Tarika Nandedkar is currently working as Associate Professor with IBMR, IPS Academy, Indore. She has over 15 years of teaching experience at the postgraduate level. Dr. Tarika served as a Resource Person in the AICTE Training and Learning (ATAL) workshop. She also coordinated AICTE-sponsored STTP on Econometrics. She has presented several research papers at National and International Conferences and published 25 research papers in Proceedings and Journals. She has been awarded the best paper awards also. She has also attended several National and International Conferences, Seminars, Workshops, and Faculty Development Programs organized by renowned institutes, including IIT Bombay, IRTM College, Kolkata, ATAL and SWAYAM.

Amit Kumar, Associate Professor at IPS Academy IBMR Indore (MP) India, is specialized in 'Marketing' with teaching experience of 12 years. He has published 34 research papers in reputed journals and five book chapters. He has been awarded twice with the best paper award at international conferences. He carries a dynamic persona with a to-do attitude.

Yvonne Kamegne is a fourth-year Doctoral candidate and adjunct faculty in the department of computer and information science at Towson University. His research interest focuses on human-computer interaction, usable security, cross-cultural design, and human-centered design. His research study involves usability testing with human participants to gather data useful in understanding user requirements, user preferences, and user experience with distinct user interfaces. The endeavour of his research is to design usable, accessible, user-friendly, secure, and inclusive technologies for all.

Rauno Rusko is a University lecturer at the University of Lapland. His research activities focus on cooperation, competition, strategic management, digitizing and social media, supply chain management and entrepreneurship, mainly in the branches of information communication technology, forest industry and tourism. In addition to several book chapters, his articles appeared in the European Management Journal, Forest Policy and Economics, International Journal of Business Environment, Industrial Marketing Management, International Journal of Innovation in the Digital Economy and International Journal of Tourism Research, among others.

Sachin Sinha, in his career spanning 25 years till now, has taught at different business schools and also worked in the field of corporate communications. His doctoral research is on the role of psychographics in consumer behaviour. His areas of teaching interest include consumer psychology and marketing communications. Dr. Sinha has been engaged in prestigious consultancy assignments, including projects commissioned by the Ministry of Defence and Ministry of Rural Development of the Government of India and also the leading advertising agency Mudra Communications. He is empanelled as Visiting Faculty with the National Institute for Micro, Small and Medium Enterprises (ni-msme), Hyderabad, an organisation of the Ministry of MSMEs, Government of India. He has authored and presented research papers at eminent institutions like IIM Ahmedabad, IIM Indore, IIT Delhi and MDI Gurgaon. He has several publications in international and national journals of repute. He is also a literature and cinema enthusiast, and in addition to his academic publications, he also has two literary books to his credit.

Deepti Sinha has an overall experience of 20 years and is currently associated with Christ (Deemed to be University), Delhi NCR. Her specialisation is in Human Resource Management, and she has carried out her doctoral work in the area of Quality of Work Life. She is on the editorial and review boards of a few journals and has published one book and more than 25 research papers in various national and international journals. She is also on the panel of evaluators of NMIMS Global Access School of Continuing Education, Mumbai, and is certified as Accredited Management Teacher in the area of Organisational Behaviour by the All India Management Association, New Delhi.

Chandra Sekhar Patro is Assistant Professor at Gayatri Vidya Parishad College of Engineering (A), Visakhapatnam, India. He was awarded a PhD in Management from Andhra University. He has a postgraduate degree in Management from JNT University and Commerce from Andhra University. Dr. Patro has more than 12 years of experience in teaching and research in the area of Commerce and Management Studies. His teaching interests include e-marketing, financial management, and human resource management. His research interests include marketing, especially e-marketing, consumer behavior and HR management. Dr. Patro has published articles and chapters in reputed national and international journals. He has participated in and presented various papers at national and international seminars and conferences. He has been associated with various social bodies as a member and life member of these associations.

Rupa Rathee is presently working as Assistant Professor in the Department of Management Studies, DCRUST, Murthal (India). She has more than nineteen years of teaching experience to her credit. She has attended 30 FDPs at various prestigious institutes like IIM-Bangalore, IIM-Calcutta, IIM-Kozhikode, MDI-Gurgaon, IITM-Gwalior, JNTU-Hyderabad etc. She has contributed papers to fifty-six international conferences and national conferences. She has 50 publications to her credit in reputed international and national journals. Her areas of interest are Marketing and HRM.

Madhvi Lamba is pursuing her Ph.D. from Deenbandhu Chottu Ram University of Science and Technology, Murthal (India). She has completed her Master's in Business Administration and Bachelor's in Computer Applications from Deenbandhu Chottu Ram University of Science and Technology, Murthal (India). She is a gold medallist in her Bachelor's. She has presented papers at national and international conferences. Her area of interest surrounds Organizational Behavior and Human Resource Management.

Xiaodan Zhang is an Associate Professor of Sociology at York College, City University of New York. Her research focuses on labor and gender. It is part of her larger intellectual inquiries into the construction and reproduction of power relations in society. The theoretical questions are centered on the intricacies between institutions, ideological influence, human action and social change. She also examines cultural factors, especially regarding how and why certain cultural elements survive different social systems. Her most recent article, "The Empowerment Revisited: Capitalist Development and Women Workers in China's Reform Era," appears in *Global Women's Work: Perspectives on Gender and Work in the Global Economy* (Routledge 2018).

Rachna Bansal Jora is a Doctorate in Human Resource Management and Organizational Behavior and MBA in HR. She has qualified. University Grant Commission's National Eligibility Test (NET) in Human Resource Management and Industrial Relations. Prof. Jora has presented more than a dozen research papers at National and International conferences. She has published research work on issues pertaining to HR and OB in UGC-approved journals and Scopus Indexed Journals. Currently, she is working as Assistant Professor at Sharda University, Greater Noida, India and has experience of more than a decade in academics and research. She is very well versed in IT skills, including PowerPoint presentation, data analysis and presentation using various tools, including Excel, SPSS, AMOS, SMART PLS, and Tablue. She has earned some certificates in HRM, CSR, Unethical Decision Making, Psychology, and Leadership from the University of Minnesota, IIM Banglore, the University of Toronto, The University of Lausanne, and The University of Pennsylvania, respectively.

Rifat Kamasak is a Professor of Management and Strategy at Yeditepe University, Istanbul, Turkey. He also holds board membership positions in several companies listed on the Istanbul Stock Exchange (Borsa Istanbul, BIST – 100). He worked in the food, confectionery, carpet, textile, aluminium, metal, retailing, trading and consulting industries for nearly twenty years. He has done research, consultancy and training at a large number of organisations and runs his family's traditional hand-made carpet business. His primary interest areas are strategic management, knowledge and innovation and diversity management. Prof. Kamasak holds master's degrees from Durham University and the University of Oxford and a PhD from the University of Exeter, UK.

Mustafa F. Özbilgin is a Professor of Organisational Behaviour at Brunel Business School, London. He also holds two international positions: Co-Chaire Management et Diversité at Université Paris Dauphine and Visiting Professor of Management at Koç University in Istanbul. His research focuses on equality, diversity and inclusion at work from comparative and relational perspectives. He has conducted field studies in the UK and internationally, and his work is empirically grounded. International as well as national scientific bodies support his research. His work has a focus on changing policy and practice in equality and diversity at work. He is an engaged scholar, driven by values of workplace democracy, equality for all, and humanisation of work.

Meltem Yavuz Sercekman is a Lecturer at the Brunel Business School, Brunel University London, UK. She completed her PhD in the Department of Management and Organization at Marmara University, Turkey. She holds a master's degree in Psychology of Work with a thesis on "Mindfulness-based interventions and their reflections on organisations" in the Department of Neuroscience, Psychology and Behaviour from the University of Leicester, UK. Yavuz Sercekman is an accredited Mindfulness-based Stress Reduction Program (MBSR) teacher and founder of the Mind Crafting Academy, which offers mindfulness-based training and consultancy services to institutions and individuals.

Kurt April is currently the Allan Gray Chair, an Endowed Professorship, specialising in Leadership, Diversity & Inclusion in the Allan Gray Centre for Values-Based Leadership at the GSB, University of Cape Town (South Africa, 1998-present), Faculty Member of Duke Corporate Education, Duke University (USA, 2008-present), and Adjunct Faculty of Saïd Business School, University of Oxford (UK, 2000-present). He is a Series Editorial Board Member of Palgrave (Springer) on EDI and Indigenization in Business (Switzerland), Associate Editor of Design Science (UK), Editorial Board Member of the European Management Review (UK), and Editorial Review Board Member of the Africa Journal of Management (USA). Outside of academia, Kurt is the Managing Partner of LICM Consulting (South Africa), Shareholder and Director of the Achievement Awards Group (South Africa), Shareholder of bountiXP (Pty) Ltd (South Africa), and Member of the Equality, Diversity & Inclusion Committee of FIFPRO (Netherlands).

Joana Vassilopoulou is a Reader (Associate Professor) in HRM and Director of Equality, Diversity & Inclusion and UN PRME Brunel University London. Her research focuses on equality, diversity & inclusion, and migration and precarious work. Joana is an editor at the Work, Employment and Society (WES) Journal. She has published in edited collections and journals such as Human Resource Management Journal, Work, Employment and Society, European Journal of Industrial Relations, International Business Review and the International Journal of Human Resource Management. Joana is a co-founder of CEFI - The Centre for Inclusion at Work in Athens, Greece. She has a PhD from the University of East Anglia and her Social Science/Sociology degree from the University of Duisburg-Essen, Germany.

Gaurav Gupta has earned a doctorate in the area of Marketing from Punjabi University, Patiala. He has also studied marketing at the prestigious Wilkes University, Pennsylvania, USA. His papers have been published in ABDC listed/Scopus Indexed Journal(s). He is also acting as an Editor with Taylor and Francis Group. He has also presented his research work at the University of Ljubljana, Slovenia and Wolkite University, Ethiopia. He is a recipient of various fellowships awarded by the European Union and IIM-Bangalore. He got an offer of a doctoral fellowship from ICSSR (Ministry of HRD, India). He has been appointed as a member of the Advisory Board for Cleveland Professional University, USA. Presently he is associated with Christ University, NCR Campus and has worked with Sharda University and Lovely Professional University. His teaching, training, researching and consulting interests include Brand Management, Marketing Research, Mythology and management, and Case writing.

Jeremy Kwok is a doctoral researcher at Northumbria University, currently working in finance and economics. He is also a Fellow of the Royal Society for the Encouragement of Arts, Manufactures and Commerce (FRSA).

Ernesto Guerra-García. Ph.D. (2005) from Higher Education Center for Research and Teaching of the State of Morelos, University of Nebraska (UNL). M.Sc. Economics from the Autonomous University of Nuevo León. Teacher and visiting professor in Mexico's universities. Co-founder of the Autonomous Indigenous University of Mexico. In this institution, General Educational Coordinator (2001-2008) and Research and Postgraduate Coordinator (2008-2010 and 2017-2020). Currently, Research Professor of intercultural education since 2021. Member of the National System of Researchers in Mexico in Social Sciences.

José G. Vargas-Hernández, Research professor at Instituto Tecnológico Mario Molina Unidad Zapopan, before at University Center for Economic and Managerial Sciences, University of Guadalajara. Member of the National System of Researchers of Mexico. Professor Vargas-Hernández has a PhD in Public Administration and a Ph.D. in Organizational Economics. He has been visiting scholar at Carleton University, Canada, the University of California Berkeley and Laurentian University, Canada. He holds a Ph.D. in Economics from Keele University; PhD in Public Administration from Columbia University; studies in Organizational Behavior at Lancaster University, and has a Master of Business Administration; he has published nine books and more than 300 papers in international journals and reviews (some translated to English, French, German, Portuguese, Farsi, Chinese, etc.) and more than 300 essays in national journals and reviews. He has obtained several international Awards and recognitions. He also has experience in consultancy. His main research is in organizational economics and strategic management. He teaches for several doctoral programs.

James E. Phelan, LCSW, MBA, Psy.D received his Master's degree in Social Work from Marywood University, Master in Business Administration from Franklin University, and Doctorate from California Southern University. He is presently a program coordinator for the Veterans Health Administration, Columbus, Ohio and field practicum instructor for The Ohio State University. He also serves as an online faculty professor for Liberty University, Grand Canyon University, and Indiana Wesleyan University.

Joyram Chakraborty holds research interest in the area of human-computer interaction. Specifically in user-centered design solutions in the areas of internationalization of user interfaces, gaming interface design, m-health, security and digital preservation. Much of the research involves experimenting with human subjects to understand user preferences in the interaction with various types of interfaces. He uses several data collection methods, such as eye tracking, virtual reality, and survey data, to better understand the end user. The findings from these studies typically allow for the development of more user-friendly and inclusive software. He collaborates closely with researchers from several fields and institutions, namely IBM Research and the Johns Hopkins School of Public Health, to develop a better understanding of user requirements that can be useful in the design and development of tools for a global audience.

Rachna Bajaj with eight years of experience teaching as an Assistant Professor and Visiting faculty in Finance and Accounting. She has taught in various prestigious colleges and universities of North like Galgotias University, Chandigarh University, SD. College, Guru Nanak Girls College (Affiliated with Panjab University), IPEM and IMS Noida. She is also having one year of corporate experience in Budget Signs as Finance Executive. She has done MBA in Finance and Marketing from Punjabi University, Patiala. She has qualified UGC-Net in Management. Apart from this, she has completed a certified course on Fundamentals of Digital Marketing from Google. She also learnt Predictive Analytics from IIMBX. In research and publications, Rachna has presented a paper on the Application of Fuzzy Logic in Credit Risk Assessment for Indian Commercial Banks at the 2nd International Conference on Business Analytics and Intelligence organised by DOMS- IISC and DCAL-IIMB. She has presented 12 other papers at various national and international conferences. She has also contributed book chapters. She has published four papers in various journals.

Index